ROUTLEDGE LIBRARY EDITIONS: THE ANGLO-SAXON WORLD

Volume 2

ANGLO-SAXON COINS

ANGLO-SAXON COINS

Studies Presented to
F. M. Stenton
on the Occasion of his 80th Birthday
17 May 1960

Edited by
R. H. M. DOLLEY

LONDON AND NEW YORK

First published in 1961 by Methuen & Co Ltd

This edition first published in 2023
by Routledge
4 Park Square, Milton Park, Abingdon, Oxon OX14 4RN

and by Routledge
605 Third Avenue, New York, NY 10158

Routledge is an imprint of the Taylor & Francis Group, an informa business

© 1961 Methuen & Co Ltd

All rights reserved. No part of this book may be reprinted or reproduced or utilised in any form or by any electronic, mechanical, or other means, now known or hereafter invented, including photocopying and recording, or in any information storage or retrieval system, without permission in writing from the publishers.

Trademark notice: Product or corporate names may be trademarks or registered trademarks, and are used only for identification and explanation without intent to infringe.

British Library Cataloguing in Publication Data
A catalogue record for this book is available from the British Library

ISBN: 978-1-032-52976-9 (Set)
ISBN: 978-1-032-53425-1 (Volume 2) (hbk)
ISBN: 978-1-032-53426-8 (Volume 2) (pbk)
ISBN: 978-1-003-41197-0 (Volume 2) (ebk)

DOI: 10.4324/9781003411970

Publisher's Note
The publisher has gone to great lengths to ensure the quality of this reprint but points out that some imperfections in the original copies may be apparent.

Disclaimer
The publisher has made every effort to trace copyright holders and would welcome correspondence from those they have been unable to trace.

Simon Blunt

SIR FRANK STENTON

ANGLO-SAXON COINS

STUDIES PRESENTED TO
F. M. STENTON
ON THE OCCASION OF HIS 80TH BIRTHDAY
17 MAY 1960

EDITED BY
R. H. M. DOLLEY

LONDON
METHUEN & CO LTD
36 ESSEX STREET · WC2

First published 1961
© *1961 Methuen & Co Ltd*
Printed in Great Britain
by Jarrold & Sons Ltd
Norwich
Cat. No. 2/6412/10

Contents

	PREFACE	page ix
	LIST OF SUBSCRIBERS	xi
I	FROM ROMAN BRITAIN TO SAXON ENGLAND by J. P. C. Kent	1
II	THE BYZANTINE EMPIRE AND THE COINAGE OF THE ANGLO-SAXONS by P. D. Whitting	23
III	THE COINAGE OF OFFA by C. E. Blunt	39
IV	THE COINAGE OF ÆTHELWULF, KING OF THE WEST SAXONS, 839–58 by R. H. M. Dolley and K. Skaare	63
V	THE CHRONOLOGY OF THE COINS OF ÆLFRED THE GREAT, 871–99 by R. H. M. Dolley and C. E. Blunt	77
VI	THE NORTHUMBRIAN VIKING COINS IN THE CUERDALE HOARD by C. S. S. Lyon and B. H. I. H. Stewart	96
VII	BOROUGHS AND MINTS, A.D. 900–1066 by H. R. Loyn	122
VIII	THE REFORM OF THE ENGLISH COINAGE UNDER EADGAR by R. H. M. Dolley and D. M. Metcalf	136
IX	SOME CORRECTIONS TO AND COMMENTS ON B. E. HILDEBRAND'S CATALOGUE OF THE ANGLO-SAXON COINS IN THE SWEDISH ROYAL COIN CABINET by G. van der Meer	169
X	THE NUMISMATIC INTEREST OF AN OLD ENGLISH VERSION OF THE LEGEND OF THE SEVEN SLEEPERS by D. Whitelock	188
XI	THE METROLOGY OF THE LATE ANGLO-SAXON PENNY: THE REIGNS OF ÆTHELRÆD II AND CNUT by V. J. Butler	195
XII	A NEW SUGGESTION CONCERNING THE SO-CALLED 'MARTLETS' IN THE 'ARMS OF ST EDWARD' by R. H. M. Dolley and F. Elmore Jones	215
XIII	SOME REMARKS ON EIGHTEENTH-CENTURY NUMISMATIC MANUSCRIPTS AND NUMISMATISTS by J. S. Martin	227
XIV	VIKING AGE COIN-HOARDS FROM IRELAND AND THEIR RELEVANCE TO ANGLO-SAXON STUDIES by R. H. M. Dolley and J. Ingold	241
XV	STERLING by P. Grierson	266
	INDEXES	285

Illustrations

HALF-TONE PLATES

SIR FRANK STENTON *frontispiece*
photographed by Simon Blunt

DR CHARLES COMBE *facing p. 232*

REV. RICHARD SOUTHGATE
from engravings in the British Museum

TAYLOR COMBE *facing p. 233*
From an oil-painting, now destroyed, formerly in the British Museum. By courtesy of the Trustees of the National Portrait Gallery.

COLLOTYPE PLATES
at end of book

I, II FROM ROMAN BRITAIN TO SAXON ENGLAND
III BYZANTINE PROTOTYPES AND FINDS
IV–VII THE COINAGE OF OFFA
VIII THE COINAGE OF ÆTHELWULF
IX THE COINAGE OF ÆLFRED THE GREAT
X VIKING IMITATIONS OF THE COINS OF ÆLFRED THE GREAT
XI, XII NORTHUMBRIAN VIKING COINS IN THE CUERDALE HOARD
XIII, XIV THE COINAGE OF EADGAR
XV THE ORIGIN OF THE 'MARTLETS' IN THE ARMS OF ST EDWARD
XVI THE 1950 HOARD FROM FOURKNOCKS, CO. MEATH

MAPS

ENGLISH HOARDS *c.* 865–900 AND LATER HOARDS WITH COINS OF ÆLFRED THE GREAT	*page* 79
ENGLISH MINTS *c.* 900–973	150
ENGLISH MINTS *c.* 973–1066	151
VIKING COINS AND ANTIQUITIES FOUND IN IRELAND	258

Preface

The papers that follow have been offered to Sir Frank Stenton as an expression of gratitude. The last decade has witnessed the emergence of a new school of Anglo-Saxon numismatists, and only those who have borne the heat of the day can appreciate to the full what Sir Frank's discerning encouragement has meant to a younger generation struggling to create academic standards in a discipline too long the preserve of the mere collector. In particular this volume is conceived as a tribute to Sir Frank's chairmanship of the Sylloge Committee of the British Academy, a chairmanship, as gentle as firm, which already within a quinquennium has borne fruit in the shape of two fascicules of quite fundamental importance for the student of the Anglo-Saxon series.

From the first it was felt to be essential that this volume should have a measure of unity, and especially since there is as yet no authoritative manual of Anglo-Saxon numismatics, and to this end it was necessary that contributions should be by invitation and their number limited. This invidious task has been rendered much easier by the generosity of all workers in the field—and of those passed over as much as of the actual contributors—and the editor feels that he should put on record the circumstance that the work has proceeded from first to last in an atmosphere of amity and co-operation far removed from the *odium numismaticum* which envy has been known to impute to the new school. To three of the contributors thanks are due for assistance which extended far beyond the scope of their own papers, to Mr Christopher Blunt and to Mr Philip Whitting for advice and intervention at more than one crisis in the volume's gestation, and to Professor Dorothy Whitelock who was kind enough to read all the papers in galley proof. The thanks of the editor are also due to Miss Joan Ingold and to Dr Michael Metcalf for undertaking the preparation of the index and of the maps respectively. Less obvious are the editor's obligations to the Keeper of Coins and Medals at the British Museum, Dr John Walker, and the attentive reader will appreciate that the great majority of the coins on Plates I–XV could have been illustrated only by kind permission of the Trustees of the British Museum. For casts and photographs of these coins, the editor is indebted to Mr K. A. Howes and to Mr L. H. Bell respectively. Messrs Spink and Son very kindly loaned certain blocks, and to them and to Messrs A. H. Baldwin and to Messrs B. A. Seaby acknowledgement is here made for the generous way in which they obtained from their customers the advance subscriptions essential to the success of a project of this kind.

It should be stressed, however, that there were many others equally generous with their time and skill, and that they are not mentioned above is simply because it did not prove necessary to impose upon their kindness to quite the same extent. For the numerous errors of omission and commission that remain—and there is perhaps no page that is perfect—responsibility attaches to the editor alone, and he can only plead with the Irish scribe of long ago:

Michael scripsit, ora pro illo peccatore.

Kingston-upon-Thames
Feast of the Purification of the BVM, 1961

List of Subscribers

L. ALCOCK	VERONICA BUTLER	M. V. DOUGLAS
N. B. ALLEN	W. A. and V. K. BUTLER	W. A. G. DOYLE-DAVIDSON
W. ALLEN	E. K. BURSTAL	P. F. DRACOTT
M. J. ANDERSON	P. W. CALLIER	J. E. DUFFIELD
P. K. ANDERSON	H. M. CAM	G. C. DUNNING
G. A. BACON	C. S. CAMPBELL	D. W. DYKES
A. E. BAGNALL	A. CANTERA	E. S. EAMES
R. N. BAILEY	R. A. G. CARSON	M. C. EDE
A. BALDWIN	G. E. L. CARTER	E. EDMONDS
A. H. E. BALDWIN	P. CARTER	E. EKWALL
A. H. F. BALDWIN	F. A. CAZEL	R. W. V. ELLIOTT
N. C. BALLINGAL	H. CHADWICK	E. ENDERBORG
M. W. BARLEY	C. A. CHILVERS	M. ESPINAISE
F. BARLOW	H. CHRISTENSEN	J. EVANS
H. C. BARNARD	R. CIFERRI	V. I. EVISON
W. BARNETT	G. E. CLARKE	R. FALKINER
R. G. BARTLETT	J. W. CLARKE	H. FEARON
P. BASTIEN	C. E. CLAY	D. B. FEATHER
E. C. BATHO	P. A. M. CLEMOES	E. H. FERDINANDO
R. T. BECK	LORD CLITHEROE	H. P. R. FINBERG
E. S. DE BEER	W. H. R. COOK	A. FJAER
B. S. BENEDIKZ	F. R. COOPER	M. FLEMING
G. BERRY	H. S. COPINGER	B. FORSTER
A. L. BINNS	B. COTTLE	S. FREY
P. HUNTER BLAIR	J. STEVENS COX	R. FRIEDBERG
CHRISTOPHER BLUNT	R. J. CRAMP	H. FULTON
ELISABETH BLUNT	E. W. DANSON	V. H. GALBRAITH
SIMON BLUNT	R. R. DARLINGTON	E. GANS
W. S. BOUNDY	H. D. DAVIDSON	T. H. GARDNER
E. G. BRADFIELD	P. R. DAVIS	G. N. GARMONSWAY
F. B. BRAMLEY	R. H. C. DAVIS	J. GARTNER
R. N. BRIDGE	M. DEANESLY	R. GOLDSTONE
G. L. BROOK	J. H. DEAS	B. GORDON
C. N. L. and R. B. BROOKE	J. M. DODGSON	A. D. GRAHAM
F. W. BROOKS	B. DODWELL	PHILIP GRIERSON
A. BROWNING	MARY DOLLEY	N. GRIFFITHS
T. B. BRUUN	MICHAEL DOLLEY	P. D. GRINKE
C. BUCKALEW	G. V. DOUBLEDAY	R. HABELT

List of Subscribers

A. HANNAH
S. E. HARDIE
FLORENCE HARMER
H. HERZFELDER
R. M. T. HILL
SIR FRANCIS HILL
D. DOBSON HINTON
P. A. HODGKINSON
B. HOPE-TAYLOR
H. L. HOPPE
A. W. J. HOUGHTON
C. H. HUGGILL
C. G. HUGHES
K. HUGHES
C. A. HULSE
L. O. HUNTER
R. L. HUSTWAYTE
JOAN INGOLD
E. M. IRONS
F. J. JEFFERY
R. F. JESSUP
H. L. JOHNSON
F. ELMORE JONES
J. O. JOYCE
J. H. JUDD
J. A. KAY.
JOHN KENT
E. J. KIBBLE
H. H. KING
M. M. S. KIRKUS
M. KNEMEYER
W. KNOWES
R. DE LACY SPENCER
L. O. LAGERQVIST
A. W. LAINCHBURY
E. J. LAKER
S. N. LANE
F. C. G. LARKWORTHY
L. V. LARSEN
W. E. LEISTNER
R. B. LEWIS
J. F. LHOTKA
D. G. LIDDELL
H. W. A. LINECAR
A. T. and M. LLOYD
L. LOWE
A. W. G. LOWTHER
HENRY LOYN
STEWART LYON
D. W. MACDOWALL
K. B. MCFARLANE
T. MCGOLDRICK
R. P. MACK
M. MACKECHNIE
M. MCKISACK
J. M. MCWILLIAMS
I. B. MADDEN
K. MAJOR
B. K. MALEN
B. MALMER
K. MALONE
J. A. MANCASTER
D. MANGAKIS
I. D. MARGARY
JOAN MARTIN
H. MATTINGLY
GAY VAN DER MEER
MICHAEL METCALF
E. MILLER
J. H. MILLER
R. J. MILWARD
S. MORISON
H. R. MOSSOP
A. S. MOTTRAM
A. R. MYERS
J. N. L. MYRES
E. NELSON
J. NORRIS
J. J. NORTH
R. W. O'BRIEN
W. E. O'BRIEN
D. A. OLIVER
H. E. O'NEIL
B. R. OSBORNE
H. C. OWEN
G. E. H. PALMER
T. M. PARKER
C. W. PHILLIPS
E. J. E. PIRIE
A. H. PLACE
T. F. T. PLUCKNETT
W. H. PRICE
F. PRIDMORE
R. B. PUGH
R. H. A. PYKETT
C. A. RALEGH RADFORD
H. M. RAND
N. L. RASMUSSON
K. A. RAUTAVAARA
E. J. P. RAVEN
R. M. REECE
V. RICH
S. E. RIGOLD
E. S. G. ROBINSON
G. S. ROBINSON
G. D. ROBSON
E. W. and M. A. ROFFEY
M. S. ROLFE
H. J. ROMDALL
I. T. ROPER
S. ROSS
C. E. P. ROSSER
K. M. and N. J. SAUNDERS
O. K. SCHRAM
J. G. SCOTT
P. SEABY
R. J. M. SELFE
D. E. SHACKLETON
B. A. SHAYLER
J. SHUTLER
K. SISAM
KOLBJØRN SKAARE
C. F. SLADE

List of Subscribers

E. SMITH	F. C. THOMPSON	V. S. WHITE
L. S. SNELL	P. TINCHANT	R. B. WHITEHEAD
F. S. SNOW	R. F. TREHARNE	K. P. WHITEHORNE
H. SPEIGHT	D. G. TRITT	DOROTHY WHITELOCK
D. F. SPINK	W. B. TURNER	PHILIP WHITTING
P. SPUFFORD	E. J. VASKAS	W. MC. C. WILSON
G. C. STACPOOLE	C. C. VERMEULE	R. M. WILSON
DORIS STENTON	W. DE VORE	H. WISCHMANN
J. STEPHAN	F. T. WAINWRIGHT	P. WOODHEAD
C. E. STEVENS	JOHN WALKER	F. WORMALD
IAN STEWART	D. G. WALKER	C. L. WRENN
J. R. STEWART	J. M. WEBBON	C. E. WRIGHT
D. STOCKWELL	G. WEBSTER	CHING-MAI YANG
B. SVENSSON	G. A. WHEELER	W. J. ZIMMERMAN
L. SYDENHAM	S. A. H. WHETMORE	

INSTITUTIONS

Aberystwyth, University Library
Adelaide, National Gallery of South Australia
Amsterdam University Engels Seminarium
Aylesbury County Museum
Bath Municipal Libraries
Belfast Museum and Art Gallery
Berkshire Archaeological Society
Birmingham City Museum and Art Gallery
Birmingham Reference Library
Birmingham University Extra-Mural Library
Birmingham University Library
Boston Museum of Fine Arts
Brierley Hill Central Library
Bristol City Museum
Burton-on-Trent Public Library
Cambridge University, Department of Anglo-Saxon
Cambridge University, Fitzwilliam Museum
Cambridge, Girton College Library
Cambridge, Gonville and Caius College Library
Cambridge, Newnham College Library
Canterbury Cathedral Library
Canterbury Public Library
Cardiff, National Museum of Wales
Carlisle Public Library
Castleford Public Library
Chester Public Library
Copenhagen, Royal Collection of Coins and Medals
Durham University Department of Archaeology
Durham University Library
Edinburgh, National Museum of Antiquities
Edinburgh University Library
Exeter City Library

Institutions

Exeter University, Roborough Library
The Hague, Kon. Penningkabinet
Hull University Library
Ipswich Museum
Leeds City Museum
Leeds University, Brotherton Library
Leicester City Museums and Art Gallery
Lincoln City Library
Liverpool University Library
Łódź Museum Archeologiczne i Etnograficzne
London, British Museum, Department of British and Medieval Antiquities
London, British Museum, Department of Coins and Medals
London, Courtauld Institute
London, Guildhall Library
London, Guildhall Museum
London, Ministry of Works, S.E.1
London, National Portrait Gallery
London, Royal Numismatic Society Library
London, Society of Antiquaries Library
London University, Birkbeck College Library
London University, Institute of Historical Research
London, Worshipful Company of Goldsmiths
Marlborough College
Munich, Staatliche Münzsammlung
New York, The American Numismatic Society
Northampton County Borough Museums Committee
North Staffordshire University Library
Nottingham University Library
Nottinghamshire Numismatic Society
Ootacamund, Government Epigraphist for India
Oslo, Universitetets Myntkabinett
Oxford, All Souls College Library
Oxford, Ashmolean Museum
Oxford, Jesus College Library
Oxford, Keble College Library
Oxford, St John's College Library
Paris, Cabinet des Médailles Bibliothèque Nationale
Peterborough Museum Society
Portsmouth Central Public Library
Reading University Library
Reading University Department of Modern History
Reading Public Libraries
Reading School
St Andrews University Library
Sheffield City Museum
Stockholm, K. Vitterhets Historie Och Antikvitetsakademiens Bibliotek
Sunderland Public Libraries
Tamworth Public Library
Warwick County Museum
Washington, Smithsonian Institution Library
Winchester City Museums
Yorkshire Philosophical Society

A. H. Baldwin and Sons Ltd.
Münzen und Medaillen
J. Thornton and Son
Whitman Publishing Co.

Abbreviations

Each contributor has been left free to adopt the bibliographical references which in his or her opinion are most likely to be intelligible to the particular class of reader envisaged. The non-numismatist, however, may not always be familiar with the following

BOOKS

BMC	*British Museum Catalogue*
Bonser	*An Anglo-Saxon & Celtic Bibliography 450–1087*
Inventory	*An Inventory of British Coin Hoards A.D. 600–1500*
RIC	*Roman Imperial Coinage*

PERIODICALS

BNJ	*British Numismatic Journal*
GM	*Gentleman's Magazine*
NC	*Numismatic Chronicle*
NNÅ	*Nordisk Numismatisk Årsskrift*
NNUM	*Nordisk Numismatisk Unions Medlemsblad*
SNC	*Spink's Numismatic Circular*

I

From Roman Britain to Saxon England

by J. P. C. KENT

[Plates I and II]

A dim mist hangs over the history of the island from the fourth to the seventh century.'[1] In the year A.D. 400, Britain was an integral part of the Roman Empire. Though already rocked by the storms that were soon to bring about its severance from the imperial government, the province was still the seat of an elaborate administrative and military structure, to maintain which heavy taxation was levied, and to pay which coin flowed into local coffers in an undiminished stream. Before the year A.D. 700, Britain had become a collection of warring Anglo-Saxon kingdoms, among some of whom at least had begun the use of national currency that was to be the ancestor of our medieval coinage. The purpose of this paper is to trace the transition between the classical and the medieval – between Roman and Anglo-Saxon. Its aim is to consider a series of important archaeological and numismatic problems whose solutions inevitably affect our interpretation of how and when Roman Britain came to an end. There remains the question of what came after. Did Roman coins continue to enter Britain after its abandonment? Were imitations of Roman coins made here on a large scale in the fifth and sixth centuries? If so, by whom were they made, and what economic and social implications can one draw from this? Then, at the other end of the scale, we must ask how Anglo-Saxon coinage began. How far does it derive from a Roman or sub-Roman predecessor? What does it owe to continental contemporaries? Above all, when did it begin? Should we associate it with the coming of Christianity to Kent, just before 600, or should it be some seventy or eighty years later? These are questions which have a peculiar relevance to Britain. Indeed, it may be said that only in Britain do these problems exist. For somewhat over a hundred years successive generations of scholars have propounded various solutions, and so fundamental has been the failure to agree even on the distinction between fact and hypothesis that I can scarcely hope that my own particular interpretation will achieve universal or unqualified acceptance. But in offering one that reconciles the supposedly conflicting claims of history, archaeology, and numismatics, it is my aim to find a measure of common ground that may perhaps serve as a basis for future advances.

Before the problems of the Dark Ages can be elucidated, it is necessary to determine what was the composition of the currency of Britain at the end of the fourth century. We are fortunate that there exists an abundance of evidence from hoards and site-finds from which it is possible to draw some general conclusions.[2] As elsewhere in the Roman Empire, there was a pronounced increase in the amount of gold coin in circulation after *c.* 370, and though finds are naturally not numerous in an absolute sense, there are enough to demonstrate that in and after 400 the coin most readily available was the *solidus* '*Victoria Auggg*' coined principally at Milan from 394 to 402, and thereafter mainly at Ravenna. Ravenna *solidi* of this type fall into three groups, of which only the first, which dates between 402 and about 409, occurs in British finds within a Roman context.[3] Britain's main wealth, however, lay in silver. She provided most of the silver for the abundant coinages of the second half of the fourth century, and herself absorbed most of the mint's output.[4] By the end of the century, though earlier pieces were still abundant, the characteristic coin was the *siliqua* '*Virtus Romanorum*' of the Milan mint. Seen rarely as site-finds, these pieces are found hoarded together in large numbers, and are at once the last considerable issue of silver from a Roman mint until the sixth century, and with rare exceptions the latest silver coins to be found in this country. It is clear that soon after 400 something happened in Britain to check the flow of silver to the imperial treasury, for the silver coined at Rome and Ravenna after 402 was both meagre in quantity and unavailable to British hoarders. The bronze coinage was necessarily more miscellaneous in character, and did not even present a uniform picture throughout the country.[5] In addition, the evidence of hoards and site-finds is not quite the same. We find that around 400 the complementary issues of '*Salus Reipublicae*' from Italian mints and '*Victoria Auggg*' from Gaul were readily available to hoarders in the south and east, and that in the great towns considerable quantities of these tiny pieces circulated freely. But though the newness of this coinage made it specially attractive to the hoarder, it formed but one part of the currency. A major part of this was composed of well-worn pieces of the later years of the House of Constantine. Even at Richborough, where late fourth century coins are notoriously common, finds suggest that the bulk of the circulation of this period consisted of '*Gloria Exercitus*' and '*Victoriae*' types, together with the coins commemorating the foundation of Constantinople, and other issues of *c.* 330–45. Of earlier coins, very few now survived – mainly a handful of radiates of the third century and their copies. Strangely enough, later coins too had become uncommon, except

From Roman Britain to Saxon England

for some of the '*Gloria*' and '*Securitas*' issues of the House of Valentinian. The '*Fel. Temp. Reparatio*' series of 345 to 360, so abundant in hoards when it first appeared, was now virtually extinct. Only the varieties bearing the 'Phoenix' type and a few of the later 'Horseman' issues still rarely persisted in currency. Such was the state of British coinage at the moment when the island was about to be cut off from Rome for ever, and the essential background against which we must consider the problems of the fifth century.

We must begin with a brief consideration of the historical circumstances under which Roman Britain came to an end, and our starting-point is the year 394, when Theodosius I reunified the Roman world for a moment, only to split it finally into two parts when at his death in 395 he divided it between his sons Arcadius and Honorius. The long and futile reign of the latter spelled disaster for the Western Empire, and when at length he died unmourned in 423, not only was Britain lost beyond recovery, but imperial rule in Gaul, Spain, and the North Balkans was rapidly declining into a meaningless fiction. It is not surprising that Honorius' reign was much troubled by usurpers. From our point of view the most important was Constantine III.[6] Britain had flared once more into revolt in the year 406. An invasion of Gaul by a confederate body of Germans seemed to have as its target the Channel ports, and giving vent to its well-founded lack of confidence in the Roman high command, the British army proclaimed its own nominee emperor, and in self-defence seized the Channel ports and successfully repulsed the invaders. Two candidates for power fell in rapid succession, but the third, Constantine, managed to survive his unpromising start. Elevated solely on account of his auspicious name, Constantine attempted to emulate the feat of his predecessor, the great Constantine of exactly a century before, and abandoned the province he was supposed to defend. He embarked on a gamble for power in Gaul, and at different times controlled (and minted at) Trier, Lyons, and Arles. At the zenith of his fortune he was master of Spain, and actually invaded Italy, but in 411 he was trapped with part of his army in Arles by the generals of Honorius, and his empire crumbled away. But Britain had already slipped from imperial hands. In 410 the civil authorities in Britain expelled the neglectful Constantine's governors, and besought Honorius to resume control. But at this very moment Rome itself was in the hands of a Gothic army and its puppet emperor Priscus Attalus, and Honorius could do no more than authorize the 'cities of Britain' – in effect the tribal aristocracies – to take measures for their own defence. With this pronouncement, the history of Roman Britain comes to an end. The famous theory of the reoccupation of a part of Britain between *c.* 417 and 428, originally propounded by Professor Collingwood in an attempt to reconcile the seemingly divergent evidence of documents and coins, need no longer be maintained.[7] Both the interpretation of the *Notitia Dignitatum* and the theories of coin-drift and survival which underlay it are now recognized to be mistaken.[8] Between 417 and c. 430 Honorius and his successors maintained precarious rule in Gaul as far as the Rhine, but Britain was lost for ever.

Apart from a very brief period under Magnus Maximus, Britain had possessed no official mint of her own since the reign of Constantine the Great, and the political severance of the province from the central government in 406 meant the practical cessation of coin import to this country. This surprises us less in these days than it did the antiquaries of a previous generation, for we have now been shown that Roman coppers seldom wandered far from their place of issue,[9] and, of course, in the late Empire circulation beyond the limits of a single province (of which there were five in Britain) was restricted by law. Furthermore, the main function of imperial bronze disbursements was the recovery of gold coin paid out to functionaries and the soldiery,[10] and the letter of 410 is a clear intimation that no further official payments were contemplated. A closer analysis of the latest Roman coins to be found here is therefore of prime importance, and the evidence of the coppers is particularly significant.[11] The issue of the types '*Victoria*' and '*Salus*' so abundant in hoards and on town sites came to an end about 396 and 402 respectively. Of the two major obverse varieties of '*Salus*', reading DN ONORIVS PF AVG or DN HONORI AVG, many thousands of specimens have come down to us. Following coinages are by contrast found but rarely, '*Urbs Roma Felix*', struck between 404 and 408, is known in Britain from two examples only. '*Gloria Romanorum*', a rare type struck in Gaul after 417, is known from but one. The large issues minted in Rome from 420 onwards in the names of Honorius, John, Theodosius II, and Valentinian III are virtually unrepresented in Britain. It is, therefore, possible to say with some certainty that the import of copper coins to Britain ceased soon after 400. In view of the 'stock-piling' of coppers by the Treasury that can be demonstrated in the late fourth century, there seems no reason to doubt that 406 is the crucial date at which this abrupt end took place. Their evidence is therefore exactly in line with that of the *solidi* already discussed. The evidence of the silver coinage is somewhat harder to assess. We have seen that the last Roman silver occurring in abundance in Britain is the Milan *siliqua* '*Virtus Romanorum*', the issue of which terminated c. 402. There are, however, found not infrequently silver coins of Constantine III, and, most significantly, the three known examples of the Trier '*Urbs Roma*' *siliqua* of Honorius all have a British provenance.[12] In the light of this it is important to remember that no single specimen of the ensuing issue, in the names of Theodosius II and Valentinian III, struck at Trier

From Roman Britain to Saxon England

between 425 and 428, comes from this country. Practically all are from the Upper Rhine.[13] Britain, I conclude, was still able to absorb much of the Gallic output of silver coin down to c. 420 – then that too came to an end.

There remains only the question of how long these latest coins persisted in circulation, and to this the answer can be subjective only. With regard to the coppers, it depends much on the interpretation of their condition. They are almost always found, even in hoards, in poor condition, and it has been disputed whether this is the result of wear in circulation or due to the extremely defective technique of the Rome mint, which generally led to substantial portions of legend and type on the '*Salus*' issues being missing.[14] Though wear is not absent in most cases, it is my opinion that poor striking is a very important factor. It is otherwise impossible to explain why the Gallic '*Victoria*' coins should so often appear to be found in better condition in the same hoards as the Roman '*Salus*' type, since the bulk of the latter coinage is beyond doubt later in date. The latest finds of silver coin generally contain a very high proportion of clipped pieces, reducing the average weight to the very low standard of the latest Trier coins. Clipped and worn *siliquae* were in fact associated with the three finds containing these pieces, which were themselves virtually uncirculated. It seems legitimate to deduce that both silver and copper coin of the latest types to enter Britain had disappeared from circulation by c. 430. No such pieces are habitually found, for example, in the earliest pagan Anglo-Saxon graves to indicate that they were more available as ornaments to the new settlers than any other of the common coins of Roman Britain. It has been suggested that the mention of *denarius* and *obolus* by Gildas is evidence that silver (clipped *siliquae*) and copper (barbarous imitations) coin was familiar in sixth-century Britain.[15] The completely coinless sixth-century royal site of Castle Dore hardly lends credence to this proposition. We should not suppose Gildas incapable of metaphor here, any more than we believe that Constantine of Dumnonia's mother was really an unclean lioness!

When in 1844 Akerman wrote his account of Roman coins relating to Britain, the possibility of a sub-Roman coinage, made by the Britons in an attempt to supply the currency suddenly denied to them by severance from the Empire, had not yet been considered. It first appears as a developed hypothesis in Roach Smith's *Antiquities of Richborough, Reculver, and Lymne*, published in 1850. Roach Smith was struck by the comprehensive nature of the Richborough coin-list, which covered the entire range of the Roman occupation, and restarted with the earliest Anglo-Saxon coins, then believed to have begun not later than the end of the sixth century. He was also faced by a mass of barbarous copies, which seemed to fill the gap, and it was natural for him to devote attention to the '*minimi*; so named on account of their small size'.[16] His conclusion was that these 'very small coins in brass . . . from their barbarous execution, or imperfect design, can only be considered as imitations, of a late date, of the commoner kinds of third brass coins', and that they should 'possibly be ascribed to unknown princes or rulers of Britain, after the departure of the Romans, and before the establishment of the Saxons'.[17] Subsequent scholars have on the whole tended to elaborate this hypothesis, though Roach Smith himself was later to reject it.[18] Sir John Evans[19] included with the *minimi* the ordinary barbarous third brass, 'like the times in which they were struck, barbarous and rude'. Two classes of prototype are copied above all others, late-third-century radiates, and one variety of the '*Fel. Temp. Reparatio* Falling Horseman' series, and though hoards of these are commonly found, the two designs are never found together in the same deposit in numbers which suggest their contemporaneous currency. This mutual exclusiveness has given rise to singular conjectures, such as that since the former were derived from pagan prototypes and the latter from coins of a Christian emperor, the ones were attributable to the pagan Anglo-Saxons, the others to the Christian Britons. Dr Mattingly went so far as to call the famous Richborough radiate hoard,[20] 'the coinage of Hengist and Horsa with their Jutes', and this in spite of the stratigraphic evidence for third-century date he himself records, and of the absence of similar pieces in pagan Kentish graves (see Appendix). Dr Sutherland has recently defended the notion of a Dark Ages coinage on the grounds that the Britons cannot soon have lost the 'habit' of using money,[21] but when it is clear that the entire administrative and economic machine was in dissolution, it is difficult to be persuaded that coinage must have continued, when there may have been no function for it to perform. Furthermore, there is a significant concentration of imitations of both classes in the southern and eastern parts of the country – not exclusive, but enough to show two facts clearly. First, that the area of circulation of both types was the same, and that in consequence of their to all intents and purposes never being found hoarded together they must be appreciably separated in date. Second, that the attribution of either class to the Anglo-Saxons is negatived by their virtual non-appearance in Anglo-Saxon graves, and to the Britons of the later fifth century by their predominantly eastern and southern distribution. Indeed, if either class were to belong to the fifth century, it could only be to a fairly early part of that century; as Roach Smith saw, they must fall 'after the departure of the Romans, and before the establishment of the Saxons'. But we have already seen that down to *c.* 430 the currency of Roman coins remains probable, and that at this date neither radiates nor '*Fel. Temp. Reparatio*'s formed more than the minutest proportion of

From Roman Britain to Saxon England

the coins in circulation in the south. With the extreme position formerly adopted by Hill in seeking to date hoards containing substantial numbers of barbarous coins to the late fifth and sixth centuries we need no longer concern ourselves. It is no longer maintained by its author, and is in any case not supported by other than subjective evidence.[22] Its corollary – the so-called '*sceatta*-like imitation' – is another snare.[23] A relationship between barbarous coins and *sceattas* suggests nearness of date, but we shall see that the latter can hardly start more than a decade before 700 – more than fifty years later than would have been admitted twenty years ago – and that their prototypes are never barbarous pieces. We are left with the fact that both are very roughly engraved and struck, evidently the flimsiest basis for associating them with one another.

The evidence that many of the third- and fourth-century copies were contemporary with their prototypes is already substantial and incontrovertible and accumulates with every publication of stratified material. It rests on the secure basis of stratification, sites with abruptly ending coin-series, overstriking of barbarous on regular pieces, and the invariable association of copies with their prototypes in hoards and on sites.[24] Not even the most ardent supporter of the Dark Ages dating has seriously challenged this body of evidence, and it is admitted that nothing can be adduced either from archaeology or numismatics to support the contrary view. In short, the onus of proof rests squarely on those who wish to date any barbarous copies of these classes substantially later than their prototypes. In my opinion, such proof is not likely to be forthcoming, and in its absence the last hope of discovering and defining a barbarous Dark Ages coinage, whether for Anglo-Saxons or Britons, must perish.

I have offered evidence that the import of Roman coins to Britain fell abruptly to negligible proportion soon after 400, and that their circulation came to an end by *c*. 430. I have shown that not only is there evidence that the barbarous pieces formerly attributed to the Dark Ages did not circulate then, but they are in fact all contemporary with the currency of their prototypes. I will now demonstrate that the characteristic coinages of the other barbarian successor kingdoms to the Western Empire were scarce, high-value issues of gold, and quite removed in kind from the common everyday coppers postulated for England. Many were simple copies of Roman *solidi*. Such was the coinage of the Visigoths in South Gaul from *c*. 440 onwards.[25] The prototype, even to the mint-mark, is closely followed, and though fineness and weight often leave something to be desired, it is not until the sixth century that style and fabric become increasingly distinct. Not until well into the second half of the sixth century did the practice of coining in the name of the reigning Roman emperor come to an end. While they lasted, the Kingdoms of the Ostrogoths and Burgundians produced even more reputable copies, no more than the royal monogram marking the piece as of non-imperial origin. Only in the urban centres of Africa and Italy did silver and copper coinages of non-imperial character flourish. In Gaul they are confined to Lyons, and can have no place in Dark Ages Britain. A transient attempt of the Merovingian Theodebert around 535 to issue *solidi* and *tremisses* in his own name failed in the face of diplomatic and no doubt commercial opinion.

However, the last quarter of the sixth century saw the emergence of national coinages in France and Spain, along quite different lines. Most distinctly national were the Visigothic *tremisses* with the name, title, and effigy of the king, combined with the name of the mint-town. The Merovingians struck few coins in the names of the kings. Not only was coinage vastly decentralized, but there is no indication of an authority other than the moneyer and the town of issue. There was naturally a great variety of design and style. Most of these pieces were *tremisses*. When *solidi* were required, it was customary until the reign of Heraclius (610–41) to coin them in the name of the reigning emperor.[26] Though on account of their situation among the latest peoples to abandon the imitation of Roman *solidi* and *tremisses*, the Lombards of Italy have a great importance in our survey. If the influence of Roman and Merovingian coins rests heavy on the earliest Anglo-Saxon pieces, yet it is from the eighth-century Lombard *tremisses* – the *solidi stellati* – that the typical *denier* coinage of the Middle Ages most directly derives its weight and design.

The marriage of the Merovingian princess Bertha with King Æthelbert of Kent *c*. 580 marks the re-emergence of England into a place in European affairs. But this country was still unready for a coinage, and it is generally agreed that the St Martin's (Canterbury) hoard, on a piece in which we read the name of Liudhard, Bertha's chaplain, is medallic in character.[27] For the start of a true coinage we are confronted by two principal pieces of evidence – the great hoards of Sutton Hoo and Crondall.[28] Since the dating of their contents by the Merovingian pieces is illusory in the absence of a firm chronology for these, we must rely on other grounds. In the first place, the complete absence of Anglo-Saxon coins from the Sutton Hoo purse seems to me to demonstrate beyond reasonable doubt that *c*. 650, the accepted date for the burial, such coins did not yet exist. The provenance of most Anglo-Saxon gold coin from Kent is demonstrated by finds, and hinted at in Bede's story of the mid-seventh-century Kentish princess in Normandy – 'aureum illud nomisma ... de Cantia'[29] – and yet in the assemblage of purely Kentish jewellery we find nothing but Merovingian coins. In support of this, we may note the use of Roman, Byzantine, and Merovingian *solidi* as jewellery, often with the characteristic gold-and-garnet

From Roman Britain to Saxon England

mounting, down to the mid-seventh century. So far as I am aware, there is no example of the use of an Anglo-Saxon gold coin by the Kentish jewellers, and this as surely denotes the non-currency of the former, as it shows that the latter did not yet exist. Our knowledge of Anglo-Saxon gold coinage is of course very imperfect. Many types hitherto unknown came to light in the Crondall hoard, while many well-known types were not represented in that find, and no doubt others will appear to fill some apparent gaps in the series. *Tremisses* only were of constant weight and could serve as coin. The so-called *solidi* were made to no fixed standard. All those of certain English origin seem to have been mounted and to have been intended as jewellers' pieces. Crondall presents some difficult problems, but its basic evidence may be stated as follows. Apart from the worn and mounted Lombard copy of a Ravenna *tremissis* of Phocas (602-10)[30] all its contents, Merovingian and Anglo-Saxon alike, are completely free from wear. Furthermore, its Anglo-Saxon element divides itself into die-linked groups, some of which seem already to have derived series showing marked typological degeneration. The question is important, because one of its groups, consisting of pieces with a facing bust, inscribed LONDVNIV, has been attributed to Bishop Mellitus of London (604-16). The issue is evidently Christian, although I can distinguish neither the pallium nor tonsure claimed by Dr Sutherland. Since London was in a virtual state of apostasy between 616 and 670, the limits outside which its date must fall are fairly fixed. For my part, I cannot believe even with the very limited amount of currency these coins must have achieved that they could have stayed together in a close die-linked group and remained without trace of wear for more than half a century. Once this series is displaced from the first quarter of the century, the last evidence for the start of an Anglo-Saxon gold coinage before *c.* 675 is removed.

The names of these coins remains uncertain. Conventionally they are referred to as '*thrymsas*', as though derived from the Roman *tremissis*. But the only authorities for the word *thrymsa* appear to be eleventh-century legal sources, which equate it with a unit of account of three pence,[31] and this seems a far cry from seventh-century Kent.

In his as yet unpublished Ford Lectures for 1957, Grierson proposes to call them 'shillings'. Perhaps he was influenced by the Western tendency to use the term *solidus* not only for the whole piece, but also for its subsidiary units the half (*semissis*) and third (*tremissis*) – a practice attested in Africa, Spain, and Italy. When we find an early eighth-century Merovingian silver coin inscribed DENARIVS, the origin of the universal West European accounting equation 1 *solidus* = 12 *denarii* becomes easier to understand, though 20 *solidi* to the pound is readily explicable only in terms of a relatively debased gold alloy, and a high valuation of gold in respect of silver. However, neither premiss is alien to our knowledge of the eighth century, and there is much to be said for the suggestion that *'thrymsas'* were none other than the *solidi* of account.

The earliest Anglo-Saxon gold naturally drew on a wide range of prototypes, the availability in England of which can either be demonstrated or reasonably assumed. Many were simple derivatives or copies of seventh-century Merovingian pieces, and their existence does nothing but to emphasize the direction whence the stimulus to coinage came. Let us rather concern ourselves with the feature of this coinage that is truly its own, the copying of Roman imperial types of the third and fourth centuries. To a large extent this copying is haphazard. We find, for example, a piece probably not itself English on which an obverse derived from an Italian gold *tremissis* of the time of Justinian (527–65) is combined with a reverse copying the late Constantinian bronze type of *'Gloria Exercitus'* with one standard.[32] The letter M on the standard enables us to define the issue copied as the Trier mint $\frac{M}{TRP\smile}$ series of *c.* 339 (**Plate I, 1–3**). Even greater confusion is revealed in my next two examples, the *'solidus'* from Markshall, and the 'Licinius' group from the Crondall hoard. The Markshall piece copies closely but illiterately the obverse of the bronze coinage of Helena of the 324–9 period. But its reverse, evidently derived from a *'Vot X'* piece of the Constantinian Caesars of *c.* 321–4, bears a legend adumbrating that of the *Beata Tranquillitas* issue of 320–1 (**Plate I, 4–6**). The Crondall examples have a tolerably correct 'Licinius' legend on obverse and reverse, of the 320 period, but the actual portrait is that of one of the sons of Constantine, as they appeared at Trier *c.* 324–6 (**Plate I, 7–9**). Such mixed copying suggests that all the prototypes drawn upon were available at the same moment to the copyist, and it is therefore significant that all were types that are regularly found together in hoards, and are by no means the commonest coins from sites. A single hoard could adequately account for the Roman elements in both the Markshall and Crondall pieces. Surely the hoard must have been laid before the puzzled copyist in its entirety as suitable material to imitate, and we have here plausible evidence for the official character of this interest. At this date Roman coins were considered more worthy prototypes for the new coinage than Merovingian, not least, perhaps, because they came to official hands more readily.

The transition from a gold to a silver coinage was a steady and, it seems, a rapid process. It is principally illustrated by a quite common, yet completely self-contained series, that imitates the *Victoria Augg* 'Two Emperors' *solidus* of the late fourth century (**Plate I, 10–11**). We find that although there is no perceptible degeneration in design, the metal varies in quality from good gold

From Roman Britain to Saxon England

to silver, with intervening gradations in electrum. The rapidity with which the standard changed is paralleled in the runic series inscribed with the name 'Pada', which occurs in various qualities of electrum, and continues well into the series of silver so-called '*sceattas*'. 'Pada's' coins have also a Roman prototype, a bronze piece in the name of Crispus of about 319, with reverse '*Virtus Exercit*'. The earliest examples show clearly the 'helmeted bust' of the original, and the legend '*Crispus Nob Caes*'. At first it looks as though the copyist produced a number of variations based on the reverse. In some, the influence of the Crondall '*Vota*' type is apparent, and it is noticeable that some of the earliest silver pieces are closer to the prototype than the electrum (**Plate I, 12–14**). Again, it looks as though the electrum coinage must have been very short lived. We turn now to a consideration of its date. An initial date for the gold of *c.* 675 has been argued earlier in this paper. We have seen that although pieces heralding the transition to electrum and silver do not occur in Crondall, ample evidence has been adduced to suggest that when either typological or metallic degeneration occurred, its progress was rapid. Either we must postulate a gap between the issue of the purely gold series and that initiating the transition, or assume that the whole process, from the start of gold coinage to the conversion to silver, took place over a brief period, for which ten or fifteen years would seem ample. The coincidence of this dating with that deduced by Le Gentilhomme for the same transition from gold to silver among the Franks (*c.* 680–700) goes far to confirm its accuracy. One group of rather base gold alone is hard to fit in with this dating, and it is itself gravely anomalous in many ways. First is its provenance – York and its immediate environs. Second is its alloy, which looks like copper and not silver. Third is its apparent date, for it seems to be imitated from a *solidus* now attributed to Justinian II's second reign, around 705–6 (**Plate I, 15–16**). Even granted the authenticity of the group, which has never been questioned and which was certainly known by the last quarter of the eighteenth century, we should not perhaps argue from the conditions prevailing in the relatively impoverished north, which to judge from such finds as the single base *tremissis* from Yeavering, and the story of King Oswald's silver dish,[33] was to all intents and purposes void of coin in the seventh century, and which could not even afford to maintain a silver coinage in the eighth.

The evidence for the inauguration of the '*Sceatta*' series around 680–90 seems conclusive, and we have to consider how long it may be supposed to have continued. English '*sceattas*', as was well shown by Hill,[34] fall into two major classes, the so-called 'Standard' group of 'Crispus' imitations, which leads straight out of the electrum coinage, and the 'London' group. The latter is miscellaneous in character, but type mules and a falling weight standard indicate that chronologically its earliest pieces succeed the latest 'Standard' varieties. Very important is the Cimiez hoard. This contained several varieties of 'Standard' *'sceattas'*, also some apparently latish examples of the 'London' group. But, according to Le Gentilhomme, this hoard must have been buried at or before the destruction of the town in 737, and it looks as though the whole life of the '*Thrymsa*'–'*Sceatta*' coinage must have been relatively short and compact. It is difficult on this chronology to protract this coinage beyond 750, if so late a date is possible, and just as a large gap looms between the Roman and Anglo-Saxon coinage, so a shorter one seems to intervene between '*sceatta*' and penny, despite the manifest influence of the one on the other, and their probable identity of denomination.[35]

Silver issues of the 'Standard' series are directly imitated from two Roman bronze prototypes. The earliest, as we have seen, is the 'Crispus *Virtus Exercit*' discussed above. Direct English descendants fail early in the series, and the ultimate derivatives (the 'Porcupine' group and cognates) are found predominantly in Frisian hoards. Our second group begins with a rare gold or electrum piece imitating a late-third-century radiate, probably Marius or Carausius. Its reverse type, 'Clasped Hands', did not persist, but the radiate obverse rapidly superseded the 'Helmeted head of Crispus', taking over its characteristic 'Standard' reverse (**Plate I, 17–19**). A rapid declension of style followed, with the radiate head acquiring first a debased runic legend EPA, APA, etc., in place of the meaningless 'Roman' TIC, and finally becoming anepigraphic. Late derivatives, specially in Frisia, combine two obverses or two reverses.

The 'London' series seems to contain three main streams. First there is the profile bust with legend adumbrating LVNDONIA, or some corruption of it. Its reverses are principally 'Man holding Cross and Bird', 'Man with Two Crosses', etc., the figure often standing in a ship that suggests the influence of the '*Fel. Temp. Reparatio* Galley' type of c. 348–50.[36] 'Men with Crosses' or 'Man with Cross' is a substantive obverse in its own right, being accompanied by the so-called 'Fantastic Animal', 'Celtic Cross', or 'Wolf-whorl'. The 'Celtic Cross' itself seems to originate with the third main obverse of this series, the moustached and bearded facing bust through a degenerate 'Bust on Shield' form. Its earliest reverse is 'Men with Cross', but it commonly occurs with 'Bird on Cross' 'Fantastic Animal', and 'Wolf-whorl'. There is to be observed a typological unity within the whole series, though it may be doubted whether it emanated from the mint of London alone.[37] It owes much less to Roman prototypes than its predecessor. The origin of the 'Facing Bust' type is probably to be sought in *solidi* of Constans II (641–68), but it is likely that the '*Fel. Temp. Reparatio*' coinage

From Roman Britain to Saxon England

played its part, and at least one rare variety has an unmistakable Roman 'Victory' (**Plate I, 20-3; II, 1-5**). Its dating we have already considered, and in support of it we may observe that the base silver Northumbrian '*stycas*' of about 750 and later exhibit the use of the same sort of 'Fantastic Animal' as the Cimiez hoard shows to have been current in the south some fifteen years before.

The subsequent development of English coinage shows that the interest in antique Roman coin-types we have noted so far did not cease with the '*sceattas*'. The rest of European coinage went its way under the influence of current Arabic, Byzantine, Italian, or Frankish prototypes. England was not unaffected by contemporary trends, but remained faithful to the direct and often renewed influence of Roman coinage to an unparalleled extent. The characteristic late Roman diademed and draped bust remained a direct source of inspiration not only for the pence of Offa, where its influence is palpable, but for a large majority of the royal heads of the late Anglo-Saxon series. Indeed, I would go so far as to assert that the predominance, and ultimate triumph, of the royal effigy in profile on the Early English coinage was conditioned by respect for Roman practice, and that groups in which aniconic types prevailed stand outside the normal pattern of development. It is, however, true that with the coming of the penny the influence of Roman reverse types becomes only sporadic. The very common 'Wolf and Twins' reverse of the Constantinian '*Urbs Roma*' was copied not only by late '*sceattas*' but also by the penny of Æthelbert of East Anglia (**Plate II, 6-8**). But apart from his direct imitation of Roman busts (**Plate II, 9-10**) and the occurrence of the Roman '*Vota* wreath', Offa seems to rely for inspiration only on the '*sceattas*'. Otherwise he looks towards contemporary Europe, and particularly Italy. The 'Celtic Cross' type seems to find its latest expression in the rosettes spacing the legend on several of his pence (**Plate II, 11**), while the 'Standard' design is clearly the source of others, and through them of the 'Three-line' series (**Plate II, 12-14**). The linear layout of the inscription has Frankish affinities, though I at least would be prepared to see in it the direct inspiration of the abundant coinage of Byzantine silver *miliaresia* introduced by Leo III (717-41) towards the end of his reign, an influence still strong as late as Ælfred. Similarly, the lettering often found on Offa's coinage (and never later), not least on his celebrated *dinar*, can be most easily paralleled on the contemporary Byzantine-Italian coinage of Rome, though a manuscript source may have furnished the actual models. Manuscripts or pictures rather than Papal coins must surely also be the inspiration for the treatment of the portraiture of the ninth-century archbishops of Canterbury. Essentially these effigies are but full-face versions of the regal portraits, the drapery, for example, remaining unaltered. But we notice that on occasional dies the archiepiscopal bust has acquired pendants below the ears derived from and only appropriate to imperial Byzantine features (**Plate II, 15–18**). Later copying does not call for much comment. The *Victoria Augg* 'Two Emperors' prototype – its later variety with the angular drapery covering the legs is clearly discernible – reappears on a famous penny of Ælfred, which was itself subsequently subject to Danish imitation (**Plate IX, 5**). The derivation of Edward the Elder's 'Burgh' type from the '*Providentiae Augg*' issue of Constantine the Great and his family is well known. Less famous but no less real is the exact imitation by the obverse of Æthelræd II's 'Radiate Helmet' penny of a pre-Reform *double denarius* of the Lyons mint, bearing the name of Maximian (**Plate II, 19–20**). Edward the Confessor looks more towards the German emperors than to Rome except on his 'Radiate Bust' type (**Plate II, 21**), but it is appropriate that the very last of our Saxon kings, Harold II, should model his effigy on a Roman bust of the first century, even though he decks it with the crown and sceptre of his own day, and the diadem tails proper to fourth-century Rome (**Plate II, 22–3**). The first type of William I was merely a modified version of Harold's bust, and effectively, all imitation of Roman coins stopped for good with the coming of the Normans.[38] The laureate effigies of the Stuart kings and the advent of Britannia are due to an antiquarianism remote from the immediacy of the tradition represented by Anglo-Saxon practice.

An endeavour to form a synthesis from the conclusions reached above forms a fitting end to my essay. We notice above all that the Anglo-Saxons had an intense interest in and admiration for things Roman. 'The Ruin', that famous poem on the remains of Bath, and the *tufa* carried before King Edwin, that he rightly or wrongly believed to be a Roman emblem,[39] continue with the coin-evidence to testify to a feeling far more profound than the qualified respect evinced by the more sophisticated barbarians for the relics of Roman greatness. St Cuthbert, we remember, was taken on a conducted tour of Roman Carlisle.[40] The unknown is always held by primitive man to be wonderful, but the phenomenon demands some explanation. That we are dealing in some way with a policy or state of mind is evident when we consider its effect on the choice of the first coin-types. Roman types abound, those of Merovingian Gaul seem to be of decreasing importance. Sutton Hoo shows that this was not due entirely to the small numbers in which Merovingian coins entered this country and the greater availability of Roman coins for copying. The very character of those copies is in itself revealing. It is clear that nothing of Roman date or type had remained in circulation. The copies have the appearance of having derived from quite a small number of hoards of limited range, for certain features emerge clearly. First, the earliest Anglo-Saxon coins do not on the whole (in

From Roman Britain to Saxon England

some cases, at all) copy either the latest Roman coins to circulate in Britain, nor those of classes of Roman imitation that are sometimes (I hope to have shown erroneously) held to have been produced by Briton or Saxon in the fifth or sixth centuries. Second, the combination on individual pieces of features, common to two or three Roman originals close to one another in date, suggests that much of the imitation was inspired by discovery at critical moments of hoards of late Roman coins, such as the words of the *Anglo-Saxon Chronicle* imply were not unfamiliar. There is no predominance of the very commonest Roman pieces such as should have occurred had casual site-finds furnished the inspiration. Third, these discoveries must have been made known to high authority to inspire coin-types, particularly in the later period, and we may perhaps venture to see in this the early stages of a law of Treasure Trove embracing *all* antique coin, as well as that authority's interest in Roman works.

The doctrine of the Dark Ages hiatus in coinage as in other classes of finds has already proved acceptable to Roman archaeologists. I hope that its implications will find favour with Anglo-Saxon scholars, and that we may come to appreciate our penny not merely as a by-product of the Merovingian *tremissis* and Carolingian *denier*, but as a true successor by descent and choice of types of the coinage of imperial Rome.

REFERENCES

1. H. M. SCARTH *Roman Britain* p. ix
2. C. H. V. SUTHERLAND *Coinage and Currency in Roman Britain (CCRB)* J. P. C. KENT 'Coin Evidence for the Abandonment of a Frontier Province' *Carnuntina* 1956 p. 85
3. e.g. at Richborough (Report IV p. 317) and Maiden Castle (Report p. 334)
4. *CCRB* pp. 90–1
5. The 1929 excavations at the Hadrian's Wall fort of Birdoswald suggest that in the north the currency developed a very miscellaneous character, with the continued circulation of obsolete pieces. Mrs Alison Ravetz, who has recently examined a large part of the north country evidence, kindly informs me that she has noted this phenomenon at other sites. However, it should be observed that the supposed association of barbarous radiates with worn coins of Valentinian at Carrawburgh (*NC* 1933 p. 81 *CCRB* pp. 116 and 121) is now recognized to be mistaken (*NC* 1937 p. 144; 1958 p. 184), and there is absolutely no reason to suppose that imitation in the north followed a different course from that in the south
6. C. E. STEVENS 'Marcus, Gratian, Constantine' *Athenaeum* 1957 p. 316
7. COLLINGWOOD and MYRES *Roman Britain and the English Settlements* ch. xviii. The late B. H. St J. O'Neil, a distinguished student of Early Dark Ages problems,

was good enough to write to me (1 February 1954) that in his experience this view, though widely publicized, achieved little recognition in academic circles

8. J. P. C. KENT 'Coin Evidence, and the Evacuation of Hadrian's Wall' *Trans. Cumb. and West. Arch. Soc.* 1952 p. 4
9. C. M. KRAAY 'The Behaviour of Early Imperial Countermarks' *Essays in Roman Coinage presented to Harold Mattingly* p. 113
10. J. P. C. KENT 'Gold Coinage in the Later Roman Empire' ibid. p. 190
11. J. P. C. KENT 'The Search for Fifth Century Coins in Britain' *Arch. News Letter* December 1954 p. 115. A forthcoming note in *NC* will endeavour to justify the redating of '*Urbs Roma Felix*' from 393–396 (*RIC* IX pp. 113–14)
12. Terling, Coleraine, 'St Pancras' (*NC* 1959 p. 15)
13. H. A. CAHN 'Trierer Siliquen des Valentinianus III. und des Theodosius II.' *Rev. Suisse de Num.* 1937 p. 425
14. C. H. V. SUTHERLAND 'Coinage in Britain in the Fifth and Sixth Centuries' *Dark Age Britain: Studies presented to E. T. Leeds* p. 5
15. GILDAS *de excidio Britanniae* ch. 66, p. 107
16. p. 151
17. p. 156
18. *Arch. Cant.* 1889 p. 72
19. *NC* 1859 p. 140
20. H. MATTINGLY and W. P. D. STEBBING 'The Richborough Hoard of "Radiates", 1931' *Num. Notes and Mon.* no. 80 p. 13
21. C. H. V. SUTHERLAND see *supra* note 14
22. P. V. HILL '"Barbarous Radiates": Imitations of Third-Century Roman Coins' *Num. Notes and Mon.* no. 112. Cf. E. J. W. HILDYARD and P. V. HILL 'A Radiate Currency Hoard from Yorkshire' *NC* 1958 p. 183
23. P. V. HILL '"Sceatta-like" Barbarous Imitations' *NC* 1949 p. 142. Cf. D. F. Allen's observations on the Richborough hoard, note 20
24. J. P. C. KENT 'Barbarous Copies of Roman Coins' *Proceedings of the Third Congress of Roman Frontier Studies (Rheinfelden)* p. 61
25. P. LE GENTILHOMME *Le monnayage et la circulation monétaire dans les royaumes barbares en occident (V^e–VIIIe siècle)* Paris 1946 provides a concise, amply documented, and reliable introduction to sub-Roman coinage on the Continent
26. S. E. RIGOLD 'An Imperial Coinage in Southern Gaul in the Sixth and Seventh Centuries?' *NC* 1954 p. 93
27. P. GRIERSON 'The Canterbury (St Martin's) Hoard of Frankish and Anglo-Saxon Coin-Ornaments' *BNJ* XXVII, i (1952) p. 39
28. Sutton Hoo: P. GRIERSON 'The Dating of the Sutton Hoo Coins' *Antiquity* 1952 p. 83. Crondall: C. H. V. SUTHERLAND *Anglo-Saxon Gold Coinage in the light of the Crondall Hoard (ASGC)*
29. BEDE *Hist. Eccl.* 3, 8. The setting of the story of her death must be, *pace* SUTHERLAND (*ASGC* p. 50 note 1), Brie in France, and not York. *Eboriacum*, the name of her monastery, has been confused in *ASGC* with *Eboracum*

From Roman Britain to Saxon England

30. As G. C. BROOKE *English Coins* p. 4, J. D. A. THOMPSON *Inventory of British Coin Hoards, A.D. 600–1500* p. 38. Sutherland's ascription to Leo I is based on his meticulously accurate transcription of the legend, but is negatived by its type, and its characteristic 'Ravenna' style
31. *English Historical Documents* I p. 432
32. For its date, see GRIERSON, op. cit. p. 43 (other examples)
33. BEDE op. cit. 3, 6
34. P. V. HILL 'The "Standard" and "London" Series of Anglo-Saxon Sceattas' *BNJ* XXVI, iii (1951) p. 251
35. A Merovingian coin of Orléans (Belfort no. 542) of generally similar size and appearance is inscribed DENARIVS AVRILIANI
36. A more immediate prototype should perhaps be sought in the Merovingian issues of Campbon (Belfort no. 1345)
37. The distribution of certain types has led to the suggestion that they were struck at Southampton also (HILL note 34 p. 271). Canterbury, too, is a probable mint from the start of the Anglo-Saxon coinage
38. Type II of Henry I is no more than a rough copy of type I of the Conqueror
39. BEDE op. cit. 2, 16. The Byzantine *tufa* was probably itself of Germanic origin
40. *Vita* ch. 27

Appendix

ROMAN COINS FOUND IN ANGLO-SAXON CEMETERIES

It was recognized many years ago by J. G. Milne* that the incidence of Roman coins and their imitations in Anglo-Saxon graves should have a considerable bearing on the question of a sub-Roman coinage in Britain, and with this in mind, the contents of some forty cemeteries have been analysed, providing a 'sample' of about one-third of the available evidence. Milne's conclusion, that *minimi* of radiate or Constantinian derivation form the characteristic coin association of the Anglo-Saxon grave, is hardly borne out by the totals revealed. In fact, it would be more accurate to say that the list exemplifies my earlier assertion,† that it contains 'a random assortment of all the commonest pieces of the Roman coinage'. It is unusual for more than two per cent of the graves to contain coins at all, and in several cases it appears that the discovery of a hoard by the family of a single individual, and its conversion into a necklace is the cause of its association with a burial. The ten early third-century *denarii* and '*antoniniani*' from Brighthampton (no. 10), pierced and found in a single grave, are a clear instance. The one grave accounts for all but five examples of this period. Much the greater number of coins have been pierced at least once, thus emphasizing their use as ornaments rather than currency. One specimen from Sleaford (no. 37, grave no. 191) retains on the back traces of the fabric to which it had been sewn, while post-Roman gold, e.g. the Merovingian pieces from Sibertswold (no. 36, grave no. 172) is often equipped with added gold loops. Not until later in the seventh century do we find contemporary, unpierced coins, evidently withdrawn from currency. The Sutton Hoo burial contains one of the earliest deposits of this character. Finds of unpierced '*sceattas*' occurred in graves at Broadstairs,‡ Sarre,§ and elsewhere. A subsidiary use for Roman coins was as weights, and in four finds, Ash (no. 2), Gilton (no. 23), Ozingell (no. 33), and Sarre (no. 34), they occurred in company with balances and scale-pans, accounting for almost half of the coins of Æ 1 and Æ 2 size.

The overall picture shows coins of the later years of Constantine I and the first years of his successors to be substantially the most common. Second in numbers come radiates of the third century. In all but a few cases these are of

---

* *JRS* 21 (1931) p. 106; cf. C. H. V. SUTHERLAND in *NC* 1934 p. 104

† J. P. C. KENT 'Barbarous Copies of Roman Coins' *Proceedings of the Third Congress of Roman Frontier Studies (Rheinfelden)*

‡ H. HURD *Some Notes on Recent Archaeological Discoveries at Broadstairs* p. 24

§ *Arch. Cant.* 1864–8 (grave no. 226)

From Roman Britain to Saxon England

the Gallic Empire, and, with a mere handful of exceptions, regular. Those few barbarous pieces are on the whole of equal size with their prototypes, and all come, by an odd coincidence, from the Oxford region.* Similarly, '*Fel. Temp. Reparatio* Horseman' imitations are notably uncommon outside that area – though no more so than one would expect from their relative scarcity on sites, as opposed to hoards – and we are entitled to wonder why such copies are comparatively unusual. In the first instance, though absolute abundance is undoubtedly reflected to some extent, we can observe that large coins, such as *folles*, seem to be over-represented. Similarly, really small coins, such as radiate *minims*, 'Falling Horseman' copies, and those of the House of Theodosius, are uncommon. It was formerly suggested that the *presence* of copies was evidence for their Dark Ages date. Now that it has been shown that this was essentially a mistaken notion, we must beware of the contrary viewpoint, that it is on account of their *absence* that their Dark Ages currency can be postulated. The presence of undoubted seventh-century coin in such graves as Sutton Hoo, Broadstairs, Sarre, and most recently Driffield, completely negatives such a view. Whatever coin was available was evidently acceptable as grave furniture. If it was current, it was kept intact, if not, then it was liable to be pierced or mounted as necklace or disk-brooch. In this telling neither regular Roman coins nor their copies achieved any currency, for the vast majority are pierced. And, if anything, copies seem to have been scarce because their insignificant size and shabby appearance led to their being overlooked and neglected, except in the 'back-woods' regions of the Upper Thames.

I conclude that this evidence confirms the absence of a coinage in Britain between the advent of the Anglo-Saxons, and the main influx of Merovingian coins in the first half of the seventh century. We have seen that distribution alone prevents the attribution of any coinage to the Britons of the post-Roman era. I hope it is now apparent that the Anglo-Saxons are equally ineligible. The contents of their graves combine with the evidence of their earliest copies to illustrate the haphazard character of their association with Roman coins.

* Abingdon (no. 1), Brighthampton (no. 10), Wheatley (no. 41). The identification of the Wheatley coin is somewhat uncertain

TABLE I

	First century		Second century		Third century					Fourth century					Post-Roman
					AR		Æ								
								Radiates							
	AR	Æ	AR	Æ	Denarii	'Antoniniani'	Aes	Regular	Barbarous	Folles	House of Constantine	'Fel. Temps.' and Magnentius	House of Valentinian	House of Theodosius	
1 Abingdon (Berks.)															
2 Ash (Kent)								1	1		4	1			
3 Barfriston (Kent)				2											
4 Barham Down (Kent)											1		1		1
5 Barrington (Cambs.)					1										
6 Bekesbourne (Kent)				1											
7 Bishopsbourne (Kent)											2				
8 Blood Moore Hill (Suff.)					no coins										
9 Breach Down (Kent)															1
10 Brighthampton (Oxon.)								1							
11 Burwell (Cambs.)					7	3		6	1	2	3		1		
12 Caistor (Norf.)				3											
13 Chartham (Kent)					2										
14 Chatham Lines (Kent)					no coins										
15 Chessel Down (I.O.W.)	1						1	3				5			1
16 Croydon (Surrey)	1			1				1		1	1				
17 Crundale (Kent)				1											
18 Droxford (Hants)				1						1	2	1			
19 Dunstable Downs (Beds.)								1					1		
20 East Shefford (Berks.)								2		1	4				
21 Fairford (Glos.)								2				7			
22 Frilford (Berks.)			1								1	5	4	2	
23 Gilton (Kent)		3		4				1		2	2				1
24 Girton (Cambs.)											5				
25 Guildown (Surrey)					coin illegible										
26 Harnham Hill (Wilts.)											1				
27 Holywell Row (Suff.)											2	1			
28 Howletts (Kent)											1		1		
29 Little Wilbraham (Cambs.)				7				1		2	20				
30 Long Wittenham (Berks.)								1		1	5				
31 Marston St Lawrence (Northants.)								2				1?			
32 Mitcham (Surrey)						1				1	2				1
33 Ozingell (Kent)	1			4				1		3	1				
34 Sarre (Kent)										1					
35 Shudy Camps (Cambs.)															2
36 Sibertswold							1	4		1	6	1			
37 Sleaford (Lincs.)											1				
38 Stapenhill (Derb.)					1	1					1		1		
39 Stowting (Kent)					6 uncertain										
40 West Stow Heath (Suff.)									1?			2			
41 Wheatley (Oxon.)															
	–	6	1	26	11	4	1	27	3	14	66	13[42]	20	3	7

From Roman Britain to Saxon England

NOTES TO TABLE

1. E. T. LEEDS and D. B. HARDEN *The Anglo-Saxon Cemetery at Abingdon, Berkshire*
2. REV. J. DOUGLAS *Nenia Britannica*: ground to serve as weights
3. B. FAUSSETT *Inventorium Sepulchrale*: includes an Ostrogothic Æ of Rome. The coin of Theodosius I in this grave is a '*Reparatio Reipub*' – a House of Valentinian type of *c*. 380
4. ex Mantell Coll. in BM
5. In BM – a probable identification
6. B. FAUSSETT op. cit.
7. Ibid.
8. REV. J. DOUGLAS op. cit. suppl. Pl. 5.2 (BM edition). This is a Late Visigothic copy of Justinian, and not a coin of Avitus as reported, and commonly stated
9. In BM
10. Ashmolean Museum
11. T. C. LETHBRIDGE *Recent Excavations in Anglo-Saxon Cemeteries in Cambridge and Suffolk*
12. C. H. V. SUTHERLAND *Coinage and Currency in Roman Britain*
13. B. FAUSSETT op. cit.
14. REV. J. DOUGLAS op. cit. Douglas's material is now mostly in the Ashmolean Museum, but the coins seem to have become separated at an early date, and cannot now be found. The seeming coin of Anthemius does not correspond in style, type, or conventions with known pieces of that Emperor and his times, and remains a puzzle
15. In BM
16. E. A. MARTIN *Anglo-Saxon Remains in and around Croydon*
17. B. FAUSSETT op. cit.
18. In BM
19. (SIR) R. E. M. WHEELER in the *Fourth Annual Report* (1928–9) of the Dunstable Museum Committee
20. No coins are quoted by H. PEAKE and E. A. HOOTON *A Saxon Graveyard at East Shefford, Berkshire* but BM acquired some in 1893
21. W. M. WYLIE *Fairford Graves*. One coin (Gallienus) in BM
22. Ashmolean Museum
23. B. FAUSSETT op. cit.: several (in grave no. 66) had been ground and marked for use as weights
24. E. J. HOLLINGWORTH and M. M. O'REILLY *The Anglo-Saxon Cemetery at Girton, Cambs.*
25. *Surrey Arch. Coll.* 39 (1931): probably a mutilated Æ 2
26. In BM
27. T. C. LETHBRIDGE op. cit.
28. In BM
29. HON. R. C. NEVILLE *Saxon Obsequies, etc.*; T. C. LETHBRIDGE op. cit.
30. In BM
31. *Arch.* 38 (1860)
32. *Surrey Arch. Coll.* 21 (1908) = *Arch.* 60 (1882)
33. C. ROACH SMITH *Collectanea Antiqua* III: most of the coins were ground and marked to serve as weights. There was also a Constantinopolitan *solidus* of Justinian I, type as *BMC* 16
34. *Arch. Cant.* 1864–8: Grave no. 26 contained a balance and scales, and twelve coins, several now illegible, ground down and marked to serve as weights
35. T. C. LETHBRIDGE *A Cemetery at Shudy Camps, Cambridge*
36. B. FAUSSETT op. cit. Roach Smith correctly read the coins, and attributed them to Verdun and Marsal. At one time, the latter was attributed, for example by Douglas, to Clovis
37. In BM. Grave no. 85 contained (out of a total of six) an example of the extremely rare 'Lugdunum' *follis* of Maxentius (see J. P. C. KENT 'Bronze Coinage under Constantine I' *NC* 1957 p. 42 no. 251), the first known to have been found in Britain
38. *Trans. Burton-on-Trent Nat. Hist. and Arch. Soc.* 1 (1889)
39. *Arch.* 31 (1846); 41 (1867)
40. *Proc. Bury and West Suff. Arch. Inst.* 7 (May 1953): six Roman coins, perforated from one to three times

Anglo-Saxon Coins

41. Ashmolean Museum. I could not find the 'Radiate' copy mentioned by C. H. V. SUTHERLAND in *NC* 1934 p. 104
42. This figure may be further broken down in chronological order as follows:

   'Fel. Temp. Reparatio Hut type': Constans 2 (Holywell Row, Sleaford)
   'Fel. Temp. Reparatio Phoenix/Pyre' type: Constans 3 (Frilford, Wheatley)
   'Fel. Temp. Reparatio Galley' type: Constans 1 (Sleaford)*
   'Two Victories' type: Magnentius 2 (Abingdon, Frilford)*
   Uncertain type: Magnentius 1 (Sarre)
   'Fel. Temp. Reparatio Falling Horseman' type: Constantius II 1 (Droxford)
   'Fel. Temp. Reparatio', but barbarous – 2 (Frilford)*
   Barbarous examples are asterisked

   The negligible impact of the *'Fel. Temp. Reparatio'* coinage and its barbarous copies is well exemplified. The classic 'Falling Horseman' copies occur in one cemetery – probably one grave – only. Their relative undesirability and non-availability stands out. The Mitcham coin is of Constantius II, but may equally belong to the preceding period

II

The Byzantine Empire and the Coinage of the Anglo-Saxons

by P. D. WHITTING

[Plate III]

The days when the deeds of the Heptarchy could be dismissed as 'the scuffling of kites and crows' have long since gone, even if the popular view of the period still retains much of Sellar and Yeatman's brilliant parody in *1066 and All That*. The change of view involves the whole character of the world of western and northern Europe after the collapse of the Roman Empire, and particularly the place of the Anglo-Saxons within that world. That the emerging civilization was different from that of Rome is obvious, but it is being looked at by men like Professor A. R. Lewis[1] as an independent growth, not as a chaotic barbarism at its best imitative of the past. Thus have the Dark Ages been transformed into a busy world of voyaging, trading, and exchange in which even the destructive Vikings played some formative part. The peaks appear in the period of the early Merovingians, the Age of Louis the Pious, and in the days of the Ottos; the low points are at the Germanic invasions, the Merovingian decadence, and the great onslaught of the Scandinavians in the ninth century. Pirenne's ideas as to the importance of the seventh-century Arab attacks in the Mediterranean have engendered such lively controversy that much new fact has been uncovered and new peoples like the Frisians have emerged as important in the world of trade.

The part played by the English outside their own land has been one of the features of the reassessment, and England has been referred to as a dominating cultural influence in tenth-century Europe. To call England an industrial centre in Carolingian times is perhaps to give a misleading impression today, but her products, especially woollen cloaks and embroidery, were wanted abroad: thus her traders were to be found all over North-western Europe and were given special privileges in Italian towns. After 991 her wealth calculated from her payments of Danegeld alone was great, both in itself and when compared with payments by neighbouring lands.

The English were well known on the Continent. There had been early

Anglo-Saxon Coins

Anglo-Saxon settlements from Britain in the Boulogne area and much subsequent intercourse, even if the slave trade formed an important part of it. Some impression of well-established communications may be conveyed by Aelfred's two visits to Rome as a boy, the frequent complaints at Pavia over English merchants evading taxation, or the Lombard King Perctarit considering refuge in England when dethroned in 662. The seventh century in particular was one of expanding trade and even greater activity in the spiritual field. Men and women of all ranks made pilgrimages to Rome, including the Wessex kings Cædwalla and Ine. The former died in Rome shortly after his baptism in 686 and Ine made the journey after his abdication: Cœnred of Mercia also went to Rome after his abdication in 709. From the early eighth century, Rome had its Anglo-Saxon quarter – today the Borgo San Spirito near St Peter's – for which Pope Leo IV erected a church and hostel after a devastating fire about 850. Both physically and spiritually the English connexion with Rome was intimate, for the decisions of the Synod of Whitby were loyally implemented, and apparently without hard feeling.

Thus securely based on the ideal of maintaining unity with Rome and uniformity with her practice, the English missions to Frisia and Germany began. In the words of Dr Levison[2] they inaugurated 'a century of English spiritual influence on the Continent' and were part of 'the expression of Anglo-Saxon expansion and influence'. The deeds of Wilfrid of York and Willibrord of Ripon among the Frisians and the long column of comrades and successors of Wynfrid carried English ideas all over Central Europe. Too little credit is given in their homeland to the courage, enterprise, and enduring influence of Englishmen like Lullus, Willibald, Willehad, Burghard, Leofwine, Beornred, and a host of others: nuns like Leofgyth, Waldburg and Hygeburg also played their part, and the last recorded the lives of the pioneers Wynnebald and Willebald.

It is against some such background as this, rather than one of isolation and backwardness, that English relationship with the Byzantine Empire should be viewed. In spite of disjointed records and much that is uncertain, there emerges a picture of England often playing an important part in western European affairs. Her kings like Offa and Æthelstan ranked with the highest of their time, and her merchants had well-recognized lines of trade, commerce, and communication. England established herself as an important component of the post-Roman world, closely connected with her neighbours in Frisia, Scandinavia, and the Kingdom of the Franks, and with Italy. The Byzantines knew something of Britain and in the sixth century Procopius refers to it as an island one-tenth the size of Thule (probably Iceland), which Belisarius was prepared to surrender, as it had once been Roman, to the Goths in exchange for Sicily which

The Byzantine Empire and the Coinage of the Anglo-Saxons

he had just captured from them in 535. Procopius, however, quotes as an instance of the unreliability of Sibylline prophecies, their tendency to mix the calamities of Britain with important imperial affairs.

Byzantium, in constant conflict with her enemies to the north and east, was already showing signs of exhaustion before Justinian I's death in 565. To citizens of the metropolis, Britain must have appeared as a distant place of little account. When the new Arab attacks gathered impetus in the seventh century the Emperor Constans II had to consider moving his capital back to Italy: this was at the moment when the Roman mission, led by Theodore from Monte Cassino and Hadrian from Naples, was leaving for England. The Franks suspected Hadrian of being an imperial agent sent to work in Britain against their interests, though the mission may equally well be explained as an attempt by Pope Vitalian to secure support against Constans II, who was uncomfortably near. The murder of Constans II in Syracuse was to end this strange and somewhat unreal entanglement of Britain in imperial policy. In the eighth century the Iconoclastic controversy was to drive a wedge between Rome and Byzantium at the very moment when the conflict against Moslems and Slavs reached such intensity that no help could be sent to ward off the new Lombard offensive in Italy. Byzantine power was perceptibly on the retreat in the west, just as England was reaching, through her missionaries in particular, a peak of influence on the Continent.

No one has as yet attempted to claim that there was any direct contact between the Anglo-Saxons and the Byzantine Empire before the Norman Conquest, as R. S. Lopez[3] has pointed out. This is in spite of a number of suggestive indications like the curious incident of Pope Vitalian and the Hadrian mission. Lopez writes that 'a strong wave of Eastern influence seems to have penetrated Anglo-Saxon cultural and artistic life from the end of the seventh century': he instances amongst other things that 'it was England that became the centre of Greek studies in northern and western Europe, surpassing even Ireland, where Greek and Coptic traditions were older still'. It is good that such lines of thought should be explored, but as yet the evidence seems slender and depends heavily on indirect transmission through Italy and the Western Empire. It is in the sphere of the arts that the influence of Byzantium in England has been most authoritatively canvassed, and it is particularly unfortunate that in the course of this, such slender attention has been paid to coins. In Sir Thomas Kendrick's[4] two volumes there are but two passing references to coins, nor does Professor Talbot Rice[5] give them any systematic treatment in his more recent analysis. It would be unfair to blame the art historians entirely for this, as numismatists have tended to keep their study in

Anglo-Saxon Coins

a watertight compartment as well as often writing with intimidating technicality. The need for exchange and integration of ideas is particularly strong in this field.

Imitation of a design does not necessarily imply that there are frequent exchanges between the peoples concerned, or that the object imitated is a common one. A single piece like the Sutton Hoo silver dish stamped in the reign of the Emperor Anastasius or a stray *solidus* of Theodosius I might catch the eye of patron or craftsman: thereby an imitative artistic tradition might begin without there being any necessary contact at all. Where regular trade and commerce was taking place, there would be more opportunity for imitation and more likelihood of its occurring in many spheres at once. Thus when Dr Adelson[6] suggests that the distinctive 'light-weight' *solidi*, struck by all emperors from Justinian I to Constantine IV, were specifically for commerce with the barbarian peoples of the north, it might be assumed that the coins would be found fairly frequently in hoards, and in jewellery. Such an issue seems to assume regular contact and from such familiarity imitation over a wide field other than coinage should arise. This has not yet been shown to be true in England, where the Wilton cross and an East Anglian find are the only known examples discovered locally. English coinage itself shows nothing but the most casual imitation of Byzantine types.

The many problems involved in the relationship of the so-called *thrymsas*, *sceattas*, and pennies to their prototypes need far more concentration of detailed study than they have yet received. In the broadest terms imitation of certain late Roman imperial types is clearly established. Roman bronze coins were plentiful in the country so that imitation would be natural and easy after the withdrawal of the army and administrative officials. The survival of the 'Radiate Bust' so frequently used by emperors in the third century, and of the 'Standard' from the Constantinian '*Virtus Exercit*' type, are plain enough in the '*Sceatta*' series. Even so, in studying these strangely distorted derivatives, the possibility of the imitation being itself one of an imitation must be borne in mind: Roman currency was being copied by many different peoples and not least by the Franks with whom the English maintained close relations. The date of the prototype – whether recent currency or hundreds of years old – is another factor in the evaluation. In dealing with possible Byzantine prototypes the problem is complicated by there being no continuous or direct relationship.

It seems certain that at no time was there any considerable quantity of Byzantine[7] coinage circulating in Britain, and so giving rise to imitation by its very familiarity. The finds of Byzantine coins in Britain are meagre in the extreme and ill-recorded. For a long time no register of such finds was maintained,

The Byzantine Empire and the Coinage of the Anglo-Saxons

with the result that information is scattered and incomplete. In J. D. A. Thompson's *Inventory of British Coin Hoards, A.D. 600–1500* Byzantine pieces figure only at Cuerdale and London (no. 253): the second is, as the compiler has noted, an exceptionally dubious 'hoard' and is dated '*c*. 1300?' as Andronicus II is the last of seven emperors spanning seven hundred years that are represented amongst the nine coins. As recently as 1958, G. C. Boon of the National Museum of Wales in Cardiff took over the material available and has since maintained a register of finds,[8] though this still seems not to be widely known. The interpretation of such a list could be of considerable importance to historians of the Dark Ages; but in fact the coins whether found singly or in groups are a most unconvincing collection when submitted to any cross-examination. Mr Boon, with everyone else who has examined the list of ninety coins, considers that the greatest caution is necessary in dealing with them. Although reports have come from Wales, Scotland, Ireland, and fourteen English counties (Devon, Somerset, Wilts., Hants, Kent, London, Suffolk, Norfolk, Cambridgeshire, Lincs., Staffs., Lancashire, Cumberland, Westmorland), only two finds at Ilchester appear to be impeccably genuine – a pierced *follis* of Anastasius and an early 'Profile' *follis* of Justinian I. The rest do not look like genuine hoards or ancient losses at all, though some of them conceivably may be. Pieces continue to be reported from such odd and unlikely places that it is permissible to suggest that they have been discarded in one way or another in fairly recent years after being acquired in the course of travel or commercial purchase. Knowledge of the Byzantine series is still not common in this country and it may have proved difficult to identify some of the well-worn bronze pieces: in the end it seems that a number were regarded as expendable. The possibility of returning Crusaders bringing back a few coins is worth entertaining, but as yet no case has arisen to justify this solution.

In spite of the unreliability of the finds contained in this list it may be useful to enumerate the reigns represented: Anastasius I, Justin I, Justinian I, Justin II, Tiberius II, Maurice, Phocas, Heraclius, Constans II, Constantive IV, Justinian II, Leo III, Constantine V, Leo V, Michael II, Michael III, Nicephorus II, John Zimisces, Basil II, Michael IV, Constantine IX, Constantine X, Nicephorus III, Alexius I, Manuel I, Andronicus II. It is an impressive list without serious breaks except after Michael III (867) and Manuel I (1180); but when some ninety coins are spread over twenty-five different reigns and fifty alleged find-spots, no significant pattern emerges.

Mr Boon's register is concerned primarily with bronze and silver coins, but the finds of Byzantine gold pieces, though fewer and better authenticated, are not very helpful. In his patient and comprehensive treatment of the problems arising out of the Crondall hoard, Dr Sutherland[9] has collected the evidence on finds of imperial coins and their number is very small: only the reigns of Justinian I (527–65), Justin II, Maurice, and Heraclius (610–41) are represented. To these may be added a find in Kent at Westerham in 1954 of a *solidus* of Leo III (717–41) which is Western in style and weight standard.[10] It makes a strange bed-fellow with those in the other fairly compact group.

The importance of the Crondall hoard in piecing together the story of the Anglo-Saxon gold coinage may be judged from Dr Sutherland's Catalogue of the series in which seventy-three, out of one hundred and thirty-one coins listed, are from the hoard. It contained no imperial Byzantine coins, although G. C. Brooke states that one piece 'a coin of the Emperor Phocas gives an approximate date for the burial of the hoard'. In Thompson's *Inventory* this piece is more accurately listed as 'Tremisses. Copy of Emp. Focas?, 1;' as it is in fact a Lombard copy of a Ravenna *tremissis* of Phocas. Akerman's account[11] did not mention the piece, and Dr Sutherland following Keary lists it as 'imitated from the imperial coinage of Leo, 451–474'. An over-scrupulous transliteration of the legend may have caused this mistake, though it is surprising that Brooke's comment was overlooked. Without the help that this coin could give Dr Sutherland dated the hoard 650–70: J. D. A. Thompson in his *Inventory* gives c. 670, and Dr Kent, in suggesting a still later date, stresses the importance of the 'Phocas' piece.[12]

In the Crondall hoard only the *tremisses* with a 'Cross on Steps' design for the reverse show clear derivation from Byzantine prototypes, and that through a Merovingian intermediary. The 'Cross on Steps' was introduced as a regular reverse design for the *solidus* by Tiberius II (578–82)[13] who also changed the reverse of the *tremissis* from a 'Winged Victory' to a 'Cross Potent'. His successors Maurice and Phocas retained the new *tremissis* design but reverted to the earlier 'Victory' (or 'St Michael') carrying a long-shafted cross in the right hand, for their *solidi*. Thereafter from Heraclius (610–41) to Leo III (717–41), who retained it for his first issue, the 'Cross on Steps' remained the major component of one side of the *solidus*: only under Justinian II was this changed in his first reign. But within the general type during its century of use there were many varieties from the four wide steps of Tiberius II to the commoner narrow, thick, and bunched ones of later emperors.[14] The prototype of the 'Ciolh' *solidus* (Sutherland, no. 76) with its 'Cross on Steps' reverse can hardly be Tiberius II's wide and well-spaced design: it is much nearer to versions used by Heraclius or Constans II. The design is important enough for the variations to receive minute attention such as must also be given to the details of helmets, diadems, and radiate crowns worn by the later Roman emperors. If the stylistic

The Byzantine Empire and the Coinage of the Anglo-Saxons

argument above has any validity the 'Ciolh' *solidus* (**Plate III, 8**) can hardly be attributed to Ceol of Wessex (591–7).

The imperial *tremissis* continued from Tiberius II to Leo III, with only one exception, as a simple 'Cross Potent' without the steps associated with it on the *solidus*. The design of the *tremissis* weighing 1·5–1·4 grammes was clearly differentiated from that of the *solidus* weighing three times that amount. Dr Lopez has referred to the Byzantine *solidus* as 'the dollar of the Middle Ages': it was, that is to say, a coin of international currency retaining its standards of weight and purity until the reign of Constantine IX in the middle of the eleventh century. The *solidus* was, however, only infrequently copied by the Merovingians and Anglo-Saxons: they found the *tremissis* more useful, and it was their basic piece. The frequent adoption of the 'Cross on Steps' design from the imperial *solidus* for their *tremisses* may indicate the importance that Merovingians and Anglo-Saxons attached to the *solidus*. They may possibly also have seen the small thick *solidi* of the Carthage mint which had the usual *solidus* reverse design: though of equal weight to the larger issues of Constantinople or Ravenna these coins had a diameter of only 12 mm. and may have suggested the suitability of transferring the design to a *tremissis*. The Carthage coins (**Plate III, 4**) were struck from the reign of Maurice until the capture of the city by Hassan's forces in 697 and were continued for a time by the Arabs in an imitated form.

It is in some ways unfortunate that the treasure associated with the Sutton Hoo ship burial contained no Anglo-Saxon or Byzantine coins amongst the thirty-seven Merovingian and three pseudo-imperial *tremisses*. A final assessment of all the material is still awaited, but the burial seems to have occurred earlier than Crondall by a few decades. The absence of imperial pieces is as important as the dominance of Merovingian ones: both are pointers to the influences current in the formative years of Anglo-Saxon coinage. Over seventy years ago C. F. Keary wrote:[15]

> We may then take it as established that the whole class of anonymous gold and silver coins which constitute the earliest English coinage, was derived from the coinage of the Franks under their Merovingian kings . . . it was from the Merovingian coins, in the first instance from the gold, later on from the silver that the earliest English coinage was derived.

Keary's solidly substantiated argument holds good today; but it allows plenty of scope for Byzantine influence, even if at second-hand or more remotely. The Merovingians inhabited a deeply Romanized area and were themselves in diplomatic, cultural, commercial, and military contact with the rulers of the late Roman Empire in Constantinople.

Anglo-Saxon Coins

A classic example of straightforward imitation of a late Roman or early Byzantine type may be seen in the *solidus* in the British Museum (Sutherland, no. 21) and a whole series of *tremisses* (Sutherland, nos. 31–44). The prototype is unmistakable – the 'two seated Emperors holding an orb between them', with a 'Winged Victory' hovering over their heads: it was a reverse type having a short existence from Valentinian I (364–75) to Theodosius I (379–95), but in that period issued in the name of at least nine associated emperors. There are a number of small varieties in the type which might be reflected in any imitation, as may be seen in volume IX of *Roman Imperial Coinage*; Dr J. P. C. Kent, however, has pointed to a characteristic turn of drapery over the leg which strongly suggests a Milan issue of Valentinian II. The imitator of this reverse has done his work well in the case of the *solidus* (though it is a whole gramme too heavy and may not be a coin at all), but the same cannot be said when he turned to the obverse, if indeed he was trying to imitate there. On **Plate I, 11 and 10** can be seen the prototype from Milan with a derivative *tremissis* also alongside. The *tremissis* shed the bottom half of the design, so that there appear to be three busts pyramidally arranged, the one at the top having wings. In spite of a number of different dies being used this *tremissis* design does not deteriorate.

Particular attention has been paid to this type because it was to be used again by Ceolwulf II of Mercia and Ælfred of Wessex almost simultaneously as the reverse design for a silver penny. Probably later the same design was used in the Danelaw by an unknown Halfdan.[16] As a reminder of the distant prototype issued five hundred years before, Ælfred's coin is characteristically the best. Sir Frank Stenton remarked that 'it was hardly possible as yet to decide which of the three kings was the first to use this type'. A satisfactory explanation is still sought for this remarkable resurrection of a type and for its immediate popularity. (See **Plate III, 10–12**.)

Before leaving early Anglo-Saxon gold coins two other pieces which for good reasons were not included in Dr Sutherland's catalogue may be briefly mentioned. The *solidus* of the St Martin's Canterbury hoard has an obverse with 'Facing Bust and Cross' in the right field, which clearly proclaims a Justinian I prototype, albeit a bronze one. But this piece is assigned by Mr Grierson to Francia rather than England. Another *solidus*, now represented by casts, is included by Mr Grierson amongst the Anglo-Saxon coins in the Fitzwilliam Collection.[17] The reverse of this piece is plainly derived from the 'Cross on Steps' design as normally used in Heraclius' reign, but this seventh-century design is accompanied by an obverse bust of elaborate fourth-century style. Two other examples of this interesting piece have been traced by Mr Grierson in Paris and Nuremberg.

The Byzantine Empire and the Coinage of the Anglo-Saxons

The same story of Merovingian and Byzantine prototypes can be told of the silver '*Sceatta*' series which began soon after the introduction of a native gold coinage and overlapped the so-called *thrymsas*. P. V. Hill[18] in gathering together much scattered material has contrived to bring more order into this baffling series which spans the late seventh to the mid-eighth century. They continued the close Merovingian connexion being virtually '*thrymsas*' in silver, which itself became ultimately so debased as to be indistinguishable from bronze. The Merovingian weight standard was maintained in the debased metal, that is to say, seven *siliquae* to the *tremissis* as against the Byzantine imperial standard of eight. The debasement of types kept pace with that of the metal with results that tax the imagination. Once more late Roman prototypes are far more in evidence than anything Byzantine. The Constantinian '*Romae Æternae*', '*Urbs Roma*', and above all the '*Virtus Exercit*' with its standard inscribed VOT XX are prominent amongst the reverses. But the 'Cross on Steps' continued, and a new and possibly Byzantine inspired type appeared in the 'Standing Figure holding a Long Cross on either side of him'. The type has affinities with the EN TŎ TO NIKA bronze issues of Constans II (641–68) on which the 'Emperor appears standing, facing with a long cross in his right hand and an orb cruciger in his left'. The folds of the imperial robe could easily be mistaken for a downward prolongation of the cross on the orb. The Byzantine issue was a large one, often badly struck, and used over a long period, if the number and worn condition of the surviving specimens is anything to go by. (**Plate III, 16**.)

One variety of this 'Standing Figure' '*Sceatta*' type (*BMC* 101) is of a 'Man with a Long Cross in his right hand and a Bird (perhaps a relic of the consular eagle-headed sceptre) in his left'; in the field beneath the bird is a T. This piece has all the elements of an early Arab-Byzantine issue, and Dr John Walker's Catalogue of these early Arab coins has also examples of 'Two Standing Figures with Crosses' such as can be found amongst the *sceattas*. These strange similarities may be worth further thought, but behind all these 'Standing Figure' types there seems to brood the figure of 'Victory' or 'St Michael' advancing with a long cross in the right hand and an orb cruciger in the left, which was introduced as the *solidus* reverse by Justin I (518–27) and continued in use for nearly a century. It must have been well known.

Yet all that has been said about Byzantine prototypes adds up to very little. In the '*Sceatta*' series especially it is difficult to find significant details like the tie behind the diadem, the turn of drapery lines, or the characteristic layout of design. The search for precise relationships behind what seem more likely to be vague memories of designs must go on and will no doubt yield results. But the more relations with Byzantium in the realm of coinage are probed, the clearer

Anglo-Saxon Coins

it seems to be that the English were not familiar with the contemporary coinage of the Eastern Empire and that it was to the Roman Empire and especially to the early emperors in fourth-century Constantinople that a return was made. In spite of its international character the golden *solidus* has left fewer traces than the silver *dirhem*. Indeed all over northern Europe it is the sparsity of Byzantine coin-finds that is remarkable. N. L. Rasmusson estimated the number of Moslem coins in Sweden as thirty-six thousand and noted how *dirhems* and a few *dinars*, including Spanish Arab pieces, dominate the scene from the ninth to the eleventh century. There are hardly any Byzantine coins in the hoards of Sweden and Norway before the mid-tenth century: the Norwegian Hon hoard is an exception, but all the pieces there were looped for suspension as ornaments. Rasmusson gives a total of four hundred Byzantine coins in Sweden in hoards of the period between 950 and 1070, and this was close to the Viking trade route that led to Constantinople itself: nor do Byzantine coins ever appear in large numbers. Scattered over the Baltic lands are a few other Byzantine pieces – some *solidi* of Romanus I and Constantine VII (913–59) in Norway, some silver of Basil II, a few ninth-century pieces at Birka, and tenth-century ones in Gotland. The pattern, however, is much the same everywhere, and even the Byzantine revival under the Macedonian dynasty made only a small impact on the northern trading area: in England it seems to have made none at all so far as coins are concerned. As Professor Lewis remarks, it is better not to overestimate the importance of the Byzantine Empire in the north as 'in all Scandinavian tenth-century hoards amongst their thousands of silver coins we find only a handful of Byzantine'. By the eleventh century the Byzantine *solidus* itself was being debased and the northern countries – all with developed silver coinages of their own – were beginning to exert pressure southwards on the weakening Empire. The silver coinages of Moslem Spain and of the Abbasids and Samanids in the east appear to have provided a medium of exchange between the Mediterranean and the northern trading areas.

The English hoards have rarely a Byzantine coin to show. The Cuerdale hoard of about seven thousand pieces surviving from the original find had a single Byzantine coin – a *hexagram* of Heraclius and Heraclius Constantine issued between 615 and 630 (see **Plate III, 17**). The hoard itself was originally connected with Æthelstan's victory over the Celtic and Norse alliance at Brunanburh in 937, but is now generally thought to be a whole generation earlier. The Heraclius coin has no significance in dating the hoard, but a *dirhem* of Al Mu'tamid (870–92) undoubtedly has. The hoard contained one of the 'Ceolwulf' coins with 'Two seated Emperors', as well as the long '*Cunnetti*' and '*Cnut Rex*' series. These last have the 'double barred Greek Cross' but the

The Byzantine Empire and the Coinage of the Anglo-Saxons

design is inverted: it immediately brings to mind the Italian issues of Theophilus (829–42), but the design was clearly not intended to be regarded in this way. Thus D. H. Haigh[19] would appear to overstate the case when he comments

> we have already seen that the moneyers of Alfred's era had some knowledge of Byzantine coins: the piece before us ['*Cunnetti*'] however proves something more – that they were familiar not only with the types but with the meaning and spirit of the designs in that interesting series.

The Croydon hoard (Thompson *Inventory* 111) was deposited about 875 somewhat earlier than Cuerdale. J. Rashleigh[20] recorded that it contained 'a rare Byzantine coin minted in Italy', and the same piece was later described to Sir John Evans as 'a Syracuse penny'. The dispersal of the coins makes the tracing of this piece an unlikely phenomenon, but the unhelpful description and its clarification point to the lack of knowledge in this country of the Byzantine series, even after Sabatier had published his *Monnaies Byzantines* in 1862. It would be most unwise to suggest Italian or Byzantine connexions on the basis of this slender evidence. The Croydon hoard shows exchange going on internally and with the Carolingian Empire but nothing farther afield.

One other hoard must be mentioned because the Byzantine piece associated with it was not recorded alongside the several thousand late Anglo-Saxon pennies of the so-called 'City hoard' (*Inventory* 255). A silver *miliaresion* of John Zimisces (969–76) is in Guildhall Museum in an envelope inscribed 'found in the hoard of silver pennies'. It has so far as is known always been associated with the rest of the hoard in Guildhall Museum and is described in the same handwriting as the others. There seems no doubt that they were all discovered together, but that this one piece was put aside as different from the others. The pennies extend from Æthelræd II to William I and the deposit is estimated as about 1070. Thus the *miliaresion* is of the same date as the earliest English pieces and has been pierced presumably for usage other than currency. Like practically all John Zimisces' *miliaresia*, it has been clipped down to the type with hardly any of the concentric rings of dots remaining. The coin had just a century to be clipped down to its present state and to reach England: it seems reasonable, and if the coin is accepted it is important and unusual in being contemporary with the other coins in the hoard.[21]

The record of English finds of Byzantine coins is indeed a sparse one from which it would hardly be expected that much imitation of design would take place. The use of monograms and of linear inscriptions on silver coins could have been copied from Byzantine originals, but is more likely to have come from the Ostrogoths and Lombards in Italy. It was only in Italy that Englishmen would be likely to meet with Byzantine currency in any quantity. If the two coinages are compared, it is the differences that are outstanding. In use of metals they were completely different and in design too. The type filling 'Facing Bust' with its often rather meanly lettered legend disposed about the edge has no Anglo-Saxon counterpart, nor have the elegantly elongated standing figures of late Byzantine issues. The eternal memory of Rome appears to flourish at the expense of anything characteristically Byzantine from the great periods of that Empire's expansion or cultural dominance. The 'Facing Bust', which dominated Byzantine coin types from the sixth to the eleventh century, was rarely used by the Anglo-Saxons and never in a Byzantine manner. The *solidus* of Archbishop Wigmund (York, *c.* 837) in the British Museum may be taken as typifying the position: neither the 'Facing Bust' nor the legend give the impression of a Byzantine prototype, although the weight standard is, exceptionally, exactly right: the reverse is characteristically Constantinian in aspect. Professor Talbot Rice, however, remarks that 'English coins are frequently modelled on Frankish and Byzantine prototypes'. It is difficult to see the frequency of Byzantine ones: where they occur at all they appear to be transmitted through other channels and quite unlike the straight copy of Al Mansur's *dinar* of 774 by his contemporary, Offa. Perhaps the Anglo-Saxons, who could produce metal-work of the highest quality in cloisonné enamel, increasingly felt that they had no need for guidance. The craftsmen were perfectly competent to go their own way.

There may be too much subjectivity about these evaluations of style. Professor Talbot Rice thinks that the bust of Ælfred was 'executed in a very Byzantine style' and that the monogram of London was 'clearly imitated from Greek monograms so popular in Byzantine art'. Æthelstan's head he regards as 'perhaps even more Byzantine than Ælfred's' and so the story continues until William I appears on his earliest coins 'done in a Byzantine manner'. These are words of authority, but in a numismatic setting they will prove difficult to justify in detail. There are hints of Byzantine prototypes in Ælfred's bust such as in Brooke's example in his Plate XII, no. 6, where a consular scarf may be intended: the busts of the 'London monogram' type are unusual and perhaps reminiscent of sixth-century Ostrogothic *folles* and of their successors after Justinian's conquest of Italy. The use of the title BASILEUS TOTIUS BRITANNIÆ by Æthelstan might indicate an interest in the position and representation of the Byzantine emperor, but, in spite of Professor Talbot Rice, it is not evident on his coins. The '*Basileus*' title was also used by Edgar who did go out of his way to copy two earlier coin-types, but they were both issues of Ælfred.[22] Features such as the prominent prependulia of the crown, the exaggerated

The Byzantine Empire and the Coinage of the Anglo-Saxons

fibula of the paludamentum, and the use of the *Manus Dei* are all worth studying as suggestive of Byzantine types, but the coins of the Carolingians and the emperors in Germany are likely to prove more valuable.

At the end of the Anglo-Saxon monarchy Edward the Confessor did issue a 'Facing Bust' type (*BMC* type XII) in different versions of which some of the details mentioned above appear. It is, however, hardly conceivable that the die-cutters had any acquaintance with a Byzantine prototype, if their work on the so-called 'Sovereign Martlets' type (*BMC* type IX) be compared. On the obverse of *BMC* type IX is a design faithfully copied from a much earlier imperial issue. The type is one of many Rome-Constantinopolis designs showing the 'personification of the city, wearing a helmet and seated on the prow of a ship with a sceptre held in the right hand and an orb in the left'. Theodosius I (379–95), his son, and grandson Theodosius II all produced *solidi* with this type, and there were bronze issues as well. The type was revived by Justin II (565–78) and used by him throughout his reign on the reverse of his *solidi*. Where so many dies and slight varieties exist, it may take time to decide which precisely provided Edward the Confessor's die-cutter with his inspiration or exemplar. Many dies of the 'Sovereign Martlets' type show important if minor differences which complicate the search. The short sceptre of Theodosius I's version could be elongated into a lance, or the plain orb surmounted sometimes by a 'Victoriola', sometimes by a Cross: the right leg could be bent or straight. But the set of Edward the Confessor's design and its main features leave as little doubt over its inspiration, as do the 'Two seated Emperors' of Ælfred and Ceolwulf. Once again it is not a contemporary issue that is copied and the sudden break with tradition in presenting the king seated on the obverse while introducing the four 'martlets' into the reverse suggests some occasion of importance rather than an archaistic or cultural whim. As the identity of the 'martlets' is also under review,[23] a more detailed analysis of the obverse will have to be undertaken to decide between Justin II – whose *solidus* seems to contain all the required elements – and the earlier Theodosian group as providing the specific prototype (**Plate III, 13-15**).

In this paper there has been no attempt to do more than make a setting for a difficult series of coins, and a background for problems still to be resolved. While the Anglo-Saxons ruled in England, the emperors in Constantinople were the most important sovereigns in the world, with the possible exception of the distant T'ang dynasty in China. When studying English history and especially when studying coins in English history, the possibilities of influence by such a Power and intercourse with it must be explored. Yet equally the

Anglo-Saxon Coins

Anglo-Saxons developed a sturdy political structure of their own, capable of resistance as well as imitation. One of their notable achievements was a coinage remarkable in the steadiness of its standard of technical production, its weight, its quality of metal, and artistic conception. This coinage bears testimony to the power of the central government over the great men in England's small and sparsely populated land, and this was a very touchstone of efficiency at the time. Such achievement can easily be submerged in a confusion of unfamiliar names, invasions, and swaying fortunes. To the reader familiar with the story and with the material here used, an apology is due: but the strange combination of microscopic observation with wide horizons, required of the numismatist, may give a certain utility to a general survey of this kind, however amorphous it may be. Now that Anglo-Saxon coinage is in course of being so skilfully and precisely delineated, it is worth underlining both the intricacies of the contemporary world picture and the dangers of hypothesis and insecure construction out of material so diverse and scattered. Interesting as are Anglo-Saxon borrowings from the late Roman Empire it is easy to exaggerate Byzantine influence in the northern, silver-based, trading area. The Germanic conquerors, while perhaps envying and certainly imitating parts of the Roman way of life, had a sturdy independence and a pride in their own achievement. The ghost of the Roman Empire was still a power in the northern lands, but Byzantium was not quite the same thing. It is this position that appears to be accurately reflected in the Anglo-Saxon coinage.

REFERENCES

1. A. R. LEWIS *The Northern Seas* (Princeton University Press 1958) – a book full of suggestive ideas and incorporating a vast amount of widely scattered information: it suffers from an inadequate index and often misleading references. H. PIRENNE's *Mahomet et Charlemagne* was published posthumously in 1937, fifteen years after his original essay, and in English translation by B. MIALL in 1940. See also *Transactions of the Royal Historical Society* 1959 for P. GRIERSON's cautionary summary of the Pirenne controversy
2. W. LEVISON *England and the Continent in the Eighth Century* (Oxford University Press 1946) – a clear picture and attractive presentation of the importance of the English in the contemporary world
3. R. S. LOPEZ 'Le problème des relations Anglo-Byzantines du septième au dixième siècle' in *Byzantion* XVIII (1946–8) – a suggestive and well-documented summary of Byzantine influence. See also T. C. LETHBRIDGE 'Byzantine influence in Late Saxon England' in *Proceedings of the Cambridge Antiquarian Society* XLIII (1950) for pottery technique

The Byzantine Empire and the Coinage of the Anglo-Saxons

4. T. D. KENDRICK *Anglo-Saxon Art* (1939) and *Late Saxon and Viking Art* (1949)
5. D. TALBOT RICE *English Art 871–1100* (*Oxford History of English Art* II 1952)
6. H. L. ADELSON *Light weight solidi and Byzantine trade during the sixth and seventh centuries* (American Numismatic Society 1957) and review in *NC* 1959 by J. P. C. KENT
7. At its widest 'Byzantine' may include anything from 330 to 1453. Historians have often sought to obtain more precise definition by shedding portions from the beginning or end of this long period. Late Roman imperial coin types naturally continued for a time and the British Museum's *Catalogue of Imperial Byzantine Coins* (1908) begins with Anastasius I (491–518). Anastasius' bronze *folles*, nearly 1½ inches in diameter, were new and, as André Grabar has noted, the number of reverse types on his gold issues reached a very low level. In Britain the crucial date is that of the Roman withdrawal in the early fifth century
8. I am greatly indebted to Mr Boon for allowing me to examine his lists, correspondence, and unpublished drafts, and for his willing co-operation over this matter. See also MR BOON's article in the *Bulletin of the Board of Celtic Studies* XVII no. 4 on the Byzantine coins at Caerwent
9. C. H. V. SUTHERLAND *Anglo-Saxon Gold Coinage in the light of the Crondall Hoard* (Oxford University Press 1948) – an indispensable guide to the tangled Roman, Merovingian, and Byzantine strands in this difficult subject, with a catalogue of the series: ninety-three types or different die combinations are listed. The later gold *dinar* of Offa and gold pennies of Æthelræd II, Edward the Elder, and Edward the Confessor are not included
10. Casts of this coin are in the British Museum
11. *NC* VI (1844), p. 171
12. *Supra* p. 9 Dr Kent pointed out the Phocas legend to me
13. A slip in attributing the new type to Maurice instead of Tiberius II should be noted on p. 34 of DR SUTHERLAND's *Anglo-Saxon Gold Coinage*. Maurice adopted his father-in-law's name Tiberius, but the change of type may well have been connected with Tiberius' own adoption of the name of Constantine (see A. GRABAR *L'Empereur dans l'art Byzantin* p. 36)
14. See Plate III, 1–7 for a comparison of Anglo-Saxon, Merovingian, and Byzantine examples
15. C. F. KEARY *Catalogue of English Coins in the British Museum*. The Anglo-Saxon series vols I (1887) and II (1893) – still a most valuable work, although as a catalogue it no longer represents the wealth of material in the National Collection
16. *Infra* p. 80 C. E. Blunt and R. H. M. Dolley argue that Halfdan's is not to be associated with 872 or with London. The coins are illustrated on Plate III, 10–12.
17. *Sylloge of Coins of the British Isles* Fitzwilliam Museum Cambridge Part I Coin no. 217. Mr Grierson's reassessment of the St Martin's Canterbury hoard is in *BNJ* 1953, and his description of the Fitzwilliam coin is in *NC* 1953 (Plate III, 9).
18. P. V. HILL has recently published several articles on the '*Sceatta*' series, notably in

Anglo-Saxon Coins

BNJ XXVI and XXVII: useful summaries are in *Congrès International de Numismatique* II (1953) p. 321 and 'Anglo-Frisian trade in the light of eighth-century coins' (*London and Middlesex Archaeological Society Transactions* XIX). See also Dr Kent. *Supra* p. 11

19. *NC* V (1842-3)
20. *NC* VIII (1868) New Series
21. Illustrated on Plate III, 18, by permission of the curator of Guildhall Museum, Mr N. C. Cook, to whom I am indebted for information about the coin and for his own views on it, which coincide with those expressed in the article.
22. I owe this example to R. H. M. Dolley.
23. The *BMC* type XII is illustrated with prototypes on Plate III, 13-15. *Infra* p. 215. R. H. M. Dolley and F. Elmore Jones write in more detail on certain aspects of this interesting type.

KEY TO THE PLATES

Plate III. Byzantine Prototypes and Finds

1. *Tremissis* of Tiberius II (578-82): obverse and reverse (Constantinople)
2. Merovingian *tremissis* of Quentovic: reverse (Sutherland 14)
3. '*Thrymsa*' from the Crondall hoard: reverse (Sutherland 6)
4. *Solidus* of Heraclius and Heraclius Constantine: reverse and obverse (Carthage dated 626/7)
5. *Solidus* of Tiberius II: obverse and reverse (Constantinople)
6. *Solidus* of Heraclius (610-41): reverse (Constantinople, period 610-13)
7. *Solidus* of Constantine IV (668-85): reverse (Constantinople)
8. 'Ciolh' *solidus*: obverse and reverse (Sutherland 76)
9. *Solidus*: casts in Fitzwilliam Museum, Cambridge: obverse and reverse (*Sylloge* 217)
10. 'Two Emperors' penny of Ælfred: obverse and reverse (London? *c.* 875)
11. 'Two Emperors' penny of Halfdan: obverse (North Midlands, *c.* 895)
12. 'Two Emperors' penny of Ceolwulf II: obverse and reverse (London, *c.* 875)
13. 'Sovereign/Martlets' ('Eagles') penny of Edward the Confessor: obverse and reverse (*BMC* type IX)
14. *Solidus* of Justin II (565-78): reverse and obverse
15. *Solidus* of Theodosius I (379-95): reverse and obverse
16. *Follis* of Constans II (641-68): obverse (Constantinople)
17. *Hexagram* of Heraclius and Heraclius Constantine: obverse and reverse (from the Cuerdale hoard)
18. *Miliaresion* of John Zimisces (969-76) observe and reverse (from the City or Walbrook hoard)

In obtaining the casts and photographs for this plate the help of the following is gratefully acknowledged: the Ashmolean Museum, the British Museum, the Fitzwilliam Museum, Guildhall Museum, C. E. Blunt, Esq., and Rev. A. Mallinson.

III

The Coinage of Offa

by C. E. BLUNT

[Plates IV–VII]

It was during the reign of Offa (757–96) that the change took place in the currency of this country from the small, thick coins known as *sceattas* to the larger, thinner penny which was to remain effectively the sole denomination in England (outside Northumbria) for the next five hundred years.

It seems clear, however, that the change was not inaugurated by Offa himself but by two minor Kentish kings, Heaberht and Ecgberht, who were his contemporaries. That so major a currency reform should have been carried out by two relatively insignificant rulers rather than by the great Mercian king must initially cause surprise, but may in fact be readily accounted for when the status of the coinage in the eighth century is considered.

The later issues of *sceattas* had, for the most part, been anonymous and such names as are found on them may probably be interpreted as those either of moneyers or, more rarely, of the London mint. If the names of Pada and Æthilræd, which are occasionally found on *sceattas*, are to be regarded as those of two Mercian kings, their coins must have come early in the 'Sceatta' series, so that the general statement that the later issues were anonymous or, at most, bore the name of moneyers or of a single mint is not invalidated. Certainly these later issues never bore the name of a king and rarely anything that could be interpreted as a royal bust.

Similarly, in Merovingian Gaul, where comparable coins existed, though gold persisted longer than in England, they only rarely bore the king's name; but the name of moneyer and mint was there a regular feature. Even those with the king's name are not regarded by French numismatists as royal issues in the normal acceptance of that term. Speaking of the Merovingian moneyer, Engel and Serrure write: 'S'il lui arrivait d'ajouter aux légendes le nom du roi, c'était une gracieuseté qu'il faisait au souverain, mais pas le moins du monde une obligation à laquelle il s'assujétissait.'[1] This view seems generally to be supported by Blanchet and Dieudonné.[2]

From this it emerges that, both in England and on the Continent, the coinage of *sceattas* and of Merovingian *deniers* was not regarded by the ruler as

Anglo-Saxon Coins

a royal prerogative but was rather a convenient and necessary tool for collecting taxes and for trade, the actual creation of which was left in large measure in the hands of the moneyers. This is not to say that the Crown derived no revenue from the coinage or left it uncontrolled. On the contrary, it is hard to believe that so well established a source of revenue would have been neglected, and it may be assumed that the moneyers had to pay for the privileges they enjoyed. Equally for the economic security of the Kingdom some control would undoubtedly have been exercised over weight and standard, though the base metal of which some of the *sceattas* are made suggest that this control cannot always have been effective. Subject to the moneyer conforming to the general format of the current coin, the type in both countries seems largely to have been left to him and his interest would be to provide one that found ready acceptance.

It is easy to see, therefore, how the change to the larger, thinner coin, which had already taken place in Gaul under Pippin in 755,[3] came in this country to be made first in Kent, the kingdom with the closest trading links with the Continent.

Pippin's coins bore for the most part on the obverse the letters ℞P for *Rex Pipinus* or ℞F for *Rex Francorum*. The reverse usually bore the name of a mint but not of a moneyer. Under Charlemagne (768–814), however, it became the general practice for the king's name to be set out in full.

In Kent, where the penny coinage seems (for reasons given later) to have started *c*. 775–*c*. 780, that is, well into the reign of Charlemagne, the king's name is invariably found in full on the obverse of the coins with, in the centre, ℞ for *Rex*. On the reverse, however, it is the moneyer's name alone that is found; no mint is given. It may be assumed that a single mint, no doubt Canterbury, would have met the needs of the relatively small Kentish kingdom in which case there would be no need to indicate it. Effective control would be exercised by requiring the moneyer responsible for the coin to put his name on it. This is what in fact was done and the practice continued for long after other mints opened.

Three moneyers worked for the Kentish kings, Eoba for Heaberht and Ecgberht (**Plate IV, 1, 3**), and Babba and Udd for Ecgberht only (**Plate IV, 2, 4**). All these moneyers worked for Offa, and the close affinities of some of their issues for Offa (e.g. **Plate IV, 7, 10**) to their issues for the Kentish kings leaves no doubt that the one followed closely on the other and that Offa's initial coinage emanated from Canterbury. The cessation of the coinage in the names of the Kentish kings indicates that Offa suppressed their right to coin.

The dates of the two Kentish kings are not precisely known. From the

The Coinage of Offa

evidence of charters it is apparent that both were reigning in 765, and it is possible that Ecgberht reigned until *c.* 780 or later.[4] But in the later years of his reign it is known that Offa treated him as a mere dependant.[5] It is when he became Ecgberht's complete overlord that Offa is likely to have taken control of the Canterbury mint and, noting that the penny coinage bore the king's name, to have given instructions that his own name should thenceforth be substituted for that of Ecgberht. This event may, for reasons given later, be tentatively dated *c.* 784–*c.* 785.

It has been suggested that Offa's control of the Canterbury mint followed the battle of Otford in 776,[6] but Sir Frank Stenton has pointed out that the evidence of charters suggests that this battle may well not have been the complete Mercian victory that has generally been assumed, and that Offa cannot be shown to have possessed any authority in Kent during the next ten years.[7] The dates now suggested for the beginning of Offa's coinage accord with this view.

GROUP I

Offa, having put the Canterbury mint into his service, did little at first to change its products. The coins continue to carry his name on the obverse, usually associated with some form of cruciform design, sometimes with his title King of Mercia (e.g. **Plate IV, 10**), but at others without even the title King (e.g. **Plate IV, 7**). Although Offa employed the regnal style *rex totius Anglorum patriae*,[8] he never went further on his coins than to describe himself as *Rex Merciorum*. To the three moneyers who had struck for the Kentish kings were added three more: Ealhmund, Ealred, and Osmod (**Plate IV, 8, 9, 19**). The issue, judging from surviving specimens, remained on a comparatively limited scale.

GROUP II

The next phase in the coinage, however, marked a radical change, namely the introduction of the king's bust on the obverse, sometimes of a quality of workmanship that entitles one to believe that an attempt at portraiture was being made. Concurrently with these there remained the issue of coins without the bust, often by the same moneyers and sometimes with the same reverse types (e.g. **Plate IV, 26, 27,** and **VI, 81, 83**). On what may be one of the earliest of the 'Bust' type the king's name is found on both sides, with the result that no moneyer's name is given (**Plate IV, 21**). On others the moneyer's name appears on the obverse, beside the king's bust (e.g. **Plate V, 47, 61**), a feature also to be found on the coins of Offa's queen, Cynethryth (**Plate VII, 116–23**).

Anglo-Saxon Coins

But it was not long before the final pattern became established, king's name on the obverse, moneyer's on the reverse (e.g. **Plate IV, 23**).

The design of these coins of Offa has long excited the admiration of both numismatists and art students. Earlier writers were disposed to attribute this sudden flowering of art on the coinage to the influence of Italian artists,[9] but Keary as long ago as 1875 pointed out that in the eighth century 'the arts in southern Europe had been suffering from an uniform and rapid decline' and added pertinently that nothing could be found in the Italian coinage of the period 'which could stand as a model for the incomparable coinage of Offa'. He calls attention on the other hand to the brilliance of the art of illumination in these Islands at this very time.[10] Oman supports this view and writes 'some of these [designs] have prototypes in the Sceatta series, but the majority are new, good examples of eighth-century English decorative art, with no debased Roman original at the back of them'.[11] It is rather surprising on the other hand to find Brooke saying that 'Offa proceeded to strike a grandiose issue of portrait coins under the influence of a romanizing tendency which he had acquired at the court of Charlemagne'. But he rapidly qualifies this by comparing the actual designs with 'the fully matured art of the Lindisfarne Gospels and of English and Irish stone and metal-work of the eighth century'.[12]

Certainly in two instances it is the Carolingian emperor who imitates Offa's coins. A coin of Lucca in the name of Charlemagne closely copies a coin of Offa's by the moneyer Ealhmund (**Plate V, 40**). That the Carolingian coin is the copy, and not the original, is clearly demonstrated by the engraver of the latter having copied the final ð of Ealhmund on to his die, under the impression no doubt that it was merely a part of the design. The second coin, also of Charlemagne and struck at Lucca, copies closely as to its reverse type the obverse of a coin of Eadberht's (**Plate V, 34**) and has a comparable obverse.[13]

The extraordinary variety of design on Offa's coins will be seen from the plates that accompany this paper. The king's bust, for instance, varies from one with elaborately dressed hair, arranged in curls to give an effect of light and shade (e.g. **Plate V, 37–9**) to another on which the diademed and draped bust is reminiscent of that of a Roman emperor (**Plate IV, 27**). At times the king is depicted wearing jewels, either as an ornament on a fine chain worn round his neck (e.g. **Plate V, 42**) or as a triple branching spray (**Plate V, 58**), such as is later found on early coins of Æthelred II.[14]

The reverses too have provided great scope for the Anglo-Saxon artist. A multiplicity of cruciform designs is found in which every variety of ornament is used. An animal-headed torque is sometimes to be seen (**Plate V, 41**), and on coins of Ciolhard there is, as the main feature of the reverse design, a

The Coinage of Offa

coiled serpent (**Plate IV, 23**) and, on some of Pendred, two serpents intertwined (**Plate VI, 78**). On coins by this last moneyer the serpent motif also occurs on the obverse (**Plate VI, 76–7**).

The delightful variety of the designs on these coins of Offa is the more noticeable when comparison is made with the contemporary issues on the Continent. These latter were purely utilitarian in design and aspired to do no more than declare the name of king and mint. The outburst of art on English coins clearly owed nothing to their continental counterparts, and the coins confirm hardly less than the manuscripts the lively state of English art in the eighth century.

Offa's new coinage called for the employment of more moneyers. The six already operating continued in office, but the names of a further fifteen moneyers are found in this group (see Table of Moneyers, p. 55). Udd is found shortly after the introduction of the 'Bust' type to change his name to Dud (**Plate IV, 25–33**), and attention should be called to what superficially seems another form of the name Æthelred on the coin illustrated (**Plate VI, 71**) where the reading Œthelred is found. Ealhmund, whose name appears in Group I as Alhmund, continues this form at first, but the initial E is soon added and on some of his coins the H is omitted, thus providing three different forms of what we may safely assume is the same name. The name Pendred sometimes appears as Rendred, but the former would seem to be the preferable reading.

The moneyer listed as Tirwald (?) may perhaps be Tidwald. Only two coins of his are known today (**Plate VI, 79–80**), but a third, said to have been found at Chesterford, Essex, was exhibited at a meeting of the Numismatic Society in 1843.[15] A somewhat similar coin in the Twisden Sale 1841 had been considered a forgery, but if the find-spot of the Chesterford is authentic, one at least is likely to be genuine. The Chesterford coin, which cannot be traced today, appears to read Tidwald, with a runic L.

The name Lulla is found in this group (**Plate V, 66**), and Lul occurs later in the group that is here associated with East Anglia (**Plate VII, 114**). Although the name may well be the same, the style of the coins suggests that two different moneyers are involved.

The coins that bear the name Eadberht on the reverse (**Plate V, 34–6**) present a puzzle. The symbol that follows the name has been read as a monogram of E and P and interpreted as an abbreviation of *Episcopus*. The coins have consequently been attributed to Eadberht, Bishop of London (d. *c.* 787–9).[16] This attribution is not without its difficulties. It would be the only recorded instance of the Bishop of London having enjoyed the right to coin. In the Grateley Decrees of Æthelstan, where the coining rights of various prelates are mentioned, eight dies are allotted to the London mint, none of which is designated for the Bishop. Coinage rights were a privilege that was highly prized and, had an earlier right existed, one would expect a claim to strike to have been revived at some later date. No record of such a claim is known. On the other hand, it is to be noted that the abbreviation M for *Monetarius*, which seems to be the alternative interpretation of this symbol, never occurs elsewhere on the early coins of Offa and is only very rarely found in Group III (e.g. **Plate VI, 85**). The question must remain an open one, but the possibility that we have in these rare coins an issue of the Bishop of London cannot be entirely rejected.

Whether acceptance of an attribution to the Bishop of London requires equally the acceptance that there was a mint there is an even more open question. Lockett was content to allow that the dies were made in Canterbury and went so far as to suggest that the coins might also have been struck there.[17] The latter contention is hard to accept: it seems unlikely that any striking authority, on whom would rest responsibility in the event of the standard failing, would allow coins to be struck outside his direct control. The dies, however, bear all the signs of having been made, in common with the bulk of Offa's dies, at Canterbury and, if these coins are in fact the Bishop's, it seems best to assume that the dies were sent to London from Canterbury.

For what, if it is genuine, must be one of the most remarkable coins of Group II we are dependent on the account of a nineteenth-century Italian numismatist. No English numismatist appears to have seen the coin or even to have had a drawing of it, though reference is made to it in early publications. The coin in question is said to show on the obverse a male head with the inscription OFFA REX-MEREOR and on the reverse a large cross in the centre with the inscription S. PETRVS around. It was published in 1863 by the then owner F. Calori Cesis of Nonantola, near Modena, and was said by him to have been found at Baggiovara, near Modena.[18] J. Evans in 1863 read to the Numismatic Society a note from Cesis on the coin[19] and a further communication in the following year,[20] but neither was published in the *Numismatic Chronicle*. There is nothing, however, to suggest that its authenticity or the validity of Cesis's reading was doubted. Haigh in a letter to the editor of the *Chronicle* dated 18 May 1863 suggests, on the analogy of the 'St Andrew' pennies of Æthelwulf which are attributed to Rochester, that Cesis's coin should be attributed to Lichfield, the church of which was dedicated to St Peter. This he regards as preferable to connecting it with the institution of Peter's Pence,[21] and he maintains this view six years later when publishing a further paper on the Old English coinage generally.[22]

The Coinage of Offa

Renewed efforts to trace this coin and secure a cast of it have so far proved unsuccessful, but, even though the legend is otherwise unknown, there seems insufficient reason to question the essential validity of Cesis's reading. Assuming, therefore, that it is more or less correctly read, the question remains as to how it is to be interpreted.

Haigh's attribution to the Archbishop of Lichfield is not entirely satisfactory because the analogy he draws is with a coin issued half a century or more later and because the coins of the archbishops of Canterbury under Offa bore, as is noted later, the name and title of the archbishop. Had a comparable issue been made by the Mercian Archbishop one might expect at the least similar treatment. There is, moreover, no evidence of there having been a mint in Mercia at this time, and a recent study by R. H. M. Dolley and D. Metcalf has shown on the basis of find-spots that the distribution area of pennies struck up to c. 820 was essentially contained within an arc drawn from the Wash to Southampton, an area that would exclude both Tamworth, the Mercian 'capital', and Lichfield.[23] Alternative explanations must accordingly be examined.

That Offa made a payment to Rome of 365 *mancuses* in gratitude 'for the victories of the Kingdom which he held by the support of St Peter' is shown from a letter written by Pope Leo III to Coenwulf in 798,[24] but Sir Frank Stenton considers that, although the letter suggests that Offa intended his successor to continue the payment annually, it would be wrong to see in this the origin of the tax afterwards known as Peter's Pence.[25] There is no reason, however, to doubt that at least one payment was made by Offa, in his personal capacity, and the question arises as to whether the coin found on Italian soil may have been issued for this purpose.

The fact that the payment is referred to as 365 *mancuses* need not be taken to indicate that it was necessarily made in gold coin. The *mancus* was essentially a money of account, comparable to our guinea today for which no coin exists and, although a unique gold coin of Offa's is known and may well have actually been found in Rome, it is suggested, for reasons given later, that this is unlikely to have been struck for payment to the Holy See. Perhaps the most significant piece of evidence in considering whether the '*S. Petrus*' penny was struck for Offa's recorded payment to Rome rests in a unique coin of his contemporary Pippin which bears as reverse legend the word ELIMOSINA. Whatever the exact purpose for which this coin was struck, and the fact that it was found in a French hoard may militate against its having been issued for a payment to Rome, there can be little doubt that it was intended for some royal offering or alms. Comparable pieces were struck in England by Ælfred,[26] but as this was a century later their relevance to a coin of Offa's must be slight.

Anglo-Saxon Coins

We have then specific evidence of a special issue by Offa's contemporary for the purpose of making an offering; we know the interdependence of continental and English currency in the eighth century – the change of weight in the latter part of Offa's reign to conform to a corresponding change in Charlemagne's coinage is discussed below; we know that Offa made at least one substantial payment to Rome; the 'S. Petrus' coin was found in Italy. All these factors should entitle us to regard the coin, always assuming it to be genuine, as having been struck for this purpose rather than as an issue of the Archbishop of Lichfield.

Other coins have, at times, been attributed to the Archbishop of Lichfield. These (**Plate V, 59-60**) bear a doubtful name on the reverse, read by Keary as HEAGR or HEARER,[27] and tentatively by Lockett as 'a blundered monogram of Higberht'.[28] Brooke rejected this attribution, remarking in an unpublished manuscript that 'Heagr' was hardly a possible form of 'Higberht' and adding that the absence of a title makes it unlikely that it is the name of a bishop.[29] Here once again the paucity of the material makes certainty impossible. Only three specimens are known. On the one in the British Museum (**Plate V, 59**) the name appears to begin HEA followed by what appears to be a ligulation of B and E. The final letter is R. On the second coin (**Plate V, 60**) it is possible to read HBEAET (the T being ligulated with the initial H). The third reads HEA..RT, the missing letters being possibly B and E ligulated. Taking these readings together it seems reasonable to postulate the name Heaberht as the moneyer.

It will be seen from the list of coins that follow this paper how many are today represented by only one or two surviving specimens. Even in cases where a larger number is shown, die-duplicates are comparatively scarce and it is clear that Offa's coinage must have been on a very considerable scale, and that what we know today is likely to represent a very incomplete cross-section of it. Were a major hoard of this period to be discovered, one could expect it to produce a crop of new and unsuspected varieties and to add to the list of moneyers, one or two of whom are today known from no more than isolated specimens.

COINAGE OF QUEEN CYNETHRYTH

During the period of Group II of Offa's coinage, coins were struck in the name of his queen, Cynethryth (**Plate VII, 116-24**). As on the king's coins, some have the bust and some omit it. This is the only instance in the Anglo-Saxon coinage of a coin being issued in the name of a consort and the reason for it has caused speculation. The most likely explanation seems that Offa was consciously imitating the classical Roman custom whereby portraits of

The Coinage of Offa

empresses figured on the coinage and that this formed the numismatic part of a policy designed to emphasize to other rulers the important position that the King of Mercia held in England. This would apply particularly to Charlemagne whom he sought to treat as an equal.

Be that as it may, the issue proved short lived and less than twenty specimens survive, all by the moneyer Eoba, who put his name on the obverse of the coins with busts. These latter generally show a head of clearly female form with long curly hair and no diadem (e.g. **Plate VII, 119**). On one specimen, however (**Plate VII, 123**), the head approximates closely to the diademed head of Offa on a coin by the same moneyer (**Plate V, 52**), and it would seem that Eoba made use, in this instance, of an obverse die intended for Offa's coinage.[30]

On the side that bears the queen's name (which appears to be the reverse on the coins with bust and the obverse on those without it) (**Plate VII, 124**), the queen's name and the title REGINA are found in full with, in the centre, the letter M, with an abbreviation mark above it, for *Merciorum*.

COINAGE OF ARCHBISHOP IÆNBERHT

Contemporary too with Group II may be placed, with one exception, the coins that combine the name of Offa with that of Iænberht, Archbishop of Canterbury (**Plate VII, 125-32**). Offa is known to have been on bad terms with the archbishop and the granting of coinage rights can only have been made unwillingly. It probably arises through there being a standing right of coinage in the '*Sceatta*' series, and everything suggests that he would not readily have granted it otherwise.

It is not possible to establish which side of the coins should be regarded as the obverse, but here the side with the king's name is treated as such. With one exception, Iænberht's coins have on the obverse the words OFFA REX in two lines. On the reverse are the archbishop's name and title surrounding a cruciform pattern that varies in detail (**Plate VII, 125-31**). That they were issued from the same mint as Offa's coins is apparent both from the similarity of style and of the obverse type to issues of Offa. The conclusive evidence, however, is the recent identification of a coin of Offa's by the moneyer Ethelnoth (**Plate V, 54**) that proves to be from the same obverse die as a coin of Iænberht's.

The exceptional coin of Iænberht's, referred to above, has the king's name in the angles of a celtic cross (cf. Offa's coins by the moneyer Tirwald(?)) (**Plate VI, 79-80**) and the archbishop's in three lines on the reverse (**Plate VII, 132**). The reverse type conforms to Offa's third group which is discussed below and, in view of the fact that Iænberht died in 792, the coin is a vital one in dating the change of type. Both the obverse type and the weight, 18·8 grains, suggest that this unique coin of Iænberht should be regarded as transitional between Group II and Group III. It was doubtless struck shortly before Iænberht's death.

GROUP III

Group III, Offa's last group (**Plate VI, 84–Plate VII, 107**), is distinguished from his earlier issues by the heavier weight and the larger flans on which the coins were struck.

In this last group nine of the existing moneyers participated, including, it is to be noted, four out of the six who struck in the first group. Among the new moneyers is found the name Eama, which also occurs on an early coin of Coenwulf. This it has been suggested may be the same name as Eanmund which is found on other coins of Coenwulf.[31]

A distinguishing feature of coins of this group is the placing of the king's name and title in three lines across the field of the coin. The bust is never found, but it was revived in Coenwulf's reign, though never of the artistic quality achieved by Offa. On the reverse the moneyer's name is usually, but not invariably, found in two lines. Evidence is again forthcoming to confirm that Canterbury was still Offa's principal minting-place. A coin by the moneyer Ethelnoth (**Plate VI, 96**) is struck from the same reverse die as one in the name of Eadberht Præn, who seized power in Kent on the death of Offa in 796.[32] This type, with what one may call a dumb-bell ornament on the reverse, must therefore have been in issue right at the end of Offa's reign, a fact further confirmed by the recent discovery of a coin in the name of Coenwulf with this reverse type.[33] The moneyer who struck it, Seberht, is, however, not known to have worked for Offa.

COINAGE OF ARCHBISHOP ÆTHILHEARD

Parallel with this issue are found coins bearing the name of Æthilheard, Archbishop of Canterbury, coupled with that of Offa (**Plate VII, 133–8**). These are all on large flans and were struck to his heavier weight standard. On his earliest coins Æthilheard is styled PONT(*ifex*), and J. Evans has suggested that this style was used in the period that elapsed between his election following Iænberht's death on 12 August 792 and the receipt of the pallium from Rome in the following year.[34] Only four coins are known with the title *Pontifex*, but there are three distinct types (**Plate VII, 133–5**). On Æthilheard's later coins, where he is styled archbishop, the 'Three-line' type associated with Offa's last group (Group III) is normally found, in most cases on both sides of the coin (**Plate VII, 136**). One has the 'Three-line' type for the name of Offa combined

The Coinage of Offa

with a reverse on which the archbishop's name is found in a circular legend, the two final letters of ARCEP being in the centre (**Plate VII, 137**). This same type is found combined with an obverse showing Offa's name and the word REX in a circular legend that is similarly continued into the centre which has M for *Merciorum* (**Plate VII, 138**).

EAST ANGLIAN GROUP

A group of coins with the name of Offa stands apart from the issues so far discussed, both stylistically and because of the more frequent use of runic letters. This group is the product of four moneyers: Botred, Hun..c, Lul, and Wihtred (**Plate VII, 108–15**). Of these, all except Hun..c are found striking coins for Coenwulf of a similar distinctive style. Brooke regarded the Coenwulf coins of Botred and Wihtred as products of a mint probably situated in East Anglia,[35] and there seems no reason not to accept that they stand apart from the products of the Canterbury mint and may well be from that area. In the subsequent development of the series they certainly link up with coins of known East Anglian kings. If the coins of Coenwulf are accepted there is no reason not to accept as well those of Offa by the same two moneyers and with the same peculiar characteristics. The addition of the moneyer Lul is at variance with Brooke's classification, but coins of Wihtred and Lul are found struck in the name of a historically unknown King Eadwald, and it must be wrong to separate the one from the other. The coins of Lul on the issue of Coenwulf are, moreover, of a style quite unlike any found emanating from Canterbury. The moneyer Hun..c is unknown elsewhere in this series, but the reading proposed seems preferable to the suggestion in Brooke that the name should be read ..chun. Hun..c could be a name such as Hunlac or Hunsig(e).

The coins of this group fall into two main subdivisions, those that seem to correspond with Offa's Group II at Canterbury, struck by Botred, Hun..c, and Wihtred (**Plate VII, 108–13**) and those with the 'Three-line' type (**Plate VII, 114–15**), clearly to be associated with Offa's last group (Group III). These latter are struck by Lul and Wihtred.

If the date of *c.* 792 for the change in the size and weight of the coins, the reasons for which are set out below, is accepted then the issue of the East Anglian mint should have started slightly before that, say 790.

East Anglian history is at this period utterly obscure. The name of only one king has come down to us in documentary sources, namely Æthilberht, whom Offa caused to be beheaded in 794. But the coinage tends to confirm Sir Frank Stenton's tentative suggestion that 'it is natural to assume that Offa killed him because he stood in some way for the independence of his kingdom'.[36] There exist coins in the name of Æthilberht struck by a moneyer Lul which may in all probability be associated with the East Anglian king of that name. Certainly the use of runic letters associates them with the coins of this group no less than does the moneyer's name.[37]

What the coins would seem to suggest – and it must be emphasized that this evidence is in no way conclusive - is that Offa established a mint in East Anglia about 790, which implies that he had effective control of that Kingdom at that time; that Æthilberht gained sufficient power to make an issue in his own name but was, as is known, killed by Offa in 794 and that Offa then resumed the coinage in his own name up to the time of his death.

There then appear the coins in the name of King Eadwald, referred to above, struck by the moneyers Eadnoth, Lul, and Wihtred. The coins of the first two are similar in type to the coins issued by Lul for Offa (**Plate VII, 114**); Wihtred's coin is also similar to his coins for Offa (**Plate VII, 115**). These coins suggest that in East Anglia a revolt against the Mercian overlordship took place on the death of Offa, as is known to have been the case in Kent where Eadberht Præn secured the crown. In each case the revolt proved short lived. In Kent Eadberht Præn was deposed in 798 and in East Anglia the moneyer Lul is soon found issuing coins in the name of Coenwulf, the reverse type of which is similar to those he had issued for Offa and Eadwald. This case of the continuation in office of a moneyer after having served a rebel king is not an isolated one and serves to show that the moneyer was not a person of sufficient political importance to have been regarded as of necessity implicated in a revolt. It is likely, however, that he was a man of some substance, and not a mere operative, and he may well have been a member of the mercantile class.

THE DINAR

The most remarkable product of this remarkable coinage is a gold coin issued in the name of Offa in imitation of a *dinar* of Caliph Al Mansur, dated 157 A.H. (A.D. 774) (**Plate IV, 5**). The coin is a reasonably accurate copy of the original, but the engraver has made certain mistakes in copying the Arabic inscriptions which make it clear that he was unfamiliar with the language. This is further confirmed by the fact that he has inserted the words OFFA REX upside-down in relation to the Arabic inscription. The weight is 66 grains.

This coin was first heard of by English numismatists when a report on it was made in 1841 to the Numismatic Society by Adrien de Longpérier. It was, he says, procured by the late Duc de Blacas during a sojourn in Rome. No doubt it was found in Italy, perhaps in Rome, but there is no specific evidence on this point.

The Coinage of Offa

Since then it has been the subject of comment by a number of authorities who have variously identified it as one of the *mancuses* referred to in Pope Leo's letter to Coenwulf, to which reference has already been made, as having been sent by Offa to the Holy See; as an ephemeral attempt on Offa's part to institute a gold currency in this country; and as a freak for some propagandist purpose, possibly payment to the Pope. There has also been the suggestion that the piece is an out and out forgery; but this must surely be rejected: its authenticity would seem apparent.[38]

That this is one of a small series of imitative pieces struck probably in France and, in this case, in England is demonstrated by J. Allan. Its purpose must remain more open. To suggest, as has been done, that Offa, desiring to institute a gold currency in this country, chose for his model the only gold coins with which he was familiar, is to ignore the fact that the whole type, let alone the legend, would have been alien to the average Englishman. Equally to suggest that Offa and his advisers would have been ignorant of the fact that the legend was an Arabic one and so would have felt the coin suitable for presentation to the Pope is to imply an ignorance which could hardly be expected on the part of the Royal Clerks, whether or not the actual writing could be interpreted.

It is known that Arab *dinars* constituted the gold currency of trade in the western Mediterranean and, in the absence of further evidence, it would seem best to accept the somewhat prosaic explanation that Offa's *dinar* was struck for the purpose of overseas trade. But the possibility must remain that it was struck for a special propagandist purpose, though not, I would suggest, for the purpose of payment to the Holy See.[39]

THE HOARD EVIDENCE

It must be said at once that the hoard evidence is disappointing in the extreme. No hoard deposited in England in Offa's reign is recorded, if we except, as we properly may, the 'Stamford Hill hoard' about which all that is known is that it is said to have contained two coins of Ecgberht of Kent.

Out of some 250+ surviving coins of Offa only seven and, of Iænberht only one, have recorded hoard provenances. None of the coins of Cynethryth or of Æthilheard-Offa has a hoard-provenance.

Hoard	Approx. date of deposit	Coins of Offa	Coins of Iænberht
Delgany (T. 117)	830	3	–
Middle Temple (T. 366)	841–2	1	–
Netley Abbey (T.—)	845 (?)	–	1
Ilanz, Switzerland	790–2	2	–
Trewhiddle (T. 362)	873–5	1	–

Anglo-Saxon Coins

The sole evidence for the Netley Abbey find (of two coins) is the Rashleigh Sale Catalogue (1909), lots 66 (b) and 88.

To these may possibly be added the coins of Offa in the 1879 Borghesi Sale, which seem likely to have come from an Italian (Roman?) hoard and may possibly be associated with a group in the Vatican. But of this there exists only the most nebulous account.[40]

There are better grounds for postulating a major hoard or hoards containing coins of Offa, one dating perhaps from the seventeenth century, another from the eighteenth century. The collection of Sir Robert Cotton (1571–1631) contained three coins of Offa and one of Cynethryth.[41] But by the time Fountaine wrote in 1705 he was able to illustrate twelve coins of Offa and two of Cynethryth, figures which compare with eight coins of Coenwulf and three of Ceolwulf I and it is to be noted that Fountaine did not restrict his illustrations to types, but seems to have sought to include all the moneyers known to him.

By 1772 Pegge was able to write 'Now Offa's coins are not scarce in general.'[42] This statement is borne out if a few eighteenth-century collections are examined. Hunter, whose collection was completed by 1783, had eighteen coins of Offa and two of Cynethryth; Tyssen, whose Anglo-Saxon coins came to the British Museum in 1802, had ten coins of Offa and two of Cynethryth;[43] the Duke of Devonshire's Collection, formed in the eighteenth century but dispersed in 1844, had seven of Offa and one of Cynethryth; Lord Pembroke's, also formed in the eighteenth century but dispersed in 1848, had three of Offa and one of Cynethryth. Other early provenances in the National Collection are *BMC* 41 ex Browne Sale (1791); *BMC* 44 ex Barker Sale (1803); *BMC* 32 or 58 ex Gostling Sale (1777); *BMC* 8 ex Strawberry Hill Sale (1842, but Horace Walpole who made the collection had died in 1797). This list could be extended, but enough has been said to show that there was a considerable supply of Offa's coins available to collectors in the second half of the eighteenth century and it is reasonable to suppose that they emanated largely from a hoard or hoards.

By the nineteenth century, numismatists had begun to record isolated find-spots of the rarer coins and the number is considerable. Some, too, have been found on the continent of Europe at places ranging from Rome in the south[44] to Voss and Rogaland in Norway. It is at least possible that one, or both, of the coins believed to be in the Leningrad Museum (of which full details are not available) was found on Russian soil.

While in a few cases coins have been found in controlled excavations, the authority for the greater part of the isolated finds rests on what the original

The Coinage of Offa

buyer was told. There is generally no reason to question the alleged find-spots, but numismatists are all too well aware that in addition to the honest mistake, alleged find-spots have at times been attached to spurious coins to bolster up the case for their authenticity.

The Offa series has been a fertile field for the forger[45] and the scarcity of hoard-material, and of coins with an unquestioned provenance, adds to the difficulty of establishing a canon of authenticity by which doubtful pieces may be judged. In the list that follows the writer has deliberately omitted one or two pieces about which he has grave doubts, even though they are not sufficient to justify outright condemnation.

DATING

The dating of the series, particularly the inauguration of the penny coinage, must remain in some doubt. Offa's own reign lasted thirty-nine years from 757 to 796; Heaberht's name is found on two charters dated 764 and 765 and on a third assigned to 765–91; Ecgberht's name appears on the last two charters and on others dated 778 and 779 and he was certainly dead by 799.[46] This would reasonably suggest that the penny was introduced between 765 and 775 and Offa's first issues might then be dated from $c.$ 775 to $c.$ 780. The difficulty that this dating involves arises from the fact that the names of two of the moneyers who struck for the Kentish kings are found on early coins of Coenwulf and, if it is permissible to equate Udd=Dud=Dud(d)a, the third is also found. It is hardly to be expected that all three moneyers would have been in office for upwards of twenty years. This suggests that the date of the initial issue of the penny must be put as late as possible, even though nothing is known at this date of Heaberht. We shall probably not be far wrong in putting it at $c.$ 775–$c.$ 780 with Offa's coinage following a few years later, say $c.$ 784–$c.$ 785.

Group I, on the classification here proposed, appears to have been issued on a fairly limited scale judging by surviving specimens.

The terminal date of Group II is fairly closely defined by the coins of the archbishops. Iænberht struck, as has been seen, a coin that verged on Group III and it may reasonably be assumed that this was inaugurated shortly before his death in August 792. A similar up-grading of the weight and increase in the size of the flan on which the coins were struck is found in Gaul, and this change has been dated by P. Grierson to the year 790. This would accord well enough with the date suggested for the change in England, as in economic, as opposed to artistic, matters the Continent was at this time in the lead.

Anglo-Saxon Coins

Group II is a substantial one and must have been spread over several years. It is tempting to associate its introduction with the memorable events of the year 787 when Offa succeeded in establishing a Metropolitan in Mercia and his own son Ecgfrith was consecrated King. This must have been a significant year in Offa's life and could well have prompted the introduction of the fine portrait coins.

Weight Standard

The following is a frequency table prepared from the weights in grains available to me of undamaged coins:

Offa	Under 15	15–15.9	16–16.9	17–17.9	18–18.9	19–19.9	20–20.9	21–21.9	Over 22
Canterbury									
Group I	1	2	1	9	6	7	2	—	—
II	5	9	17	26	36	30	9	—	—
III	2	1	—	2	4	12	10	4	3
East Anglian									
Group II	—	1	—	1	2	—	—	—	—
III	—	—	—	—	—	—	—	3	—
Cynethryth	—	—	4	5	2	3	1	—	—
Iænberht									
Early	1	—	1	2	4	—	1	—	—
Late	—	—	—	—	1	—	—	—	—
Æthilheard	1	1	—	—	—	4	3	1	1

This table brings out clearly the increase of weight that accompanied the introduction of Group III. For the first time coins of over 21 grains are found, and it will be seen that in this group (which consists of the Canterbury and East Anglian coins of Group III and those of Æthilheard) only a minority of the coins is found to weigh under 19 grains.

In the earlier groups the bulk of the coins come within the bracket 17–1.99 grains.

It would appear that a weight of something over 19 grains was the standard for Groups I and II and that for Group III it was distinctly over 20 grains.

Table of Moneyers

East Anglian Group

Moneyer	Offa Group II	Æthilberht	Offa Group III	Eadwald	Coenwulf
Botred	x				x
Hun..c	x				
Wihtred	x		x	x	x
Lul		x	x	x	x

The Coinage of Offa

Kentish Group

Moneyer	Heaberht/Ecgberht	OFFA Group I	OFFA Group II Bust	OFFA Group II No Bust	OFFA Group III	Eadberht Præn	Coenwulf
Babba	x	x			x	x	x
Eoba	x	x	x	x	x		x
Udd (Dud)	x	x	x	x			x (Duda)
(E)alhmund		x	x	x	x		
(E)alred		x	x				
Osmod		x		x	x		
Beaghard				x	x		
Ciolhard			x		x		x
Cuthberht				x			
Eadberht				x			
Eadhun			x				
Ethelnoth				x	x	x	
Ethelwald			x	x			
Heaberht(?)				x			
Ibba			x		x		x
Lulla			x				
Œthilred			x				
Pehtwald			x	x			
Pendred			x				
Tirwald(?)				x			
Winoth			x	x	x		
Deimund					x		
Eama					x		x
Ethelmod					x	x	x
Ludomon					x		x
Wilhun					x		x
Wulfhath					x		

PLATES

In the plates, a key to which follows, an attempt has been made to illustrate all the significant varieties of the coins of Offa and Cynethryth and of the two archbishops who combine their names with Offa's. To give the non-numismatist an idea of the relative extent to which the material has survived today, the number of specimens known to the writer is added at the end of each item. In view of the scarcity of die-duplicates and of the liberty accorded to the die-cutters, complete uniformity in any of the coins so grouped is not necessarily to be expected, but the general type conforms to the illustration.

Acknowledgement is gratefully made to the various owners who have facilitated the illustration of their coins and have permitted their publication here. Where practicable coins outside the British Museum have been selected in the knowledge that a number have never been illustrated before, whereas the coins in the National

Anglo-Saxon Coins

Collection are always readily available for study. My thanks are particularly due to the Keeper of Coins at the British Museum and his staff for much valued help and to Professor D. Whitelock who has read this paper in proof and made a number of valuable suggestions.

KEY TO THE PLATES

The number in brackets at the end of each item indicates the number of specimens of the type known to the writer.

PLATE IV

KINGS OF KENT. c. 775–c. 784

Heaberht
1 Eoba   Blunt, ex Grantley 878 (1)

Ecgberht
2 Babba   Chur, ex Ilanz hoard (4)
3 Eoba   Vatican (2)
4 Udd   Bagnall, ex Ryan 584 (5)

KINGS OF MERCIA

Offa
5 Dinar   BMA 14 (1)

Group I   c. 784–c. 787
6 Babba   Hunter 318 (1)
7 Babba   Margate. Some add *Rex* (6)
8 (E)alhmund   BMC 32 (1)
9 Ealred   Lockett, ex Roth 53 (1)
10 Eoba   Blunt, from Italy (3)
11 Eoba   BMA 32 (3)
12 Eoba   Lockett, ex Durden 18 (1)
13 Eoba   Copenhagen (2)
14 Eoba   BMC 46 (1)
15 Eoba   Vatican (1)
16 Eoba   Copenhagen (1)
17 Eoba   Cambridge (2)
18 Eoba   BMA 31 (1)
19 Osmod   Oxford (4)
20 Udd   BMA 44 (2)

Group II   c. 787–c. 792
21 No moneyer   BMC 30 (1)
22 Beagheard   BMA 29; name spelt Bahhard or Beoghard (4)
23 Ciolhard   Berlin; name spelt Ciolhard or Celhard (9)
24 Cuthberht   Lockett, ex Grantley 832. Appears to be of base silver (1)
25 Dud   BMC 40 (4)

The Coinage of Offa

26 Dud   BM, from Richborough, 1925 (1)
27 Dud   BMC 13 (1)
28 Dud   Paris (1)
29 Dud   BM, ex Lockett 351 (1)
30 Dud   Mack, ex Drabble 319 (1)
31 Dud   Mack, ex Lockett 350 (6)
32 Dud   Coats 308 (1)
33 Dud   BMC 28; name spelt Udd (1)

PLATE V

34 Eadberht   BMC 41 (3)
35 Eadberht   Berlin, bought 1875 from Hirsch (2)
36 Eadberht   Vatican (1)
37 Eadhun   BMC 14 (2)
38 Eadhun   BMC 15 (3-4)
39 Eadhun   Cambridge (3)
40 (E)alhmund   BMC 33 reads Alhmund (7)
41 (E)alhmund   Copenhagen, ex Montagu 222, reads Alhmund (1)
42 (E)alhmund   Coats 307 reads Alhmund (10)
43 (E)alhmund   Chur, ex Ilanz hoard (1)
43a (E)alhmund   Hunter 305, similar to 43 but moneyer's name Alhmund on the reverse (2) (not ill.)
44 (E)alhmund   Blunt, reads Ealmund (3)
45 (E)alhmund   Lockett 2642, reads Ealmund (3)
46 Ealmund   BMA 19 reads Ealmund (1)
47 Ealraed   BMC 17 reads Ealraed (1)
48 Ealred   BMA 16, reads Alred (1)
49 Ealraed   Hunter 311, reads Ealred, Ealraed or Alred (6)
50 Eoba   BMC 47 (1)
51 Eoba   Hunter 322 (1)
52 Eoba   BMA 20 (3)
53 Ethelnoth   BM from Richborough, 1925 (3)
54 Ethelnoth   Phillips, reads Ehelnot (1)
55 Ethelwald   Brighton (3-4)
56 Ethelwald   Copenhagen (6-7)
57 Ethelwald   Berlin, reads Ethilwald or Ethelwald (9)
58 Ethelwald   Lockett 2643 (2)
59 Heaberht (?) BMC 51 (2)
60 Heaberht (?) Blunt, ex Lockett 358 (1)
61 Ibba   BMA 21 ⎫ (4)
62 Ibba   BMC 19 ⎭
63 Ibba   Reading, ex Ryan 610 (3)

Anglo-Saxon Coins

64	Ibba	BMC 20; there are several variants in the obverse legend (10)
65	Ibba	BMA 22 (1)
66	Lulla	BMC 22 (1)
67	Lulla	Cambridge 392 (1)
68	Lulla	Edinburgh (7)

PLATE VI

69	Lulla	Berlin, ex Gansauge Collection (1)
70	Lulla	BMA 24 (2)
71	Œthilred	BMC 25 (1)
72	Osmod	BMA 43 (1)
73	Pehtwald	Hunter 323 (3)
74	Pehtwald	Lockett 2644 (1)
75	Pehtwald	Oxford (4)
76	Pendred	Hunter 316 (2)
77	Pendred	Lockett 3566 (1)
78	Pendred	BMC 27 (2)
79	Tirwald (?)	BMA 49 (1)
80	Tirwald (?)	Blunt, ex Ryan 617, reads Tidwald (1)
81	Winoth	Mack, ex Lockett 2645 (1)
82	Winoth	BMC 29 (1)
83	Winoth	Oxford (5)

Group III   c. 792–769

84	Babba	Grantley 825; the second coin (BMC 36), varies in detail (2)
85	Babba	BMC 35 (4)
86	Beagheard	Copenhagen (3)
87	Ciolhard	Hanham (1)
88	Deimund	Lockett 355 (1)
89	Ealhmund	BMC 44 (2)
90	Eama	Baldwin (1)
91	Eoba	BMA 34 (1)
92	Eoba	BMA 35 (1)
93	Eoba	BMA 36 (2)
94	Eoba	BMA 37 (1)
95	Ethelmod	Sharp, read Ethelmod, Etheelmod, or Etheelmd (4)
96	Ethelnoth	BM, ex Bruun 20. Same reverse die as a coin of Eadberht Præn (4)
97	Ethelnoth	BM, ex Carlyon-Britton 1604 (1)
98	Ethelnoth	BMC 49 (1)
99	Ethelnoth	Sharp (2)
100	Ethelnoth	Mack, ex Ryan 619 (1)

The Coinage of Offa

101	Ibba	*BMA* 42 (1)
102	Ludomon	Copenhagen, ex Montagu 212 (1)
103	Osmod	*BMC* 53 (2)

PLATE VII

104	Wilhun	*BMA* 48 (3)
105	Winoth	Lockett 2649; the name is also found as Winoth (6–7)
106	Winoth	*BMC* 58 (1)
107	Wulfhath	Cast in BM (1)

EAST ANGLIAN

Group II   c. 790–c. 792

108	Botred	*BMA* 30 (1)
109	Botred	Stockholm, found in Kent *c.* 1729 (1)
110	Hun..c (?)	*BMC* 31 (1)
111	Wihtred	*BMA* 46 (1)
112	Wihtred	*BMA* 45 (1)
113	Wihtred	Hunter 324 (1)

Group III   c. 792–796

114	Lul	*BMC* 52 (3)
115	Wihtred	*BMC* 55; all vary slightly in the reverse design. On all except the BM specimen the ϒ on the obverse is of the normal form (4)

QUEEN CYNETHRYTH (all moneyer Eoba) between *c.* 787–*c.* 792

116	Hunter 328 (1)
117	Lockett 360 (2)
118	Berlin, ex Murdoch 22 (1)
119	*BMC* 60 (5)
120	Cambridge, ex Lockett 361 (2)
121	Mack, ex Ryan 620 (1)
122	Oxford, ex Lockett 2651 (1)
123	Reading, ex Grantley 837 (1)
124	BM from Richborough 1931 (3)

IÆNBERHT, ARCHBISHOP OF CANTERBURY

125	*BMC* 20 (2)
126	BM bought Dominy 1924 (1)
127	Cambridge 435 (1)
128	*BMA* 189 (2)
129	*BMA* 188 (1)
130	Mack, ex Lockett 331 (1)

Anglo-Saxon Coins

131	Hunter 391 (2)
132	BM, ex Lockett 2632 (1)

ÆTHILHEARD, ARCHBISHOP OF CANTERBURY

(*a*) with title *Pontifex*

133	*BMA* 190 (1)
134	Blunt, ex Ryan 591 (1)
135	Hunter 392 (2)

(*b*) with title *Archiepiscopus*

136	Blunt, ex Ryan 590 (6)
137	*BMC* 23 (1)
138	*BMC* 22 (1)

Collections, etc., referred to above:
 Bagnall: A. E. Bagnall, Esq.
 Baldwin: A. H. F. Baldwin, Esq.
 Berlin: State Museum, Berlin.
 Blunt: Author's collection.
 BMA: Anglo-Saxon Acquisitions of the British Museum, *NC* 1922 pp. 214–44; *NC* 1923 pp. 243–59.
 BMC: A Catalogue of Coins in the British Museum, Anglo-Saxon Series, vol. I.
 Brighton: Brighton Art Gallery and Museum.
 Bruun: L. E. Bruun Sale, 1925.
 Cambridge: Fitzwilliam Museum. References are to *Sylloge*.
 Carlyon-Britton: P. W. Carlyon-Britton Sale, 1913–18.
 Chur: Rhät. Museum, Chur, Switzerland.
 Coats: Coats Collection, Glasgow. References are to *Sylloge*.
 Copenhagen: Royal Danish Coin Cabinet.
 Drabble: G. C. Drabble Sale, 1939 and 1943.
 Durden: H. Durden Sale, 1892.
 Edinburgh: National Museum of Antiquities of Scotland, Edinburgh.
 Grantley: Lord Grantley Sale, 1943–5.
 Hanham: the late Sir John Hanham, Bt.
 Hunter: Hunterian Museum, Glasgow. References are to *Sylloge*.
 Lockett: R. C. Lockett Collection. Sale in progress.
 Mack: Commander R. P. Mack.
 Margate: Margate Public Library.
 Montagu: H. Montagu Sale, 1895–7.
 Murdoch: J. G. Murdoch Sale, 1903–4.
 Oxford: Ashmolean Museum.
 Paris: Bibliothèque Nationale.
 Phillips: A. L. Phillips, Esq.

The Coinage of Offa

Reading: Reading University.
Roth: B. Roth Sale, 1917–18.
Ryan: V. J. E. Ryan Sale, 1950–2.
Sharp: Collection of Archbishop Sharp (d. 1714) now in possession of his descendants.
Stockholm: Royal Coin Cabinet.
Vatican: Apostolic Library of the Vatican, Rome.

REFERENCES

1. *Traité de Numismatique du Moyen Age* I (1891) p. 98
2. *Manuel de Numismatique Française* I (1912) pp. 235 ff.
3. Ibid. p. 359
4. POWICKE *Handbook of English Chronology* (1939) p. 9, BCS 196, a charter of Ecgberht's confirmed by Heaberht, with a second confirmation by Offa, shows that both Kentish kings were in subordination to Offa in 765
5. SIR FRANK STENTON *Anglo-Saxon England* (1947) p. 206
6. BROOKE *English Coins* (1950) p. 21
7. Op. cit. p. 206
8. POWICKE op. cit. p. 17
9. The views of earlier writers are neatly summarized by Assheton Pownall in *NC* 1875 pp. 196–205. But although the writer seeks to disprove Offa's journey to Rome, he does not entirely reject the Italian influence on his coinage
10. *NC* 1875 pp. 206 ff.
11. *Coinage of England* (1931) p. 19
12. Op. cit. p. 21
13. See *BNJ* xxv pp. 282–5
14. e.g. *Sylloge of British Coins* Hunter and Coats Collections nos. 776 and 777
15. *Proc. Num. Soc.* (23 November 1843) p. 5 (ill.)
16. *NC* 1920 p. 68 and BROOKE op. cit. p. 22
17. *NC* 1920 p. 68
18. *Di una rara moneta di Offa re de Merciani* Bologna 1863 (pamphlet). A letter to J. Evans in the Ashmolean Museum, Oxford, shows that this coin was in Cesis's Collection
19. *Proc. Num. Soc.* (19 March 1863)
20. Ibid. (18 February 1864)
21. *NC* 1864 p. 223
22. *NC* 1869 p. 193
23. *BNJ* xxviii iii (1957) pp. 459–66
24. DOROTHY WHITELOCK (ed.) *English Historical Documents* I (1955) pp. 793–4
25. Op. cit. p. 215 n.

Anglo-Saxon Coins

26. *Infra* p. 77
27. *BMC* I p. 32
28. *NC* 1920 p. 69
29. MS. in possession of the writer
30. It is interesting to note that Fountaine took the view that it was Offa who was depicted on this coin. *Numismata Anglo-Saxonica & Anglo-Danica* (Oxford 1705) 173
31. *BNJ* XXIX i (1958) 9
32. *BNJ* XXVIII ii (1956) pp. 243 ff.
33. It is hoped to publish full particulars of this coin shortly
34. *NC* 1865 pp. 356 ff. Evans uses the uncorrected date 790 for Iænberht's death, but acceptance of the revised date need not invalidate his argument, although it materially curtails the interval between the two events
35. Op. cit. pp. 22–3
36. Op. cit. p. 209
37. Brooke, however, prefers a Kentish attribution op. cit. p. 15
38. For the various views see P. W. CARLYON-BRITTON in *BJN* V (1909) pp. 55 ff.; J. ALLAN in *NC* 1914 pp. 77 ff.; C. OMAN *The Coinage of England* p. 19; D. F. ALLEN in *BNJ* XXV iii (1948) pp. 267–9; P. GRIERSON in *Revue Belge de Philologie et d'Histoire* XXXII (1954) pp. 1059–74; P. BELTRAN in *Centennial Publication of the American Numismatic Society* (1958) pp. 83–8; J. MENADIER in *Berliner Münzblätter* (1932/3) X pp. 533, 563; XI pp. 4, 17, 41, and 59
39. A later papal reaction to eastern coin-types is found at the time of the crusades. Innocent IV received a report from the pontifical legate who accompanied Louis IX on his crusade to the effect that the crusaders were issuing besants and drachmas with the name of Mahomet and dated with the musulman era. The Pope endorsed the legate's action in excommunicating the Christians of St John of Acre and of Tripoli and ordered that this abominable practice should cease forthwith. (G. Schlumberger *Numismatique de l'Orient Latin* (1954) p. 139)
40. See *BNJ* XXVIII iii (1958) p. 457
41. *BNJ* XXVII iii (1954) pp. 308 and 311
42. *Assemblage* p. 2
43. *BNJ* XXVIII i (1954) pp. 37–8
44. This coin cannot, however, now be identified, see *Proc. Num. Soc.* (25 May 1843) and *NC* VII (1845) p. 202. It was shown with a coin of Pippin and may be one of the coins referred to in *BNJ* XXVIII iii (1957) p. 457 n.
45. *BNJ* XXVIII i (1955) pp. 18–25 and works there cited
46. POWICKE op. cit. p. 9
47. 'Cronologia delle riforme monetarie di Carlo Magno' *Riv. It. di Numismatica* 1954

IV

The Coinage of Æthelwulf, King of the West Saxons, 839–58

by R. H. M. DOLLEY and K. SKAARE

[Plate VIII]

The purpose of this paper is to essay a reasoned chronological arrangement of the extant coins of Æthelwulf of Wessex. History has scarcely done justice to Æthelwulf, who had the misfortune to be overshadowed both by his father and by one of his sons. Yet, as Sir Frank Stenton has pointed out, he maintained intact Ecgbeorht's virtual annexation of the whole of South-eastern England, and he was by no means uniformly unsuccessful in meeting the new Danish menace.[1] For the numismatist there are certain dates in his reign which may or may not be suggestive. In 842 occurred a great slaughter of the Londoners, presumably at the hands of the Vikings, and in 851 Canterbury and London were sacked before Æthelwulf was able to inflict upon the Viking host their heaviest defeat in the memory of man. It will be the suggestion of this paper that there is some connexion between these two events and the concealment of the two critical finds from the Middle Temple and Sevington respectively. In 855 Æthelwulf went to Rome, and in the autumn of 856 he broke his journey home to marry the daughter of Charles the Bald. This Frankish marriage would seem to have been the pretext for a secession of Wessex as such, and for the last two years of his reign Æthelwulf was content to share the kingdom with his eldest son Æthelbald. In this context it should be observed that it is now universally admitted that no authentic coins of the latter are known.

Coins of Æthelwulf have occurred in a number of English hoards. In order of date of deposit they are as follows:

(a) Middle Temple (London), 1893.
(b) Sevington (Wiltshire), 1834.
(c) Croydon Palace (Surrey), in or shortly before 1907.
(d) Dorking (Surrey), 1817.
(e) Southampton (Hampshire), 1837.
(f) Gravesend (Kent), 1838.
(g) Trewhiddle (Cornwall), 1774.

Anglo-Saxon Coins

All these hoards appear in the recent *Inventory* (nos. 366, 328, 110, 123, 182, 176, and 362 respectively), but as it happens in almost every case there is something that can still be said. A few words on the subject of each find may not be out of place, and especially since the hoard-evidence is so critical for any scientific rearrangement of the series.

(a) MIDDLE TEMPLE (LONDON), 1893

This is the so-called 'Franks hoard'. The *Inventory* lists it under 'Unknown Site' and does not specify the date of finding, although in 1932, Brooke referred to a 'London (1893)' find 'buried early in his [i.e. Æthelwulf's] reign'.[2] More recently an even closer indication of the find-spot has been found in the MS. registers of the Department of Coins and Medals at the British Museum.[3] The hoard is believed to have been recovered intact. Little more than ten per cent of the coins were of Æthelwulf, and there were present only four of the twenty-six types distinguished in *BMC*. The *Inventory* dating c. 841–2 is acceptable.

(b) SEVINGTON (WILTSHIRE), 1834

The *Inventory* lists no more than fourteen out of some seventy coins, only two of them of Æthelwulf. In the British Museum, however, there are a further twelve coins, eight of them of Æthelwulf, which until 1937 had been kept with the archaeological material from the find. Moreover, an analysis of the relevant portion of the Loscombe Collection as recorded in the 1855 Sale Catalogue reveals that the twenty-eight coins concerned include all ten of those illustrated by Hawkins in 1838.[4] When it is appreciated that these twenty-eight coins form a definite entity, and that the eighteen not described in detail in *Archaeologia* are in every way consistent with the ten that are *and* with the twelve in the British Museum, the *Inventory*'s statement that Loscombe's 'collection probably included a number of coins from Sevington' may seem unnecessarily guarded. Incidentally, some of the coins concerned, for example, the Winchester penny of Æthelwulf by the moneyer Eanwald (lot 1068), remain unique to this day. We would suggest, therefore, that we can be reasonably certain concerning the types of forty-two of the coins, i.e. approximately sixty per cent of the hoard, something of an advance on the twenty per cent of the *Inventory*. Since there is no reason to think that coins of Æthelwulf amounted to less than half of the whole hoard, the probability is that there were originally present between thirty and forty of them. It is likely, however, that the twenty-two which are identifiable today represent a very fair sample of the whole. The *Inventory* dating '840–50' is unacceptable for reasons that will emerge later, and we would prefer one 'c. 850'.

The Coinage of Æthelwulf, King of the West Saxons, 839–58

(c) CROYDON PALACE (SURREY), IN OR SHORTLY BEFORE 1907

The *Inventory* gives no date for the discovery, but in fact it must have been very recent at the time of its publication. In Croydon Public Library are the MS. notes of Corbet Anderson who died in January 1907, and who had been a most diligent collector of all material relating to the Palace and to the borough as a whole. It is true that his book on the Palace was published in 1879, but the MS. notes include a drawing of the famous 'Two Emperor' type of Ælfred, also apparently a Croydon Palace find, which was not discovered much if at all before its publication – without provenance – in the *Numismatic Circular* for December 1892. There is nothing in Bliss's 1907 account of the small find with which we are here concerned to suggest that it was not comparatively recent, and the fact that it escaped Corbet Anderson's net would favour a date after 1895 at the very earliest, and more probably one after 1900. The *Inventory* date for the deposit – '*c.* 845' – seems impossibly early. Two of the three Æthelwulf coins are of the type (*BMC* type XVII) continued by Æthelbearht, and the Ceolnoth coin must surely be placed after rather than before 850. Our own dating of the hoard would be 'after 855 and before 860'.

(d) DORKING (SURREY), 1817

Taylor Combe's *Archaeologia* report on the bulk of the hoard remains fundamental if only because the *Inventory* omits altogether one hundred and five Æthelwulf pennies of *BMC* type XVII. The date of the hoard is not altogether easy to establish. Taylor Combe remarked that there were present in the portion of the hoard seen by him no coins of Æthelbearht's second coinage. He does describe, however, a penny of Burgred, and Puttock, writing many years after the event, claimed to have seen coins of Ælfred. This would suggest that the hoard was not concealed until after 871, but there are inconsistencies which demand careful consideration. Brooke, who may well have had access to some verbal or written, but now lost, tradition in the Department of Coins and Medals, is quite explicit that the hoard was concealed 'in the reign of Æthelberht', i.e. before 866, and this is despite the fact that in the same work he was peculiarly insistent that Burgred did not strike until that year. Several possibilities come to mind. The first is that Taylor Combe was mistaken when he identified one coin as of Burgred. If, however, there is one English numismatist of the nineteenth century who is unlikely to have made a mistake of that description it is Taylor Combe, and we feel that the hypothesis is to be rejected, even though the moneyer of the Ruding coin cited is one known in an earlier period. A second possibility is that the Burgred coin was a stray unconnected with the original deposit, and this possibility is one that has much to commend it. In particular it receives support from the fact that there seem to have been absent from the hoard not only coins of *BMC* type II of Æthelbearht but the corresponding issue of Ceolnoth. Admittedly such coins are still comparatively rare, the newly rediscovered example of Ceolnoth being in fact unique, but it is precisely a hoard deposited soon after Æthelbearht's death that might have been expected to contain them in appreciable numbers.[5] Thirdly there is the possibility that Burgred's coinage began earlier than Brooke supposed, and that the West Saxons adopted a type which had already been current in Mercia for a number of years, albeit on an exiguous scale. In support of this hypothesis we would point out that in hoards such as those from Gravesend and Southampton, which were deposited deep in West Saxon territory and within a year or two of 871, Mercian coins of Burgred preponderate. Moreover, there are considerably more varieties of the main type among the coins of Burgred than there are among the coins of Æthelred I and of Ælfred put together. It is by no means impossible that Wessex should have adopted a Mercian type when the decision was made to strike a unified coinage on behalf of both kingdoms when they were locked in life-and-death battle with the common enemy. In other words, there is really no reason why the hoard should not be dated to *c.* 865 as Brooke supposed – we are not inclined to take very seriously Puttock's claim more than twenty-five years after the discovery that he had seen a small parcel which happened to have contained coins of Ælfred. The occasion for the hoard's deposit is not apparent. One may wonder, however, whether it is not connected with the Viking assault on Winchester mentioned in the *Anglo-Saxon Chronicle s.a.* 860. In this case the coins could suggest that the sack of Winchester is to be dated nearer 860 than 865, and the date of 861 implied by Hincmar's narrative is by no means improbable. Slight discrepancies will be noted between the *Inventory* summary and our own. These are not due in every case to our rejection of the *Inventory* interpretation, as we have also added a few coins, presented to the British Museum by Taylor Combe's widow, which seem to have formed part of a small parcel brought to his notice after the *Archaeologia* publication.

(e) SOUTHAMPTON (HAMPSHIRE), 1837

This is the 'Hampshire find' of the *Inventory*. Greater precision has been given in respect of the find-spot by Mrs J. S. Martin.[6] Of the six coins of Æthelwulf recorded by Lindsay, one is in fact illustrated as such in his *Coinage of the Heptarchy*, and it is not clear why the type (*BMC* type I) and moneyer (Welheard) could not have been given in the summary. Incidentally, the coins passed, in the

The Coinage of Æthulwulf, King of the West Saxons, 839–58

first place at least, to Sainthill and not to Lindsay, as claimed in the *Inventory*, and it is on the basis of the Sale Catalogues of both these men that we have ventured to suggest identifications of some of the remaining coins. In the matter of the date of deposit, however, the suggestion of the *Inventory* – '*c*. 870' – seems impeccable.

(*f*) GRAVESEND (KENT), 1838

One little slip in the *Inventory* is the attribution of the first account of the find to Borrell and not to Hawkins. The date of deposit suggested – '*c*. 875' – seems a little on the late side if only because of the presence of only one coin of Ælfred, and we would prefer to date it '*c*. 872'. It is interesting that the coins of Æthelwulf should all be of 'pre-Reform' (i.e. pre-*BMC* type XVII) issues.

(*g*) TREWHIDDLE (CORNWALL), 1774

It has recently become possible to check the accuracy of the received tradition against some unpublished contemporary MS. notes in the hand of Philip Rashleigh himself. The date of deposit given in the *Inventory* – '*c*. 871–5' – is probably correct, but only if one rejects as we do the presence in the hoard of the *BMC* type XIV penny of Ælfred. In this connexion it should be observed that current work suggests that Jonathan Rashleigh identified as from Trewhiddle coins in the family cabinet which in fact were from other sources – but prima facie suspicion does not attach to any particular coin of Æthelwulf.[7]

The classes of Æthelwulf penny present in the above finds are set out in the following tables, but first we should perhaps note a few isolated finds from these islands and from the Continent.

(1) London Wall (London). *BMC* type V, D(iar). [*Num. J.* II (1837) p. 109]
(2) Croy (Inverness). *BMC* type IX, Deiheah (with a coin of Coenwulf, brooches, beads, etc.). [*Inventory* 109]
(3) Rome (or neighbourhood). *BMC* type I, Biarnnoth. [*BNJ* XXVIII iii (1957) p. 453]

Typologically the coins of Æthelwulf falls into three main groups: coins with a true monogram (i.e. *BMC* types I, Ia, II (in fact a mule), III, IV, V, and Va), coins with a portrait (i.e. *BMC* types VI, VII, VIII, IX, IXa, X, XI, XII, XIII, XIV, XV, XVI, and XVII), and lastly coins without monogram or portrait (i.e. *BMC* types XVIII (in fact a mule), XIX, XX, XXI, XXII, and XXIII). According to the rather simpler and more scientific Brooke classification, the same three groups are repeated, the 'Monogram' coins being of his types 5, 6, 9, 10, and 11, the 'Portrait' coins of his types 1, 2, 3, 7, and 8, and the 'Non-portrait' coins of his type 4. In the following tables each group is treated separately.

(A) 'Monogram' Types

	BMC							Brooke				
	I	Ia	II	III	IV	V	va	5	6	9	10	11
Middle Temple	–	–	–	–	–	2	4	–	–	–	2	4
Sevington	4	1	–	–	1	–	1	5	–	1	–	1
Croydon	–	–	–	–	–	1	–	–	–	–	1	–
Dorking	33	3	2	2	–	28	6	38*	2	–	28	6
Southampton	2?	–	–	–	–	2?	–	2?	–	–	2?	–
Gravesend	1	1	–	1	–	–	–	2	1	–	–	–
Trewhiddle	2	–	–	–	–	1	–	2	–	–	1	–

(B) 'Portrait' Types

	BMC											
	VI	VII	VIII	IX	IXa	X	XI	XII	XIII	XIV	XV	XVI	XVII
Middle Temple	–	–	–	8	14	–	–	–	–	–	–	–	–
Sevington	1	1	–	–	–	–	4	–	–	6	1	1	–
Croydon	–	–	–	–	–	–	–	–	–	–	–	–	2
Dorking	2	1	2	1	2	–	44	1	12	4	2	–	105
Southampton	–	–	–	–	–	–	1?	–	–	–	–	–	2?
Gravesend	–	–	–	–	–	–	–	–	–	–	–	–	–
Trewhiddle	–	–	–	–	–	1	1	–	1†	–	1	–	3

	Brooke				
	1	2	3	7	8
Middle Temple	1	7	14	–	–
Sevington	–	2	–	12	–
Croydon	–	–	–	–	2
Dorking	–	4	3	65	105
Southampton	–	–	–	1?	2?
Gravesend	–	–	–	–	–
Trewhiddle	Var.	1	–	1	3

(C) 'Non-portrait' Types

	BMC						Brooke
	XVIII	XIX	XX	XXI	XXII	XXIII	4
Middle Temple	–	–	–	–	–	–	–
Sevington	–	–	–	–	–	1	1
Croydon	–	–	–	–	–	–	–
Dorking	5	1	3	8	2	2	21
Southampton	1?	–	–	–	–	–	1?
Gravesend	–	–	–	–	–	–	–
Trewhiddle	–	–	–	–	–	–	–

* Including two 5/4 mules   † In Fact an VIII/XIII mule

The Coinage of Æthelwulf, King of the West Saxons, 839–58

The Middle Temple hoard, although rich in Mercian coins generally, contained none of Berhtwulf who came to the throne in 840 and who can scarcely have been in a position to strike coins after the great Viking assault of 850-1. Doubtless in part this absence of coins is to be explained by the supposition that Berhtwulf did not begin minting until a year or so after his accession – and here we must not forget that it was Wessex and not Mercia which possessed Canterbury – but a hoard such as that from Sevington makes it clear that quite a considerable volume of Mercian coinage has to be fitted in before c. 850. Moreover, an even greater volume of West Saxon coinage belongs to the same decade, and, as we shall see, there is reason to think that virtually all the coinage of Berhtwulf was contemporaneous with quite an early phase of West Saxon striking. All the evidence, then, is that the Middle Temple hoard was deposited early in Æthelwulf's reign, and certainly the slaughter of the Londoners in 842 would seem to provide a plausible explanation of its non-recovery. In consequence it must be accepted that *BMC* types V, Va, IX, and IXa (Brooke 1, 2, 3, 10, and 11) are among the earliest in the reign.

The simple fact that *BMC* type XVII (Brooke 8) was continued by Æthelbearht would alone suggest that it was the last type of the father and confirmation of this comes from a scrutiny of the moneyers. Fourteen moneyers are known for Æthelwulf, and no fewer than ten reappear among the forty-six recorded for Æthelbearht. More than a third of the Æthelwulf coins in the Dorking hoard, moreover, are of this type, and further arguments can be based on such minutiae as the lettering which leave no room for doubt that *BMC* type XVII was in fact the last of the reign. At this stage, too, we may profitably take into account the evidence of Sevington. Details are known of twenty-two coins of Æthelwulf. They embrace eleven of the *BMC* types, only one of them represented in the Middle Temple find. The absentees are *BMC* types II and III (Brooke 5/4 and 6), the first of which at least cannot properly be considered a substantive issue, *BMC* type V (Brooke 10), an early issue present in the Middle Temple hoard, *BMC* type VIII (Brooke 2) which epigraphically and prosopographically also must be quite early, *BMC* types IX and IXa (Brooke 1 and 3), both represented in the Middle Temple hoard and in consequence early, *BMC* type X (Brooke —) known from a unique coin in the Trewhiddle hoard and typologically very early, *BMC* type XII (Brooke 7) another great rarity, *BMC* type XIII (Brooke 7), the absence of which may or may not be significant, *BMC* type XVII (Brooke 8) which must be, as we have seen, the last issue of the reign, and, finally, *BMC* types XVIII, XIX, XX, XXI, and XXII (Brooke 4), all of them types represented in the Dorking hoard by fewer than ten specimens. To us it would seem that the principal importance of the Sevington hoard is its provision of a basic canon of moneyers operating in the period c. 840–50, and we believe that it would be dangerous to read too much into the absence of any type other than *BMC* XVII (Brooke 8).

On the other hand, it does seem legitimate to draw attention to the fact that in the Dorking hoard coins of *BMC* types I, V, and XI (Brooke 5, 7, and 10) were present in substantial quantity. In the case of *BMC* type V (Brooke 10) we are faced with an apparent anomaly in that the Middle Temple find makes this one of the earliest types of the reign, but the probable explanation is that the type continued for some considerable time. In this connexion it should be noted that coins of this type, though generally homogeneous, present many minor diversities of type and lettering. As regards *BMC* type XI (Brooke 7) the position is that it outnumbers all types except *BMC* type XVII (Brooke 8) which might suggest that it was the penultimate issue of the reign. However, as we shall see, there are reasons for placing it somewhat earlier, and it seems worth remarking that coins of *BMC* type I (Brooke 5) appear to have been present in the trifling Æthelwulf element from the late hoards from Gravesend, Southampton, and Trewhiddle. It is not impossible, therefore, that the proper position for *BMC* type I is between *BMC* type XI and *BMC* type XVII, and that its under-representation in the Dorking hoard is accidental.

It is at this point that epigraphy begins to be decisive, and we believe that there is both epigraphical and prosopographical evidence to warrant a division of the coinage of Æthelwulf into four distinct phases.

PHASE I (839–c. 843?)

In this phase the Canterbury coins fall into three types, each with its own epigraphy and each confined to certain moneyers. A 'Portrait' type (*BMC* types IX, IXa, and X=Brooke 1, 2, and 3) is struck by Beagmund, Dun, and Wilheah. Two varieties exist (**Plate VIII, 1** and **2**), the bust in the latter breaking the inner circle. The name of the King is written EDELVVLF, and there is no initial cross at the head of the obverse legend. A 'Monogram' type (*BMC* type V=Brooke 10) with the word SAXONIORVM in three lines occupying the whole of the reverse field (**Plate VIII, 3**) is struck by Diar, Herebeald, Manna, Osmund, and Torhtwald. Here the name of the King is written EÐELVVLF, and an initial cross at the head of the obverse legend is the rule. A second 'Monogram' type (*BMC* type Va=Brooke 11) substitutes OCCIDEN-TALIUM for the name of the moneyer (**Plate VIII, 4**). The name of the King is spelt AEÐELVVLF, and again an initial cross is an integral part of the obverse legend. It was a variant obverse die cut by this engraver which was sent to Winchester and used with a local reverse die to produce the only coin of Æthelwulf (*BMC* type IV=Brooke 9) certainly struck at a mint other than Canterbury (**Plate VIII, 20**). As it happens, too, an obverse of this same issue is also found muled with a 'Portrait' obverse of the Mercian king Berhtwulf (**Plate VIII, 21**). The Canterbury types of this phase all occur in the Middle Temple hoard, and a further clue to its early date is to be found in the circumstance that Beagmund and Osmund – and possibly Dun(un) – had struck for Ecgbeorht late coins which typologically are closely connected with Æthelwulf's earliest issues.

PHASE 2 (*c.* 843–*c.* 848?)

Whereas in Phase 1 no fewer than three distinct schools of die-cutting are at once apparent, in Phase 2 there is a reduction to two, the absentee being that which had produced the 'Portrait' coins in the previous phase. Beagmund, Dun, and Wilheah do not strike 'Portrait' coins in this phase – an indication of overlapping of the two phases? – but receive a variety of 'Non-portrait' dies from the same source that had produced the '*Occidentalium*' dies (*BMC* types XVIII, XIX, XX, XXI, XXII, and XXIII=Brooke 4). The reverse types are usually some form of cross (**Plate VIII, 5**) or an elaborate letter A (**Plate VIII, 6**), and there are also two distinct founts of lettering, the smaller (**Plate VIII, 7**) being apparently earlier than the larger (**Plate VIII, 8**). The sequence is well borne out by the circumstance that only the new moneyers in this type, Brid, Ethelhere, Maninc, and Welheard, strike coins with the late lettering. It is for the last three of these moneyers alone that a new 'Portrait' type is evolved (*BMC* types VIII, XI, XIV, XV, and XVI=Brooke 2), which is also struck by Biarnnoth. Again the reverse types are a cross or a letter A (**Plate VIII, 9 and 10**). On the 'Portrait' coins of this grouping the King's name is spelt EÐELVVLF and the initial cross is omitted, but on 'Non-portrait' coins we find also the AEÐELVVLF spelling with initial cross that distinguished the '*Occidentalium*' coins in the previous phase.

A smaller version of the portrait also occurs in this phase where it is struck by Diar, Herebeald, Manna, and Osmund who had struck '*Saxoniorum*' coins in Phase 1, and also by Deiheah, Eanmund, Hunbearht, and Liaba. These coins (*BMC* types VI, VII, XI, XII, XIII, and XIV=Brooke 7) have three principal reverse types, the cross and A common to the other grouping (**Plate VIII, 11 and 12**), and also a *chi/rho* monogram (**Plate VIII, 13**). There is a quite characteristic small epigraphy, and any risk of confusion with the 'Portrait' coins of the other grouping is prevented by the circumstance that the initial cross precedes the King's name though it too is spelt EÐELVVLF.

Anglo-Saxon Coins

As in Phase 1, then, the moneyers fall into two distinct groups, but whereas before they were divided three and five the division is now eight and eight. On the one hand we have Beagmund, Biarnnoth, Brid, Dun, Ethelhere, Maninc, Welheard, and Wilheah; on the other, Deiheah, Diar, Eanmund, Herebeald, Hunbearht, Liaba, Manna, and Osmund. To the best of our knowledge muling between the two groups is never found, and this despite the fact that they are clearly contemporaneous. It is indeed tempting to postulate two 'mints' operating in Canterbury simultaneously. On historical grounds there would be every reason for two or even three distinct schools of die-cutting to have evolved during the half-century that had passed since the introduction of the penny. Whereas originally archiepiscopal minting-rights seem to have been purely permissive, the quarrel between Coenwulf and Archbishop Wulfred meant that the latter had to strike on his own account and in flat defiance of the Mercian King whose name was now expunged from the archiepiscopal series. Obviously there would be tensions when men served both masters, and in the same way we might see the germ of a third mint when Ecgbeorht, though in a position to exact obedience from either of the existing mints, may have thought it more consonant with his position to have some at least of his coins struck at Canterbury by his own moneyers. Under Æthelwulf, of course, many of the old tensions no longer existed, and we venture to postulate a general 'tidying up' with the erection of two secular *officinae* of equal size. As far as can be told the Archbishop seems to have patronized one of the two engravers for the small number of dies required for his coinage, and it is perhaps significant that Berhtwulf seems usually to have gone to the other. That Æthelwulf was firmly in control may seem indicated by the fact that the two moneyers he shared with Berhtwulf, namely Brid and Liaba, were divided between the two *officinae*.

PHASE 3 (*c.* 848–51–*c.* 855)

Phase 2 had seen the introduction and later the progressive elimination of 'Non-portrait' types and the emergence of a more or less standardized 'Portrait' issue, though considerable freedom remained in respect of reverse types. In Phase 3, on the other hand, the portrait is abruptly swept away, and both the new *officinae* strike coins of uniform type, the so-called '*Dorib/Cant*' issue (*BMC* type I=Brooke 5). Of the fourteen moneyers who are known, only two had not struck in the preceding phase, and a further proof of the close connexion between the two issues is the existence of a unique mule (*BMC* type II) by the moneyer Diar (**Plate VIII, 14**). Of the fourteen moneyers who strike the type proper, one group, Biarnnoth, Brid, Ethelhere, Maninc, Welheard, and

The Coinage of Æthelwulf, King of the West Saxons, 839–58

Wilheah, survivors from Phase 2 where they had all belonged to the same *officina*, is joined by Ethelmund. The lettering is still large (**Plate VIII, 15**), but the spelling of the King's name now appears as EÐELVVLF, and not AEÐELVVLF as on the earlier 'Non-portrait' coins. The second *officina* is composed of the following survivors from Phase 2, where again they had belonged to the same *officina*, Deiheah, Diar, Eanmund, Hunbearht, and Osmund, together with a new-comer Ealhmund. The lettering is notably smaller (**Plate VIII, 16**), and not surprisingly the spelling EÐELVVLF is retained with the result that the division of the moneyers of Phase 3 between the two *officinae* has to be made on the basis of the size of the lettering alone. The distinction is not the less valid for that, and we can be hopeful that any new coins of this period which might be thrown up by some future Sevington will fit naturally into place. There is in fact a seventh moneyer to be attributed to this second *officina*, Herebeald, who with Hunbearht strikes a rare and not very significant variety where the monograms are transposed (**Plate VIII, 17**). Also to this phase of the coinage belongs another 'Monogram' type of quite exceptional rarity (*BMC* type III=Brooke 6) by a moneyer Hebeca (**Plate VIII, 18**) who struck otherwise only for Archbishop Ceolnoth, the only royal moneyer in Phases 1, 2, and 3 to serve two masters. Clearly Hebeca stands in a class by himself, and all the evidence must be that his 'Monogram' coins are later than those of the '*Dorib/Cant*' issue proper. It is here that we must draw attention to a most singular lack of continuity between the '*Dorib/Cant*' coins and the prolific 'Portrait' issue (*BMC* type XVII=Brooke 8) which forms Phase 4 of Æthelwulf's coinage and is clearly the last of the reign. Of the fourteen names that appear on the '*Dorib/Cant*' coins, only four figure among the fourteen found on the 'Portrait' coins. Our belief is that the '*Dorib/Cant*' coinage came to an abrupt end with the great Viking assault of 850/1. The Hebeca coins represent a flicker of activity after the disaster, perhaps even a gesture of recognition of the royal rights by the archiepiscopal mint, before a complete reorganization brought about the creation of the new cadre of moneyers who struck *BMC* type XVII.

PHASE 4 (c. 855–9)

As we have seen, continuity with Phase 3 exists only in the persons of four moneyers, Diar, Ethelhere, Hunbearht, and Maninc. New-comers are Dægberht, Dudwine, Ethelgeard, Ethelmod, Ethelnoth, Hunred, Manna, Tirwald, Torhtulf, and Wermund. The portrait adopted (**Plate VIII, 19**) is a greatly improved version of that found on certain coins of Phase 2, but there is no direct influence and significantly the obverse legend reads +AEÐELVVLFREX.

Anglo-Saxon Coins

Although as it happens the four Phase 3 moneyers had been divided equally between the two *officinae* then at work, it is impossible to find any such division in the new coinage. Clearly all the dies are the product of a single school, if not of a single hand, nor is it without significance that it is at this juncture that the Archbishop begins to strike coins of the same type even though for the present the hieratic facing bust is still retained.[8] Unity had at last been brought to the coinage of England south of the Thames, and it would not be much more than a decade before a wider unity emerges only to be disrupted by the great Danish invasions of Ælfred's reign.

In this paper we hope that we have traced in not too unconvincing a fashion the broad outlines of the coinage of by no means the least effective of the successors of Cerdic. To some extent the paper may claim the merit of novelty no similar study of Æthelwulf's coinage having appeared in any of the numismatic journals, and, though much work remains to be done on the details, we sincerely believe that the structure is sound. The English National Collection is particularly rich in the coins concerned and it may well be that there are only two combinations of moneyer and type that are not there represented, and both of these we have checked and found to fit naturally into the broader framework. The arrangement of the accompanying Plate has been especially designed to permit the student confronted with a coin of the period to fit it readily into the chronological sequence, and even if the exact variety of bust or of reverse type is not illustrated it should still be possible to place the coin by the lettering. The archaeologist in particular may find it useful to have these new close datings, and if they claim to be no more accurate than within five years we feel that they do mark a certain advance on earlier work in this field. The numismatist, on the other hand, will doubtless be more exercised by our reattribution to the Canterbury mint of Brooke types 10 and 11, a reattribution that we believe inevitable in the light of Mr Blunt's recent study of the coinage of Ecgbeorht.[9] Primarily, however, it is for the historian that we have been seeking to muster the evidence of the coins, and it is with a certain relief that we find our story of progressive unification of the coinage according reasonably well with the picture of Æthelwulf which emerges from the pages of *Anglo-Saxon England*. As we have seen, by 850 Æthelwulf had secured a unity of type, recognized for the first time we would claim in these pages, and it is a nice question whether the process was facilitated or hindered by the sack of 851. Vested interests must inevitably have been injured by the new order, and we suggest that not the least significant portions of our paper are those where we claim to have shown that unification was in the air before the 'Reform' of *c.* 855.

The Coinage of Æthelwulf, King of the West Saxons, 839-58

REFERENCES

1. F. M. STENTON *Anglo-Saxon England* p. 242
2. G. C. BROOKE *English Coins* p. 43
3. *BNJ* xxviii i (1955) p. 31
4. *Archaeologia* xxvii (1838) Plate xxiii
5. For the Ceolnoth fragment cf. *BNJ* xxviii ii (1956) p. 405
6. On the basis of references in *GM*
7. The problem of the Jonathan Rashleigh interlopers is discussed in the numismatic part of C. E. Blunt and D. M. Wilson's forthcoming *Archaeologia* study of the Trewhiddle find. For similar scepticism concerning the Ælfred coin of *BMC* type XIV see a recent note by R. H. M. Dolley in *BMQ* xxi pp. 94-7
8. For the clearest statement of the significance of the common type see Mr Blunt's paper (see note 5 *supra*)
9. C. E. BLUNT 'The Coinage of Ecgbeorht, King of Wessex, 802-839', *BNJ* xxviii iii (1957) pp. 467-76

Appendix

SUMMARY TABLE OF TYPES, LETTERINGS, AND MONEYERS

	Early			Second Coinage			Third Coinage				Late
	Portraits 1 and 2 Occidentalium Saxoniorum	Saxoniorum	Portrait 3	Non-Portrait	Portrait 4	Dorib/Cant	Cant/Dorib	Sack of Canterbury	Cant/Cumm		Portrait 5
Anonymous		B.1									
Manna		C.1			C.2						D
Beagmund	A			B.1 and 2							
Torhtwald		C.1									
Dun	A			B.1 and 2							
Diar		C.1			C.2	C.2					D
Wilheah	A			B.1 and 2		B.2					
Herebeald		C.1			C.2	C.2					
Biarnnoth					B.2	B.2					
Osmund		C.1			C.2	C.2					
Ethelhere			B.2		B.2	B.2					D
Deiheah					C.2	C.2					
Maninc			B.2		B.2	B.2					D
Eanmund					C.2	C.2					
Ethelmund						B.2					
Liaba					C.2						
Brid				B.1 and 2		B.2					
Hunbearht					C.2	C.2	C.2				D
Welheard				B.2		B.2					
Ealhmund						C.2					
Hebeca									C.2		
Daegberht											D
Dudwine											D
Ethelgeard											D
Ethelmod											D
Ethelnoth											D
Hunred											D
Tirwald											D
Torhtulf											D
Wermund											D

A — Early lettering
B.1 and 2, C.1 and 2 — Intermediate lettering
D — Late lettering

V

The Chronology of the Coins of Ælfred the Great 871–99

by R. H. M. DOLLEY and C. E. BLUNT

[Plates IX and X]

In this paper an attempt will be made to arrive at a satisfactory if very approximate chronology for the extant coins of perhaps the greatest of all the English kings. Many of our conclusions will have to be guarded, but we believe that misconceptions concerning Ælfred's coins are so fundamental and so widespread that a reassessment has become a matter of urgency. The mainly relative chronology that follows may be of some use, therefore, to the archaeologist as well as to the historian, but we also hope that numismatists will be encouraged to re-examine the problems posed by certain issues in the expectation that a detailed scrutiny of the evidence of the coins themselves will permit of more detailed conclusions being drawn than we believe to be justified by a preliminary survey.

All the coins of Ælfred known today are struck in silver, but we would not rule out the possibility that there might have been a very limited coinage in gold for certain specific purposes.[1] Certainly three and perhaps four denominations of the silver are known, and in descending order of weight they are as follows:

(a) THE 'OFFERING PIECES' [Plate IX, 1]

There have been many theories concerning the probable purpose and use of these coins which are without parallel in the coinage of western Europe. A recent paper, however, has come down heavily in favour of the expansion of the reverse legend as ELIMO (*sina*) and the consequent interpretation of the coins as royal alms.[2] More tentative and perhaps more controversial is the suggestion that they were intended as 'sixpences' on the Carolingian standard. A possibility that will have to be explored in the near future is that they may have been used as part of the royal contribution to early Romescots, but it seems unlikely that they can be dated early enough to allow of their having been struck for the first recorded payment in 887. Their closest affinities are with the *'Win'* and *'Exa'* pennies described on p. 87, and on the available evidence they seem to belong to the last years of the reign, the presumptive mint being Winchester. Only two specimens are known, one occurring in the Goldsborough hoard from Yorkshire (Thompson *Inventory* 175), a Viking hoard that seems associated with the tussle for York between the Hiberno-Norsemen and the Danes twenty years after Ælfred's death, and the other as a single-find from near Poole in Dorset.[3]

(b) THE PENNIES [Plate IX, 2–17]

I WITH PORTRAIT

The following distinct classes are known:

(a) *The 'Burgred' type* [Plate IX, 2]

Coins of this issue are relatively common, and have occurred, generally in fair numbers, in hoards from Beeston Tor (*Inventory* 40), Croydon (*Inventory* 111), Dunsforth (*Inventory* 146), Gainford (*Inventory* 167), Gravesend (*Inventory* 176), Hook Norton (*Inventory* —), Leckhampton, *alias* Cheltenham (*Inventory* 82), and Trewhiddle (*Inventory* 362). There is just a possibility, too, that the odd coin of this type may have occurred in the ill-documented nineteenth-century find from Waterloo Bridge (*Inventory* 256), and in this connexion it may be observed that Ælfred coins have always tended to command considerable prices so that their abstraction from finds before notification to the authorities is a possibility that has always to be taken into account. Most of the above hoards are adequately published, but much additional material is now available concerning the Croydon hoard, while the *Inventory* summaries of the finds from Leckhampton and Trewhiddle stand in need of urgent emendation. The Hook Norton find is unpublished but the coins concerned are identifiable in the trays of the National Collection.

All the above hoards must be dated during the first three or four years of Ælfred's reign, and a glance at the accompanying map (Map 1) shows that the majority of them fall in an arc coincident with the farthest extent of effective Danish penetration of England. That the coins of this type are not found in later contexts must suggest that they were effectively demonetized, and in this connexion it may be significant that they have the reputation for being base – though it would not seem that any representative number of specimens has ever been submitted for quantitative assay.

The type is a continuation of one struck by his elder brother and by his Mercian brother-in-law. When it was introduced is a little doubtful, but it was either at the very end of the reign of Æthelbearht – assuming the relevance

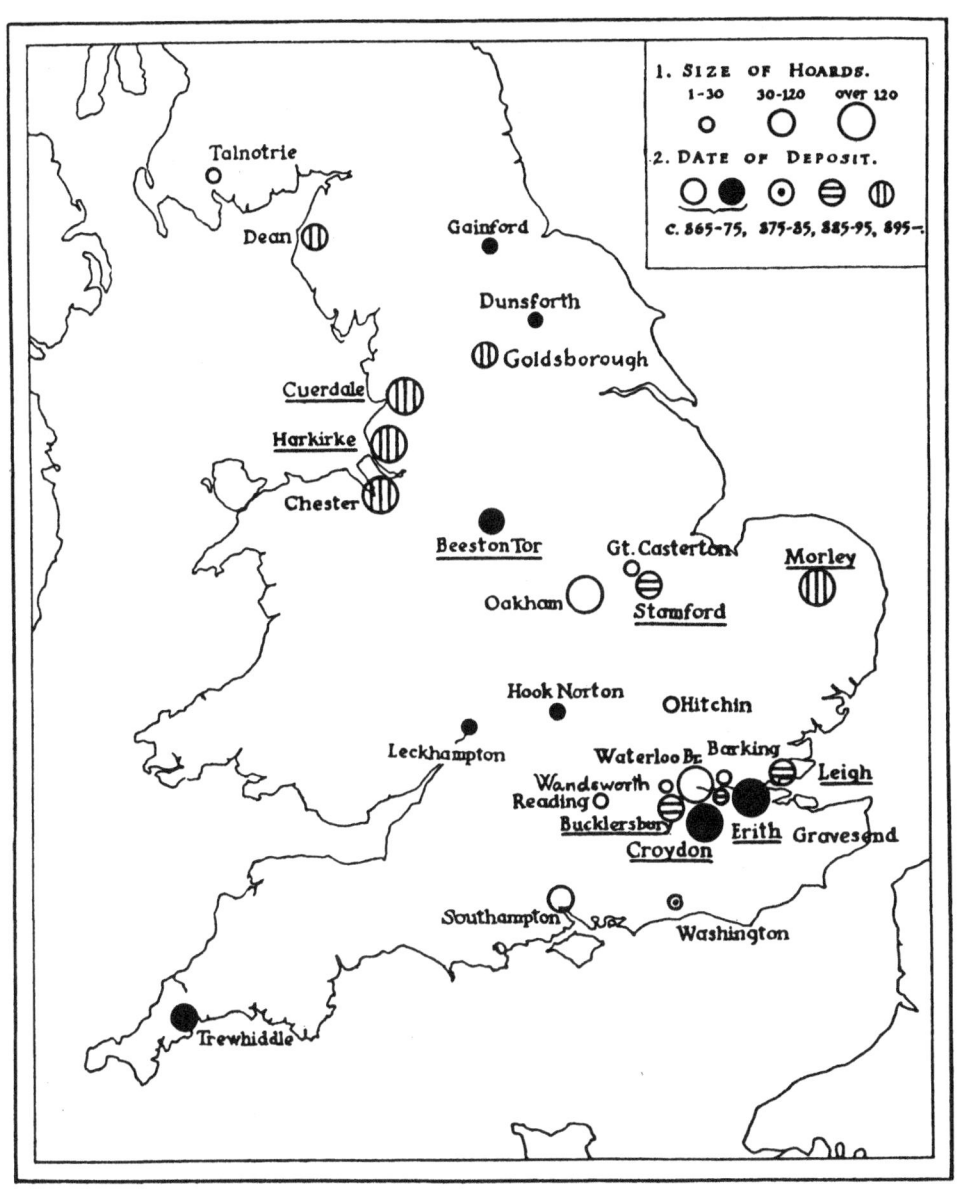

MAP I

English Hoards after 865 with coins of Burgred and/or Ælfred. Underlined hoards are critical for chronology.

of one controversial coin – or immediately after Æthelred's accession.⁴ The new King's name is usually rendered AELBRED, and comparable 'phonetic' spellings (e.g. ELBERE for AELFHERE) occur among the names of the forty or so moneyers of the type who almost without exception are found already to have struck either for his brothers or for his brother-in-law. There can be no doubt whatever that this was Ælfred's first issue, and it is worth noting that hoards where coins of this type occur seem to contain no other coins which can be dated later than Burgred's abdication in 874. The type is one that had also been struck by Archbishop Ceolnoth, and it has usually been assumed that all the coins of the whole issue were minted at Canterbury. One may suspect, though, that many of the coins were struck at London. The hoard-evidence and the large number of moneyers concerned must suggest that the issue was continued for several years into Ælfred's reign, though as it happens no coins are known for Archbishop Æthered who had been consecrated in 870.

The principal objection to the theory of a major mint at London so early in Ælfred's reign has been taken to be the existence of a handful of coins, a penny and two halfpennies, with the name Halfdene or Halfdan. For some reason these have almost always been associated with the Halfdene who wintered in London in 871/2, but, as we shall see, these coins imitate Ælfred coins that cannot possibly be earlier than 886, and we must endorse Mr Grierson's conclusion that they are coins of quite another Halfdene.⁵ It is also becoming clear that the Danes did not begin striking on their own account much before *c.* 888, and we may wonder whether in point of fact the presence in London of a part of the Great Army during the winter of 871/2 would necessarily have terminated the production of coin by the English mint.

(b) *The 'Ceolwulf' type* [Plate IX, 4]

Whereas on coins of the previous type an ethnic after the royal title was normally omitted, in this issue a fairly consistent attempt is made to continue the legend. As far as can be judged the norm is s, presumably for *Saxonum*, but there are coins where the reading is A, presumably for *Anglorum*, and even SM (? for *Saxonum et Merciorum*). Coins of the issue are quite rare, and appear to have occurred in no more than two hoards, the great Cuerdale hoard (*Inventory* 112) deposited *c.* 903 and very probably to be associated with newly intensified Hiberno-Norse penetration north of the Mersey, and a small and formally unpublished find from Washington in Sussex (*Inventory* —).⁶ All the same, the issue must have been on a substantial scale as the names of seventeen moneyers have been recorded. The type was also struck by Ceolwulf II of Mercia, the King set up by the Danes in 874, not known to history after 877 and certainly

The Chronology of the Coins of Ælfred the Great, 871–99

vanished from the scene by 883, and by Archbishop Æthered who occupied the see of Canterbury from 870 until 888. Again the numismatic tradition is to associate the issue with the mint at Canterbury, but a block of lead – usually considered a trial-piece but perhaps a mint-weight – with the imprint of a pair of Ælfred dies of this type has been found in St Paul's Churchyard, and we feel that it is by no means impossible that the mint of a major part of the whole issue may have been London. The status of London between 871 and 886 is not known, and there seems no good reason why it should not have been a species of 'open city'. As we have seen, the land-hungry Danes of the Great Army at this time had little interest in minting as such, and for them as much as for the English there would have been advantages in a free flow of new coin. If this hypothesis be accepted, and we are well aware of its novelty, Ælfred's occupation of London in 886 should be interpreted as the military seizure of a strong-point that hitherto had been technically 'neutral'.[7]

That the 'Ceolwulf' type immediately followed the 'Burgred' issue is not at first sight obvious – at most six of Ælfred's 'Ceolwulf' moneyers have been recorded in the 'Burgred' type – but this arrangement raises the fewest difficulties when we come to consider the remaining coins which have to be fitted in before *c.* 885. There is, too, a critical single-find from Southampton (**Plate IX, 3**) which appears to combine a 'Burgred' obverse with a 'Ceolwulf' reverse, though on closer examination the obverse would be better described as a transitional (=early) variety of the 'Ceolwulf' obverse, retaining many features (e.g. the inner circle) from the old design.[8]

(c) *The 'Two Emperors' type* [Plate IX, 5]

Only one coin of this issue is known. It was first published, without hoard-provenance or find-spot, almost exactly seventy years ago. However, it is now possible to label it as a presumptive single-find from the Old Palace at Croydon, a sketch of it endorsed to this effect having been found among the Corbet Anderson papers in Croydon Public Library.[9] This new and impeccable provenance is not without importance because the form of the ethnic is so exceptional that doubts might have been cast upon the authenticity of the coin. The obverse legend ends quite unequivocally ANGLO, presumably for *Anglorum* unless we accept alternative expansions *Anglorum Saxonum* or *Anglo-Saxonum*.[10] A unique coin of Ceolwulf II, by another moneyer and of rather coarser style, occurred in the Cuerdale hoard, but on this coin the ethnic is omitted. As W. H. Stevenson so very clearly saw, the English title is one that we would not have expected to find on a penny of this period, and its arrogation may be thought inconsistent with Ælfred's solicitude for Mercian susceptibilities. The

Anglo-Saxon Coins

Ceolwulf coin is closer in style and in lettering to both the Ælfred and the Ceolwulf coins of the preceding issue, but we are reluctant to believe that the new design was not technically at least a joint issue of the two Kings. The reverse type may be copied from a fairly common Roman *solidus* of a type often found in this country (cf. **Plate III,** where the Ceolwulf coin is illustrated), but it is also a design which is particularly appropriate for a joint coinage by two rulers – fortunately recognition of the Halfdene imitation (**Plate X, 7**) as a later copy means that it is no longer able further to bedevil the issue as it has done in the past.[11] We are also impressed by the fact that there are certain affinities between the Ælfred coin and certain rare pieces not known for Ceolwulf, but the balance of the evidence must be that it and the Ceolwulf piece of the same type are broadly contemporary.

(d) *The 'Archbishop Æthered' type* [Plate IX, 6]

There exists one fragmentary coin of this type, of uncertain provenance.[12] The obverse legend in fact reads no more than .....ED REX, so prima facie the coin could equally well be (Burgr)ED as (Ælfr)ED. However, the lettering and portrait are totally unlike any found on coins of Burgred, but have very close parallels on certain London coins from the period *c.* 886. Moreover, the type was also struck by Archbishop Æthered, no coins of whom are known which belong to Ælfred's joint issue with Burgred, and so there can be little doubt that the traditional ascription of the fragment to Ælfred is correct. The mint, or at least the source of the dies, would presumably still be Canterbury.

(e) *The 'London Monogram' type* [Plate IX, 8 and 9]

As well as being present in proportionately small numbers in the great Cuerdale hoard already mentioned, coins of this class, invariably omitting the potentially controversial ethnic, comprised the whole of a medium-sized hoard from Bucklersbury in the City of London (*Inventory* —), probably figured in a small hoard from Erith (*Inventory* —), and certainly occurred in the Morley St Peter hoard (*Inventory* —), and in two hoards from Rome. In the case of the Bucklersbury and Erith finds no other coins would seem to have been present, but the great Morley St Peter hoard with its one coin of Æthelstan can be dated securely *c.* 925.[13] The earlier of the Rome finds, from the area of the Vatican (?), is little later in date, while the even richer hoard from the Forum (House of the Vestal Virgins) can be dated *c.* 945.[14] These last three hoard-provenances would suggest that the issue was the last of the 'Portrait' types, but equally the poverty of its representation could argue that the type was not one in issue at the very end of the reign. The obvious historical occasion for this noble coinage would have been Ælfred's military occupation of London in 886, a conscious turning-point in English history, and certainly this date is far from being inconsistent with the numismatic evidence.

Two distinct phases of issue may be detected. The earlier and more prolific coins omit the name of the moneyer, but on a few late pieces there appears the name TILEWINE. Presumably it was intended to increase the size of the issue – though coins of this type purporting to be by other moneyers are all Danelaw imitations – but the idea was abandoned with the introduction of a 'Non-portrait' type so that these London coins can be dated with considerable precision. The *terminus post quem* is, as we have seen, 886, and not only are no 'Portrait' coins known of Archbishop Plegmund who was consecrated in 890, but the new 'Non-portrait' type must have been in issue already by 888 as one coin of it is known with the name of Archbishop Æthered who died in that year. It is also noteworthy that Edward the Elder's first issue of 'Portrait' coins, an issue which can be dated quite early in his reign, does not exhibit the least degree of stylistic, prosopographical, or epigraphical continuity with any of the 'Portrait' coins of Ælfred. Alone of Ælfred's 'Portrait' pennies the London coins were the subject of extensive imitation in the Danelaw, a pointer to the improbability not only of their antedating the *démarche* of 886 but also of their being later than *c.* 895. That, too, the London pennies are comparatively late and presumptively the last of the 'Portrait' coins of Ælfred is further suggested by the existence of halfpennies of this type, the first coins of this denomination ever to be struck in England and the victims of such eager and extensive imitation in the Danelaw that it is only recently that English primacy in the field has come to be recognized.[15]

Finally it should be remarked that Ælfred in 886 would have had good precedent for the issue of coins bearing the name of the English metropolis. Sixty years before, after the battle of *Ellendun* (Wroughton), his grandfather had struck coins at London with the reverse legend +LVN/DONIA/CIVIT(as).[16]

(f) *The 'Gloucester' type* [Plate IX, 10]

The unique coin of this type extant today is from the Cuerdale hoard. On general grounds it is perhaps roughly contemporaneous with the London coins, if anything a little earlier, but it would be dangerous to pontificate concerning a piece which obviously lies outside the main stream of Ælfred's coinage. Possibly significant on a coin struck outside Wessex and in territory that was indisputably Mercian is the omission not only of the ethnic but also of the royal title itself.[17]

To sum up: three main periods of 'Portrait' coinage may perhaps be distinguished. The first (**Plate IX, 2**) was certainly over by *c.* 875, the second (**Plate IX, 3–6**) embraces the years *c.* 875–*c.* 885, and the third (**Plate IX, 8–10**) seems to have begun in 886 and to have been of comparatively brief duration. Coins of the first period are not uncommon, even though they do not occur in hoards deposited after *c.* 875, but coins of the middle period are always rare, their paucity being due in part to a virtual absence of hoards from the decade in which they were presumptively current. In contrast, coins of the third period are rather less uncommon, though their apparent number has been inflated by the reluctance of numismatists to exclude from the regal series the very numerous Danelaw imitations. These 'London' imitations occur in a number of 'late' contexts, the Stamford find (*Inventory* 339), apparently to be dated *c.* 895 or a little later, the Dean find (*Inventory* —), concealed perhaps twenty years later, and of course the great Cuerdale hoard itself, the imitations providing further corroboration of the place of the prototypes in the sequence of Ælfred's issues.[18] There could indeed be no better illustration of what the Treaty with Guthrum meant to England.

II WITHOUT PORTRAIT

(a) *The 'Quatrefoil' type* [Plate IX, 7]
The unique coin of this type occurred in the Cuerdale hoard. On stylistic and epigraphical grounds, it clearly belongs to the period of the immediately post-Ceolwulf 'Portrait' coins, and so it may perhaps be dated *c.* 880. Among 'Non-portrait' coins of Ælfred it stands in a class all by itself. The mint is unknown, but Canterbury is perhaps a more likely candidate than London or still less Winchester.

(b) *The 'Guthrum' type* [Plate IX, 11–13]
Coins of this relatively common class have been recorded in the case of a number of hoards. In date-order of deposit they are probably to be arranged as follows: (1) a critical but unpublished find from Leigh-on-Sea (*Inventory* —) which was probably the source of the small parcel described as from Ingatestone (*Inventory* 197); (2) the Stamford find; (3) the Cuerdale hoard; (4) the Harkirke find (*Inventory* 184); (5) the Morley St Peter hoard; (6) the 'Vatican' hoard from Rome; (7) the Forum hoard from Rome; (8) the Terslev hoard from Denmark; (9) the 1950 Chester hoard (*Inventory* 86). One coin of this type has also been claimed for the Trewhiddle hoard, but the evidence is unsatisfactory and the presence of such a coin in such a context would be against all

probability.[19] In the same way, we would not contest any suggestion that the examples in the Stamford hoard were all in fact imitative pieces from one or more centres in the Danelaw.

There are three very distinct styles of lettering, and it would seem that the coins emanate from at least three centres. One grouping (**Plate IX, 11**) has an epigraphy identical with that which occurs on one coin, and one only, of Archbishop Æthered, on a large number of coins of Archbishop Plegmund, and on a number of mint-signed coins of Ælfred. The type is not common, though Danelaw imitations exist, and there is reason to think that it was of no great duration. The obvious mint is Canterbury, and the presumptive bracket of issue is *c*. 887–*c*. 894, the latter limit being suggested by the Viking pincers attack on Kent and by the fact that there is absolutely no continuity with the earliest issues of Edward the Elder.

A second grouping (**Plate IX, 12**) is identical in style and in epigraphy with certain coins with a blundered rendering of the name Æthelstan which have been associated quite convincingly with the historical Guthrum. Indeed, the two issues are even die-linked. Again the grouping can be dated quite convincingly within very narrow limits. An attractive *terminus post quem* is afforded of course by Guthrum's baptism at 'Aller' in 878, but the whole feel of the coinage is that it belongs a decade later. Moreover, it is a London coinage – as is shown by the fact that one of the moneyers is the Tilewine who struck the latest of the London 'Portrait' coins – and examples seem to have been entirely wanting from the finds from Erith and Bucklersbury. It would seem, therefore, that this 'Non-Portrait' coinage was introduced at London and at Canterbury at about the same time, there being a most useful *terminus ante quem* for the London coins' first issue in the death of Guthrum in 890. At Canterbury, as we will see, there is a presumption that the issue may have ceased *c*. 893, but at London it may well have continued at least until after the final departure of the Viking host from England in 896.

A third stylistic grouping (**Plate IX, 13**) has recently been recognized as Mercian. Coins of this style were present in the Cuerdale and Harkirke hoards, but were absent from those from Stamford, Morley St Peter, and Leigh-on-Sea.[20] There is not as yet the hoard-evidence which would allow of their being dated with the same precision as the coins from Canterbury and London, but it does seem a fair presumption that their issue did not begin before *c*. 890. Moreover, there is quite an element of continuity with the earliest issues of Edward the Elder from the same area, and it is clear that they were still being struck when Ælfred died in 899. The identity of the Mercian die-cutting centre and of the mint or mints remains a mystery. On numismatic grounds Chester would be the most obvious candidate, but this raises the whole question of the intensity of English habitation of the site not only in 893 when a Danish army sheltered there and it was described as already a deserted 'waste', but also in 907 when Ætheflæd 'fortified' it to counter the new menace from the Hiberno-Norsemen established in Wirral.

(c) *The 'Canterbury' type* [Plate IX, 14]

Coins of this type overwhelmingly preponderate in the as yet unpublished find from Leigh-on-Sea, and are also present in the Cuerdale hoard (along with numerous imitations), in the Harkirke find, in the Morley St Peter hoard (without any imitations), and in the earlier of the two hoards from Rome. Even were it not for the occurrence of the letters D O R O at the end of the obverse legend, they would have to be ascribed to Canterbury on account of their identical appearance with coins of Archbishop Plegmund. The obvious occasion of the deposit of the Leigh-on-Sea hoard is to be found in the English operations against the Danes who had established themselves along the Essex coast, and it seems that it is a fair presumption that the coins had been obtained during the great pincers attack on Kent which opened in 892. Again there is no continuity with the earliest coins of Edward the Elder, and we should also bear in mind recent recognition of the fact that there is absolutely no continuity, not even of moneyers, between Plegmund's 'first' coinage under Ælfred and his 'second' under Edward the Elder. It would come as no surprise to us to discover independent evidence that the Canterbury mint, greatly expanded *c.* 887, had to be closed down again after five years because of its exposed position. It may even have been sacked, as one particular group of imitations, apparently Northumbrian, is much more readily explicable on the assumption that a mass of coins, if not indeed some of the mint-personnel as well, were carried back to Northumbria by 'Sigeferth'.[21]

(d) *The 'Edward the Elder' type* [Plate IX, 15]

This is essentially a neater version of the 'Guthrum' issue, and it is even debatable whether it should constitute a separate type. No distinct styles are known, and all the coins seem to be from a southern mint or mints. They are identical with the earliest coins of Edward the Elder from the same area, and even on grounds of style alone could be placed without hesitation at the very end of Ælfred's reign. London is the presumptive mint of most if not all of the coins extant today, though mention must be made of a Plegmund coin with a variant obverse recorded by William Blundell in his account of the now-vanished Harkirke find.[22] The hoard-provenances of the Ælfred coins are

The Chronology of the Coins of Ælfred the Great, 871–99

likewise 'late', namely Cuerdale, Harkirke, Morley St Peter, and both the Rome finds.

(e) *The 'Exeter' type* [Plate IX, 16]

The exceptionally rare coins of this class have occurred only in the 'late' hoards from Cuerdale and Morley St Peter. The absence of the moneyer's name – we may compare the earliest post-886 coins of London – must suggest that one man was responsible for the entire output of the mint. The probable source of the dies is Winchester, and noteworthy on these purely West Saxon coins is the resumption of the title *Rex Saxonum* discreetly omitted from Ælfred's coins struck in Mercia and Kent. The fact that the same types are found on an early issue of Edward the Elder from Bath must suggest that the Ælfred coins belong very late in the reign, and a dating after *c*. 895 would be consistent with the absence of Danelaw imitations.

(f) *The 'Winchester' type* [Plate IX, 17]

Again the type is one of the very greatest rarity, and the handful of extant coins, from four pairs of dies incidentally, are all from the 'late' Cuerdale and Morley St Peter hoards. There is no name of a moneyer, and there is no continuity of style with the Edward the Elder coins that on prosopographical grounds are to be associated with Winchester. Even so, a date after rather than before *c*. 895 seems indicated, and especially if it were possible to regard the 'Multiples' as a posthumous eleemosynary issue like that of Pippin's on which it seems to be modelled.

To sum up: with one exception – represented significantly enough by a unique coin (**Plate IX, 7**) – the non-portrait coins of Ælfred (**Plate IX, 11–17**) are to be dated after *c*. 887, and the great bulk of them between *c*. 890 and *c*. 895. There is thus relatively little overlapping between the 'Portrait' and 'Non-portrait' pennies of the period, a discovery which we believe to be not entirely without significance.

(c) THE HALFPENNIES [Plate IX, 18 and 19]

I WITH PORTRAIT

(a) *The 'London' type* [Plate IX, 18]

Genuine English coins of this type are exceptionally rare, and perhaps no more than three exist today, all of them apparently from the Erith hoard.[23] Viking imitations from the Danelaw occur in the Stamford find and the Cuerdale hoard, hoard-provenances which corroborate the presumptive dating of the prototypes *c*. 886 to coincide with the pennies with the selfsame types. These undoubted halfpennies must, therefore, rank as the very first halfpennies to be struck in these islands, and, if only because imitations cannot precede in point of time their prototypes, we must abandon once and for all the old tradition which gave primacy in this respect to the Vikings.

II WITHOUT PORTRAIT

We must admit at the outset that we are not entirely in agreement on the issue whether there are in existence today any 'Non-portrait' halfpence with the name of Ælfred which are indisputably the products of an English mint. We do agree, however, that the balance of the evidence is overwhelmingly in favour of the view that Ælfred's coinage of pennies of 'Guthrum' type was accompanied, at least in its early stages, by an issue of complementary halfpence. Accordingly we have decided to illustrate (**Plate IX, 19**) beneath the undoubted English coins, but on the same plate, an example of a halfpenny in Ælfred's name which is almost certainly English. It must be remarked, however, that this is the only halfpenny with Ælfred's name that has yet been found on which there occurs a spelling of his name with initial digraph, and Mr Dolley feels unable to guarantee the English origin of any pieces without this feature.[24]

(a) *The 'Guthrum' type* [Plate IX, 19]

The model for this coin is clearly the 'Non-portrait' penny introduced shortly after Ælfred's capture of London in 886. A dating *c*. 890 is further indicated by the presence of a large number of Danelaw imitations not only in the Stamford find but also in the Cuerdale hoard, but the whole question of where to draw the line between English and Viking work is at present open. A dating after *c*. 895 seems precluded by the fact that there seem to be no coins, English or imitative, which are complementary to the Edward the Elder issue of pence, nor is there any continuity between any of the Ælfred 'halfpence' and certain rare coins of that denomination which formed part of Edward the Elder's first coinage.

At this juncture we should perhaps remark that one of Ælfred's 'Portrait' halfpennies of London was imitated by Eadgar.[25] The same great-grandson also struck a halfpenny with the letters WIN disposed horizontally across the reverse field. It is by no means impossible, therefore, that Ælfred may have issued halfpennies from Winchester (and possibly even Exeter as well) which have not survived to this day, but which were available in the tenth century to serve as a model for one of Eadgar's engravers.

The Chronology of the Coins of Ælfred the Great, 871–99

(d) THE SUPPOSED THIRD-PENNIES

In his fundamental paper cited above[26] Mr Grierson has commented on the undoubted lightness of many of the Ælfred 'halfpence' which he suggests go well beyond what could be accounted for by a desire to give the moneyer the same profit on two halfpence as he would have received on two pennies. He has suggested that many of them may have been struck as third-pennies, and this is not the place to enter on a detailed review of all the evidence for and against what must be considered a very plausible hypothesis. Fortunately we are not called upon to express a final verdict, as we believe we are right in claiming that none of the coins which could be considered a third-penny stands any chance of being English. Since, however, the *Laws of Alfred* have been cited with their references to penalties where the sum exacted seems to be a third of a 'decimal' wergeld and involves in consequence an odd third of a penny, we do feel it only proper to remark that there is an exactly parallel passage quoted by Ruding[27] from the legislation of Henry I. As far as we know, it has not been suggested that a 'third-penny' of Henry I ought on that telling to exist.

We believe that the coins illustrated on the first of our plates (**Plate IX, 1–17**) represent every significant variety of the silver coinage of Ælfred. Mention has already been made of Danelaw imitations, and there can be little doubt but that the inclusion of these among the genuine coins of Ælfred has delayed for more than a century recognition of the true sequence of his types. Perhaps one hundred and fifty of the four hundred and fifty coins attributed to Ælfred in the 1893 *British Museum Catalogue* must be considered contemporary imitations, and it is instructive to review those issues where such copying is specially prevalent. We find that there are three issues in particular which attracted the attention of the Viking imitators, the 'London' pennies and halfpennies (**Plate IX, 8, 9** and **18**), which can be dated immediately after 886, the London and, to a lesser extent, the Canterbury – but not the Mercian – versions of the 'Guthrum' pennies and halfpennies (**Plate IX, 11, 12** and **19**), which seem all to be contained within a period of at most a decade from *c.* 887, and the 'Canterbury' pennies (**Plate IX, 14**), which seem to fall *c.* 890.

IMITATIONS OF THE 'LONDON' PENCE AND HALFPENCE

[Plate X, 1–11]

Proportionately these are the most numerous of the imitations in respect of *extant* prototypes, examples in the National Collection outnumbering the

Anglo-Saxon Coins

originals by something like three to one. Some of the imitations are very close (**Plate X, 1**), but others are progressively more barbarous (**Plate X, 2 and 3**) until the depths of degradation are touched with crude caricatures (**Plate X, 4**), which seem to emanate from the Northern Danelaw. One of the better imitations (**Plate X, 5**) has a variant of the monogram that has been read ROISENG (for Castle Rising?), and on other imitations (**Plate X, 6**) there is another version of the monogram which is clearly to be read LINCOLLA for Lincoln. Other pieces mule the 'London' reverse with obverses or reverses from other issues, and we may instance the unique penny of Halfdene (**Plate X, 7**) on which the obverse is a crude version of the 'Two Emperors' obverse (**Plate IX, 5**) – this being the coin so persistently associated with 871/2! – as well as a competent adaptation of one of the rare signed reverses of Tilewine (**Plate X, 8**) and a crude Lincoln coin (**Plate X, 9**), where it is the name of the moneyer and not that of the mint which is rendered as a monogram. Two 'halfpennies' (**Plate X, 10 and 11**) are typical of the run of these controversial fractions. The provenances of these 'London' imitations seem all from northern England, Cuerdale, Dean, and Stamford, and it is likely that the great majority were produced in the general area of Lincoln and Stamford.

IMITATIONS OF THE 'GUTHRUM' PENCE AND HALFPENCE

[Plate X, 12–15]

Proportionately to their *extant* prototypes these coins are not unduly common, and we estimate that in the National Collection the imitations are outnumbered approximately eight to one. It is possible, however, that the exact criteria for distinguishing the authentic English coins have still to be established. The 'London' imitations are those more generally met with (**Plate X, 12 and 13**), and especial interest attaches to the 'halfpenny' – as Mr Grierson has shown a blundered imitation of a coin of Cuthberht – because the reverse legend has been fantastically misread EIL BAD and associated with a no less far-fetched interpretation ELI M-O of the reverse of the ELIMO (*sina*) multiple (**Plate IX, 1**) to produce a new (Jewish?) moneyer for a mint at Bath. Again the provenances for these coins are northern, and the majority seem to have been produced in the area south of the Humber. In contrast the majority if not all the imitations of the 'Canterbury' coins (**Plate X, 14 and 15**) are very clearly to be associated with a mint north of the Humber, and they are conspicuously absent from the Stamford find.

The Chronology of the Coins of Ælfred the Great, 871–99

IMITATIONS OF THE 'CANTERBURY' PENCE AND (?) HALFPENCE

[Plate X, 16–20]

Reasonably close copies of the originals are relatively common, and in the National Collection today outnumber the prototypes by five to two. The disproportion in the 1893 *British Museum Catalogue*, on the other hand, is far greater, as the collection has been filled out with authentic coins of the issue from the East Anglian hoards from Leigh-on-Sea and Morley St Peter where, significantly, we believe, the imitative pieces appear to have been absent. They are likewise absent from Stamford, and in fact have occurred in no more than two hoards, Cuerdale and Harkirke. The bulk of them (**Plate X, 16** and **17**) 'reproduce' the name of only one moneyer – Bernwald – and it is suggestive that he is also the moneyer of the so-called 'Orsnaforda' variant (**Plate X, 18–20**) which have been persistently associated with Oxford despite the determined efforts of Stainer to disown them.[28] The third of these coins (**Plate X, 20**) also imitates a type of the post-895 Viking coinage of Northumbria (cf. **Plate XI, 31**), and it is significant that the only find-spot other than Cuerdale and Harkirke that has been recorded is the river Ouse at York.[29] All the evidence points to the whole coinage emanating from a second Viking mint in Yorkshire, and the possibility of it being at Horsforth is one that is being canvassed though here the last word must lie with the philologists.

For the sake of completeness we have thought it best to illustrate six further coins, all attributed by the *British Museum Catalogue* to Ælfred and all of the very greatest rarity, which do not fit readily into the above scheme but which are, nevertheless, of considerable potential importance. Two coins can be dismissed at once as certainly not English (**Plate X, 21** and **22**). The former is a crude muling of a barbarous parody of a late Ælfred obverse and no less coarse a version of a Northumbrian reverse. The latter is an only less crude muling of a degraded late Ælfred obverse and of an obverse of the so-called 'St Eadmund' coinage of the East Anglian Danes. Neither coin has any claim on the attention of the historian. In a very different category falls a third coin (**Plate X, 23**) where a 'Canterbury' obverse of excellent workmanship is combined with an equally fine obverse from the 'St Eadmund' series. It is hard to dismiss this coin as an imitation, and one may even speculate whether the 'St Eadmund' coinage was not begun with Ælfred's blessing – at least it appears to have nipped in the bud any tendency to large-scale imitation of English coin in East Anglia proper. The remaining three coins all present problems of quite another order. The first (**Plate X, 24**) would seem to be a normal 'Guthrum' penny but for its reverse legend which appears to read EDEL.S R GELDA. The *British Museum Catalogue* suggests an interpretation which necessitates our postulating two moneyers, Æthelstan and 'Gelda', but we are not happy about this, though equally we can conceive formidable objections against any macaronic expansion such as EDELSTANI REGIS GELDA. The second coin (**Plate X, 25**) is of good workmanship, and seems to elaborate the last of Ælfred's types. Again it is the reverse legend that defies interpretation, and according as to how one 'reads' the curiously cursive lettering one can put forward theories involving personal names as diverse as those of the Prince of the Apostles and of the God of Thunder. Presumptively it is to be dated after *c.* 895, and it has affinities with the Northumbrian rather than the Danelaw series. On our last coin (**Plate X, 26**) the name of Ælfred is not to be read, though the reverse is a tolerable copy of a coin of Ælfred's last type albeit by a moneyer not known for the issue. The coin has more than a few affinities with one or two of the 'St Eadmund' pennies, and is probably East Anglian. How the legend is to be read is another matter, but we must here register an emphatic protest against the suggestion that the coins have anything whatever to do with Regnald vi Ivar and still less with Regnald Guthfrithsson, attributions that are totally incompatible with the Cuerdale provenance.

As stated at the outset, this paper has been conceived as an essay – in the full sense of that word – towards the better ordering of the surviving coins of perhaps the greatest of all the English kings. One consequence has been the excision from the English series of virtually a third of the coins which Grueber and Keary included under Ælfred in the 1893 *British Museum Catalogue*, not too heavy a price to pay perhaps for the comparatively simple sequence of types which we set out schematically in the table that follows (Appendix). If it is thought that our paper represents any advance on the arrangements already propounded, progress has been made possible largely by new evidence. It must not be forgotten that it is only in the last few years that it has been feasible to reconstruct the very largely unpublished hoards from Leigh-on-Sea and Stamford, while the Morley St Peter hoard was only discovered in 1958.[30] It is the Stamford hoard, however, that is the key to so many of the Danelaw imitations, while the two finds from East Anglia are no less critical for establishing the norm of coin-production in England proper. What is needed now is a hoard from southern England deposited a year or two before Ælfred's occupation of London, towards the end, that is, of a quinquennium from which the surviving coins of Ælfred can be counted quite literally on the fingers of one hand.

The Chronology of the Coins of Ælfred the Great, 871–99

REFERENCES

1. The possibility that a gold coin may actually exist today is discussed in *BNJ* xxv iii (1948) pp. 278–9. Since this paper was written the gold coin found on the Hatherop Castle estate has been identified as in fact a gold *tremissis* of the seventh century now in the British Museum, cf. *BNJ* xxviii i (1955) p. 36 (*BMC* 8). Nor do we see any reason to suppose that the gold coin (presumably Roman) found at Plas Gwyn was in any way associated with the silver penny of Eadgar found in the same neighbourhood, cf. *infra*, p. 166
2. *NC* 1954 pp. 76–92
3. For Mrs Martin's solution to the mystery of the provenance of *BMC* 158 *vide infra*, p. 231
4. *BNJ* xxvii i (1952) pp. 54–6
5. *BNJ* xxviii iii (1957) p. 489
6. But see *NC* 1925 p. 349
7. London was not formally incorporated in Wessex until 911
8. *BNJ* xxvi ii (1951) pp. 213–15
9. *Supra* p. 65
10. Cf. W. H. STEVENSON ed. *Asser's Life of King Alfred* Oxford 1904 pp. 151–2
11. e.g. BROOKE *English Coins* pp. 25, 33, and 45–7
12. *BMC* 179
13. Cf. *SNC* May 1958 pp. 113–14
14. *NC* 1931 pp. 133–5 ('Vatican'); *NC* 1884 pp. 225–55 (Forum). Both hoards stand urgently in need of detailed republication
15. In 1933, for example, Brooke could still write of Halfdene: 'To him may be ascribed the introduction of two features which now appear in the English coinage, the halfpenny denomination and the design of the London monogram, both of them probably suggested by Frankish models' (op. cit. p. 33)
16. Ibid. p. 42. Ecgbeorht, however, did not scruple to assume the Mercian title as well, though this he would seem later to have renounced
17. There is a reference in *BNJ* vi (1909) p. 153 to a second specimen described as in the cabinet of Major P. W. Carlyon-Britton, but it did not figure in his Sale and may be presumed to have later been condemned as false. Extremely dangerous cast forgeries of a number of the Cuerdale rarities plagued nineteenth-century Sales and still occasionally are submitted to the British Museum
18. For the Dean hoard cf. *BNJ* xxviii i (1955) pp. 177–80
19. *Supra* p. 67
20. A coin of this style formerly in the Taffs collection with the Leigh-on-sea proverance we believe may be an interloper
21. *NNÅ* 1957–8 pp. 38–9
22. *NC* 1955 pp. 189–93
23. *BNJ* xxviii iii (1957) p. 480

24. We are not unduly disturbed by the weight of the coin illustrated though admittedly it is on the low side
25. *BNJ* xxvii ii (1953) p. 136
26. *BNJ* xxviii iii (1957) pp. 477-93
27. *Annals of the Coinage* I Third Edition 1840 p. 110
28. *Oxford Silver Pennies* 1904 pp. xxxiii ff.
29. *NC* 1958 p. 94 – by a curious quirk this coin from the Ouse, apparently the only pre-Cuerdale coin of 'Orsnaforda' still extant, has reposed since the eighteenth century in the collections of Oxford University (information from Mr J. D. A. Thompson)
30. In *BNJ* xxix ii (1959) we are publishing summaries of known Ælfred hoards

Appendix

CHRONOLOGICAL TABLE OF THE ISSUES OF ÆLFRED THE GREAT

	871	875	880	885	890	895	899
Multiples WITHOUT PORTRAIT					ELIMO *sina* (S) 2		
Pennies WITH PORTRAIT	'BURGRED' (S) 46	'CEOLWULF' (S) 15	'TWO EMPERORS' (S) 1 'ARCHB. ÆTHERED' (S) 1 'GLOUCESTER' 1	'LONDON' 12	'GUTHRUM' (L) → 'EDW. ELDER' (S) 23 → 250+ { 'GUTHRUM' (M) 'GUTHRUM' (C) 'CANTERBURY' 24 'EXETER' 2 'WINCHESTER' 4		
Pennies WITHOUT PORTRAIT				'QUATREFOIL' 0			
Halfpennies WITH PORTRAIT					'LONDON' 3		
Halfpennies WITHOUT PORTRAIT					'GUTHRUM' 1+		

Underlined types alone are extensively imitated in Danelaw and Northumbria

S = A Mint (or Mints) on or South of the Thames
L = London
C = Canterbury
M = A Mercian Mint (or Mints)

Figures following or preceding types indicate number of coins in BM – 'Guthrum' type cannot as yet be finally broken down

VI

The Northumbrian Viking Coins in the Cuerdale Hoard

by C. S. S. LYON and B. H. I. H. STEWART

[Plates XI and XII]

This remarkable hoard was found on the property of W. Assheton, Esq., at Cuerdale, near Preston, Lancashire, in May 1840: it comprised more than seven thousand coins and nearly one thousand ounces of silver. The official report on the contents of the hoard was contributed by Edward Hawkins,[1] and his analysis of the coins may be summarized as follows:

Wessex:		Continental:	
Ælfred	915	'Charles'	727
Edward the Elder	51	Eudes	197
Archbishops of Canterbury:		Others	65
Ceolnoth	1	Unclassified, but probably	
Æthered	1	mostly 'Charles' and Eudes	35
Plegmund	65	Vikings:	
Mercia:		Cnut, Siefred, and associated	
Ceolwulf II	2	(including 23 of Quentovic)	3039
East Anglia:		St Edmund memorial	1815
Æthelred	3	Earl Sihstric	2
Æthelstan (Guthrum)	24	Oriental:	27

Total 6969

Hawkins made it clear that a small proportion of the coins was dispersed before the bulk was seized for the Crown: one of these was undoubtedly the unique 'Two Emperors' type penny of Halfdene, acquired by the British Museum from the Montagu Collection. The halfpenny of Halfdene (*BMC* 869) in the National Collection appears not to be described by Hawkins in his report, but will be found under Ælfred.

The Viking series which is the subject of this essay is particularly important

The Northumbrian Viking Coins in the Cuerdale Hoard

in that, while it accounts for more than three thousand of the coins found at Cuerdale, it is almost unknown from other sources. It would, in fact, be a conservative estimate to state that at least ninety-nine per cent of extant examples have come from this hoard.[2] Controversy immediately arose among eminent antiquaries and numismatists about the significance and origins of these coins. Hawkins ascribed them to France on the strength of the 'Quentovic' coins and a hypothetical association of the mint-name *Ebraice Civitas* with Evreux; D. H. Haigh, however, attributed the coins in the name of Cnut to Guthred or Guthfrith of Northumbria, and other writers sided with one or the other point of view.[3] The attribution of the series to Northumbria is now generally accepted, but historians have cast serious doubts on the identification of the Cnut of the coins with King Guthfrith.[4] The time is ripe for a critical re-examination of the evidence, and in view of the conflicting opinions expressed by previous writers we propose to consider the whole question from first principles.

Considering first the general composition of the hoard, it is worth noting that, with the probable exception of the coins in the name of a King Æthelred, generally assigned to East Anglia, and the single specimen of Archbishop Ceolnoth, the English coins in the hoard all date from the last thirty years of the ninth century and the earliest years of the tenth century. Of the Frankish coins, those of Eudes are satisfactorily identified, and are consistent in date with the English coins in the hoard: nearly two-thirds of them are of the Limoges mint. The classification of the coins of the kings named Charles is most unhappy; Prou[5] freely admitted that he was unable to distinguish with certainty the issues of Charles the Bald, Charles the Fat, and Charles the Simple, and he ascribed most of the Cuerdale coins to Charles the Bald. This does not seem probable, especially when one considers their excellent state of preservation, the close stylistic resemblance of certain coins of Charles – especially those of the Angers and Limoges mints – to those of Eudes, and the presence of at least five hundred and sixty-one coins of Charles from a single mint (Metullus, i.e. Melle in Aquitaine). Hawkins considered that the majority of these coins should be assigned to Charles the Simple, and with this dating we concur: this is not the place, however, to discuss whether they should be dated before or after the death of Eudes. On the other hand, Hawkins no doubt erred in ascribing the handful of coins reading HLVDOVVICVS PIVS to Louis the Pious; Prou assigned them to Louis the Child, which in view of their condition is acceptable, and makes them among the latest Frankish coins in the hoard, with a *terminus post quem* of 899. In this event, the earliest Carolingian coins found at Cuerdale can probably be dated *c.* 880, which is entirely concordant with the dating of the

Anglo-Saxon Coins

English coins. It is worth noting, incidentally, that over ninety per cent of the coins of Charles, and ninety-seven per cent of those of Eudes, are from an area of western France bounded by Le Mans to the north, Limoges to the south, Orleans and Bourges to the east, and Angers and Melle to the west: no mint outside this area contributes more than ten coins and most mints, if represented at all, only contribute single specimens.

On the evidence of the English and Frankish coins in the hoard, therefore, the date of deposit can be established as early in the tenth century, and Mr C. E. Blunt has suggested a date *c*. 903 on the strength of the relatively small proportion of coins of Edward the Elder as compared with those of Ælfred.[6] It seems probable that the hoard represented the treasure-chest of a Viking ruler or army, and its loss may not be unconnected with the influx of Scandinavian settlers into Lancashire at the beginning of the tenth century.[7] It is quite certain that, by preserving over three thousand coins of the Viking series, the Cuerdale hoard has grossly distorted their commonness in relation to contemporary English coins of Ælfred and even perhaps to the 'St Eadmund memorial' issues.

In previous descriptions of the types of the Viking series, obverse and reverse have often been confused, the distinction having been made primarily by reference to the inscription. We have found it an invariable rule that the lower die was engraved with a circular inscription around a 'Small Cross' or, rarely, the '*Karolus* monogram': the upper die was engraved with a variety of designs, generally embodying some form of cross, but occasionally taking the form of a plain inscription in two lines. The position of the dies relative to one another has become apparent from a study of the respective numbers of dies used in the coinage, the ratio of upper to lower dies averaging about 1·5:1. It will thus be noted that, contrary to accepted tradition, the royal names and titles were generally engraved on the upper, or reverse, die. We admit that this may appear confusing, but we believe that insistence on the 'Small Cross/*Karolus*' type being the obverse clears up many points of difficulty about the interchanging of dies and the so-called muling of two obverse or two reverse dies; it has the added merit of offering the simplest basis for a general classification. Whether the placing of the royal titles on the upper die was a feature of either the contemporary English or the contemporary Frankish coinage we are not in a position to state, but research into this subject might throw further light on the origin of the engravers and moneyers who produced this Viking coinage.

The obverse inscriptions consist of two personal names – *Siefredus* and *Alvaldus*; two mint-names – *Ebraice Civitas* and *Quentovici*; two religious mottoes – *Dominus Deus Rex* (abbreviated to DNS DS REX) and *Mirabilia Fecit*; and an

The Northumbrian Viking Coins in the Cuerdale Hoard

unidentified word – *Cunnetti*. The reverse inscriptions include various royal names and/or titles – *Cnut Rex, C Siefredus Rex, Siefredus Rex, Sievert Rex*, and simply *Rex*; one mint-name – *Ebraice C*; and one religious motto – *Dominus Deus Omnipotens Rex* (abbreviated to DNS DS O REX). The various types and inscriptions are illustrated on **Plate XI,** and they will be discussed in detail in the course of this essay. For the present we would emphasize that, where an inscription can occur on either obverse or reverse, it is never found on both sides of the same coin.

Frankish influence on the coinage is at once apparent from the inscriptions, and from the use of the '*Karolus* monogram'. Religious mottoes are found frequently on Frankish coins (e.g. *Christiana Religio, Misericordia Dei*), though not the mottoes used in the Viking coinage: on the other hand, English pennies invariably have the name of the moneyer and/or mint. Even in the case of the 'St Eadmund memorial' coinage the moneyers' names are shown, although many of them disclose a Frankish origin. Possibly there is some reflection of the design of Ælfred's pence in the division of inscriptions into three or four segments, and the abundant use of groups of pellets in the field and as stops is more English than Frankish; but the only direct English type influence appears to be in the two-line inscription, which, it should be mentioned, is not uncommon in the Frankish series also. A notable feature is the angular ◊ for *Omnipotens*, which is found also (though with a different meaning) on late ninth-century coins of Canterbury and on coins of the Frankish King Eudes, as well as on some pence of the early tenth-century 'St Peter' coinage of York.

The origin of the other reverse designs is less apparent. The forms of cross appear to have a Byzantine derivation, and it is significant that the hoard contained a *double miliaresion* of Heraclius and Heraclius Constantine which depicts a 'Cross on Steps'.[8] This design is also featured on those coins of Ælfred which read ORSNAFORDA and which have been shown to be of northern origin.[9] The disposition of *Cnut Rex* around a 'Plain Cross' or an inverted 'Patriarchal Cross' is ingenious, and may have had, as its immediate inspiration, the '*Karolus* monogram'.

The quality of workmanship, both in engraving and in striking, is high, though the accuracy of the inscriptions can sometimes be faulted. This is particularly true of the '*Mirabilia Fecit*' and '*Ebraice Civitas*' obverse inscriptions: the former is frequently much blundered, and the latter is generally contracted to the form EB IAI CEC IVI – which may be merely an attempt at a forced symmetry. The ingenuity of the '*Cnut Rex*' inscription has already been mentioned, but the engraver who cut the dies on which the inscription appears around a 'Cross-crosslet' was copying without the knowledge of the origin of its form, since it is meaningless in the form in which he has engraved it (**Plate XI, 23**). Slavish copying, however, is most conspicuous in the 'Quentovic' issue, which is crude in the extreme (**Plate XI, 44, 67** – obverse and reverse).

This coinage is clearly Christian rather than pagan in conception; it is original in design and competent in execution. It is not a coinage which a Viking ruler could have been expected to originate without some external assistance. The many problems which it presents are difficult if not impossible to solve in the absence of major historical documentary evidence; they may be summarized as follows:

1 The time, duration, and *raison d'être* of the coinage.
2 The authority for its issue, and in particular the identity of *Cnut, Siefredus, Sievert*, and *Alvaldus*.
3 The minting-place or -places.
4 The origin of the craftsmen who designed and executed the coinage.
5 The significance of the religious mottoes.
6 The meaning of the enigmatic *Cunnetti*.

We will endeavour to define, from numismatic and such other evidence as is available to us, the limits within which we believe the respective answers to these problems should be sought, conscious that they cannot be solved from a consideration of such evidence alone. With this object in mind, the coins themselves will now be discussed in detail.

CLASSIFICATION AND ANALYSIS OF THE COINAGE

A brief indication of the basis of classification has already been given. Details of the types, and principal varieties, of obverse and reverse designs are as shown below (unless otherwise stated, only pennies are known).

OBVERSE TYPES

These fall into two groups:
1 Small Cross, with or without pellets in angles.
2 '*Karolus* monogram'.

They combine with the various inscriptions as follows:
Ebraice Civitas and contractions:
   EC-1 Small Cross
      (a) no stops in legend

The Northumbrian Viking Coins in the Cuerdale Hoard

       (i) no pellets in angles of Cross; inscription continuous or broken (pennies and halfpennies) (**Plate XI, 1–3**)

       (ii) group of three pellets in each angle of Cross; broken inscription (**Plate XI, 4**)

   (b) groups of pellets as stops

       (i) no pellets in angles of Cross; inscription almost always broken (**Plate XI, 5, 6**)

       (ii) one pellet in two or four angles of Cross; broken inscription (pennies and halfpennies) (**Plate XI, 7, 8**)

EC-2 '*Karolus* monogram'

   (a) no stops in legend; continuous inscription (**Plate XI, 9**)

   (b) groups of pellets as stops; broken inscription (halfpennies only) (**Plate XI, 10**)

Cunnetti

C-1 Small Cross; groups of pellets as stops; broken inscription (pennies and halfpennies)

   (a) no pellets in angles of Cross (**Plate XI, 11**)

   (b) pellet in two or four angles of Cross (**Plate XI, 12, 13**)

C-2 '*Karolus* monogram'; groups of pellets as stops; broken inscription (halfpennies only) (**Plate XI, 14**)

Siefredus

S-1 Short or Small Cross; no stops; inscription generally broken

   (a) groups of two or three pellets in each angle of Cross (**Plate XI, 15**)

   (b) pellet in two angles of Cross (**Plate XI, 16**)

Alvaldus

A-1 Small Cross; pellet in two angles; continuous inscription (**Plate XI, 17**)

Dns Ds Rex

DDR-1 Small Cross; pellet in two angles; usually single pellets or groups of pellets as stops, but one die is without stops (**Plate XI, 18**)

Mirabilia Fecit

MF-1 Small Cross; pellet in two angles; inscription frequently blundered, but generally continuous and without stops; certain re-cut penny dies, and both halfpenny dies, have groups of pellets interrupting the legend (pennies and halfpennies) (**Plate XI, 19, 20**)

Anglo-Saxon Coins

REVERSE TYPES

These have been divided into seven groups:

- A Two-line inscription.
- B Two-line inscription, Cross on Steps between.
- C Plain Cross, pellet in each angle.
- D Cross-crosslet, extending to edge of coin.
- E Cross-crosslet, within legend.
- F Plain Cross, no pellets in angles.
- G Patriarchal Cross, generally inverted, pellet in each angle of subsidiary Cross.

They combine with the various inscriptions as follows:

Cnut Rex

- CR-C Generally only one group of pellets as stop (pennies, and crude halfpenny) (**Plate XI, 21, 22**)
- CR-D Pellet in angles of main Cross, and in outer angles of subsidiary Crosses; usually no stops, but one die has one group of pellets as stop; legend copied from CR-C and meaningless in this form (pennies and halfpennies) (**Plate XI, 23, 24**)
- CR-F One, two, three, or rarely, four or five groups of pellets as stops (**Plate XI, 25**)
- CR-G A variety has pellets in angles of main Cross also; occasional reversed R on upper limb; other minor varieties; many combinations of stops (pennies and halfpennies) (**Plate XI, 26-29**)

C Siefredus Rex

- CSR-A Name and title in two lines; group of pellets above, below, and between the lines (**Plate XI, 30**)
- CSR-B Group of pellets above and below the lines (pennies and halfpennies) (**Plate XI, 31, 32**)
- CSR-C Two pellets at end of each limb of Cross; broken inscription; group of pellets between each segment, but slightly below (**Plate XI, 33**)

Siefredus Rex

- SFR-E Inscription generally continuous, without stops, but one die has inscription broken, with groups of pellets as stops (**Plate XI, 34**)

Rex

- REX-E Letters REX and initial cross disposed at ends of limbs of Cross; groups of pellets between (**Plate XI, 35**)

The Northumbrian Viking Coins in the Cuerdale Hoard

REX-F   Letters REX and initial cross disposed at ends of limbs of Cross; no stops (**Plate XI, 36**)

Sievert Rex

SR-B   No groups of pellets (**Plate XI, 37**)

SR-D   Groups of three pellets in each angle of Cross; letters of *Sievert R* permuted in pairs in the segments of the Cross (pennies; halfpennies without pellets) (**Plate XI, 38, 39**)

SR-G   Legend begins in various positions; broken inscription; groups of pellets as stops on some dies (pennies and halfpennies) (**Plate XI, 40, 41**)

Ebraice C

EC-G   Legend begins in various positions; broken inscription; generally pellets or groups of pellets as stops (**Plate XI, 42**)

Dns Ds O Rex

DDOR-A   Contraction marks generally omitted; usually small cross, with or without two pellets, between the lines

(i) omitting letter o (**Plate XI, 43**)

(ii) including letter o (pennies and halfpennies) (**Plate XI, 44, 45**)

We have not included in this classification the coins with obverse inscription QUENTOVICI (**Plate XI, 46, 47**). These are of inferior workmanship, and we believe that they imitate the 'Northumbrian' coinage; the reverse type appears to be derived from *CR*-C. We have no reason to doubt the opinion of previous writers, that they emanated from the old French port of Quentovic, at the mouth of the Canche, and we consider them to be only incidental to our study.

The classification above may seem arbitrary at first sight: in fact, it is quite deliberate, and the order of the reverse types A to G is intended to be roughly chronological, as will become apparent when the combinations of obverse and reverse types have been considered. These combinations can be summarized as follows:

Obverse type			*Associated reverse types*
EC-1	(a)	(i)	*CSR*-A, B; *SR*-D; *CR*-C
		(ii)	*CSR*-A, B; *SR*-D; *SFR*-E
	(b)	(i)	*CSR*-A, B, C; *SR*-B, D; *CR*-C, D, G
		(ii)	*CR*-D, F, G
EC-2	(a), (b)		*CR*-G
C-1	(a)		*CR*-C, G
	(b)		*CR*-D, F, G

Anglo-Saxon Coins

Obverse type	Associated reverse types
C-2	CR-G
S-1 (a)	REX-E
(b)	REX-E, F; CR-G
A-1	DDOR-A (i)
DDR-1	SR-G; EC-G; CR-G
MF-1	DDOR-A (ii); SR-G; EC-G; CR-G

This scheme is also shown diagrammatically in Figure I.

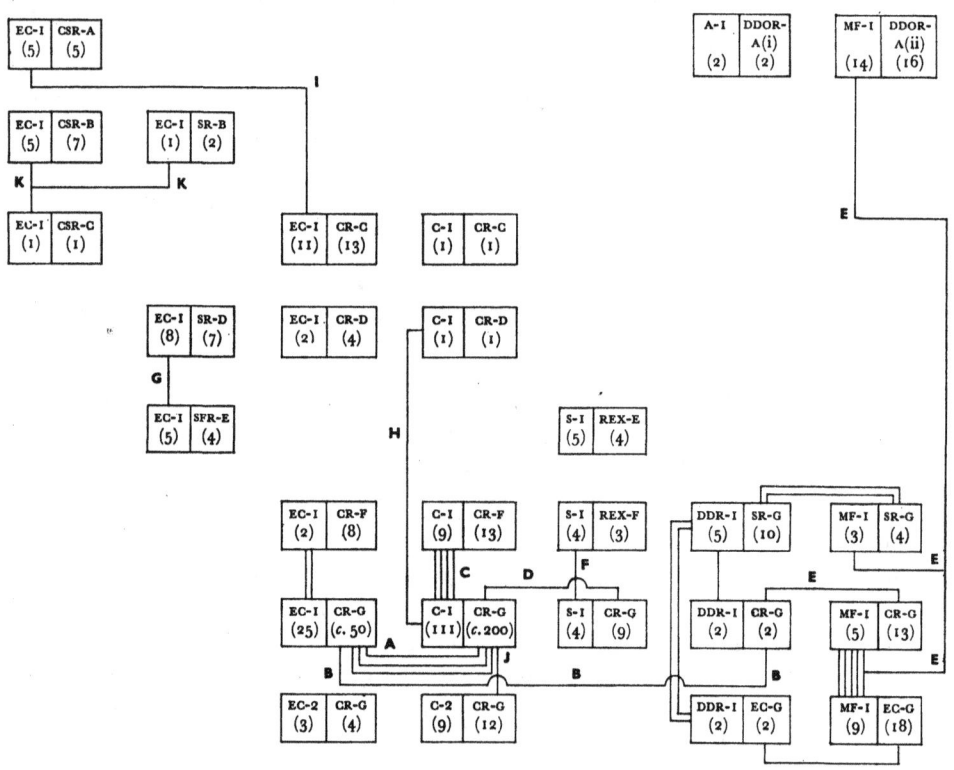

FIGURE I. *The Northumbrian Viking Coins in the Cuerdale Hoard. Diagram showing the combinations of obverse and reverse types, with the number of dies recorded to date. Dies common to two or more combinations of types are denoted by joining lines. Die-link references are to Plate XII.*

We were faced with a difficult task in attempting to determine the order in which the various types were issued, as to all intents and purposes our only source of information was the hoard itself. The condition of the coins, while in some respects confirming other evidence, was of little value in this analysis,

The Northumbrian Viking Coins in the Cuerdale Hoard

since so many of them are in mint condition; this fact did, however, lead us to suspect that the duration of the greater part of the coinage was very short. Little further progress could have been made had the number of coins of each major type occurring in the hoard not been recorded so faithfully by Hawkins; as it was, we were able to make a detailed analysis of a substantial proportion of the Viking coins in the hoard and not only to determine the number of dies represented in our sample, but also to estimate for each type the average number of coins surviving in the hoard from each die.

The sample examined included the coins in the National Collection, and those in the collection of the late Dr Philip Nelson – now housed in the Liverpool Public Museums; each of these collections comprises more than two hundred coins. The coins in the Assheton cabinet, numbering more than one hundred and fifty, and those in the museums at Preston and St Ives, were examined from photographs kindly made available to us by Mr Blunt, and we also included an important collection belonging to Messrs Baldwin, to whom we are indebted. Taking into account the Fitzwilliam *Sylloge*,[10] we had access, directly or from photographs, to nearly a quarter of the Viking coins found at Cuerdale; the proportion was considerably higher among the rarer types.

As our study progressed, it became apparent that the British Museum had chosen its selection of coins from the hoard with great care, so as to include every possible variety. This has meant that relatively few new dies have been recorded from other collections, except in the case of the '*Cunnetti*' series, and we are convinced that, if we were able to examine the remaining three-quarters of the coins, the pattern which has emerged from our sample would be very little altered. We, therefore, have considerable confidence in the survival rates of obverse dies which are shown in the table on p. 106.

Other things being equal, a high survival rate suggests recent minting, and the table indicates very clearly that those coins in the name of Cnut which incorporate a 'Patriarchal Cross' must be regarded as among the latest in the hoard. The '*Mirabilia Fecit*' (*MF*-1/*CR*-G and *MF*-1/*EC*-G) coins, which have the highest survival rate, prove to be remarkably closely die-linked; all nine of the *MF* dies used with these reverse types have been linked together with all nineteen *EC*-G dies in one complex chain of die-links, which also includes three *DDR*-1 dies, three *SR*-G dies, and a number of *CR*-G dies. Clearly these types were of very short duration. It is possible that the survival rate of coins from the latest dies of the prolific '*Cunnetti*' and '*Ebraice Civitas*' series would be found to be equally high if we could separate them from those struck from earlier dies.

It would seem to be established beyond reasonable doubt from the figures in

TABLE I

TABLE I shows, for each group of reverse types, the maximum number of coins surviving on the average from each obverse die used with these types. A high survival rate is indicative of relative lateness in date.

Obverse type (and number of dies recorded)	Reverse type	No. of coins in hoard	No. of coins examined	No. of obverse dies recorded	Maximum survival rate
EC-1	CSR-A	11	7	5	
	-B	18	13	5	
(59)	-C	6	1	1	
	CSR-all	35	21	10	3·5
	SR-B	6	3	1	
	-D	45	12	8	
	SR-all	51	15	9	5·7
	SFR-E	62	10	5	12·4
	CR-C	?	24	11	
	-D	?	5	2	
	-F	?	8	2	
	-G	?	52	25	
	CR-all	500+	89	38	13·2
EC-2 (3)	CR-G	?	5	3	?
C-1	CR-C	?	1	1	
	-D	?	4	1	
(117 recorded; 135 assumed)	-F	?	26	9	
	-G	?	220	111	
	CR-all	1900+	251	117	14·0
C-2 (9)	CR-G	?	17	9	?
S-1	REX-E	26	12	5	
(12)	-F	27	10	4	
	REX-all	53	22	9	5·9
	CR-G	57	18	4	14·2
A-1 (2)	DDOR-A (i)	3	2	2	1·5
DDR-1	SR-G	43	20	5	
(6)	CR-G	10	3	2	
	EC-G	10	5	2	
	All-G	63	28	6	10·5
MF-1 (24)	DDOR-A (ii)	66	35	14	4·7
	SR-G	4	4	3	
	CR-G	125	39	5	
	EC-G	124	42	9	
	All-G	253	85	11	23·0
All	All	3043+	598	250	12·2

The Northumbrian Viking Coins in the Cuerdale Hoard

NOTES

1. Where the total number of obverse dies recorded for a group of types differs from the sum of the totals for the individual types, this indicates that one or more obverse dies are common to more than one reverse type (*vide* Fig. 1).
2. The maximum survival rate for a group of types has been determined by dividing the number of coins in the hoard by the number of obverse dies recorded in the course of this study, except in the case of C-1/CR-all, where the survival rate has been based on an estimated number of obverse dies likely to have been represented in the hoard.
3. The figures for the maximum survival rates based on the number of obverse dies recorded in our sample would not be a reliable indication of the actual survival rates which would emerge if the whole hoard could be examined, were it not for the fact that the sample is not random, but is highly selective (*vide* p. 105).

---

the table that the coinage in the name of Cnut outlasted that in the name of Siefred and Sievert. That is not to say that the whole of the former coinage is later than the latter; in fact, those coins which have the inscription SIEFREDUS on the obverse combined with CNUT REX on the reverse are comparatively late. The key to the whole coinage clearly lies in the '*Ebraice Civitas*' obverse type, which spans its entire duration. One might postulate, on the evidence of survival rates, that the earliest '*Ebraice Civitas*' coins are those with the *CSR* reverse types; this may be true, but the survival rates must be interpreted with caution in view of the fact that Hawkins, in his analysis, did not distinguish between the *CR*-C, F, and G types. There are reasons for believing that the *CR*-C type preceded the other two, in which case the survival rate of *CR*-C coins, if it could be determined separately, might well be of the same order as that of the *CSR* types.

The problem can only be solved if we can deduce which form of the '*Ebraice Civitas*' inscription was used first. The complete, continuous form might be expected to have preceded the broken, abbreviated form, particularly the symmetrical variety; but the complete inscription appears only in conjunction with the *CR*-C and *CR*-G types, the second of which has already been shown to be late. In fact, the very rare pennies (as distinct from halfpennies) bearing the '*Karolus* monogram' may well be among the latest coins in the hoard; not only are they quite unworn, but the type continues into the 'St Peter' coinage. The *CR*-C coins with a complete obverse inscription do not necessarily date from the same period: the lettering is much smaller, and they have a worn appearance. There is also a die-link between the *CR*-C and *CSR*-A types (**Plate XII, 1**), through an obverse of type 1 (b) (i) – i.e. of symmetrical form with groups of pellets as stops. It is not possible to demonstrate convincingly that the '*Ebraice Civitas*' dies with complete inscription and *CR*-C reverses are the earliest of all; in fact, it seems likely that they are later than some, at least, of the dies having a broken inscription which were used with *CSR* reverses. The only positive conclusions we can put forward about the order of the '*Ebraice Civitas*' types are that 1 (b) (ii) is late and contemporary with the '*Cunnetti*' series, and that large obverse lettering is generally later than small lettering.

We are of the opinion, however, that the coinage in the name of Cnut began at much the same time as that in the names of Siefred and Sievert, but that the bulk of it was struck after the names of Siefred and Sievert had ceased to appear on the coins. While we have not arranged the obverse types in any definite chronological order, we believe the reverse types A to G to be arranged in an order which is indicative of their true chronology so far as is possible in our present state of knowledge. In arriving at our arrangement, we have taken account of survival rates and die-links, as well as of the appearance of the coins themselves. Several reverse types seem to have been in simultaneous use; types A, B, and C may be regarded as an early group, closely followed by types D and E, with types F and G latest of all, but the groups must have overlapped to some extent. The number of groups of pellets interspersed among the letters of the '*Cnut Rex*' reverse inscription may have some chronological significance; it appears that there was an increasing tendency to multiply these groups, which are fewest on coins of type C and most plentiful on those of type G.

A possible exception to this general pattern is presented by the *DDOR*-A reverse type. Several of the '*Mirabilia Fecit*' dies used in conjunction with *DDOR* reverses are blundered – which would suggest that they were late. Survival rates, however, indicate that they were earlier than those used with 'Patriarchal Cross' (type G) reverses, and certainly the degree of die-linking is much less. Only one '*Mirabilia Fecit*' die is found in conjunction with reverses of both series, and the die is quite new when used with *DDOR* reverses. If the *DDOR* type came first – and by analogy with the *CSR* Two-line types this is by no means impossible – the '*Alvaldus*' coins (two and a fragment are known) must be early, too, and the attribution of these coins to the ætheling Æthelwald becomes more improbable.

The extent of the die-linking between types is shown in Figure I. The '*Dns Ds Rex*' and '*Mirabilia Fecit*' obverse types are closely associated, as has been demonstrated above, and probably the '*Alvaldus*' coins belong to the same group. There is a single die-link between the '*Dns Ds Rex*' and '*Ebraice Civitas*' obverse types, via a *CR*-G reverse die (**Plate XII, B**), but the later '*Mirabilia Fecit*' type has not so far been die-linked directly to any of the non-religious obverse types. There is a die-link, via *CR*-G, between '*Siefredus*' and '*Cunnetti*'

The Northumbrian Viking Coins in the Cuerdale Hoard

(**Plate XII, D**), and three die-links between '*Cunnetti*' and '*Ebraice Civitas*', all through *CR*-G, have so far been found (**Plate XII, A**).[11] There is little doubt that, although the '*Mirabilia Fecit*', '*Siefredus*', '*Cunnetti*', and '*Ebraice Civitas*' types were apparently in concurrent use, the obverse dies were not freely interchangeable, otherwise they would be die-linked on a larger scale. The die-linking which exists, and the similarity of style between *CR*-G dies used with the various obverse dies, strongly suggests that there was only one mint in operation, although there may have been more than one workshop within that mint.

A review of the evidence afforded by the coins themselves would not be complete without an indication of the size of the coinage. It seems probable, from the sample which we examined, that the number of obverse dies used in the coinage did not exceed two hundred and fifty. The number of reverse dies may be half as much again. Of these dies, probably half were used in striking the '*Cunnetti/Cnut Rex*' coinage. We do not know how many coins were struck, on the average, from an obverse die at this time. If, for purposes of illustration, a figure of ten thousand is taken – which may well be on the high side – this indicates a total coinage of some two and a half million pence, representing rather less than four tons of silver, of which the coins in the hoard accounted for about one per mille. The size of the coinage can thus be seen in perspective: it was definitely limited, and can only have lasted for a few years – perhaps five at the most. The Cuerdale hoard probably contained a cross-section of the whole coinage: it is tempting to speculate that the disaster which resulted in the loss of the treasure also put an end to the coinage. We know of no direct link between this coinage and the 'St Peter' coinage which apparently followed it, and there may well have been a gap of a few years between the two.

CONCLUSIONS

We have so far looked at the Viking coins in the context of the Cuerdale hoard; and by analysis of the combinations of types, of the die-linking within and between these types, and of the survival ratio of coins per die, reached certain broad conclusions about the issue as a whole and the sequence of the various types. This purely numismatic evidence is, we would emphasize, both limited and limiting: we must neither claim that it proves too much, nor on the other hand, in seeking to place the coins in their historical context, admit any theory which contradicts the results of our numismatic analysis. In attempting, therefore, to solve our original questions about the coinage, we shall hope to reconcile our numismatic conclusions with the documentary evidence, of

Anglo-Saxon Coins

which the inscriptions and types of the coins themselves comprise an important part.

The duration of the coinage was not long. So widespread is the die-linking that we may assume a short period of intense and highly organized minting activity with many types being struck concurrently and a considerable overlap in the time during which dies of consecutive types (if such they were) were being used. Though the *'Cunnetti'* type is so overwhelmingly the most abundant, yet it is the *'Ebraice Civitas'* type which is perhaps the most significant, for it unites the whole series. Furthermore, it is linked with the subsequent 'St Peter' and *'Raienalt'* coins of the Danelaw both by the inscription itself, and by the use of the *'Karolus* monogram'. The fact that, in the later hoards from Harkirke and Morley St Peter, *Cunnetti* was the only type present, does not necessarily argue for an extended issue of the *'Cunnetti'* type beyond the body of the issue: it could be explained by reference to the large scale of the *'Cunnetti'* issue within the coinage as we know it.

Accurate dating depends upon when the Cuerdale hoard was deposited. Earlier writers thought as late as 910, but *c.* 903 would allow sufficient interval for coins of Edward the Elder to travel north from southern mints. Haigh thought as early as 901, only two years after Ælfred's death: certainly the Viking coins raise no objection to this. The coinage as a whole was probably near its close by the time of the burial of the Cuerdale hoard; the compactness of the main issue suggests a period of not more than five years for its duration and extension of the date of deposit much beyond *c.* 901 becomes increasingly improbable. As we shall see from the documentary evidence, a date *c.* 897 for the inception of the coinage would accord happily with historical tradition. Their very recent issue would explain why several of the coins in the Cuerdale hoard, notably of the *'Mirabilia Fecit'*, *'Ebraice Civitas'*, and *'Cunnetti'* types, retained their original bloom from the mint.

Because of their types, Hawkins, and later Bergsoë, believed that the Viking coins in the Cuerdale hoard were of French rather than English origin. Moreover, the one undoubted mint-name identifiable was that of Quentovic. There are strong, and we believe conclusive, objections to this. So far as types are concerned, two imitative coins support the idea of an English origin – the type in the name of Ælfred, inscribed ORSNAFORDA, which copies the 'Cross on Steps' design from Siefred's coins,[12] and the semi-barbarous coin which combines the names of Cnut and Ælfred.[13] Hawkins himself says, 'All the varieties are so intimately connected with each other by the types and legends, that all must have been struck about the same time, in the same country, and by the same authorities.' Now, if the coins had been struck in France, the group buried

The Northumbrian Viking Coins in the Cuerdale Hoard

in Cuerdale must have been brought in one parcel, from France to Lancashire, and kept in one parcel until buried; otherwise there could hardly have been such an abnormally high proportion of die-links and die-identities. If this had been the case, it is most unlikely that the coins could have circulated sufficiently to have been imitated in the English Danelaw, from which the two coins just mentioned almost certainly emanated.

Provenance, too, is against a French origin. As we have seen,[2] the only recorded continental provenances are of single specimens found in North Germany, Denmark, and Sweden: the two coins in French private collections at the time Lelewel described them are of unknown provenance, which may just possibly be French. On the other hand, although the exceptional Cuerdale hoard is not – for example, in the case of the large number of '*Metullus*' coins – by itself valid evidence for the country of origin of its contents, the other known provenances are all in the British Isles. If the coinage were French, the single '*Cunnetti*' coin in the Morley St Peter hoard would be the only continental coin in that hoard, which is scarcely probable in a hoard deposited so late as the beginning of the reign of Æthelstan.

Finally, it seems improbable that so large an issue of coins would have been struck in France weighing, in almost every case, between 19 and 22 grains when the average weight of the Frankish *denier* at the time was quite 26 grains. Admittedly, the 'Quentovic' coins are at the same lower weight standard (which exactly corresponds with that of the later coinage of Ælfred), but this seems to have been a small and isolated issue. We believe that considerations of weight, provenance, and imitation establish beyond doubt that the issue belongs to the English Danelaw during the years before, and perhaps just after, the end of the ninth century.

We can now look anew at the coins as historical documents in their own right, and see to what extent they confirm or conflict with the independent tradition of the chroniclers. The inscriptions are in accurate, consistent Latin. It is quite apparent that the coinage was well planned and organized; the types and legends are clear, and where the inscriptions can be understood today they suggest that they were carefully and deliberately chosen, and were comprehensible at least to the die-sinkers and workmen in the mint, even if not to all of those who used them. For instance, though certain words or phrases can appear on either reverse or obverse dies, coins with similar inscriptions – e.g. *Ebraice C*/*Ebraice Civitas* – or redundant combinations such as *Cnut Rex*/*Rex* or *Siefred*/*Siefredus Rex*, which might have resulted from illiterate or haphazard pairing of dies, are never found. In fact, we may assume deliberate and literate sinking and use of dies, and since the Latin elements of the inscriptions which we can understand are logical and correct, elements of which we are not certain, whether Latin or not, are likely to be logical and correct also.

The two liturgical mottoes are, in themselves, self-evident, and, as has been mentioned, belong firmly to the tradition of continental coin-types; there is nothing comparable on any Anglo-Saxon penny. When the two are combined on one coin, they may be intended to be read as one inscription; obviously, however, there can be no suggestion of a blasphemous consecutive rendering when, for instance, *Cnut Rex* and *Mirabilia Fecit* are on the same coin. Earlier writers have demonstrated (though the point has not been widely received) that the angular serifed o in DNS DS O REX stands for *Omnipotens* – 'The Lord God Omnipotent Reigneth': it is not easy, nor perhaps important, to explain why the o should be omitted when DNS DS REX is written in a circular inscription on obverse dies.

In view of these religious legends, it is not surprising to find the one definite mint-name with the title of *Civitas*, which implies an episcopal see. If this was in France it might be Evreux, the name of which appears on Merovingian coins as *Eboro Vico* or *Ebroce Cast*, is designated *Oppidum* by Adam of Bremen, but is styled *Civitas* on Carolingian coins. If in the English Danelaw, it must be York: no other see in the area has even a remotely comparable name. The well-known ecclesiastical coinage dedicated to St Peter struck certainly at York, a few years after the Cuerdale Viking coins, spells the mint-name usually *Eborace*, but some specimens read (without the o) EBRACE C, EDRACE CI, BRACE, etc., and one, bearing the '*Karolus* monogram', reads EBARICE CT. The similarity is too close to be coincidental.[14] We have no hesitation in saying that York must have been the only mint of the coinage on the evidence of die-linking alone. In that case, we are led to wonder why some of the coins bear the mint-signature, some liturgical mottoes, and others the obscure word *Cunnetti*.

Typologically we have noted that the '*Karolus* monogram' links the later '*Cunnetti*' and '*Ebraice Civitas*' coins with the 'St Peter memorial' issues and the coins in the name of *Raienalt*, which seem to have formed the subsequent Danish coinage of Northumbria. It seems legitimate to consider the possibility that these two later groups *may* represent an ecclesiastical and a regal issue from the York mint; and analogously that the Cuerdale Viking coins may fall into the same division. During the earlier York coinage, *sceattas* and *stycas* were struck simultaneously for kings and archbishops, and this was normal practice at Canterbury also. We consider this a possible, but by no means certain, reason why a considerable proportion of the Cuerdale Viking coins should have religious inscriptions and why a number should combine legends which include no royal name or title.

The Northumbrian Viking Coins in the Cuerdale Hoard

We have yet to interpret the word *Cunnetti* and to consider who were Siefred, Cnut, and Alvaldus. There is little we can say of Alvaldus; we have already noted the improbability on numismatic grounds of his identification with Æthelwald, who, we are told,[15] was accepted as King by the Northumbrians in 900. Alvaldus is not styled *Rex* on the coins: he could have been a moneyer, particularly if his coins could be shown not to be an integral part of the coinage which we are discussing. In the present lack of adequate evidence, we prefer to leave the question quite open.

Because of the intimate and consistent die-linking within and between types we have seen that all the coins must have been struck at the same mint. Thus *Cunnetti* cannot be a mint-signature. It can hardly, even in a contracted form, be a quotation from the liturgy. Numismatic and philological considerations do not allow it to be a moneyer's name: on the one hand, it is most highly improbable that the bulk of such a varied coinage could have been struck under the direct responsibility of a single moneyer, and, if it had been, there would have been no reason for his name to appear on a majority of the coins; and, on the other hand, *Cunnetti* is not a form of any word which might represent a plausible moneyer's name. Furthermore, a moneyer's name would be quite contrary to the Frankish design and concept of the issue. We are driven to the conclusion that *Cunnetti* must in some way be connected with the name or title of the ruler.

Certain coins read SIEFREDUS on one side and REX on the other, so it must be assumed that the two inscriptions on a coin *may*, in any other case, be intended to read continuously. *Cunnetti* is the only major type to be combined with a single reverse – *Cnut Rex*. If it is connected with the ruler's name, the literal resemblance between *Cunnetti* and *Cnut* should be noticed. But if, in fact, *Cunnetti* is a form of the name Cnut, it is difficult to understand why it appears in the genitive, or even why it appears at all, in view of the care which seems to have been taken in the rest of the series to avoid redundant or tautological combinations of inscriptions.[16] The fact that *Siefredus Rex/Cunnetti* is never combined cannot necessarily be endowed with more than a chronological significance – i.e. '*Siefredus Rex*' reverse dies were probably out of use before most of the '*Cunnetti*' coins were struck. Nevertheless, the association of *Cunnetti* with *Cnut Rex* only, at a period during a part of which reverse dies reading other than *Cnut Rex* were certainly available, does appear deliberate; and its significance may lie in that the two inscriptions are complementary. Can *Cunnetti* only accompany *Cnut Rex* to make sense? The possibilities for a continuous inscription are *Cunnetti Cnut Rex* or *Cnut Rex Cunnetti*. Grammatically *Cunnetti* in this context looks like the genitive or locative of a district (or town) *Cunnettum*, i.e. 'Cnut

Anglo-Saxon Coins

King of (or in) Cunnettum.' This explanation we feel to be far from certain, but we would stress that the solution cannot be a mint's or moneyer's name, must take into account the limitations which we have put forward, and must allow for the obvious contemporary importance of the '*Cunnetti*' type, which the number of original dies and of extant coins shows to have been unparalleled within the series.

Considerable obscurity surrounds the individual identities of Siefred and Cnut, and more particularly their relationship to each other. Certain coins – certainly not early in the series, and in fact probably the latest in the name of Siefred – combine the inscriptions SIEFREDUS/CNUT REX. It is worth noting that though *Siefredus/Rex* can stand alone, and *Siefredus/Cnut Rex* can be combined, there is no combination *Siefredus Rex/Cnut Rex* and, when Siefred's and Cnut's names are combined, the singular *Rex* is written, not *Reges*.

Sometimes the inscription C SIEFREDUS REX is found, though when the name is in the unlatinized form *Sievert* the C is never present; the significance of this apparently deliberate distinction is obscure. What does C stand for? It could be a name, a title, or a place. If the last, it would have to be an abbreviated genitive: if *Cunnetti* is such, the inscription *could* be expanded to mean 'of Cunnettum Siefred King'. This seems improbable, but the parallel of *Cnut Rex/Cunnetti* must be remembered. *Siefredus Rex C* would, however, be a much more normal order. If the C represented a title, *Comes* and *Cununc* spring to mind. But *Cununc* is extremely improbable in a Latin inscription, especially as it merely reduplicates *Rex*; *Comes* is almost impossible, because it is less than *Rex* and should in any case come last – *Siefredus Rex Comes*.

If C stands for a name, it could perhaps be another name of Siefred; but it is worth considering that the only name found in this series beginning with C is, in fact, combined with Siefred's – namely *Siefredus/Cnut Rex*. If that combination is possible there is no reason why it might not have been combined and abbreviated on one side of the coin as *C(nut) Siefredus Rex*. Both these cases would involve the combination of the Latin *Siefredus* with the unlatinized form *Cnut*; we shall have to consider whether this clue is any evidence for the relationship between Siefred and Cnut. In the first place, the absence of *Rex* on the obverse of the '*Siefredus/Cnut Rex*' coins suggests emphatically that this was not a joint issue of two contemporary kings. Yet these same '*Siefredus*' obverse dies were also designed to be used with the plain '*Rex*' reverses – no other obverse makes sense in conjunction with *Rex*, nor is any found; from which we induce, with certainty, the authority of a King Siefred. On the other hand, some dies contemporary with these in the name of King Siefred, some dies earlier than them, and a great many later, proclaim, with no less emphasis, the authority

The Northumbrian Viking Coins in the Cuerdale Hoard

of a ruler who could be styled (with the name never latinized) *Cnut Rex*. It is to be noted that, whereas Siefred is, as we shall see, historically identifiable with some certainty, the bulk of the coins with a royal title are in the name of Cnut alone. We are forced to concede that the numismatic possibility Cnut=Siefred would happily explain the mysterious *C Siefredus*, the inscription *Siefredus/Cnut Rex* (not *Reges*), and the simultaneous manufacture of dies in the names of *Siefredus Rex* and *Cnut Rex* when joint royal authority is apparently precluded. In these circumstances Cnut may be thought to have had, as a name, something of the quality of a patronymic, or at any rate more than a specific personal application: for example, at a later date Harthacnut, son of Cnut the Great, is styled on a high proportion of his Anglian coins simply as *Cnut Rex*.[17]

Any investigation into the historical identities of Siefred and Cnut must take account of these inscriptions. Its conclusions must also be consonant with the approximate date and sequence of the coins, which we believe is firmly established by the analysis of dies, and by the context of the Cuerdale hoard. Such is the newness of the Viking coins from that hoard, and so great the quantities of coins from each die, that we can hardly push the date of issue of the earliest coins back more than five years before 900; and that we must assume that the later types were probably still being struck at that date, and perhaps for some time afterwards. Now we have seen from the comparative frequency of coins from each die found at Cuerdale that there are consistently less per die, in the name of Siefred, than there are of Cnut: which indicates that the coinage in the name of Siefred had, on the average, been in circulation for longer than that of Cnut. Further, in the cases where a single obverse die is coupled with reverses in the names of both Siefred and Cnut, the evidence is generally that those of Cnut were struck later. We must then seek an historical Siefred *c*. 895 or a little later, and a Cnut who could have been the same man, his contemporary or successor, but not his predecessor. Both (if they were two persons) are more likely to have been pirates than statesmen: sudden supplies of silver for coinage would most probably accumulate in Northumbria as a result of successful looting, for York still was not primarily a focus of civil life nor a centre of trade. At a later period of Viking dominance at York, the most successful adventurers – notably Anlaf Guthfrithsson – struck the largest and most regular coinage.

As far as Sievert-Siefredus is concerned it is reasonable to suppose that these two names both represent the same man. Siefredus could be latinized Frankish, while Sievert appears to be derived from the English form Si(ge)ferth. Æthelweard refers to a Sigeferth, 'a pirate from the land of the Northumbrians', and describes him raiding Devonshire in 893–4, presumably at the head of the

Anglo-Saxon Coins

Danish force which the Parker MS. of the *Anglo-Saxon Chronicle* records as having attacked Exeter in 893 (the original and, Miss Whitelock points out, the correct dating). It is possible that this Siefred or Sigeferth succeeded Guthfrith on the latter's death on the Feast of St Bartholomew (26 August), 895,[18] although Adam of Bremen's reference to 'Nordmanni' having invaded Gaul in 884–5 'cum regibus Sigafrido et Gotafrido' may have some significance in this context.[19]

If Siefred did, in fact, succeed Guthfrith (who is apparently the same person as Simeon of Durham's Guthred) he could hardly have begun coining before the beginning of 896, which agrees well with the date that we have, on numismatic grounds, postulated for the start of the Viking coinage of the type found at Cuerdale. Had it not been for their chance preservation in the Cuerdale hoard, Siefred's coins would probably be unknown today; as it is, they are not outstandingly rare, but the issue was probably very short lived. There is no indication as to how and when Siefred disappeared from the scene, unless we infer that Danish acceptance of the atheling Æthelwald in 900 was connected with the death or expulsion of a king, which was not necessarily the case.

The one categorical statement which we are confident to make about the identity of Cnut is that he cannot possibly have been Guthfrith. Whatever was the real name of this person (or persons), the coins inscribed CNUT REX have been attributed to him by Haigh, Rashleigh, Keary, Nelson, Oman, Brooke, and others.[20] They would thus have had to be struck some two or three years before 895 when Guthfrith died. But the coinage in the name of Cnut definitely outlasted that in the name of Siefred: Cnut's coins (from the Cuerdale hoard) in particular have a fresh mint bloom; and they, if any of the series, are typologically connected with later coinages from York and survive from later hoards. Thus, on numismatic grounds, it is quite impossible that they should have been issued c. 893–5, and not later than 895, even allowing the quite arbitrary interpretation of Cnut as a baptismal name for Guthfrith, on the analogy of Guthrum-Æthelstan.[21]

Reluctantly we have admitted the numismatic possibility of Cnut being the same man as Siefred. Otherwise all we can suggest from the evidence of the coins is that he could have been a contemporary and successor of Siefred. As such his historical identity is obscure. No Cnut known to history remotely fits the context of time and place. However, we must look for a ruler who appeared on the Northumbrian scene c. 897, and was at the height of his power from then until c. 900; who (if he was not one and the same man) succeeded Siefred at York, having perhaps for a time held joint authority with him; who had enough silver for a considerable coinage; whose authority, or at least whose influence,

The Northumbrian Viking Coins in the Cuerdale Hoard

was such that coins were struck in his name in France as well as in Northumbria; which authority must therefore have come from sea-power.

In the *Annales Vedastini*, from the monastery of Arras, Haigh found reference to one Hundeus, whose exploits should be examined in this light. In 896 'Nortmanni cum duce Hundeo[22] nomine' sailed down the Seine, despoiling the country in that area; in 897, 'Karolus vero Hundeum ad se deductum Duninio monasterio in pascha eum de sacro fonte suscepit.' After wintering by the Loire, the Northmen (presumably Hundeus' band) harried part of Aquitaine and Neustria in the spring of 898; they were intercepted by the King's army, but got through to their ships.

There is no certain indication that the marauders of 898 came from Northumbria; but it is to such a raid that we must look for an explanation of the high content of Carolingian coins from precisely this area and period of time in the Cuerdale hoard. Perhaps, in view of the apparent occurrence of a few coins of Louis the Child in the hoard, the ravages of the Northmen of the annals are a year or two too early to account for the Carolingian content of the hoard, but it would be unwise to pass final judgement on this point until the Carolingian coinages generally have been satisfactorily classified.

The baptism of Hundeus is not without interest. As we have already noted the coinage from York, in the names of Siefred and Cnut, is, for the most part, of the highest quality in workmanship and production – it presupposes considerable expertise on the part of the moneyers and die-sinkers. Since York had not issued coins since the demise of the '*Styca*' coinage of the old English kings of Northumbria in the early 850's, we are led to wonder whence this technical skill was acquired. It was a coinage, too, involving several tons of silver, coined into pennies of Frankish design, with Christian types and inscriptions. A Viking marauder, converted to Christianity and baptized by Charles the Simple, could have had large supplies of silver; it would not be surprising if he had persuaded French engravers to return with him to mint the silver into coins of Frankish type with Christian inscriptions.

Tempting though it might be for numismatists to try to equate the Latin name Hundeus with Cnut, there are philological objections which must first be overcome. Nor is there any likelihood of Cnut or Siefred having been the baptismal name of Hundeus. Nevertheless, the numismatic evidence for a connexion between the Carolingian and Northumbrian Viking coins in the Cuerdale hoard and the cited entries in the *Annales Vedastini*, though admittedly circumstantial, is so strong that we are convinced it cannot be ignored. It may not necessarily have been Hundeus' campaign of 896–8 which was responsible for the Carolingian content of the Cuerdale hoard, and for the Viking coinage itself, but if not, there must surely have been a similar set of circumstances at the most a year or two later involving a Northumbrian leader who was, or who was responsible to, the Cnut or Siefred of the coins. It is unfortunate that the annals cease with the turn of the century; had they continued, we might have been able to identify the raid with some certainty. Even so, it is by no means certain that we could have identified our Cnut, still less have solved the problem of the *Siefredus/Cnut Rex* and *C Siefredus Rex* inscriptions.

We are forced to admit that many of the problems of the early Viking coinage at York are not yet capable of definite solution, though we believe that we have narrowed the field in which the various solutions can lie. The problems must, however, be approached as one complex puzzle; attempts to answer them in isolation have led, and must always lead, to confusion.

REFERENCES

1. 'An Account of Coins and Treasure found in Cuerdale' *NC* 1843
2. A handful was discovered in 1611 at Harkirk(e), near Sefton, Lancashire, and isolated specimens are recorded on very dubious authority as having been found in 1846 at Drogheda, Co. Louth, and in 1902 at Stamford, Lincolnshire (*vide* J. D. A. THOMPSON, *Inventory of British Coin Hoards, A.D. 600–1500*, 1956, pp. 67, 50, and 127 respectively); more recently, a single specimen of the '*Cunnetti*' type was in the Morley St Peter hoard of 1958. From the Continent, three coins in the name of Cnut ('*Cunnetti*', '*Mirabilia Fecit*', and '*Quentovici*' types) are described by V. Thomsen of Copenhagen in *Blätter für Münzkunde*, 1836, pp. 206–9 and Plate XIV; these were in the author's collection at the time, but the provenance is not stated. Two more ('*Cunnetti*' and '*Mirabilia Fecit*' types)are recorded by Lelewel in *Numismatique du moyen-âge*, Paris, 1835, Part II, pp. 86–9; these were in French private collections and of unrecorded provenance: the latter coin is illustrated on Plate XVII, and the reverse reading is *Cnut Rex*. Single specimens of the '*Cunnetti*' type have occurred in hoards from Dransau, North Germany, and Koldemosen, Denmark (for the references to these and for a general discussion of the Northumbrian Viking coinages see R. H. M. DOLLEY, 'The Post-Brunanburgh Viking Coinage of York', *NNÅ* 1957–8), and a '*Cunnetti*' halfpenny was found in excavations at Birka, Sweden (N. L. RASMUSSON, 'Kring de västerländska mynten i Birka', in *Från Stenålder till Rokoko*, Lund, 1937). HAWKINS in 'Account of Coins and Treasure found at Cuerdale', *Arch. J.* 4, 1847, pp. 193–4, referred to a find at Vaalse in the island of Falster in 1835 which contained objects resembling those found at Cuerdale, and included English coins. Mr Dolley has checked the reference to this hoard, and states that the hoard was deposited *temp.* Æthelræd II, and that none of the English coins were early

The Northumbrian Viking Coins in the Cuerdale Hoard

3. e.g. *NC* 1843 (Haigh, de Longpérier), 1869 (Rashleigh), 1880 (Bergsöe); *BNJ* 1903-4 (Andrew), *BMC* A/S I (1887) pp. 201-30 (Keary). See also C.-A. SERRURE *Les monnaies de Canut et de Sifroid, rois pirates normands* Paris 1858; and D. H. HAIGH 'The Coins of the Danish Kings of Northumberland' *Arch. Æl.* N.S. VII (1876) pp. 21-77
4. F. M. STENTON *Anglo-Saxon England* Second Edition 1947 p. 260
5. M. PROU *Les monnaies carolingiennes* Paris 1896
6. This is not inconsistent with the Kufic *dirhams*, while the attribution of a Papal coin, as with the French coins of 'Charles' rests on the date ascribed to the hoard, and not vice versa
7. *Vide* e.g. F. T. WAINRIGHT 'Æthelflaed Lady of the Mercians' p. 63 in *The Anglo-Saxons* ed. P. A. M. Clemoes, Cambridge, 1959
8. *Supra* p. 32
9. *Supra* p. 91
10. PHILIP GRIERSON *Sylloge of Coins of the British Isles, 1. Fitzwilliam Museum, Cambridge, Part I* 1958
11. Various short notes by PHILIP NELSON in *NC* 1943-50 (*vide* index to 1950 volume for full list)
12. *BMC* A/S II (1893) Plate V no. 11
13. Ibid. Plate VI no. 18
14. The name of York has a complete history, *vide* A. H. Smith, *The Place-Names of the East Riding of Yorkshire* pp. 275-80
15. *Anglo-Saxon Chronicle s.a.* 900 C; 901 D, E; no date in B. The A manuscript carefully refrains from mentioning his acceptance as king
16. It comes to mind that *Cunnetti*, if a form of the name Cnut, might just possibly be used to denote a specifically regal coinage
17. P. J. SEABY 'The Sequence of Anglo-Saxon Coin Types, 1030-1050' *BNJ* XXVIII (1955) p. 111 ff.
18. This date is based on the original date in the Parker MS. for the arrival of the Danes from Boulogne (892). Æthelweard puts Guthfrith's death a year after an event which he dates two years after this
19. *Gesta Pont.* ed. Pertz 1846 lib. I c. 41.
20. HAIGH, RASHLEIGH, KEARY, NELSON, opp. citt. SIR CHARLES OMAN *The Coinage of England* 1931 p. 47; G. C. BROOKE *English Coins* 1950 Edition p. 34
21. It is extremely unlikely that Cnut was ever a baptismal name for anyone; Guthrum, baptized as Æthelstan, was given a name which had already been borne by Christians of the Ælfredian house. Miss Whitelock points out that Guthfrith's father was called Hardacnut and that if a man thus named could also be called Cnut (*supra*, p. 115), there is just the possibility that Cnut of the coins might be a son of Guthfrith, called after his grandfather
22. *Variae lectiones – Huncdeo et Hunedeo*

Anglo-Saxon Coins

KEY TO THE PLATES

Plate XI

The various types and major varieties are shown on Plate XI, obverse and reverse types separately. References are given in the text. The coins illustrated (in order of illustration) are *BMC* 870, 875, 1040, 1023, 882, 1035, 878, 907, 906, 911, 922, 920, 991, 997, *BMA* 308, *BMC* 1021, 1078, 1063, 1056, 1076 (obverse only); 876, 913, 905, 910, 878, 906, a duplicate of 984, 962, 997, 1026, 1031, 1032, 1025, 1023, *BMA* 308, *BMC* 1033, 1039, 1035, 1040, 1041, 1042, 1056, 1078, 1069, 1076 (reverse only); 1007 and 1015 (obverse and reverse).

Plate XII

Several examples of die-links are illustrated on Plate XII. They are as follows:

A. Die-link between *Ebraice Civitas* (*EC*-1 (b) (i)) and *Cunnetti* (*C*-1 (b)) through *CR*-G. (1, *BMC* 882; 2, *CSSL*.)
B. Die-link between *Ebraice Civitas* (*EC*-1 (b) (ii)) and *Dns Ds Rex* (*DDR*-1) through a reverse die which is a curious mixture of *CR*-G and *EC*-G, though predominantly the former. The reverse die is linked, through the same '*Dns Ds Rex*' obverse die, to *SR*-G. (1, *BMC* 896; 2, *BMC* 918; 3, *BMC* 1048.)
C. Die-link between *CR*-G and *CR*-F through *Cunnetti* (*C*-1 (b)). It appears, from the relative clarity of the letter c on the obverse die, that the coins were struck in the order illustrated – despite the condition of the *CR*-G coin. (1, *BM* Burnett bequest 385; 2, *BM* Barnett bequest 379.)
D. Die-link between *Cunnetti* (*C*-1 (b)) and *Siefredus* (*S*-1 (b)) through *CR*-G. Note the wrongly engraved reverse inscription. (1, *BMC* 965; 2, *BMA* 307.)
E. Die-link between 1, *DDOR*-A; 2, *SR*-G; 3, a mixture of *CR*-G and *EC*-G; 4, *EC*-G; 5, *CR*-G, in probable order of striking; the common obverse die is '*Mirabilia Fecit*' (*MF*-1) type. This group is part of a very extensive and complex chain of die-links; for example, 6 shows a die-link to *Dns Ds Rex* (*DDR*-1) through the reverse die used in 3. (1, *BMC* 1069; 2, *BMC* 1041; 3, *BMC* 1062; 4, *BMC* 1056; 5, *BMC* 914; 6, *BMC* 1064.)
F. Die-link between *REX*-F and *CR*-G through *Siefredus* (*S*-1 (b)). (1, *BM* Barnett bequest 360; 2, Nelson 1298.)
G. Die-link between *SR*-D and *SFR*-E through *Ebraice Civitas* (*EC*-1 (a) (ii)). (1, *BMC* 1036; 2, Assheton.) Another link between the '*Sievert*' and '*Siefredus*' forms is illustrated in die-link K.
H. Die-link between *CR*-D and a variety of *CR*-G having a 'Double Patriarchal Cross'; the obverse is *Cunnetti* (*C*-1 (b)). Note the crude and retrograde '*Cunnetti*' die, and the equally crude execution of the *CR*-G die. The *CR*-D die may be a stray; this type is usually found in conjunction with *Ebraice Civitas*. (1, *BMC* 986; 2, *BMC* 987.)

The Northumbrian Viking Coins in the Cuerdale Hoard

I. Die-link between *CSR*-A and *CR*-C, through *Ebraice Civitas* (*EC*-1 (b) (i)). The *CR*-C coin may be the later striking; the reverse die is subsequently used with an obverse die of type *EC*-1 (a) (i) having a continuous inscription. (1, *BMC* 1026; 2, *BMC* 876; 3, *BMC* 870.)

J. Die-link between halfpennies of *Cunnetti* C-1 (b) and C-2 types, through *CR*-G reverse. (1, *BMC* 991; 2, Nelson 1291.)

K. Die-link between *CSR*-B, *CSR*-C, and *SR*-B through *Ebraice Civitas* (*EC*-1 (b) (i)), in probable order of striking. (1, *BMC* 1031; 2, *BMC* 1025; 3, *BMC* 1039.)

NOTE: The photographs may not seem fully to warrant the claim for the existence of Die-link F, but actual inspection of the coins will be found conclusive.

VII

Boroughs and Mints A.D. 900–1066

by H. R. LOYN

There is some need for a word of explanation for the unenterprising nature of the title of this paper. The early history of our boroughs has been thoroughly worked over in connexion with their courts, their tenures, and indeed to some extent their minting-rights. But new material and new thought have gathered together around the problems of late Anglo-Saxon boroughs and mints to such an extent in the last decade or so, that perhaps the time has come for a brief statement of some of the new conclusions and new puzzles that seem to be emerging in relation to these institutions. New material has come in part from finds such as that from Chester in 1950, or more sensationally that of Morley St Peter in early 1958.[1] New thought has been provided by what is virtually a new school of Anglo-Saxon numismatists.

Indeed, a subsidiary but important objective of this paper is to pay tribute from an historian's point of view to the valuable work of our coin-experts, particularly in their treatment of the late Anglo-Saxon period. No one would deny that the major inspiration behind the work, itself the product of some half-dozen researchers and writers attached to our great museums, universities, and learned societies, has been Sir Frank Stenton. He has been heard to say in public that an Anglo-Saxon penny can be bought for a pound, and to ask further where else an historical document for that period can be bought for such a price. This is very true. The little Anglo-Saxon silver penny is an historical document. It gives the name of a king, how he spelled his name, the name of the borough in which it was struck, the name of the moneyer responsible for the striking, to say nothing of more intangible information concerning the techniques of coining and the artistic inspiration that determined the type and form. It is hard to tease as much information out of much more verbose documents. Fortunately the new school of numismatists has been fully aware of the historical nature of its material. With so much good work in progress it would be invidious perhaps to mention more than the neat little paper, 'Carolingian Europe and the Arabs; the Myth of the Mancus', in which Mr Grierson demolished many long-cherished ideas concerning the nature of the gold currency known to the Anglo-Saxons.[2] For our own immediate period and problems a little 'school'

Boroughs and Mints, A.D. 900–1066

centred on the British Museum has done much in the course of the last decade to rewrite the history of the late Anglo-Saxon coins.

Perhaps the first and most potent impression made on the historian of late Anglo-Saxon England as he approaches the problems of the coinage comes from the sheer quantity of coins involved. Only silver pennies were minted for ordinary use, in itself a fact of significance, but there were many of them. Literally tens of thousands lie in the great repositories of London and of Stockholm, and the giant task of re-editing and reclassifying the major collections is in progress at the moment. The second impression made upon the historian is the immediacy of the problems as men with fresh minds approach plentiful material with new questions to address to it. This sense of immediacy is heightened as new discoveries are made; and it would be idle to deny that the incongruous nature of some of the discoveries adds piquancy for an historian operating in a field where hope of fresh documentary evidence has long since dwindled. There is great satisfaction in reading of the excitement of discovery; of men digging drains, turning up gravel-pits, sometimes mistaking the precious coins for lemonade-bottle tops, sometimes dispersing the hoard among themselves, of sober numismatists touring the public houses of a district in an effort to regroup a scattered hoard. Such a hoard can lie snug for a thousand years. Its moment of greatest peril comes when the workman's pick or shovel upturns it.

All the sorting and classifying and absorption of new material appears highly technical, not to say abstruse, to the non-numismatist. Important work has been done on detailed topics like the state of the die-axis, or the distribution of dies, or the study of what are inevitably called mules, with the obverse of such-and-such a type and a reverse of a different nature. The special vocabulary of 'Short Cross' and 'Long Cross', of 'Lozenges' and 'Rosettes', of 'Facing Busts' and 'Radiates' is at first sight intimidating. But from the detail and technicalities certain general points begin to emerge of interest to all. The following four propositions seem of special moment to all who concern themselves with the development of late Anglo-Saxon society.

1. *The coinage was good*

Apart from ceremonial issues no gold appears to have been minted, and no silver coin above the penny. In some ways the familiarity of the word *penny* is positively misleading to the modern. During the reign of Æthelstan a sheep could be valued at five pence. The blood-price of an ordinary freeman was reckoned at two hundred shillings, or one thousand West Saxon pence.[3] Exact equivalence of value is impossible, but there is much to be said for thinking of an Anglo-Saxon penny more in terms of a pre-1914 half-sovereign; that is to say, of a coin of considerable value, not lightly to be spent or lost, rather than in terms of any silver coin familiar to us. The weight of silver in the coin was maintained at a reasonable and consistent if variable level. The strictures of late chroniclers do not tally with numismatic facts. Roger of Wendover, for example, tells how Eadgar's great reform of the currency was needed because the weight of silver had sunk so low that a penny was worth scarcely more than a halfpenny. The coins themselves disprove this statement. Eadgar's reform was a remarkable achievement, but it was not caused by a disastrous falling off in his earlier coinage.[4]

2. *Royal control of the currency was firm*

The strength of the legal evidence for this has long been appreciated. It is, therefore, doubly convincing to find that the numismatist's technical evidence points also decisively to such a conclusion.

3. *Royal control was exercised through the supply of dies, normally from a well-organized central die-cutting workshop, exceptionally, and this applies notably to the reign of Æthelræd II, from a number of regional die-cutting centres*

Again this is a proposition that could be made on documentary evidence, and it is comforting to find it substantiated by modern numismatic research. Changes of type applied quickly throughout the country, and such changes were of course effected by the cutting and distribution of new dies.

The question of the existence or non-existence of regional centres at which dies could be cut is one of considerable importance and great interest. In the period before *c*. A.D. 900 it is likely that die-cutting was normally the preserve of the craftsmen of Canterbury. Their monopoly was shaken during the reign of Ælfred, and probably did not survive the shock of Viking attack. London took the place of Canterbury as the premier die-cutting centre. By the reign of William I it was unusual for any die to be cut outside London. Recent subtle and intuitive work on the coinage of Æthelræd II has suggested, however, that there may well have existed seven or eight die-cutting centres during the years 1009–25: at London, Canterbury, Winchester, Exeter, Chester, Lincoln, York, and possibly Thetford. Others may be inclined to agree with Mr Grierson that the evidence so brilliantly analysed by Mr Dolley points rather to a division of interest on a regional basis amongst craftsmen employed at a central die-cutting workshop in London.[5] Such an interpretation would certainly afford a better explanation of some of the anomalous strikings to which Mr Dolley himself draws our attention. The question remains undecided. It says much for modern

Boroughs and Mints, A.D. 900–1066

numismatics that it could ever be asked. The major premiss, that royal control was exercised through control of the dies, is of course untouched by possible differences over the regional die-cutting centres.

4. There were regular changes in types, and therefore in dies directed from the centre

The importance of such changes, simply as a financial perquisite, is immense. 'Domesday Book' leaves us in no doubt on the matter. The account of the borough of Hereford tells how the King received eighteen shillings from each of the seven moneyers for their new dies which they collected, probably in London. He received a further twenty shillings from them one month after their return home. One of these moneyers belonged to the Bishop, who received twenty shillings of his minter, again one month after the return from London with fresh dies. Moneyers at Worcester (who definitely went to London), Chester, Shrewsbury, and Lewes gave twenty shillings for their new dies, and reference elsewhere, notably in the Dorset boroughs, to moneys received 'quando moneta vertebatur', confirms that here is record of a formal financial process of great significance to the King.[6]

Recent critical investigations, both here in England and also in Sweden, into changes of type have led to conclusions little short of sensational in regard to the regularity of such change. It is plain sober fact that one now expects to be able to date most late Anglo-Saxon coins with a precision that would have been unthinkable a generation ago. Twenty-four successive types were issued between 973 (?) and October 1066; each main type ran for a fixed period, originally of six years; later in the series the period was shortened, in some instances to two or three years. Taking internal variations within a type into account, some coins can be dated positively within a matter of months. For example, a new type could be the subject of experiment and then withdrawn as seems to have been the case with the rare and beautiful '*Agnus Dei*' penny of Æthelræd II, to all appearance struck in the summer of 1009.[7]

The final picture that emerges from an acceptance of these propositions is of a coinage of remarkably fine quality, technically competent, subject to a central direction that transcended superficial political disaster, subject also to consistent and regular changes of type, with the old type smoothly recalled as the new type was issued. Such a picture demands a toning-down of the historian's instinctive unhappiness when he looks at the variety of mints available in Anglo-Saxon England. There were between sixty and seventy mints operating in the reigns of Edward the Confessor and of Harold. Close on eighty have left traces of their activity during our period. Yet though the mints were decentralized the coinage was not. Carolingian parallels are positively misleading. The reforms of Charles the Great himself, which included a cutting down of the number of mints in operation, were needed to safeguard standards. In Frankish lands the great danger consisted in the spread of private moneyers, leading in point of fact to a debased feudal coinage in the course of the tenth and eleventh centuries. The English situation was quite different. Here the function of coining remained in practice as in theory a royal preserve. Decentralization of mints was a matter of convenience, of royal as well as local convenience.

From the legal records of the tenth and eleventh centuries comes full proof of royal concern to hold and to retain control of the mints. The savageness of the penalties imposed on the false coiner, coupled with a certain tendency to repeat legislation, suggests that the kings were not uniformly successful. Æthelstan decreed that the hand of a false coiner should be struck off and set up over his workshop. Æthelræd II inveighed against those who struck coins in the woods or elsewhere in out-of-the-way districts.[8] Most revealing of all the penal legislation are the clauses bearing on the matter in the document known as 'Æthelræd's Fourth Code'.[9] The King appears to make quite a sharp distinction between the moneyers who strike false or inferior coins and those who work in woods or other secret places. The former, presumably duly accredited moneyers or moneyers' craftsmen, operating in formal mints, are to lose their hands; the latter are to lose their lives unless the King has mercy on them. A difficult clause earlier in the 'Code' may give the key to a distinction which though denied by the citizens of London in theory was observed by the King in practice:

Also they [the citizens] said that there appeared to be no distinction between the *falsarii* and the merchants who bring good money to the *falsarii* and bribe them to produce (from it) impure and underweight coins, and therewith chaffer and bargain, and those also who make dies in secret places and sell them to the *falsarii* for money and cut on them the name of another moneyer, and not that of the guilty one.

A veritable hierarchy of offence is disclosed by this clause: the false coiner, the merchant who supplies the false coiner with good pence out of which bad are fabricated, the backwoodsman making his dies in secret places. Without straining excessively at this tortuous code, it may well be the last of the three groups that meets the full venom of the King, and whose members are fully culpable as to their lives. The fabricator of dies struck hard at vital spots in the royal income.

Apart from penal sanction and from inveighing against forgery and poor

Boroughs and Mints, A.D. 900–1066

workmanship, there were two further intertwined threads in royal policy. The first of these was to control the number of mints, and the second to associate mints with boroughs. This policy is on the whole consistent and successful. Æthelstan in his 'Grately Decrees' gave a list of mints, together with the number of moneyers to operate in them in the lands of Greater Wessex, rounding off his tally of named boroughs with the simple but important observation that in other boroughs there was to be one moneyer. 'Æthelræd's Fourth Code', very concerned as has already been shown with the purity of the coinage, went further and attempted unsuccessfully to limit the number of moneyers to three 'in omni summo portu' and to one in 'omni alio portu'.[10] The vital consistent thread in all royal activity in the matter consists in an association of mints and boroughs. The mint and the borough may 'just have growed', like Topsy; but they 'growed' together.

Again this is a field of study where the numismatist is of great help to the historian, and can fill out the dry bones of legal record.

From the reign of Æthelstan it began to be customary, and after Eadgar's Reform it was obligatory, for the name of a mint and the name of a moneyer to appear on a coin. Identification of mints is not always easy. Ambiguous abbreviations, doubtful letters, difficult readings, set traps for the unwary and give stimulus to the ingenious. Attribution of coins with common elements like NIWAN and BRYG(G)IN is a matter for the expert.[11] But these are peripheral cases. For the main part identifications are straightforward, and the mere accumulation of data offers valuable information about the size and importance of the late Anglo-Saxon boroughs. From the percentage of total output, based on a reasonable statistical sample of coins which have survived, and from the number of moneyers at work at any given time, it is possible to deduce that some boroughs had a thriving mercantile element, while others had not. As shall be seen later, the preponderance of London comes out well from an analysis of such figures. With the growing precision of knowledge of the chronology of the coinage it is possible also to point to variations in mintage output that suggest variable local demand and variable local prosperity. Chester at one time, Exeter at another, enjoyed a somewhat disproportionate share of the Anglo-Saxon mintage. Though careful handling is needed it may be possible to go one stage further and to say that such output is a reflection of the prosperity of Chester and Exeter at these given periods.[12] Large enough numbers of coins are involved to give a reasonable statistical guide, though the accident of survival is still a factor to reckon with. Sir Frank Stenton, from 'Domesday' evidence alone, has been able to suggest that Norwich, Thetford, Lincoln, and Hereford have been unfortunate in their hoarders, and that these towns were more prosperous than estimates based on their coins and moneyers would allow.[13]

To some degree caution is also necessary in assessing how much weight should be given to coinage and currency in any discussion of the more general late Anglo-Saxon problems concerning kingship and unity. But if basic principles are brought into question then quite obviously there are two fundamental reasons for the existence of coinage in this period, convenience and confidence, and both have bearing on the general problems. The stamp of the King's head upon the coin guaranteed a certain weight of silver and a certain uniformity in issue. Upon the possession of convenient units of exchange depended the whole apparatus of trade. The consistent reckoning of legal penalties, of wergeld payments, of the value of goods left by will, of the proceeds of estates, mills or woods in terms of pounds, of marks, of *mancuses, oras*, shillings, and pence does not mean that more primitive means of payment were not in use; it does suggest that currency and weight of silver and gold were the medium through which such payments were thought. When Ælfric Bata asks in his *Colloquy* how payment shall be made, the sensible reply is given that 'there is nothing dearer to me than that you should give me pennies, for he who has pennies or silver can get anything he pleases'.[14]

Nor was the marketing involved in such monetary transactions exclusively local. The English silver penny was respected overseas, notably in Scandinavia. From as far back as there is record the Baltic and the North Sea were silver-loving areas; gold for jewels and specie, silver for use was early the aim. Many of the hoards in Sweden and in Gotland where such a mass of the coins of Æthelræd II have been found, bear the mark of traders' hoards rather than of straight deposit of Danegeld or of seamen's wages. But though this external trade through the medium of English pennies lends an exotic note to coinage problems, much more important from the immediate point of view is the question of internal trade within these islands.

This is an exceedingly vexed question. Every reference to trade and to merchants in the tenth and eleventh centuries is seized on avidly, sometimes to the neglect of the obvious fact that for the bulk of the population the agrarian round remained the be-all and the end-all of existence. Yet it is possible that the amount of internal trade demanded by the agrarian round itself has consistently been under-estimated. Iron and salt are the commonplaces of those who deal with the economy of pre-Norman England, but trade in cattle, seed, and surplus must also have involved many people, only a small proportion of whom, to be sure, would be professional merchants. Such steady intercourse will explain the concern of even our earliest law codes with regulation of trading

Boroughs and Mints, A.D. 900–1066

activities. The very process of vouching to warranty itself is symptomatic of anxiety over possible abuse of trade. The King through the royal officers took the suppression of disorder and violence as a prime duty; nothing contributed to disorder so readily as theft; the surest safeguard against theft lay in the formulation of procedures that would guarantee good witness to each and every trading transaction of importance. References to markets and to tolls and to the royal interest in them suggest that the rural communities were not as shut in as tradition has it. A coin-hoard found at Shaftesbury consisted mostly of coins minted in the Danelaw, a fact which speaks of some inter-regional trade.[15] Above all, the royal care for the merchant and for the proper conduct of trade is a pointer to the significance of the chaffering and bargaining element in late Anglo-Saxon society.

Yet the question might well be asked at this stage why a discussion of currency and of trade should lead so directly to the king. Why do so many appear monarchists, looking for justice to the king, using with approbation phrases like royal discipline where tyranny might be nearer the case, extolling even the harsh first William for the good peace he gave? Part of the answer rests in the nature of eleventh-century society itself. The hope for a just society lay in the king over against a tyranny all the more pernicious for being local. This fact alone explains why the spectacles are rosy when regard is paid to the late Anglo-Saxon monarchy. In England certainly the documentary evidence tends to reinforce in theory the beneficent aspects of kingship: the coronation *Ordo* of Eadgar, the homilies of Ælfric, the work of Wulfstan impregnating the legislation of Æthelræd and Cnut, the vigour of Cnut the convert, the piety of the Confessor. A benign picture is given of kingship in action, different from the force and violence of the Angevin world, and different too from the tales of treachery and duplicity of the Æthelrædian *Chronicle*, in themselves enough to offset the apparent calm assurance of the royal theocratic position. There is more to it, however, than merely a contrast between high-flown theoretical claims and brutal reality. Institutionally there was genuine advance. Under Cnut there was clear reservation of important pleas to the royal interest. The writ was developed, the geld was effective; above all, from the immediate point of view, there was an increased emphasis on royal control of trade. The twin agents through which this control was effected were regulation of currency and regulation of boroughs. It is at this royal level that the two institutions of our title really cohere: the mint and the borough are the major institutions through which the king could benefit the trader, and could himself benefit from the trader's activity.

The laws of the late Anglo-Saxon period are particularly informative on the question of the borough. A conscientious attempt was made to canalize trade into boroughs, into fortified centres where royal officers could be present and men of good repute could bear witness to trading transactions. The attempt was not completely successful, owing in all probability to an absolute increase in the volume of trade as the political unity of England became a reality. Cnut had to recognize the legitimate exercise of transactions that involved goods to the value of over four penny-worth outside the boroughs. By inference lesser transactions 'upp on lande' must have been commonplace.[16] The existence in 'Domesday Book' of many market towns which did not aspire, nor were ever to aspire, to borough status is a further reminder that the developed borough was too cumbersome an institution for such minute regulation. To the present writer many of the 'simple' boroughs of 'Domesday Book' are similarly symptomatic rather of extended economic activity than of extension of institutional life. The handfuls of *burgenses* operating around an abbey, a lord's house, or a new Norman *caput* of a new Norman honour are proof of vitality in a community, and proof also that any attempt to conscribe trading to formal boroughs was doomed to fail. But the attempt was logical. Even the seventh-century Kentish laws show trade transacted at the royal hall in London.[17] Good witness and forced honesty are the keys to the situation. When Æthelstan relaxed his strict laws concerning trading outside boroughs, he continued to insist on full and true witness. Eadgar was at pains to ensure that even rural hundreds should provide their twelve chosen witnesses competent to vouch for the validity of trading transactions, the same number as was required for a 'small' borough, whereas a borough with no qualification was expected to possess a panel of thirty-six such witnesses.[18] Behind the shaping of the Old English borough lies royal administrative activity and royal concern with the peace.

The moulding force of royal administration is apparent in the days of Edward the Elder when the 'Burghal Hidage' recorded the arrangements by which the walls of the *burhs*, the defensive headquarters of the locality, were to be manned by a levy imposed on the surrounding landowners. It is apparent too in the very distinction between boroughs and 'small' boroughs, made by Eadgar, and carried further by Æthelræd. Under Cnut indeed an attempt was made to standardize one law of exculpation for all boroughs, a sign of the prominence given by the King to honesty and good witness in his dealings with the borough. Eadgar again with one of the classical and controversial texts of tenth-century history tells how a *burhgemot* shall be empowered to meet three times a year. An eleventh-century tract concerning the duties of a bishop distinguishes between borough-right and land-right.[19] By the time of 'Domesday Book' the differentiation of the borough from the hundred is far advanced, and the elaborate royal and earlish rights over the borough accurately delineated. But variety is great; the borough is a growing, developing institution. Any attempt at precise definition is likely to create anomalies. The facts of historical change fit uneasily, if at all, into neat legal theory.

Of all the possible tests of borough status the possession of a mint is in many ways the most satisfying and complete. It is the one obvious feature that Wareham has in common with York, that the eleven or twelve favoured residences of the king in Somersetshire have in common with Lincoln. A market could flourish and become a borough, if fortified and in possession of a mint. A fortified royal residence with a mint could develop into a permanent borough, if suitably placed to act as a focus for trade in its area. There is inevitably a cloudy border-line of argument between posing the presence of a mint as a mark of borough status and stating the simple proposition, given directly by the law-codes, that a borough was to have a mint. The situation is further complicated by the impermanence of some boroughs and of some mints. The term *burh* itself undergoes semantic change during our period, and many of the fortifications referred to in the 'Mercian Register' do not develop into recognizable boroughs.[20] Coins were struck for a brief period at Cadbury hillfort, at a time when the more regular mints of Bruton, Crewkerne, and Ilchester were disrupted by Danish raiding. With more settled conditions the minters returned home from their draughty hill-top, and Cadbury can claim no more than temporary burghal status on their account.[21] The termination *burh* or *byrig* in the dative was still used at the end of the period and beyond to describe a fortified estate, and as such survives, for example, in the Gunnersbury of Middlesex.[22] To deal with living institutions like the English borough much patience is needed. Neat theoretical patterns fail the modern observer as they would have failed the contemporary if he had tried over-zealously to define his borough.

Nevertheless, there are some characteristics to be expected in a borough of the late Anglo-Saxon period: mints and fortifications; special legal procedures; in the early stages at least, garrisons; the earl's share, the third penny, of borough revenue; royal administration. Boroughs are official. The mediatized borough is rare and of minor importance before 1066. But if boroughs are to acquire permanence then they must also be towns and more than mere administrative centres. The very size of the population recorded in the bigger boroughs of 'Domesday Book' shows how far this process of growth had advanced by the latter half of the eleventh century. By contrast many of the smaller boroughs of the south-west, so well regarded by the Anglo-Saxon kings, are losing their distinctive status as their importance within the kingdom declines. Here again the numismatist helps the historian as he plunges from the relative certainties of 'Domesday Book' to the uncertainties of the Beyond. For there is scarcely a single 'Domesday' borough of importance in 1066 that has failed to preserve at least some coins as evidence of its activity in the late Anglo-Saxon period.[23] The problem lies rather in analysing the Anglo-Saxon minting-places that for one reason or another failed to develop into permanent boroughs. Horndon in Essex, for example, put out coins during the reign of Edward the Confessor, but remained a relatively undistinguished village, assessed at a little more than ten hides, not even a royal manor in 1066.[24] All manner of local reasons could lead to a lack of viability in minting-places. Yet when all is taken into account possession of a mint remained a spectacular test of immediate borough status and a hint at the hope of permanence.

But it was not the only test. Tait in his brilliant analysis of the growth of urban institutions placed the mint as one of a solid quadrilateral of special features that distinguish a borough: the mint itself, a market, a court, and heterogeneity of tenure. His judgement is eminently sane. The borough is a complex institution growing from an economic need, spurred on by administrative activity. And it is with the recognition of the economic necessity lying behind the creation of the town that the strength of Tait's analysis rested, as against, for example, the ideas of Carl Stephenson which, interesting as they always are, seem somewhat legalistic and abstract.[25] For a clear distinction between town and borough, *Dorf und Stadt*, useful though it is for teaching purposes, should not be carried too far in our period. The mint may provide here an essential clue. Royal control of the mints is of a piece with royal anxiety to supervise trade and the process of vouching to warranty. Any considerable body of people needed a mint; and a mint demanded royal supervision and protection. The association of mint and borough was a natural response to such demand, twin manifestations in their different ways of growing complexity and cohesion in English society. Borough status was not in itself coveted; it grew as a natural growth. Not until the twelfth century with the desire for exclusion of sheriffs and the granting of charters does the magic of corporate sense begin to transform urban institutions. In the tenth century, and to great measure in the eleventh also, it is easier to conceive borough without town than town without borough.

A borough inside which market and mint would be protected offered conditions well suited for urban growth. If a township flourished outside the borough network, then in turn it might aspire to take on the concrete duties and somewhat nebulous status of borough. Towns needed mints; mints helped to confirm towns as boroughs.

Boroughs and Mints, A.D. 900–1066

Finally it must be pointed out that for an assessment of the relative size and importance of late Anglo-Saxon towns, the percentage of the total output coming from any particular mint and the number of moneyers operating at that mint provide valuable criteria. One mint is pre-eminent, that of London, which seems to have produced close on a quarter of the whole of the country's output. York, with perhaps a tenth, and Lincoln and Winchester, with slightly less, follow in order of importance. With variations from period to period, Chester, Norwich, Exeter, and Thetford take pride of place after the four major mints.[26] Population figures teased out of 'Domesday Book' tally with reasonable accuracy. The overall picture is of one big town, half a dozen or so of intermediate size, and many small towns. It is a realistic picture quite in accord with the part played by London in national affairs and with the general picture of Anglo-Saxon economy. Town life was stable, rooted in the soil. Where overseas trade touched it, across the North Sea, from the whole stretch of North-west Europe into London, across the Irish Sea, then town life flourished. This picture is also a reminder that it was not a question of come 1066, come the light. The tenth and eleventh centuries were times of great political upheavals and troubles which, nevertheless, led to a solid enrichment of western Europe. The last barbarian invaders fell back or were absorbed. Christianity was extended to the Slavonic and Scandinavian world. Under royal patronage the borough grew from its dim, partly military, beginnings to the substantial centres of population of 'Domesday Book'. In any attempt to unravel this tangled story the modest English silver penny with its record of mint and moneyer offers new hope; at worst the joy of the chase, at best fresh insight into the detailed working out of the complex evolution of English urban society.

REFERENCES

1. C. E. BLUNT and R. H. M. DOLLEY 'The Chester (1950) Hoard' *BNJ* XXVII ii (1953) pp. 125–60; R. RAINBIRD CLARK and R. H. M. DOLLEY 'The Morley St Peter Hoard' *Antiquity* 1958 pp. 100–3
2. *Revue Belge de Philologie et d'Histoire* XXXII (1954) pp. 1059–74
3. VI Æthelstan c. 6.2; an ox was to be paid for at 30*d*, a cow 20*d*, a pig 10*d*, and a sheep a shilling (that is to say 5*d*). On wergeld payment there is an interesting elaboration of a pre-Conquest document in *Quadripartitus* where the wergeld of a 'two hundred man' is given as two hundred shillings: 'id est ducenti sol. ex v scilicet denariis, qui faciunt iiii libros et xl denarios' F. LIEBERMANN *Die Gesetze der Angelsachsen* I p. 393
4. ROGER OF WENDOVER *Flores Historiarum* ed. H. O. Coxe Eng. Hist. Soc. 1841–4 s.a. 975; MATTHEW PARIS *Chron. Maj.* I ed. R. Luard R.S. 1872 p. 467

Anglo-Saxon Coins

5. R. H. M. DOLLEY 'Some Reflections on Hildebrand type A of Æthelræd II' *Antikvariskt Arkiv* 9 Kungl. Vitterhets Historie och Antikvitetsakademien Stockholm 1958; P. GRIERSON, a notice of the above, *EHR* 1959 pp. 715–16
6. 'Domesday Book' i 179a (Hereford), 172a (Worcester), 262b (Chester), 252a (Shrewsbury), 26a (Lewes), 75a (the Dorset boroughs of Dorchester, Bridport, Wareham, and Shaftesbury)
7. R. H. M. DOLLEY 'The Shaftesbury Hoard of Pence of Æthelræd II' *NC* 1956 p. 267; P. SEABY 'The sequence of Anglo-Saxon coin types, 1030–1050' *BNJ* XXVIII i (1955) pp. 127–9
8. II Æthelstan c. 14.1; III Æthelræd c. 16
9. IV Æthelræd, in particular c. 5 and c. 5.3 (which gives the substance of II Æthelstan c. 14.1) and c. 5.4 (substantially III Æthelræd c. 16)
10. IV Æthelræd c. 9
11. R. H. M. DOLLEY 'Three Late Anglo-Saxon Notes' *BNJ* XXVIII i (1955) pp. 92–9 where the possible attribution of these coins to Newport (Salop) and Bridgenorth is discussed
12. R. H. M. DOLLEY 'The Mint of Chester' *Chester Archaeological Society's Journal* Chester 1955 pp. 3–4
13. F. M. STENTON *Anglo-Saxon England* Second Edition O.U.P. 1947 pp. 529–30
14. W. H. STEVENSON (ed.) 'Ælfric Bata's Colloquies' *Early Scholastic Colloquies* O.U.P. 1925 p. 50
15. R. H. M. DOLLEY 'The Shaftesbury Hoard of Pence of Æthelræd II' *NC* 1956; see note 7 *supra*
16. II Cnut 24; no one was to buy anything worth over fourpence unless he had the witness of four true men, be it within a 'burh' or 'upp on lande'.
17. Hlothære and Eadric c. 16, 16.1
18. IV Æthelstan 2; VI Æthelstan 10; IV Eadgar 5 and 4 (one MS. gives thirty-three as the number of witnesses expected in a borough) LIEBERMANN op. cit. I p. 210
19. The 'Burghal Hidage' *Anglo-Saxon Charters* ed. A. J. Robertson pp. 246–8; IV Eadgar 3–6.2; IV Æthelræd 9; II Cnut 34; III Eadgar 5.1; Episcopus 6. LIEBERMANN op. cit. I p. 477
20. J. TAIT *The Medieval English Borough* Manchester 1936 p. 24: 'only eight (of the twenty-one *burhs*) are found as municipal boroughs later in the Middle Ages'
21. R. H. M. DOLLEY 'Three Late Anglo-Saxon Notes' *BNJ* XXVIII i (1955) pp. 99–105
22. A. H. SMITH *English Place-Name Elements* I E.P.N.S. XXV (1956) *burh* (e) p. 59; *The Place-Names of Middlesex* E.P.N.S. XVIII (1942)
23. A. BALLARD *The Domesday Boroughs* O.U.P. 1904 pp. 118–20 listed forty 'Domesday' boroughs for which, at the date he wrote, pre-Conquest coins were unknown. The forty included two 'county boroughs', Bridport and Northampton, both of which are now known to have struck coins in Anglo-Saxon days. Twenty-five were so-called 'simple boroughs', that is to say settlements of tenurial

Boroughs and Mints, A.D. 900–1066

homogeneity which had grown up or were growing up on the demesne of the king or of a great landowner, and which can only with many qualifications be classed with the established, fully developed boroughs. Even among this group, which includes many new agglomerations of traders around new feudal *capita* like Castle Clifford, Clare, Eye, Rhuddlan (where Robert divided the render of the mint with the Earl of Chester in King William's day), Pontefract, and Tutbury, there are to be found little boroughs like Bedwyn, Pershore, Warminster, and possibly Quatford where coins were in fact minted in Anglo-Saxon days. Of Ballard's remaining thirteen 'quasi-county' boroughs, that is to say boroughs enjoying heterogeneous tenure but not ranking with the 'counties', Axbridge, Barnstaple, Milborne, and Twineham are now known to have been Anglo-Saxon mints, while Pevensey was set up as a mint by the Conqueror. Arundel, Dunwich, and Fordwich were mediatized. Droitwich, a likely candidate for a mint as the centre of the West Midland salt industry, was very near to the powerful mint and borough of Worcester. There remain Calne, Wimborne, Yarmouth, and possibly Grantham, for all of which reasonable though not conclusive geographical or tenurial reasons can be given for the absence of a mint. To the present writer Droitwich and perhaps Grantham seem the two conspicuous exceptions which probe without proving the rule that all fully developed Anglo-Saxon boroughs possessed a mint. Numismatists might well ponder, however, the coins with mint-name apparently PICNEH in the Rotherham find, the Winchester attribution of which is no longer acceptable on purely numismatic grounds

24. F. M. STENTON op. cit. p. 529. More work on the so-called 'mediatized' boroughs of the eleventh century may reveal the sense behind many of the trials and experiments of the age
25. J. TAIT *The Medieval English Borough*, particularly Chapter VI, which gives the substance of his acute review of STEPHENSON's 'Borough and Town' *EHR* XLVIII pp. 642 ff.
26. These figures are based on the analysis by R. H. M. DOLLEY 'The Mint of Chester' *Chester Archaeological Society's Journal* 1955 p. 4

VIII

The Reform of the English Coinage under Eadgar

by R. H. M. DOLLEY and D. M. METCALF

[Plates XIII and XIV]

> Deinde per totam Angliam novam fieri praecepit monetam, quia vetus vitio tonsorum adeo erat corrupta, ut vix nummus obolum appenderet in statera.
>
> ROGER OF WENDOVER *Flores Historiarum* s.a. 975

In these words a thirteenth-century monk of St Albans has recorded, almost certainly on the strength of a passage in some pre-Conquest source, now lost to us, a great recoinage which was also a monetary reform.[1] It could well be said that Eadgar's reform was a turning-point in the monetary policy of the English State as significant as Offa's endorsement of the new penny or the successful adoption of a bimetallic currency under Edward III, and that it marked the beginning of a chapter of monetary history which was to continue, uninterrupted by the Norman Conquest, until the reign of Stephen. The description given by Roger of Wendover is the sole surviving written account, and only in the light of numismatic research has the considerable importance of the event become clear. It rests, indeed, with the numismatist both to provide the confirmation that there is a basis of truth to Roger's statement, and also to adduce evidence suggesting that the date given is the wrong one and that he has misunderstood or, more probably, embroidered his source. The date of Eadgar's reform, although very late in his reign, certainly was not 975, and the state of the English coinage prior to the reform certainly was not so bad that the weight of the penny in circulation had fallen by almost a half, for it can be shown without difficulty that his earlier pennies were not significantly lighter than those struck during the last two years of his reign.[2] There can be little doubt but that Roger was, in fact, 'improving' on his source, by adding to a simple statement to the effect that there was a new coinage the explanation that would have been apt in his own day.

The most important of the primary sources for our knowledge of Eadgar's coinage are the hoards, discovered in the British Isles, that include issues of his reign. It is possible to gather information about no less than twenty-eight such

The Reform of the English Coinage under Eadgar

hoards (see Appendix A). Eleven of them are from Ireland, seven are from Scotland, two each come from Wales and the Isle of Man, while only six are from England.[3] The task of the student is not made any the easier by the fact that very few of these hoards have received adequate publication, while fewer still have been recovered in their entirety. In these respects the finds from Iona and Tetney stand in a class by themselves, both being major hoards containing a very large number of coins of Eadgar, both reaching the national museum concerned substantially intact, and both having been published in an extremely competent manner. The inadequacy of so much of the earlier publication makes it difficult to attempt any rigorous classification of the finds, but it may perhaps be useful at the outset to distinguish three categories of hoard, on the basis merely of size, accordingly as they contain more than one hundred and twenty, more than twenty but fewer than one hundred and twenty, or fewer than twenty Anglo-Saxon coins,[4] and briefly to survey the evidence for each of the three groups.

Seven of the hoards contained more than one hundred and twenty Anglo-Saxon coins (see Table 1). As we have just said, the student may be reasonably confident that he knows exactly what coins were present in the Tetney and Iona finds when they were concealed. In the case of the two finds from Chester and that from Douglas not all the coins concealed were recovered by the authorities,

TABLE I

British hoards including coins of Eadgar which contained more than one hundred and twenty Anglo-Saxon coins in all.

Hoard	Reigns represented
From England	
TETNEY, Lincolnshire, 1945	Eadred–Eadgar
CHESTER, 1914 (Pemberton's Parlour)	Eadgar–Æthelræd II
CHESTER, 1950 (Castle Esplanade)	Ælfred–Eadgar
From the Isle of Man	
DOUGLAS, 1894 (Ballaquayle)	Æthelstan–Eadgar
From Scotland	
IONA, 1950 (Abbey)	Æthelstan–Eadgar, Æthelræd II
TIREE, Hebrides, 1782	Edward the Elder–Eadgar
From Ireland	
DERRYKEIGHAN, Antrim, 1843	Æthelstan–Eadgar

but the publications are adequate and there is no reason to think that there were present any major classes of the pennies of Eadgar which have escaped the record. The same seems to be true of the find from Derrykeighan, which can be very largely reconstructed on the basis of early accounts and of a number of coins in the Belfast Museum.[5] Concerning the Tiree hoard very little is known, but a recent note has suggested its general composition,[6] and there is welcome corroboration of the main outlines in another paper in this volume.[7]

Almost half the hoards fall into the middle group, of those that contain more than twenty but fewer than one hundred and twenty Anglo-Saxon coins (see Table 2). There are quite satisfactory publications of the 1857 hoard from Chester and of those from Lough Lene and Smarmore, which appear to have been recovered substantially intact. Confidence may also be placed in the

TABLE 2

British hoards including coins of Eadgar which contained between twenty and one hundred and twenty Anglo-Saxon coins in all.

Hoard	Reigns represented
From England	
CHESTER, 1857 (Eastgate Street)	Eadred–Eadgar
UNKNOWN SITE, c. 1750 (?) (North-east Midlands)	Eadgar–Æthelræd II
From Wales	
LAUGHARNE, Carmarthen, c. 1930 (Churchyard)	Eadgar
From the Isle of Man	
ANDREAS, 1867 (Churchyard)	Eadwig and Eadgar
From Scotland	
MACKRIE, Islay, 1850–2 (Kidalton)	Æthelstan–Eadgar
INCHKENNETH, Hebrides, c. 1830	Eadgar and Æthelræd II
From Ireland	
LOUGH LENE, Westmeath, 1844	Plegmund, Æthelstan–Eadgar
SMARMORE, Louth, 1929	Edward the Elder–Eadgar
UNKNOWN SITE, 1862	Edward the Elder–Eadgar
BURT, Donegal, 1864 (Carrowen)	Eadgar
DALKEY, Dublin, 1838 (?)	Edward the Elder–Eadgar
Western County KILKENNY, c. 1823?	Edward the Elder (?)–Eadgar
KILLINCOOLE, Louth, 1864	Æthelstan–Eadgar

account of the Irish hoard of unknown provenance, and it is likely too that the great bulk of the Mackrie hoard was recovered, albeit in two parcels. There are soon to appear notes on the hoards from Burt,[8] Dalkey,[9] and Co. Kilkenny,[10] which go some way towards repairing deficiencies in earlier accounts. It is fairly certain that the Laugharne hoard was composed entirely of late coins of Eadgar.[11] Intensive study of the coins in the National Museum of Antiquities at Edinburgh and the Manx Museum at Douglas will probably throw further light on the hoards from Inchkenneth and Andreas respectively.[12] In contrast the record of the find from Killincoole is disappointingly incomplete, and the

The Reform of the English Coinage under Eadgar

composition of the early discovery from the Lincoln–Stamford area can only be inferred from a detailed study of the coins in certain eighteenth-century cabinets such as those of Hunter and Tyssen.

The remaining eight finds probably contained fewer than twenty Anglo-Saxon coins in all. Except in the case of two pennies of Eadgar found in excavations at York,[13] records of these minor finds are fragmentary,[14] but a

TABLE 3

British hoards including coins of Eadgar which contained fewer than twenty Anglo-Saxon coins in all.

Hoard	Reigns represented
From England	
YORK, 1951 (Pavement)	Eadgar
From Wales	
BANGOR, Caernarvon, 1845–6 ('Senior Vicar's garden')	Eadgar
From Scotland	
TARBAT, Ross, 1889 (Churchyard)	Eadgar
BURRAY, Orkney, 1889	Eadgar and Æthelræd II
QUENDALE, Shetland, c. 1830 (Fitful Head, Dunrossness)	Eadgar and Æthelræd II
From Ireland	
GLENDALOUGH, Wicklow, 1835–6	Eadmund–Eadgar
DUNGARVAN, Waterford, 1911 (Knockmaon Castle)	Eadgar and Æthelræd II
County MEATH, c. 1845	Eadred and Eadgar

forthcoming note on that from Glendalough[15] shows that there is often something of value still to be extracted from the most unpromising material.

Hoards in which the latest coins are those of Eadgar are far more numerous than those in which Eadgar's coins occur along with others struck by his successors. From the Tables above, it will be seen that only seven of our hoards (Chester (1914), Unknown Site (c. 1750), Iona, Inchkenneth, Burray, Quendale, and Dungarvan) fall into the latter group, while there are twenty-one in the former. This disparity is fully large enough to be significant, and reflects, we believe, not merely variations from year to year in the concealment of hoards, but a real difference in monetary organization and in the control of the currency. Within the small group of later hoards, a further distinction must be made. Even though the finds are often incomplete and the records of them inadequate, one cannot but observe that the two English finds appear to have included no foreign coins whatever, and that they contained substantial numbers of one issue only of Eadgar's (presumably his last), of Edward the Martyr's sole type, and of the first and second types only of Æthelræd II. By contrast, the five Scottish and Irish finds contain no coins of Edward the Martyr, and a mere handful of pennies of Æthelræd's first and second types, while at least four out of the five contain coins from the Continent. Obviously the two hoards from England have a very different evidential value from the five from areas not under the effective control of the English Crown. Indeed, these five hoards seem all to be connected with Viking activities. In the Hiberno-Norse settlements there would of course have been no prejudice against foreign coin as such, and obsolete English coin would have been able to circulate freely. In point of fact, too, we can be quite certain that the two English finds contain Eadgar's last issue: not only is there typological continuity with the 'Portrait' coins of Edward the Martyr, but this issue, and this alone, is represented in quantity in the great coin-hoards from Scandinavia.

Five substantive types of pence of Eadgar may be distinguished among the several thousands of his coins which have survived (see Table 4). In addition to the 'Portrait' type (*BMC* type VI; **Plate XIII, 15**), already mentioned as having been continued under his sons, there was an earlier 'Portrait' type (*BMC* type V; **Plate XIII, 5–7**) which seems to have been struck fairly consistently in East Anglia, and more sporadically in southern England. Except for the King's name, coins of this type are indistinguishable from those of Eadgar's predecessors. The commonest coin of Eadgar is, however, a 'non-portrait' type (*BMC* type I; **Plate XIII, 1–4**), with the name of the moneyer in two lines on the reverse, which seems to have been struck at mints throughout the country with the probable exception of East Anglia. There are four main varieties, two with thick lettering to be associated with north-eastern England, one with small, neat lettering to be associated with southern England, and one with quite different lettering which is associated with north-western England by the inclusion in the reverse type of two or more rosettes. This 'Two-line' type, like the early 'Portrait' type, is essentially a continuation of an issue struck by earlier kings. Another type (*BMC* types III and IV; **Plate XIII, 8–13**), generally much less common except in the north-east, has the moneyer's name disposed in a circle. Several varieties of it can be distinguished; thus there are two in the north-west and one in the north-east, while in the south there seem to be three styles associated with the south-west, the south-east, and the Midlands respectively. The type is a revival of one struck by Æthelstan, and the fact that most of the coins, except those from the north-east, essay a mint-signature is perhaps an argument for placing them somewhere about the middle of Eadgar's reign. The remaining type (*BMC* type II; **Plate XIII, 15**), at first sight, seems to continue one of Eadwig, a mint-signature being added to the

The Reform of the English Coinage under Eadgar

'Two-line' type, but in the publication of the Smarmore hoard it has already been pointed out that this 'Three-line' variety, the issue of which was confined to the Chester area, belongs comparatively late in the reign. Prosopographically it is tied very closely to the 'Reform' coinage of the end of the reign, and in the republication of the Dalkey hoard the suggestion will be made that the two types may in fact be parallel issues, the 'Three-line' type (of which no specimen seems ever to have been found in England) being a 'trade dollar' intended for dealings with the Ostmen.

It would be difficult to attach too much weight to the paucity of 'Portrait' coins of Eadgar in hoards from Ireland, the Isle of Man, and Scotland. There were apparently none at all in those from Andreas, Burray, Burt, Dungarvan, Glendalough, Inchkenneth, Killincoole, Mackrie, Quendale, Smarmore, and Tarbat, and odd examples only in the major finds from Douglas, Iona, and Tiree, the substantial finds from Dalkey, Derrykeighan, and Co. Kilkenny, and the smaller hoards from Lough Lene and Co. Meath. It is curious, too, that the one 'Reform' coin of Eadgar found in this area is from the same mint and by the same moneyer as the one 'First Small Cross' coin of Æthelræd II, while 'Portrait' coins of Edward the Martyr seem to be completely wanting.

If portrait and non-portrait types were issued concurrently in different parts of the country at the end of Eadgar's reign, one may wonder whether the same was no less true of the beginning of his reign as well, and whether the 'Early Portrait' or 'Bust' type, struck mainly in East Anglia, and the 'Two-line' type, probably not struck in East Anglia, may not have been issued concurrently, even if the periods of their emission did not exactly coincide. Without wishing to commit ourselves to a firm chronology for the coinage of Eadgar's reign, we suggest very provisionally that one can envisage its division into three periods, and the attribution of the five substantive types among them in the way shown in Table 4.

The strikingly unequal, and unexpected, distribution of the hoards is illustrated by the map at Figure I, in which different symbols are used to show the size and date of deposit of the hoards. Fewer than a quarter of the twenty-eight hoards come from England, and all of those that do are from the northern part of the country, three being from a single place. It should not be a matter for surprise, therefore, that the British hoards give a distorted view of Eadgar's coinage. An examination of the very few single-finds of coins of Eadgar from southern England goes some way to show that the hoards are indeed far from typical of the currency of England. Mrs J. S. Martin has been good enough to put at our disposal her notes, which include mention of only four find-spots on

Anglo-Saxon Coins

TABLE 4

Diagram to show the suggested attribution of Eadgar's five substantive issues.

959

'EARLY PORTRAIT' TYPE
BMC type V
(Pl. XIII, 5–7)
 	
(i) East Anglia (Pl. XIII, 5)
   (*sole type*)
(ii) S.E. England (Pl. XIII, 6)
(iii) S.W. England (Pl. XIII, 7)
	'TWO-LINE' TYPE
	BMC type I
	(Pl. XIII, 1–4)
	(i) York – *very thick lettering* (Pl. XIII, 1)
	(ii) N.E. England – *thick lettering* (Pl. XIII, 2)
	(iii) Southern England – *neat small lettering*
	   (Pl. XIII, 3)
	(iv) N.W. England – *rosettes* (Pl. XIII, 4)
	
	'CIRCULAR' TYPE
	BMC types III and IV
	(Pl. XIII, 8–13)
	(i) N.W. England (Pl. XIII, 8, 9)
	(ii) N.E. England (Pl. XIII, 10)
	(iii) S.W. England (Pl. XIII, 11)
	(iv) S.E. England (Pl. XIII, 12)
	(v) Midlands (Pl. XIII, 13)

'REFORM' (PORTRAIT) TYPE BMC type VI (Pl. XIII, 15)	'THREE-LINE' TYPE BMC type II (Pl. XIII, 14) *Chester area only*

973

975

or south of the line of the Thames. A coin of Eadgar was found at Southampton in the course of excavations in the nineteenth century, but further information is completely lacking. There is an eighteenth-century engraving of another coin, found at Salisbury; it is a penny of the 'Early Portrait' or 'Bust' type (*BMC* type V) by the London moneyer Æthered. The British Museum has two coins with provenances which can be added to the brief list: a 'Circular' (*BMC* type III) type penny was found at Lympne (moneyer Burhstan but mint uncertain) and an 'Early Portrait' or 'Bust' coin is thought to have been found in London (*London*, Ælfnoth). Also from London came the now disintegrated round halfpenny of Winchester. It is only when we reach Northampton that we find a *BMC* type I penny of 'Mania' – presumably one of the 'York' coins of

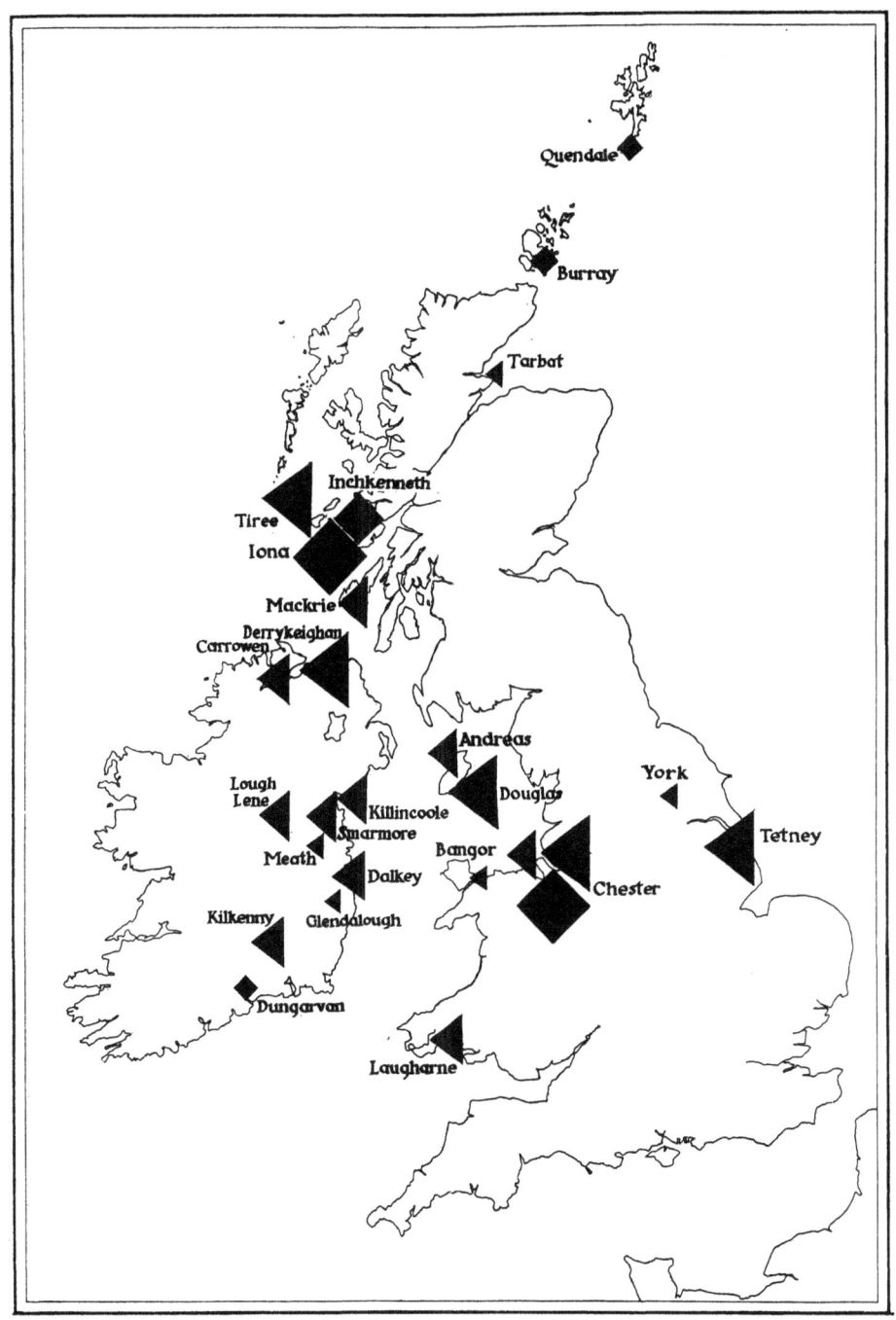

FIGURE 1. *Map of hoards from the British Isles containing coins of Eadgar. (The symbols are of two shapes and three sizes: triangles mark hoards terminating with coins of Eadgar, diamonds, those which are later; large symbols mark hoards with over one hundred and twenty Anglo-Saxon pennies, medium symbols, twenty to one hundred and twenty, small symbols, fewer than twenty.)*

Man(n)a(n). In short, coins of *BMC* types III and V alone have been recorded from southern England, whereas if the hoards from the British Isles reflected the coinage struck throughout the country, our single-finds ought all, or very nearly all, by the laws of probability, to have been of *BMC* type I. Although there are far too few southern finds as yet recorded for one to be quite certain, it looks as though 'northern' types may have been as scarce in the currency of southern England as portrait coins undoubtedly were in the currency of the north and west.[16] The obvious barrier to penetration into southern England by 'northern' coins would be local self-sufficiency, itself a pointer to a considerable output from the mints: *BMC* types III and V may well have been struck in southern England on a scale comparable with the output of *BMC* type I in northern England, and the two classes of coin may have remained largely separate in their circulation areas. Only a hoard from southern England could prove the validity of this suggestion. The absence of such a find may indicate that Eadgar's *frith* was so absolute that there were few occasions during his reign when hoards were concealed in emergency and never recovered.

It was only with the introduction of *BMC* type VI, the 'Reform' type, that a mint-signature became the rule on Eadgar's coins, and only for the last years of his reign, therefore, that one can draw up a list of the mints in operation, in the assurance that it is as complete as the run of coins of the type that have survived. Table 5 shows forty such mints, as compared with no more than twenty-three for the rest of Eadgar's reign.[17] All the earlier mints are present in the list of those working after 973, so that there are seventeen new mint-signatures, three-quarters as many again, among the coins of the 'Reform' type. The figures of twenty-three and forty, however, by no means tell the whole truth about the mints in Eadgar's reign, since important additions need to be made to each total. To begin with, some of the unsigned coins from the years before 973 may have been struck at mints not in the shorter list; one notes that in Æthelstan's reign ten further mints (Dover, Gloucester, Hereford, Leicester, Lewes, Norwich, Rochester, Stafford, Wareham, Warwick) had struck signed coins, and since all ten were active again after 973, they may well have struck, albeit sporadically, in the intervening period. The Tetney hoard provides a sufficient basis on which to argue that at least one major mint, presumably Lincoln itself, was operating in Lincolnshire, and a study of moneyers' names and of provincial styles makes it seem likely that Stamford as well was striking by 960 if not earlier.[18] Thus, Cambridge, Ilchester, Ipswich, Lympne, and Winchcombe would appear on the evidence so far to be the only places where entirely new mints were set up in 973.

The Reform of the English Coinage under Eadgar

TABLE 5

List of mint-signatures from the reign of Eadgar, before and after 973 (including names still to be identified).

Before 973	After 973	Before 973	After 973
Bath	Bath	Oxford	Oxford
Bedford	Bedford		Rochester
	Cambridge	Shaftesbury	Shaftesbury
Canterbury	Canterbury	Shrewsbury	Shrewsbury
Chester	Chester	Southampton	Southampton
Chichester	Chichester		Stafford
Derby	Derby		Stamford
	Dover	Tamworth	Tamworth
Exeter	Exeter	Thetford	Thetford
	Gloucester	Totnes	Totnes
	Hereford	Wallingford	Wallingford
Hertford	Hertford		Wareham
Huntingdon	Huntingdon		Warwick
	Ilchester	Wilton	Wilton
	Ipswich		Winchcombe
	Leicester	Winchester	Winchester
	Lewes	York	York
	Lincoln		
London	London	DARENT	
	Lympne	MI	
Malmesbury	Malmesbury	NIWANPO	NIWU ?
Northampton	Northampton	WEARDBYRH	
	Norwich		

The number of coins of the earlier types which have survived is probably sufficient for one to suppose that they represent virtually all the mints which were in operation. For the 'Reform' coinage, on the other hand, this is an assumption which it would be very unwise to make. The survival rate for the type has been so low that there are perhaps no more than two or three hundred specimens in cabinets today.[19] When allowance is made for the proportion of these which come from the more active mints, the number of coins now in existence from most of the 'scarce' mints is small indeed. Bearing in mind the additions to the list of forty mints that can be made by including those which are known to have begun operation only a few years later than 973, the chances of at least one coin of every mint having survived and being among the couple of hundred or so pieces now known are poor, and it seems easily possible that even one quite small hoard of the 'Reform' type discovered in southern England would enable significant additions to be made to the list of Eadgar's mints.

The progressively more plentiful coinage of the last twenty-five years of the tenth century includes issues from no fewer than thirty mints not on the list of those known for Eadgar's 'Reform' coinage. These thirty places (of which three or four had mints before the time of Eadgar) are the ones from among which any such additions are likely to be made. One may expect that in this way the origin of quite a few more mints will eventually be put back to the date of the reform. It is necessary, therefore, to look at the additions which complete the tally of mints as it was at the end of the tenth century. Within a decade of 973 we have coins from Barnstaple, (?) Bridgnorth, Bridport, Buckingham, Caistor, Cricklade, Guildford, Horncastle, Launceston, (?) Louth, Lydford, Maldon, Nottingham, Peterborough, Torksey, Warminster, Watchet, and Worcester. 'Pre-Eadgar' coins are known from Barnstaple and Nottingham, and more doubtfully from Maldon, and there is documentary evidence that the extraordinary privilege of a mint had been conceded to the Abbot of Peterborough before 973. By the year 1000 the list of 'new' mints has again been substantially increased with the accession of Axbridge, Aylesbury, Bruton, Colchester, Crewkerne, Dorchester,[20] GOTHABYRH (= Castle Gotha, Cornwall?), Hastings, Milborne Port, Romney, Southwark, and Sudbury. Excepting 'Gothabyrh', which seems to have been a replacement for Launceston, all the additions seem to represent entirely new mints.

The history of mint-organization in the eleventh century presents a contrast with the sudden and considerable increase in numbers which can be traced to the few years after 973. For half a century there were very few changes, and only in the reign of Edward the Confessor, when nine more small mints were authorized, is there anything which can be construed as a definite move to increase the number of the English mints. Thereafter the total declined. It may be worth while to review briefly the position as regards the rest of the Anglo-Saxon period. Late in the reign of Æthelræd II 'emergency' mints sprang up at Cadbury (replacing Bruton, Crewkerne, and Ilchester),[21] Cissbury,[22] and Salisbury, but only the last achieved permanence. At about the same time or a little later Bristol and Taunton began striking, and there was a resumption of activity at two mints, Langport and Newark,[23] which had been active in the tenth century. Long before this Horncastle and Caistor had ceased striking – at the same time, apparently, as work at Lincoln and York had been suspended for the duration of the 'Second Hand' type[24] – so that one wonders what this may not reflect. Towards the end of Cnut's reign are first found coins which can be attributed to Steyning, perhaps the successor of Cissbury, which in turn may ultimately have derived its status from the apparently abandoned burgh at Burpham, and there are other coins from a puzzling mint at FRO, which could be Frome in Somerset.[25] Finally, under Edward the Confessor, there is a new crop of little mints at places which are mostly of no real importance, Bedwyn,

The Reform of the English Coinage under Eadgar

Berkeley, Bury St Edmunds, Horndon, Hythe, Pershore, Petherton, Reading, and Sandwich. The reasons for this sudden burst of activity are obscure, and the coins from many of the mints concerned are extremely rare. From Reading, for example, only one, and from Berkeley no more than three coins are known.[26] It may be that the coming of more peaceful days gave an opportunity to attend to local affairs which had been denied during the troubled reign of Æthelræd II.

It is a matter of fact that something between twenty-five and say thirty-five mints had been at work in the years before Eadgar's reform, and that by the end of the tenth century their number had been increased to seventy. It is a view for which good support can be found that the mints in operation directly after 973 probably numbered more than the forty which are at present known. It is an interpretation, the correctness of which the reader must judge for himself – but some explanation of the facts is most certainly called for – to say that, even though the plan may not have been fully implemented at once, the establishment of new mints was conceived as an integral part of the reform of 973, and that the surprising increase in their already large number, together with certain details about their geographical distribution, and about the history of the 'new' mints, throw no little light on the scheme which lay behind their creation.

After the time of Stephen the number of the English mints was never greater than sixteen, and as few at times as four were able to issue the currency of the thirteenth and fourteenth centuries. By comparison, seventy mints, or even forty, must be seen as a total far in excess of what was needed simply to strike the coinage, and one must suppose that the government had some good reason for multiplying its mints so extravagantly. It has generally been accepted that a mint was one of the marks of a borough, and, with the reservation that a substantially complete list of the mints at work at any particular date in the tenth or eleventh century can be compiled, whereas a correspondingly reliable list of boroughs cannot be given, we would agree that the two lists were very largely the same at the end of the Anglo-Saxon period, and that it is probable that they were largely the same from about the year 1000 onwards. There are, however, a few mints which seem never to have been boroughs, and, perhaps more important, boroughs where coins seem never to have been struck. Some of the implications of this state of affairs have been discussed already in this volume,[27] and we accordingly leave the topic, claiming simply that it is going beyond and indeed contrary to the evidence to accept the 'Grately Decree' of Æthelstan as applicable to the whole country and to the whole of the late Anglo-Saxon period. We would suggest that when a place had both burghal status and a mint, the real connexion is that many of the same considerations governed the establishment and geographical distribution of each. If the coins show anything, it is that under Eadgar there was a new régime, and that practical considerations once more prevailed over tradition and sentiment. Æthelræd's insistence in his *Laws* that his coins should be struck only in a town could in itself be used as an argument that mints had been operating in places which were not towns, and had been doing so with the royal *fiat* implicit in the supply from a central source of the necessary dies. Even if it were demonstrably true, then, which it is not, to say that every borough always had a mint, the significant question would still need an answer: Why were there so many mints?

The 'new' mints of the years after Eadgar's reform were created, we submit, not to compete with but to supplement the work of the mints already at the disposal of the English Crown; it is significant that not one of them attained an importance comparable with that enjoyed by the first dozen or so among the mints previously in existence. This could of course suggest no more than that vested interests and tradition were too strong to be overcome, but if this had been the case one might expect many of the newly created mints to have withered away. A few did in fact fail to achieve real permanency – for example, Launceston – but the majority exhibit a remarkable persistence, even though they can hardly have been an economic proposition. Often, too, when a mint disappears, one notices a new creation in the immediate vicinity – for example, Castle Gotha seems to have taken over the work of the Launceston mint during a period of some forty years.[28] Often, again, one may suspect that particular mints are only seemingly dormant because of the accident of discovery. An instance is provided by Bruton, a mint which in the reign of Cnut is quite well attested by coins from Swedish, Danish, Norwegian, and English hoards. On the evidence from such standard works as Hildebrand's *Anglosachsiska Mynt* and the *British Museum Catalogue* it had no prior existence, and a few years ago one of the present writers suggested that the mint may have been founded when the emergency mint at Cadbury was closed at the very beginning of Cnut's reign.[29] In Bergen, however, there is a unique but quite unimpeachable penny of Æthelræd II which shows that there was a mint at Bruton a whole decade before the Cadbury mint was even established, let alone dismantled.[30]

The geographical distribution of mints in late Anglo-Saxon times affords very clear evidence of the monetary policy of the English Crown, for they occur so regularly throughout the country that their establishment cannot have been other than systematic. Our claim is that a network of mints was part of the plan of the reform of 973, and that it was the intention that men should not have to travel an unreasonable distance in order to reach a mint. Many of the smaller 'new' mints seem to have been designed to fill gaps in the network, and their

The Reform of the English Coinage under Eadgar

failure to achieve any importance is understandable when it is seen that they were established not to meet a real economic need but to implement a policy. The facts are graphically represented on the map at Figure III. It shows all the mints which have been identified with any degree of certainty as working in the period 973–1066. Around each place where there was a mint a circle has been drawn with a radius of fifteen miles, marking out the area within which it might be expected that a man could walk to the mint and back again in a day, without being put to the trouble and expense of seeking a night's lodging. Even if we have not hit upon the legally enacted distance (supposing that the administration had a particular figure in mind), the fifteen-mile radius is still adequate for the purposes of the argument, and it will be seen that there are remarkably few areas within the English kingdom which were unreasonably distant from a mint. Without attempting a detailed analysis of the map, one may point to the coasts of Norfolk and the Fens as the largest 'blank' area, and to the Weald as the clearest illustration of the absence of mints in a thinly populated region. There are other blanks on the map which coincide with inhospitable areas, such as, for example, Exmoor. Also to be remarked is the way in which a chain of (mostly small) mints stretches all the way from Ipswich to Totnes, so that no one could have pleaded the remoteness of a mint in exculpation of a charge of having brought into the country the foreign coin which from the time of Æthelstan at least had been forbidden to circulate; there seems in the Anglo-Saxon period to have been no division between a *cambium* and a mint, a single institution serving both purposes, and one may well recall that barely a dozen continental coins from the tenth and eleventh centuries are known to have been found in England south of a line from the Mersey to the Humber. Very possibly, too, the mint at Bristol, apparently not established until after the battle of Clontarf, was meant to block a potential loophole when the Ostmen of Dublin and Waterford were driven by military adversity to concentrate on the commercial side of their activities. In the same way, the absence of mints from the Lincolnshire and Norfolk coasts may have been because they were the natural landfall for Viking raiders and were so unsafe that any trader who came that way found none to do business with him until he had sailed up the rivers to the well-fortified ports at York, Lincoln, or Norwich.

There is a remarkable concentration of minor mints in and around Somerset. A full explanation of their number would have to take into account the history of the region from the ninth century at latest,[31] but one possibility is that when the West Saxon king was no longer able to spend the greater part of the year on the old royal 'demesne', there arose a small but constant need for coin for the commutation of food-rents.

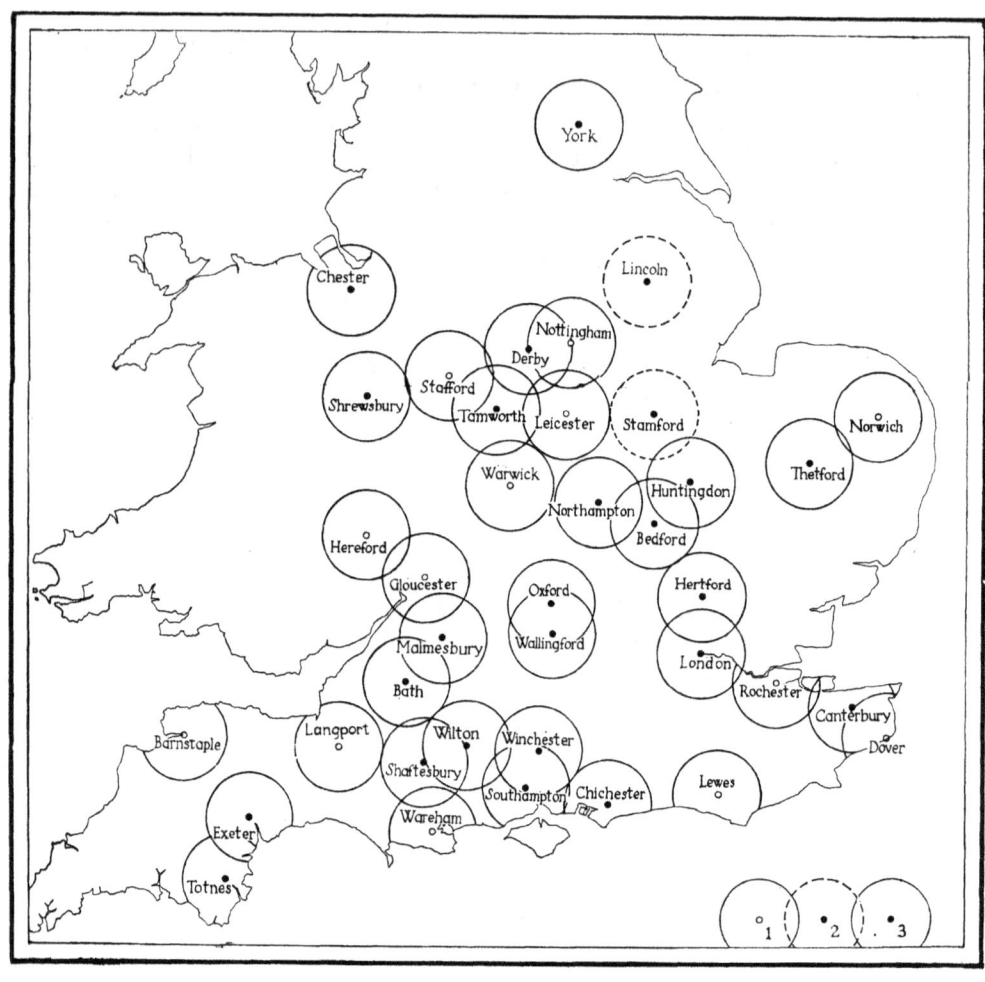

FIGURE 11. *Map of mints at work in the years before 973. The symbols indicate: 1, mints not known for Eadgar before 973, but known for Æthelstan or successors; 2, mints believed to have been in operation under Eadgar, but from which no early signed coins of his are known; 3, mints of Eadgar (BMC types I–V). The circles are of fifteen-mile radius.*

FIGURE III. *Map of mints at work in the years after 973. The symbols indicate: 4, mints of Eadgar (BMC type VI); 5, mints from which coins are known from the following years, and which may be suspected to have been at work under Eadgar; 6, mints established later than the reform, by way of* (a) *additions,* (b) *changes. The circles are of fifteen-mile radius.*

For comparison, a second map has been drawn (Figure II), using the same fifteen-mile radius for circles around mints which were in operation before Eadgar's reform. It shows that there were considerably more areas, not all of which can be supposed to have been desolate, where the nearest mint was more than fifteen miles away. If with only these mints at work an attempt had been made to implement a major recoinage, there would have been many who would have suffered considerable inconvenience, not to say hardship, when they were required to exchange their old coin. Since, too, the intention seems to have been from the first that the recoinage of 973 was to be followed by others at regular intervals, the recurrent inconvenience could not but have hardened justifiable resentment against the new programme, and might have caused its breakdown. On practical grounds a government which wishes to reform the coinage needs to convince the great majority of its subjects that the new measures are equitable, and the type of reform that Eadgar contemplated was one that certainly would not have worked if there had been widespread opposition. The success with which the system was introduced was such that, as appears elsewhere in this volume, by the time that a quarter of a century had elapsed, the regular change of type was so accepted a feature of English life that a homilist could touch on it as something that simple congregations would comprehend readily.[32]

As far as can be established at the present, it was originally envisaged that change of type should take place every sixth year. Later, in the reign of Edward the Confessor, the interval was halved, and the system continued to work, with some modification, until the reign of Stephen. In a paper of this kind it is not possible to set out all the evidence, but it may be as well briefly to indicate the principal lines of argument that are available. On the basis of the Scandinavian hoards, for example, it is possible to show that Æthelræd II, who reigned for just over thirty-seven years, struck six substantive issues, while Cnut, who reigned for just over nineteen years, struck three. On this telling, and on the assumption that each type had the same duration, each issue should have lasted six or seven years. The latter figure is superficially the more attractive, but presents almost insuperable difficulties when one tries to fit in seven substantive issues between the last year or so of Eadgar's reign and the accession of Cnut. If, however, we adopt the year 973 as our point of departure – remembering the date of Eadgar's solemn and long-delayed coronation[33] – and postulate a sexennial cycle, there are some remarkable coincidences between change of type and well-attested historical events, of which five examples may be given. First, the 'Small Cross' type introduced by Eadgar should have given way to the 'First Hand' type in the course of 979. It was in the winter of 979–80 that Cheshire was

The Reform of the English Coinage under Eadgar

ravaged,[34] and the 1914 Chester hoard in fact contains a majority of coins of the earlier issue which was in process of withdrawal, together with a proportion of the new coins; the first change of type cannot, therefore, have been as long as seven years after any date in 973. Secondly, the 'First Hand' type should in the same way have begun to be withdrawn at some time in 985, and by 986 the 'Second Hand' issue should have been in general circulation. In 986 Iona was sacked,[35] and there is a hoard from that island in which, very obviously, a handful of current coin has been added to a family treasure of a decade earlier. The new element is composed of 'First Hand' and 'Second Hand' coins. Thirdly, in 991, the decision was taken to pay Danegeld on a national scale; the '*Crux*' type, introduced, on this reckoning, at some date in 991, is nearly four times as common in Hildebrand's Catalogue as the 'Second Hand' type, and there is reason to think that the proportion in which the two types occur in the Scandinavian hoards is really of the order of five to one at the very least. Fourthly, 'Long Cross' coins of Æthelræd II are known from Wilton, but not from Salisbury, while coins of the succeeding 'Helmet' type by the same moneyers are known from Salisbury but not from Wilton.[36] It is clear, therefore, that the transition from 'Long Cross' to 'Helmet' must have coincided with the closing of the Wilton mint and the foundation of that at Salisbury. By referring to the *Anglo-Saxon Chronicle*, one finds that it was in 1003 that Wilton was burnt by a Viking force which 'then went to Salisbury' (but presumably did not devastate that place too) 'and from there back to the sea'. Here is the obvious historical occasion for the transfer of the mint, and a sexennial cycle calculated from 973 in fact makes the 'Helmet' type succeed the 'Long Cross' type in 1003. Fifthly, a change of type at some date in 1009 allows us to associate the decision not to proceed with the '*Agnus Dei*' issue, and to reduce almost immediately the weight standard originally chosen for the 'Last Small Cross' type, with the apparently unlooked-for arrival of the army under Thorkell the Tall.[37]

Finally, we may note how one piece of evidence which appears to be inconsistent with the scheme can be made to fall satisfactorily into place, and can point in the process to some interesting conclusions which are to be drawn from the varying weight standards of the sexennial penny. In 1863 there was discovered in the Butter Market at Ipswich a large hoard of 'First Hand' pennies of Æthelræd II. They seem to have been associated with a layer of burning, and one is tempted to assume that the occasion of their loss was the Viking attack of 991. This may be a dangerous assumption to make, as fires were not very uncommon among the wooden buildings of tenth-century towns; it is not beyond the bounds of possibility that the Butter Market area of Ipswich had been the scene of a fire several years earlier which was quite unconnected with the attack by the victors of Maldon. Accepting the view, however, that the coins were lost in 991, we can still suggest a reason for the coins being of a type which was withdrawn in 985. In that year the 'First Hand' coins were replaced by the appreciably lighter 'Second Hand' issue, and this was the first time under the new system that a 'heavy' type had been followed by a 'light' one.[38] It is not difficult to imagine that some at least of the population were left unconvinced of the desirability of changing their money on such terms: a merchant may have decided to retain his obsolete coin, which would have a greater bullion value than the new, as the most attractive form of savings that was available to him. The raising of the weight of the penny to 27 grains in 997 and again in 1009 may have been intended to draw back into circulation bullion that was being hoarded in this way.

Within no more than the duration of two sexennial types, the government of Anglo-Saxon England is seen to have not only grasped but implemented the idea that the weight of the coinage could be manipulated as a matter of monetary policy. The clearest example of this policy is the withdrawal, already referred to, of the '*Agnus Dei*' type in the summer of 1009, and the hasty reduction in the weight standard of the 'Last Small Cross' type. The main concern of the government during much of the period under review was probably to maintain a plentiful currency so as to facilitate taxation, and the way in which a reduction in the weight of the penny would contribute to this end is somewhat as follows. The English economy was predominantly agrarian and local in character, and one of the chief uses of coinage by the ordinary man was probably for the payment of rents and taxes. As long as the assessment of these was not adjusted in accordance with the weight of the penny, and as long as the government would accept light coin at its face value when the type was changed, the ordinary man probably cared little if his penny in one year weighed only three-quarters of what it had weighed the year before, and the monetary system accordingly tended to be anchored against inflation. The merchant trading on the Continent, on the other hand, would care very much, since to him the value of the penny would be closely related to its weight; abroad, he would have to pay more pennies for the goods that he bought, while he should have been able to sell the commodities that he was exporting more advantageously. In other words, by devaluing the penny in relation to its continental (i.e. bullion) rate, the government was able to discourage imports, encourage exports, and thereby improve the balance of trade and cause silver to flow into the country. A reduction in the weight of the penny would also, of course, allow the number of coins in circulation to be increased. It was thus that England was able to sustain the burdens of the Danegeld and the Heregeld; the abolition of the latter

The Reform of the English Coinage under Eadgar

impost coincides with a dramatic shrinkage in the numbers of English pence that found their way to Scandinavia, and with a major increase in the weight of the penny.[39] The weight standards of medieval coins as a rule were reduced far more frequently than they were raised, and its says much for the government of the country, and for the flourishing condition of its economy, that such a step, with its less obvious advantages, should more than once have been taken.

An attempt at such elaborate control of the coinage was almost unprecedented in a medieval State: one would probably have to look as far as the Byzantine Empire to find a more complex monetary policy. We must not forget, however, that the stage had been set long before Eadgar began his great reform. The necessary powers were already gathered into his hands, for he held a close control both over the sources of silver and the production of coin. In the first place, foreign coin was forbidden to circulate, and was not allowed to penetrate beyond the seaport *cambia*, where it came into the possession of the king's officers. Royal mining rights are too well known to need more than a mention here; it was the military strength of the English king that secured from the Welsh the more or less disguised tributes which must have supplemented very handsomely the production of the mines in Cornwall, Devon, Somerset, and Derbyshire. Again, it seems clear that the Crown already enjoyed rights of Treasure Trove.[40] Private persons, therefore, had little chance of acquiring any quantity of silver to jeopardize the royal monopoly, and the fact that the Anglo-Saxon penny appears to have been overvalued would have deterred individuals from melting down coin, even if they could have found means of reconverting it back into currency at some favourable opportunity. Secondly, the Crown regulated the production of coin very closely indeed. Moneyers were appointed by the Crown; they were dependent for their dies on a strictly controlled die-cutting agency, and each man's name was stamped on his work. The reality of the king's hold over the coinage is shown, even more clearly than by legislation seeking to limit the number of moneyers and the places where they might work, by the fact that we have not a single coin with the name of Eadmund Ironside. Until the king ordained it, no die-engraver dared so much as to substitute the name of the new sovereign, still less to vary the type of the coin. Finally, the king could exercise a considerable degree of control over the use of coinage, for all transactions except the most trifling had to be conducted within *port* in the presence of official witnesses, and the reeve no doubt kept his eyes open at times when appreciable sums of money were changing hands.[41]

It remains to be argued that Roger of Wendover was in error when he wrote that the purpose of Eadgar's recoinage was the remedy of abuse. One has only to examine major hoards, such as the 1950 find from Chester or that from

Tetney, neither of which can have been deposited more than a year or so before 973, to see that the English coinage was in a satisfactory condition. There may have been malpractice here and there, but it was of little general importance; the English penny circulated freely, and it was certainly neither debased nor clipped. Stray finds, for what they are worth, tell the same story. It is scarcely conceivable, therefore, that Eadgar should have gone to the great trouble of initiating a recoinage merely to end the trivial depredations of petty malefactors, and here, too, is a hint as to the nature of the scheme. Eadgar, very conscious that he was the great-grandson of King Ælfred, was consciously looking back into the past: before the crisis of Athelney, Wessex had had a monetary policy of regular recoinage. Certain of the designs of Eadgar's earlier coins show him already seeking inspiration in the glories of the past; the halfpenny of London (**Plate XIV, 16**), for example, is directly copied from some of the most impressive coins of his great-grandfather (**Plate IX, 7, 8** and **18**).[42] In 973 the reformed coinage of the third quarter of the ninth century was beyond living memory, but there were men – for example, Archbishop Dunstan himself – who had been intimate with the elder statesmen of the West Saxon Kingdom, who, in turn, would have heard tell of the abandonment of the old system under the pressure of the Danish onslaught. As early as the time of Æthelwulf the beginnings of the policy can be seen; that it conferred advantages seems to be indicated by Mercia's joining with Wessex in a kind of monetary convention.[43] The continuance of this common coinage under Ælfred and Ceolwulf II, at least as late as 875, again suggests that there were advantages in the system of a regular type-sequence, and chief among them must have been the possibility of effective control of the currency.

In the course of this paper it has been claimed that the essence of the reform of 973 was the introduction of a system by which the English coinage was regularly called in and reissued. Far reaching as this may be, there is the strongest evidence not only that the system was introduced, but that it worked successfully for many years. That evidence lies in the composition of the many hoards of the period which have been found. Those containing Anglo-Saxon pence struck between 973 and 1066, and deposited between c. 975 and c. 1075, total no fewer than fifty-four; of this number, thirty-three are from territory under the effective control of the late Anglo-Saxon monarchy (see the lists in Appendix B). At least fifteen of them are composed substantially of coins of a single issue,[44] and a further seven seem to be made up of no more than two successive issues.[45] Rather more than two-thirds of the English hoards, in other words, are consistent with the proposition that under the reform of Eadgar each new type was virtually a recoinage. No less significant is the circumstance

The Reform of the English Coinage under Eadgar

that until the reign of Edward the Confessor, some seventy years later, none of the English hoards contain more than two types in any appreciable quantity. Even then, single-type hoards continue to occur in numbers which must confirm the impression that one type only was meant to be current at any particular time – although of course there must have been a moratorium at the beginning of a new type's currency when the old money was still legal tender.

The twenty-one hoards deposited in territory where the English king's writ did not run afford corroboration of these inferences. In the north and west there was, naturally, nothing to prevent old money being used and hoarded according to individual preference, but even so there are nine finds where English coins of no more than one type are present. Particularly impressive are the major hoards composed predominantly of English coins from Halton Moor and Caldale. It is instructive, too, to examine the eight hoards which do not conform to the pattern. Only one, that from Iona, contains more than one hundred and twenty English coins, and among them there are no more than a handful of 'Reform' pennies.[46] In the Dunbrody hoard, English coins made up only a very small proportion of a vast treasure. The remaining six hoards each contained fewer than a hundred coins, and in all of them the 'Reform' element is insignificant. The figures can best be studied from Table 6.

TABLE 6

Analysis by composition and size of the hoards from the British Isles, containing examples of the 'Reform' coinage of 973–1066, and deposited *c.* 975–*c.* 1075.

	Before 1017				1017–42				1042–66			Totals
	A	B	C	Total	A	B	C	Total	A	B	C	
'One-type' hoards: from 'England'	1	3	3	7	1	–	–	1	3	2	2	7	15
from the rest of the British Isles	2	·2	1	5	2	1	1	4	–	–	–		9
'Two-type' hoards: from 'England'	2·	1	–	3	–	2	–	2	1	–	1	2	7
from the rest of the British Isles	–	1	–	1	–	–	–	–	–	–	–		1
'Multiple-type' hoards: from 'England'	–	–	–	–	–	–	–	–	8	3	–	11	11
from the rest of the British Isles	1	–	5	6	–	–	–	–	–	2	–	2	8
Totals	6	7	9	22	3	3	1	7	12	7	3	22	51

A Hoards with more than one hundred and twenty coins.
B Hoards with thirty to one hundred and twenty.
C Hoards with less than thirty coins.

Anglo-Saxon Coins

The pronounced tendency for hoards of the period 1042–66 to be 'multiple-type' is perhaps a sign that a breakdown was threatening the system of regular renewal of the coinage, and may also reflect a decline in public morality of which there is evidence in other aspects of English life. The late Anglo-Saxon hoards need to be considered in the light of those from the years after the Norman Conquest, for there is a tendency after 1066 to revert to hoards consisting of only one or two types. The improvement may in part have resulted from an effort towards more efficient administration under the new rule, but its main cause may well have been the decision to 'peg' the weight of the penny at 22.5 grains or thereabouts in an attempt to suppress speculative hoarding, perhaps by individuals who saw the way to personal profit in the increased connexions between England and the Continent. One must be careful, however, not to read too much into the evidence as it stands: the Sedlescombe hoard omits the issue current at the presumed time of its concealment, and should perhaps be considered not as the deposit of a private person but as part of the bullion reserve of the Hastings mint, hastily carried inland and concealed at the approach of the Norman army; nor can we be certain that the great treasures from Chancton and Walbrook were not likewise official bullion.

In conclusion, we suggest that a substantially greater value was placed on the penny, throughout the late Anglo-Saxon period, than on the silver it contained. A sufficient illustration of the small importance that was attached to the weight of individual coins is provided by a hoard concealed early in 1066 at Harewood which contained coins of one type not merely struck on two different weight-standards, but obviously so struck.[47] It is suggestive, too, of quite substantial overvaluation of coin in the world of the northern seas that two of the first Scandinavian coinages, those of Sihtric Silkbeard at Dublin and of Olaf Skotkonung at Sigtuna, began with imitations of pennies of Æthelræd's '*Crux*' type which weigh appreciably more than their prototypes.

KEY TO THE PLATES

On **Plate XIII** are illustrated the principal regional varieties of the five substantive issues of Eadgar. In the top row are set representative examples of four regional varieties clearly discernible in *BMC* type I, indisputably the first type of the reign, though perhaps persisting parallel with *BMC* types III and V until the great reform of 973. No. 1 is a coin from the area of York with thick coarse lettering, and no. 2 a coin from the area of Lincoln. Pennies of both styles are extremely common, whereas coins with the small, neat lettering found on no. 3 are of very rare occurrence indeed. Presumably they are from southern England. No. 4 is a penny from north-western England, but it should be observed that there are two distinct styles of lettering found

The Reform of the English Coinage under Eadgar

in this area, the other being coarser (cf. **Plate XIV, 4**). Coins of both groupings are relatively common. A mint-signature is virtually never found.

The coins in the second row are the generally scarce pre-'Reform' 'Portrait' coins where the bust breaks the obverse legend. No. 5 is typical of East Anglia, no. 6 of south-eastern England, and no. 7 of south-western England. Examples of the first grouping are relatively common; of the second, not rare; but of the third quite exceptional. Mention should also be made of a few anomalous coins of cruder style which have still to be associated with a particular area. Mint-signatures are found on about fifty per cent of the extant coins.

The coins in the third row represent the principal regional styles so far established in the case of *BMC* types III and IV, and seem to reflect reasonably faithfully the 'Non-portrait' coinage of the middle years of Eadgar's reign. Nos. 8 and 9 are from north-western England, the 'Rosette' coins being much the more common. A mint-signature is sometimes found on either obverse or reverse. No. 10 is a typical and relatively common coin from north-eastern England. Here a mint-signature is quite exceptional and confined to the obverse. Nos. 11, 12, and 13 are examples of the much rarer coins from southern England, and are typical of the products of the West Country, of the area south of the Thames, and of the Midlands respectively. It will be noticed that in each case the obverse legend attempts the ethnic ANGLORUM, while the reverse normally essays a mint-signature, a pointer to the place of this issue between the 'Two-line' type and the 'Reform' coins of 973. The weights also differentiate the majority of these coins from those of *BMC* types I and V.

In the bottom row, no. 14 is one of the 'trade coins' struck in the north-west – and almost exclusively at Chester – late in the reign. They may be considered rare. No. 15 is one of the 'Portrait' coins struck after the reform of 973. They are probably less common than is generally thought, and the great majority in British public collections are from two hoards. In Scandinavia one or two examples often occur as the earliest English coins in a large number of hoards from the tenth and eleventh and even the early twelfth centuries.

On **Plate XIV** are illustrated a number of varieties of the coins of Eadgar which, with one exception (no. 4), are extremely rare, and, with certain exceptions (nos. 11 and 13 to 17), of little direct historical significance. No. 1 is a variety known from a handful of coins by four moneyers which substitutes a pellet for each of the trefoils found on a normal reverse of *BMC* type I. It is noteworthy that the obverse legend includes the initial letters of the *Anglorum* ethnic, and this may suggest that the variety belongs fairly late in the currency of the type in question. A late date is likewise suggested by the inclusion of a coin of this variety among the four pre-973 coins of Eadgar recorded in the 1881 edition of Hildebrand – another of them (of *BMC* type III) also including in the royal style a contraction of the *Anglorum* ethnic. The lettering has southern affinities which are no less pronounced in the case of no. 2, an even rarer variety probably of slightly earlier date. Here the Crosses are replaced by Trefoils. A unique coin in the Smarmore find is illustrated as no. 3, and here the

Anglo-Saxon Coins

variety is constituted by the replacement of two of the three Crosses by Annulets. Nos. 4–8 are similar minor varieties from north-western England, and illustrate incidentally certain differences of lettering found in the case of coins from that area of 'Two-line' type generally. Coins corresponding to no. 4 are fairly common, being in fact little if any rarer than those of the grouping represented by no. 4 on **Plate XIV**. No. 5, on the other hand, is perhaps known from a single coin, and only two moneyers are believed to have struck no. 6. Only less rare are examples of no. 7, while no. 8 may well be unique. At this point mention should be made of a ninth variety of *BMC* type I which is believed to exist, although it has not been possible to trace the coin despite the co-operation of the auctioneers and coin-dealers concerned. In this case (cf. Rashleigh Sale, lot 280) the variety consists in the ornaments in the reverse field being arranged 'Rosette/Cross-Rosette-Cross/Rosette', the moneyer being Manin.

Not altogether surprisingly *BMC* types III and IV are found muled, though the coins are of the greatest rarity. No. 9 illustrates the combination of a *BMC* type III ('Small Cross') obverse with a *BMC* type IV reverse, and no. 10 that of a *BMC* type IV ('Rosette') obverse with a *BMC* type III reverse. What may be significant is that in neither case does a *BMC* type I obverse appear to have been used, though formally the distinction has to be made on style rather than on a purely objective criterion.

No. 11 is a very rare variety of the 'Early Portrait' with the 'Bust' contained within the inner circle. Two specimens only are known, one from the Douglas hoard, but the use of the ethnic suggests that we are faced with a transitional issue immediately prior to the reform of 973. The coins, only less rare, corresponding to no. 12 were promoted to the status of a variety in the *British Museum Catalogue*, but it is arguable whether in fact the addition of symbols in the reverse field of a coin strictly warrants its erection as a typological variant. Nos. 13 and 14, on the other hand, represent what may be thought a substantive issue contemplated but never put into official currency. Both coins are unique, and both are from Ostmannic hoards, no. 13 being from Iona and no. 14 from Douglas. The lettering suggests a comparatively late date, and it is possible that no. 14 may represent a recasting of the design to allow the inclusion of the initial letters at least of the new desirable *Anglorum* ethnic. Unfortunately the mint of no. 13 is enigmatic, and the name of the moneyer gives no clue to its place of origin. On balance, however, we would not exclude the possibility of its being Leicester – LIHA(R) being a well-attested if rare signature in the tenth and early eleventh centuries.

Nos. 15–17 must count as examples of Anglo-Saxon 'antiquarianism'. No. 15 is the restitution of a quite exceptionally rare coin of Eadwig. The inclusion of a rosette means that it is presumptively from north-western England. Two specimens, perhaps, are known. Only four round halfpennies of Eadgar have been recorded. Two hark back to types of Ælfred, the 'London' halfpenny (without name of moneyer) from the 1950 Chester hoard which can be shown to be copied from a coin in the unsold portion of the Lockett Collection (cf. *BNJ* XXVII ii (1953) p. 136) and a halfpenny

The Reform of the English Coinage under Eadgar

of Winchester (also without moneyer's name) which was found in London c. 1840 (ibid. p. 135). The former is here illustrated as no. 16, the latter having disintegrated in an age which had not evolved the new British Museum technique of mounting such friable rarities in perspex. Two other halfpennies imitate the 'Floral' type penny of Edward the Elder struck by the Shrewsbury moneyer Eofermund, the moneyers being Hildulf and Oswine. No. 17 shows the coin of the latter, and it will be noticed that the engraver has included in the design the last two letters of Eofermund's name, the semi-cursive letters flanking the stem of the 'flower' which on the prototype had overflowed from the line below. Unfortunately it is not possible to date the halfpennies more precisely within the bracket 959–73, but the evocation of the Ælfred types does make us wonder whether they may not perhaps have been struck quite consciously to mark the abandonment of a denomination – never popular – which had been initiated by the great-grandfather whose work of liberation and consolidation Eadgar can be said to have completed.

NOTE: All coins illustrated are in the British Museum with the exception of the following.

Plate XIV, 3 – National Museum of Ireland
9 – C. E. Blunt, Esq.
13 – National Museum of Antiquities, Edinburgh

The authors are also indebted to Mr Blunt for access to his unrivalled card-index of tenth-century pennies and to the typescript of his as yet unpublished check-list of Eadgar's types, mints, and moneyers.

POSTSCRIPT

MS material seen in the Royal Irish Academy suggests that there were also early coins of Eadgar in the hoards from Armagh (*Inventory* 13) and Ballitore (*Inventory* 29). Consequential emendations are necessary on pp. 138, 139, 143 and 162, but the argument is not affected.

Appendix A
LIST OF FINDS WHICH INCLUDE COINS OF EADGAR
(from the British Isles)

Date of discovery	Find-spot	Thompson 'Inventory' no.	Earlier Coins	I	V III,IV	II	VI	Later Coins
A. Hoards								
c. 1750	UNKNOWN SITE (North-east Midlands?)	–	–	–	–	–	+	+
1782	TIREE (Hebrides)	357	+	+	+	+	–	–
c. 1823 (?)	County *Kilkenny*, western part	207	+	+	+	+	–	–
c. 1830	Quendale (Shetland), Fitful Head, Dunrossness	144 & 161	+	+	–	–	–	+
c. 1830	*Inchkenneth* (Hebrides)	196	+	+	–	+	–	+
1835/6	Glendalough (Co. Wicklow)	174	+	+	–	+	+	–
1838 (?)	*Dalkey* (Dublin)	115	+	+	+	+	–	–
1843	DERRYKEIGHAN (Co. Antrim)	119	+	+	+	+	+	–
1844	*Lough Lene* (Co. Westmeath)	260	+	–	+	–	–	–
c. 1845	County Meath	–	+	?	+	?	–	–
1845/6	Bangor (Caernarvon), 'Senior Vicar's garden'	–	–	+	–	–	–	–
1850/2	*Mackrie* (Islay), Kidalton	201 & 202	+	+	–	+	–	–
1857	*Chester*, Eastgate Street	84	+	+	–	–	–	–
1862	*Unknown Site* (Ireland)	–	+	+	–	+	–	–
1864	Burt (Co. Donegal), Carrowen	75 & 261	?	+	–	+	–	–
1864	*Killincoole* (Louth)	212	+	+	?	?	–	–
1867	Andreas (Isle of Man), Churchyard	8	+	+	?	+	–	–
1889	Burray (Orkney)	61	+	+	–	–	–	+
1889	Tarbat (Ross), Churchyard	351	–	–	–	+	–	–
1894	DOUGLAS (Isle of Man), Ballaquayle	127	+	+	+	+	+	–
1911	Dungarvan (Co. Waterford), Knockmaon Castle	–	–	+	–	–	–	+
1914	CHESTER, Pemberton's Parlour	85	–	–	–	–	+	+
1929	*Smarmore* (Louth)	333	+	+	–	+	–	–
c. 1930	Laugharne (Carmarthen), Churchyard	–	–	–	–	–	+	–
1945	TETNEY (Lincolnshire)	355	+	+	–	–	–	–
1950	CHESTER, Castle Esplanade	86	+	+	+	+	–	–
1950	IONA, Abbey	198	+	+	+	+	+	+
1951	York, Pavement	–	–	+	–	–	–	–

162

Appendix B

HOARDS FROM THE BRITISH ISLES DEPOSITED *c.* 975-1075
and believed to contain one or more English coins struck between 973 and 1066.

NOTE: Thompson's *Inventory* lists some forty hoards which apparently fall under the above heading. For this purpose we disregard, of course, the little group of Ostmannic finds which end with *BMC* type II of Eadgar. In the Tiree hoard (no. 357) the alleged coins of Edward the Martyr must be attributed to Edward the Elder, while in the finds from Kirkmichael, Scaldwell, and York, Jubbergate (nos. 224, 323, and 388) the alleged Anglo-Saxon element is mythical. Four of the *Inventory* entries, moreover, are duplicated; the Sullington find (no. 345) is the same as that from Chancton (no. 81), the Penarth Fawr find (no. 306) being that from Drwsdangoed (no. 131), the Thwaite hoard (no. 360) being that wrongly associated with Campsey Ash (no. 69), and Dunrossness (no. 144) and Fitful Head (no. 161) being alternative names for the find best known as that from Quendale. Thus, in effect, the *Inventory* yields thirty-three hoards for our purpose. A further score or so hoards can now be added from other sources, and a more complete picture is as given below:

Hoards marked *** are thought to have contained one hundred and twenty or more English coins.

Hoards marked ** are thought to have contained between thirty and one hundred and twenty such coins.

Hoards marked * are thought to have contained fewer than thirty such coins.

The evidence about hoards marked (?) is not conclusive.

(*a*) Hoards where the English coins appear to be predominantly of one issue:

(i) from England south of a line from the Ribble to Flamborough Head:

Find-spot	Size	Date of deposit	Reference
DENGE MARSH, Kent	***	1067/8	*NC* 1957, 186
GREAT BARTON, Suffolk	**	*c.* 1003	*NC* 1958, 102
HAREWOOD (Yorkshire)	**	1065	*NC* 1959, 189
HARTING BEACON, Sussex	*	*c.* 1003	*NC* 1958, 104
IPSWICH, Suffolk	***	*c.* 991	*Inventory* 199
KINGSHOLM, Gloucestershire	***	*c.* 1020	*NC* 1958, 82
LONDON (St Martin's-le-Grand)	**	*c.* 1016	*Inventory* 249
LONDON (Honey Lane)	*	*c.* 1003	*NC* 1958, 99
NOTTINGHAM (Barkergate)	*	*c.* 1058	*Inventory* 294

Anglo-Saxon Coins

Find-spot	Size	Date of deposit	Reference
OFFHAM, Sussex	(?) **	c. 1066	Inventory 297
OVING, Sussex	***	c. 1066	NC 1957, 198
ROTHERHAM, Yorkshire	**	1067/8	Inventory 318
SHAFTESBURY, Dorset	**	c. 1003	NC 1956, 268
SOBERTON, Hampshire	***	1067/8	Inventory 334
YORK (Micklegate Bar)	*	c. 1003	Archaeologia XCVII 69

(ii) from the rest of the British Isles:

Find-spot	Size	Date of deposit	Reference
BALLYCASTLE, Antrim	*	c. 1035	infra p. 255
CALDALE, Orkney	***	c. 1035	Inventory 66
DERRYMORE, Westmeath	*	c. 1000	infra p. 246
HALTON MOOR, Lancashire	***	c. 1025	Inventory 181
KILKENNY (neighbourhood)	(?) **	c. 1035	GM 1792, 122, etc.
LAUGHARNE, Carmarthenshire	**	c. 975	BNJ 1959 (in press)
MARL VALLEY, Westmeath	***	c. 985	Inventory 265
PENRICE, Glamorgan	**	c. 1008	NC 1959, 187
RUSHEN, Isle of Man	***	c. 995	Inventory 320

(b) Hoards where the English coins appear to be predominantly of two consecutive issues:

(i) from England south of a line from the Ribble to Flamborough Head:

Find-spot	Size	Date of deposit	Reference
BARROWBY, Lincolnshire	(?) **	c. 1025	Inventory 35
CASTOR, Northamptonshire	***	c. 1048	SNC 1960, 211
CHESTER (Pemberton's Parlour)	***	979/80	Inventory 85
CONSTANTINE, Cornwall	(?) **	c. 1020	Unpublished
ISLEWORTH, Middlesex	**	c. 991	Inventory 203
NOTTINGHAM (northern outskirts)	*	c. 1058	NC 1956, 297
Unknown Site (Lincolnshire?)	***	979/80	supra p. 138

(ii) from the rest of the British Isles:

Find-spot	Size	Date of deposit	Reference
KILDARE (neighbourhood)	**	c. 991	Inventory 134

(c) Hoards where the English coins range generally over more than two consecutive types:

(i) from England south of a line from the Ribble to Flamborough Head:

The Reform of the English Coinage under Eadgar

Find-spot	Size	Date of deposit	Reference
CHANCTON, Sussex	***	1066	Inventory 81 and 345
LONDON (Gracechurch Street)	**	c. 1061	Inventory 244
LONDON (St Mary Hill)	***	c. 1070	Inventory 250
LONDON (Wallbrook) ('City')	***	1066	Inventory 255
MILTON STREET, Sussex	**	c. 1055	Inventory 270
SEDLESCOMBE, Sussex	***	1066	Inventory 327
STAFFORD ('a tanyard')	***	after 1042	Inventory 338
THWAITE, Suffolk	***	c. 1050	Inventory 69 and 360
WEDMORE, Somerset	***	c. 1043	Inventory 374
WHITCHURCH, Oxfordshire	(?) **	c. 1070	Inventory 376
YORK (Bishophill)	***	1066	Inventory 386

(ii) from the rest of the British Isles:

ANDREAS, Isle of Man	**	c. 1050	Inventory 9
BURRAY, Orkney	*	c. 1000	Inventory 61
DUNBRODY, Co. Wexford	(?) **	c. 1050	Inventory 141
DUNGARVAN, Co. Waterford	*	c. 1000	Bonser, 9245
FOURKNOCKS, Co. Meath	*	c. 1000	*infra* p. 250
INCHKENNETH, Hebrides	*	c. 1000	Inventory 196
IONA, Inner Hebrides	***	986	Inventory 198
QUENDALE, Shetland	*	c. 1000	Inventory 144 and 161

(*d*) Hoards of which the general composition cannot safely be inferred on the evidence at present available:

BETHAM, Westmorland	(?) **	1067/8 (?)	*Archaeologia* XXXIV 446
DRWSDANGOED, Carnarvonshire	*	c. 1030	Inventory 131 and 306
KIRK MAUGHOLD, Isle of Man	(?) **	c. 1000 (?)	Inventory 222
NORTH UIST, Hebrides	(?) ***	c. 990	SNC 1959, 159

Anglo-Saxon-Coins

REFERENCES

1. *Flores* ed. Coxe 1 p. 416
2. A frequency table constructed on the basis of unbroken coins of Eadgar in the 1950 Chester hoard gives the following picture:

	BMC I	*BMC* V	*BMC* III and IV
less than 18·6	6	2	3
18·6–19·5	5	2	1
19·6–20·5	7	5	6
20·6–21·5	17	6	9
21·6–22·5	12	2	8
22·6–23·5	10	2	9
23·6–24·5	1	1	12
24·6 or more	—	2	2

Of the eleven coins which fail to tip the scale at 18·6 grains only four (or three per cent of the total) weigh less than 18 grains. Not one weighs less than 16 grains, whereas the *obol* of Roger's narrative must have a theoretical weight not higher than 12 grains, and very probably as low as 10

3. The two finds from Mackrie are treated as parcels from one hoard, and there are two cases where two *Inventory* entries clearly relate to the same find. The alleged hoard from Anglesey (*Inventory* 10) in fact represents two disassociated single-finds, probably of very different periods, and the reference to 'silver of Cnut' in the Introduction to that work (p. xxiv) seems to have its origin in a further conflation with the find from Drwsdangoed which itself figures under two heads (*Inventory* 131 and 306). In this way an apparent *Inventory* total of twenty-five is brought back to twenty-one, but the balance is more than redressed by the inclusion of seven further finds
4. These figures are not as arbitrary as they may seem, one hundred and twenty being chosen for this purpose as the half-pound reckoned by tale, while twenty is the larger of the two *orae* in use in the Danelaw. It is interesting to note that very few alterations would be necessitated by substituting for the lower limit the *mancus* of thirty pence, or the earlier computation of the *ora* at sixteen pence
5. We are under a heavy obligation to Mr W. A. Seaby for allowing us to consult the typescript of his forthcoming (*BNJ*) study of the Derrykeighan hoard
6. *SNC* September 1959 p. 159
7. *Infra* p. 231
8. In the *Ulster Journal of Archaeology* (1960)
9. In the *JRSAI* (1961)
10. In *NC* 1959 (in the press)
11. Cf. *BNJ* 1959 (in the press)
12. Again we are under a heavy obligation to Mr B. R. S. Megaw, who has made

The Reform of the English Coinage under Eadgar

available to us photographs of the Anglo-Saxon coins in the Manx Museum and also a number of his own notes

13. *NC* 1952 p. 118
14. Bangor, cf. *SNC* April 1959 p. 76; Tarbat *Inventory* 351; Burray *Inventory* 61, but the suggestion that the Æthelræd II coins could have been of *BMC* type VII cannot be taken seriously; Quendale *Inventory* 144 and 161 and – for the pre-973 coins – the forthcoming Hunter and Coats fascicule of the British Academy *Sylloge*; Dungarvan, Bonser 9245; Meath *infra* n. 16
15. *JRSAI*, 1960, pp. 41–47
16. It may or may not be significant that the sole penny of Eadgar in the Vatican Collection, presumptively a random sample from the Romescot collected up and down the whole country, is a *BMC* type III coin of an Oxford moneyer (*BNJ* XXVIII iii (1957) p. 455)
17. Uncertain mint-signatures at the end of each list bring the totals to 27 and 41
18. Cf. *BNJ* XXII (1934–7) pp. 35–77 etc.
19. In Great Britain *BMC* type VI coins occur in appreciable numbers only in the British Museum, the Hunterian Museum, Glasgow, and the Grosvenor Museum, Chester
20. A *Quadripartitus* addition to the Grately canon, as Professor Whitelock has been kind enough to point out to us
21. Cf. *BNJ* XXVIII i (1955) p. 99
22. Cf. *BNJ* XXVIII ii (1956) p. 277
23. Cf. *NNUM* 1956 p. 215
24. Cf. forthcoming paper in the first Swedish volume of papers devoted to the elucidation of particular problems involved in the publication of the Swedish Viking Age hoards
25. Cf. *BNJ* XXVIII iii (1957) p. 504
26. Reading, unique coin in Stockholm (Hildebrand 635); Berkeley, unique coins in Copenhagen (of which Hildebrand 18 is an electrotype), London (from the Dunbrody find) and Gloucester
27. *Supra* p. 122
28. Cf. *BNJ* XXVIII ii (1956) p. 270
29. Cf. *BNJ* XXVIII i (1955) p. 99
30. Cf. *NC* 1959 p. 183
31. In this connexion we should not neglect to take into account wider patterns, and what is very urgently needed is an index of single-finds compiled on a county by county basis by local enthusiasts under expert guidance
32. *Infra* p. 188
33. On which see F. M. STENTON *Anglo-Saxon England* p. 363
34. *Anglo-Saxon Chronicle* s.a. 980
35. Cf. *PSAS* LXXXV (1950–1) p. 170
36. Cf. *NNUM* 1954 pp. 152–6

37. The '*Agnus Dei*' type seems to have been struck on the same standard (27 grains?) as the earliest 'Last Small Cross' pennies; cf. *infra* p. 208
38. *Infra* p. 200
39. Cf. *BNJ* xxviii i (1955) p. 128
40. *Infra* p. 189
41. *Supra* p. 129
42. Cf. *BNJ* xxvii ii (1953) p. 136
43. *Supra* p. 72
44. Stragglers must be disregarded, and in many cases are to be explained by a confusion of single-finds or even of small secondary hoards with the main hoard proper, such confusion being due either to the carelessness of unskilled workmen or to a desire to share some promised reward
45. The emphasis must be on *issue*; in certain circumstances three *types* could form one *issue*, for example, the 'Pyramids' pence of Edward the Confessor, the coins of Harold II, and the 'Profile/Cross Fleury' coins of William the Conqueror together comprise one issue embracing the triennium 1065 to 1068
46. *Supra* p. 153
47. *NC* 1959 p. 189

IX

Some Corrections to and Comments on B. E. Hildebrand's Catalogue of the Anglo-Saxon Coins in the Swedish Royal Coin Cabinet

by G. VAN DER MEER

It is now nearly eighty years since Bror Emil Hildebrand published the second much enlarged edition of his *Anglosachsiska Mynt*.[1] In spite of its age it is still the most important work of reference for students of the late Anglo-Saxon coinage for the exceptional richness of the material alone which surpasses that of any other collection in the world. Of still greater importance is the brilliant way in which the material has been handled. When one has had the opportunity, as the present writer has had, to work with the Anglo-Saxon coins of the so-called 'Systematic Collection' in the Royal Coin Cabinet of Stockholm which form the material described in Hildebrand's Catalogue, one is struck time and again by the clarity and reliability of Hildebrand's great work. However, in the course of time a great deal of new material has come to light, and it is inevitable that this should have resulted in a number of reattributions. Not only has it been possible to prove from fresh evidence that many types and individual coins which Hildebrand supposed to be English are in reality Scandinavian or Irish (though research on this subject is still very much in its infancy), or that certain mint-signatures, such as COR, USTLA, or WIBR stand for non-English towns, but also by checking hardly legible readings against those of better preserved specimens from new hoards or single-finds the true readings of many names of mints and moneyers have been discovered. In some cases die-duplicates of coins which Hildebrand only knew as fragments have enabled us to complete fragmentary legends and to establish hitherto unknown names of mints or moneyers. Of course there are also a number of mistakes which Hildebrand could easily have avoided, but even these cannot diminish our admiration for his brilliant scholarship. His reasons for his arrangement of the sequence of types were sound, based as they were on the material then at his disposal. Later researches, however, based on new material, have led to a revision of his type-sequence on some points. For instance, Cnut's type I is now attributed to Harthacnut, and the present sequence of the first four types of

Anglo-Saxon Coins

Edward the Confessor is different from Hildebrand's, but on other points, such as the type-sequence for Æthelræd II, his judgement has been proved right. To quote a recent paper:

> Bror Emil Hildebrand . . . was an academic giant, and the present generation of researchers into a field which he still dominates more than seventy-five years after his death feels instinctively that it is his shade which urges it on to remove from his masterpiece those minor blemishes that were inevitable in a work conceived and executed on a scale without parallel in its own age.[2]

A large proportion of the corrections which follow below have been published before in numismatic periodicals, many other ones on the other hand are published here for the first time. It will be clear from the references to publications that most of the corrections have been made in the last six years and that the majority of them were discovered by R. H. M. Dolley. (This also holds true for most of the hitherto unpublished corrections.) It is around the Coin Room of the British Museum in fact that under the inspired tutelage of C. E. Blunt and F. Elmore Jones a group of students of the Anglo-Saxon coinage has formed itself and their work has produced a rich crop of interesting new discoveries, especially for the period which is covered by Hildebrand's Catalogue. New methods of research have been applied, such as systematic searching for die-links between mints and the use of regional styles of die-cutting in limiting the area in which a certain die may be found. As an example may be mentioned the identification of 'Gothabyrig' as a West Country mint. The wildest theories about the site of this mint had been advanced in the course of the years, until it was proved on style and from an obverse die-link with an Exeter coin that the mint had to be sought in the general direction of this city.[3]

To a very great extent the renewed interest in Anglo-Saxon numismatics has been inspired and stimulated by Sir Frank Stenton's masterpiece *Anglo-Saxon England*, which has made our knowledge of the history of the Anglo-Saxons so much more detailed and accurate. Its influence is felt in many numismatic papers in which arguments have been based on facts which are now known through Professor Stenton's work, and at least one important monograph was written as a direct answer to a problem stated by him.[4]

However, in spite of all these favourable circumstances, it would not have been possible to check so many of Hildebrand's readings and to study the new Viking Age hoards which have been found in Sweden since Hildebrand's day and which have almost doubled the amount of Anglo-Saxon coins in the Royal Coin Cabinet in Stockholm, if it had not been for the generosity of the Swedish authorities. Nearly ten years ago the Swedish 'Royal Academy of Letters,

Some Corrections to and Comments on B. E. Hildebrand's Catalogue

History, and Antiquities'[5] decided to initiate the publication of all the Viking Age hoards found in Sweden. The publication of the Anglo-Saxon coins was entrusted to R. H. M. Dolley, who has spent many months in Sweden since then. He has been able to go through nearly all the new hoards and to work out many intricate problems with consequent revisions of Hildebrand's Catalogue. The many references, too, in his subsequent papers on Anglo-Saxon coins to his indebtedness, especially to Dr N. L. Rasmusson, the Director of the Royal Coin Cabinet in Stockholm, and to *fil. kand.* L. O. Lagerqvist for information or photographs supplied, bear witness to the generosity of the help they have extended to all students in this sphere. Since this paper went to Press Miss V. Butler has discovered further additions to the list, and these have how been incorporated in it.

In the list of corrections the following abbreviations have been used:

Ant. Arkiv 9=*Some Reflections on Hildebrand Type A of Æthelræd II* by R. H. M. Dolley, *Antikvariskt Arkiv* 9, Stockholm, 1958
BNJ = *The British Numismatic Journal*
NC = *The Numismatic Chronicle*
NNUM = *Nordisk Numismatisk Unions Medlemsblad*
SNC = *Spink's Numismatic Circular*

REFERENCES

1. The full reference is: B. E. HILDEBRAND *Anglosachsiska Mynt i Svenska Kongliga Myntkabinettet funna i Sveriges jord* Ny tillökt upplaga Stockholm 1881
2. R. H. M. DOLLEY 'Three *Long Cross* Pennies of Æthelræd II *c.* 1000, misattributed to the mint of Winchester' *Spink's Numismatic Circular* 1959 pp. 200, 201
3. R. H. M. DOLLEY and F. ELMORE JONES 'The Mints "Æt Gothabyrig" and "Æt Sith(m)estebyrig"' *BNJ* XXVIII ii (1956) pp. 270-7
4. R. H. M. DOLLEY *Some Reflections on Hildebrand Type A of Æthelræd II, Antikvariskt Arkiv* 9 Stockholm 1958
5. Kungl. Vitterhets Historie och Antikvitets Akademien

A. CORRECTIONS TO THE BODY OF THE WORK

(a) *general*

Coins belonging to types which are described as non-English in the analysis of the Plates are not mentioned in the list of corrections of the individual coins. The numbers are as follows:

Æthelræd II: 209, 1493, 2215, 2897, 2944, 3018, 3105, 4001, 4203
Cnut: 49, 154, 253, 419, 639, 865, 1446, 1447, 1843, 2049, 2050, 2062,

Anglo-Saxon Coins

2114, 2123, 2200, 2508, 2511, 2675, 2732, 2733, 2734, 2735, 2736, 2739, 2741, 2743, 2744, 2749, 2896, 2907, 2908, 2909, 2911, 2912, 2961, 2962, 2971, 3050, 3065, 3066, 3079, 3118, 3243, 3553, 3567, 3624, 3625, 3626

Harold I: 419, 445, 473, 492, 597, 653, 719, 720 (die-duplicates), 965

Harthacnut: 87, 88, 103, 104, 105, 106, 107, 108, 109, 110, 116, 135, 137, 139, 142, 143, 144, 145, 153, 169

Edward the Confessor: 431

(b) *particular*

EADGAR

42   The moneyer is Byrhtric

EDWARD THE MARTYR

17   The mint is Lydford, cf. *SNC* 1958 col. 162

ÆTHELRÆD II

3	The mint is perhaps Hastings, cf. *BNJ* VI (1909) pp. 19, 20
4	The mint is probably Hastings, cf. *BNJ* VI (1909) p. 20
5	The mint may be Axbridge or Exeter, cf. *BNJ* VI (1909) pp. 18, 19
6–36	The mint is Barnstaple, cf. *NC* 1897 pp. 302–8, and *NC* 1898 pp. 274–7
17	The type is 'Intermediate Small Cross', cf. *Ant. Arkiv* 9 pp. 7–9
19	The coin is of type B I var. c
63	The coin is not English
64	The coin is Irish (same obverse as 380)
71	The mint signature reads BADF (Bedford?)
77	The type is 'First Small Cross', cf. *Ant. Arkiv* 9 pp. 4–7
84	The mint is perhaps Lydford, cf. *BNJ* XXVIII iii (1957) p. 502, and *Ant. Arkiv* 9 p. 18
102	The mint may be Bridgnorth, cf. *BNJ* XXVIII i (1955) pp. 92–9, and *Ant. Arkiv* 9 p. 19 note 26
103 and 105–114	The mint is Bridport, cf. *BNJ* XXVIII i (1955) pp. 92–9
104	The mint is perhaps Bridgnorth, cf. *BNJ* XXVIII i (1955) pp. 92–9
118	The mint is Lewes, cf. *BNJ* XXVIII i (1955) p. 100
194	The coin is of type A var. f (not English)
205, 206	The coins are not English

Some Corrections to and Comments on B. E. Hildebrand's Catalogue

251	The coin is Scandinavian
303	The mint is Canterbury (same obverse as 152)
329	The coin is not English
348	The coin is Irish
362–383	The coins are Irish, except:
367, 382	The mint is probably Thetford
429	The mint is Derby (die-link with 358)
433	The coin is Scandinavian
440	The mint is London, cf. *SNC* 1955 col. 470 1958 pp. 229, 230, and *Ant. Arkiv* 9 p. 20
461	The type is 'First Small Cross', cf. *Ant. Arkiv* 9 pp. 4–7
537	The mint is Lydford (duplicate of 3053)
541	The type is 'First Small Cross', cf. *Ant. Arkiv* 9 pp. 4–7
605, 606	The coins are Scandinavian
620	The type is 'First Small Cross', cf. *Ant. Arkiv* 9 pp. 4–7
644	The coin is a 'Long Cross/Helmet' mule, probably Scandinavian (same obverse as 1380)
688	The coin is Scandinavian
689	The mint is probably Warwick
696, 697	The mint is not York, cf. *BNJ* XXVIII iii (1957) p. 504 note 1
698	The mint is Norwich
731	The coin is Irish
793	The coin is Scandinavian (same obverse as 2142 and 3362)
805–813	Most of these coins, if not all, are Scandinavian
866	The type is 'First Small Cross', cf. *Ant. Arkiv* 9 pp. 4–7
870	The coin is Irish
1033	The coin is probably not English
1036	The type is 'Intermediate Small Cross', cf. *Ant. Arkiv* 9 pp. 7–9
1051	The mint is Colchester, cf. *SNC* 1960 p. 131
1063	The mint is Ilchester (duplicate of 1038)
1100	The type is 'Intermediate Small Cross', cf. *Ant. Arkiv* 9 pp. 7–9
1131–1137	The mint is in the West Country, perhaps Castle Gotha in Cornwall, cf. *BNJ* XXVIII ii (1956) pp. 270–7
1138	The moneyer is Elfwig (same reverse as 1176)
1146, 1147	The coins are not English
1183	The mint signature reads HRT (probably Hertford)
1217	The moneyer is Elfwig
1218	The mint is Cambridge, cf. *BNJ* VI (1909) pp. 25, 26
1235	The attribution is very doubtful

Anglo-Saxon Coins

1236–1269, 1274, 1275, 1277–1292	The mint is Northampton
1270–1273	The mint is Southampton, cf. *SNC* 1955 cols. 159–61
1276	The coin is not English
1293	The moneyer is Oswold and the mint is Nottingham, cf. R. H. M. Dolley's forthcoming study of the '*Agnus Dei*' type
1294–1301	The mint is Southampton, cf. *SNC* 1955 cols. 159–61
1311	The moneyer is Byrhtlaf
1343	The mint is York
1380	The coin is not English, cf. 644
1400	The mint is Hertford, cf. *BNJ* VI (1909) p. 27
1401	The coin is not English, cf. *BNJ* VI (1909) p. 43
1420	The type is 'First Small Cross', cf. *Ant. Arkiv* 9 pp. 4–7
1475–1573	The mint is Chester, cf. *NC* 1885 pp. 258, 259; *NC* 1891 pp. 12–24, except:
1488, 1519	The coins are Irish
1574	The coin is not English
1575–1602	The mint is Leicester, cf. *NC* 1885 pp. 258, 259; *NC* 1891 pp. 12–24
1603	The coin, if English, is of Worcester, but may well be Irish
1604–1607, 1609–1618	The mint is Lymne, cf. *BNJ* VI (1909) p. 29
1604	The type is 'First Small Cross', cf. *BNJ* XXVIII i (1955) pp. 89, 90, and *Ant. Arkiv* 9 pp. 4–7
1608	The coin is not English
1644	The mint is London
1674	The coin is Scandinavian
1726–1729	The coins are not English
1754	The mint is Ipswich
1756	The coin is Scandinavian
1791, 1888	The type is not type A var. b, cf. *Ant. Arkiv* 9, pp. 38, 39
1809	The coin is not English (duplicate of 206)
1810	The mint is Lewes
1841	The coin is Irish
1888	The type is not type A var. b, cf. *Ant. Arkiv* 9 pp. 38, 39
1896	The mint is York (same obverse as 871)
1897–1899	The mint is Leicester (1899 reads LIGE)
2015–2018	The coins are not English

Some Corrections to and Comments on B. E. Hildebrand's Catalogue

2141–2144	The coins are Scandinavian
2194	The type is 'First Small Cross', cf. *Ant. Arkiv* 9 pp. 4–7
2234	The coin is a die-duplicate of 2308 and both read DRHWOLD
2245, 2288, 2434	The coins are not English
2492, 2494, 2495, 2497	The coins are Scandinavian
2542	The moneyer is Edwerd (same reverse as 2469)
2635	The moneyer is Edwine and the coin is Scandinavian (duplicate of 2495)
2845	The coin is not English
2858	The coin is probably Scandinavian
2898	The coin is Irish (same obverse as 375)
3017	The mint signature reads LUID and the coin is doubtfully English
3064	The coin is of a transitional type which was struck at the beginning of the '*Crux*' issue, cf. forthcoming article by Dolley and Elmore Jones: 'The transition between the "Hand of Providence" and "*Crux*" types of Æthelræd II'
3081, 3087	The type is 'Intermediate Small Cross', cf. *Ant. Arkiv* 9 pp. 7–9
3092	The coin is not English, cf. *BNJ* VI (1909) p. 44
3093	The mint is Milborne Port, cf. *BNJ* VI (1909) pp. 30, 31, and *NC* 1956 p. 274
3094	The mint is Newark, cf. *NNUM* 1956 pp. 215–19
3104, 3105	The coins are not English
3205	The coin is not English, cf. *BNJ* VI (1909) pp. 44, 45
3267, 3268	The coins are Irish, cf. *BNJ* VI (1909) p. 44
3358	The coin is Irish
3362	The coin is Scandinavian (same obverse as 793 and 2142)
3406 and 3407–3409	The mint is Cissbury, cf. *SNC* 1956 cols. 165, 166, and *BNJ* XXVIII ii (1956) pp. 277–82
3410, 3411	The coins are not English, cf. *BNJ* XI (1915) pp. 3–7
3429	The type is 'First Small Cross', cf. *Ant. Arkiv* 9 pp. 4–7
3447	The mint-signature is NIPAN and the coin is from the same obverse die as 104, cf. *BNJ* XXVIII i (1955) pp. 92–9
3501, 3503, 3506–3508	The coins are not English
3527, 3532, 3533, 3538, 3539	The coins are probably not English

Anglo-Saxon Coins

3562, 3563, 3573	The type is 'First Small Cross', cf. *Ant. Arkiv* 9 pp. 4–7
3575–3577, 3582, 3587, 3588–3599, 3600–3604, 3620–3626	The mint could be Southwark. For attributions to Southwark and Sudbury, cf. *BNJ* xxviii ii (1956) pp. 264–9 and my forthcoming study of the mints of Southwark and Sudbury
3578–3581, 3583–3586, 3605–3619, 3627–3632	The mint is Southwark, cf. preceding reference
3643, 3644	The mint is Sudbury, cf. *BNJ* xxviii ii (1956) pp. 264–9
3682	The mint is Derby (same reverse as 346)
3717	The moneyer is Edwig (duplicate of 3724)
3741	The type is type A var. c with 'Right-facing Bust'
3828	The mint is Tamworth, cf. *BNJ* vi (1909) p. 39, and *SNC* 1956 p. 26
3829	The mint is Totnes, cf. *SNC* 1959 p. 26
3830, 3831	The Torksey attribution is now accepted, cf. *NC* 1956 pp. 293–5
3862	The mint is Hertford, cf. *BNJ* xxix i (1958) pp. 54–8
3863, 3864	The coins are not English
3908	The coin is transitional '*Crux* 'type, cf. *BNJ* xxviii i (1955) pp. 81 ff.
3933	The mint is Guildford, cf. forthcoming article by Dolley and Elmore Jones: 'The transition between the "Hand of Providence" and "*Crux*" types of Æthelræd II'
3947	The coin is of a transitional '*Crux*' type, cf. *BNJ* xxviii i (1955) pp. 81 ff.
3949	The mint is Warwick, cf. *SNC* 1959 p. 4
3957	The mint is Warwick, cf. *SNC* 1959 p. 4
3966	The mint is Leicester, cf. *SNC* 1958 p. 35
3982	The type is 'First Small Cross', cf. *Ant. Arkiv* 9 pp. 4–7
4008, 4021, 4022	The type is 'Intermediate Small Cross', cf. *Ant. Arkiv* 9 pp. 7–9, and *NNUM* 1954 p. 154 note 4
4035	The mint is Winchcombe and the type is 'Intermediate Small Cross', cf. *Ant. Arkiv* 9 p. 9
4057	The mint is Lincoln, cf. *SNC* 1959 pp. 200, 201
4131	The mint is Lincoln (die-duplicate of 1691)

Some Corrections to and Comments on B. E. Hildebrand's Catalogue

4146, 4159, 4168, 4240	The coins are of a transitional *'Crux'* type, cf. *BNJ* xxviii i (1955) pp. 81–3
4246	The coin is Irish, cf. *SNC* 1959 pp. 200, 201
4249	The coin is from the same dies as 2656 and the mint is London, cf. *SNC* 1959, pp. 200, 201
4310–4312	The coins are not English
4344–4346	The mint is Warminster, cf. *BNJ* vi (1909) pp. 41–3
4347	The coin is from the same dies as Cnut 639

CNUT

1	The mint is Axbridge, cf. *BNJ* vi (1909) p. 17
5, 6	The mint is Axbridge, cf. *BNJ* vi (1909) pp. 18, 19
7–13	The mint is Barnstaple, cf. *NC* 1897 pp. 302–8, and *NC* 1898 pp. 274–7
51	The moneyer is Leofwine
112, 113	The mint is Bridport, cf. *BNJ* xxviii i (1955) pp. 92–9
118	The mint is 'Eanbyrig', cf. *BNJ* xxviii i (1955) pp. 100, 101, and *SNC* 1956 cols. 322, 323
125	The mint is Leicester
163	The mint is perhaps Chester (same obverse as 1404, crude English imitation)
182, 183	The mint is Leicester
193, 194	The mint is perhaps Caistor
197	The mint is Ipswich, cf. *BNJ* xxviii i (1955) p. 65 note 2
205	The mint is Ipswich, cf. *BNJ* xxviii i (1955) p. 64, note 2
249	The mint is 'Fro', cf. *BNJ* xxviii iii (1957) pp. 504–8
252, 253	The coins are not English
271	The mint is Chester
280–283	The coins are Irish
284	The mint is not English, cf. *BNJ* vi (1909) p. 43
354–356	The mint is Derby, cf. *SNC* 1956 col. 323, and *BNJ* xxviii ii (1956) p. 273
361	The mint is Huntingdon or Buckingham, cf. *SNC* 1958 pp. 229–30
370	The coin is of type E var. d, cf. *SNC* 1956 col. 323
794	The moneyer is Swota and the mint is Shrewsbury
901	The mint is Ipswich, cf. *SNC* 1956 col. 323, and *BNJ* xxviii ii (1956) pp. 273, 274
960	The mint is Ilchester

998–1003	The mint is in the West Country, perhaps Castle Gotha in Cornwall, cf. *BNJ* xxviii ii (1956) pp. 270–7
1014	The mint is Bruton
1108	The mint is Winchester
1116–1120, 1122, 1123	The mint is Southampton, cf. *SNC* 1955 cols. 159–61
1121, 1124–1128	The mint is Northampton, cf. previous reference
1129, 1130	The coins are not English
1131–1141	The mint is Northampton, cf. *SNC* 1955 cols. 159–61, and *NC* 1958 pp. 125–7
1142	The mint is Southampton, cf. previous reference
1143–1147	The mint is Northampton, cf. previous reference
1148, 1149	The mint is Southampton, cf. previous reference
1215	The coin is not English
1288, 1289	The mint is Langport, cf. *BNJ* vi (1909) pp. 27, 28
1290–1308	The mint is Chester, cf. *NC* 1885 pp. 258, 259; *NC* 1891 pp. 12–24
1307	The mint is Lewes
1309	The mint is Shaftesbury
1310–1337, 1340–1363	The mint is Chester, cf. *NC* 1885 pp. 258, 259; *NC* 1891 pp. 12–14
1338	The coin is not English
1339, 1364	The mint is Lewes
1365	The mint is Canterbury
1366–1386, 1388–1403, 1405–1434, 1436–1439	The mint is Chester, cf. *NC* 1885 pp. 258, 259; *NC* 1891 pp. 12–14
1387	The mint is Lewes (duplicate of 1284)
1404	Crude English imitation (same obverse as 163)
1435	The mint is Leicester
1440–1459	The mint is Leicester, cf. *NC* 1885 pp. 258, 259; *NC* 1891 pp. 12–24
1460–1462	The mint is Lymne, cf. *BNJ* vi (1909) p. 29
1483	The moneyer is Ælfsige and the mint is Winchester (die-duplicate of 3670)
1484	The mint is Chester
1503	The coin is of type E var. c

Some Corrections to and Comments on B. E. Hildebrand's Catalogue

1510	The mint is Ipswich, cf. my forthcoming paper on the mints of Sudbury and Southwark
1834, 1835, 1847	The mint is London, cf. *SNC* 1958 pp. 90–1
1961	The mint is Southwark (die-duplicate of 3389)
2021	The mint is Canterbury (duplicate of 129)
2032	The coin is of type G
2130	The moneyer is Dursig
2135	The moneyer is Godman
2210–2212	The coins are not English
2275	The moneyer is Lewerd (duplicate of 2613)
2509, 2510	The mint is Lydford and the moneyer Hunewine, cf. *BNJ* xxix i (1958) pp. 66–8
2723, 2724	The coins are of type E var. d, but not of the true regional E.d. variety
2729	The coin is not of the true E.d. variety
2810	The moneyer is Dunstan
2879	The mint is Ilchester, cf. *SNC* 1957 cols. 535–6
2896	The mint is not English
2897, 2898	The mint is Milborne Port, cf. *BNJ* vi (1909) pp. 30, 31, and *NC* 1956 p. 274
2898	The moneyer is Swetric, cf. *BNJ* xxix i (1958) pp. 61–4
2910	The coin is not English
2943	The mint is Oxford
2998	The coin is not English, cf. *BNJ* vi (1909) pp. 44, 45
3057–3059	The mint is Hertford, cf. *BNJ* vi (1909) pp. 35, 36
3060–3067	The coins are not English, cf. *BNJ* vi (1909) p. 45
3082	The moneyer is perhaps Godwine
3163, 3193	The mint is probably Shrewsbury
3194	The mint is Cissbury, cf. *SNC* 1956 cols. 165, 166, and *BNJ* xxviii ii (1956) pp. 277–82
3214	The mint is Stafford
3283	The first N of GONWINE has been changed into D
3369	The mint is Romney
3370–3373	The mint is Southwark, cf. my forthcoming paper on the mints of Sudbury and Southwark
3385, 3386	The coins are of type E var. i
3395	The mint is Sudbury, cf. *BNJ* xxviii ii (1956) pp. 264–9
3406	The moneyer is Eadwerd and the obverse is 'a 7'

3415	The moneyer is Swegnn
3419–3422	The mint is Sudbury and the mint-signatures are SUÐB, ZUÐB, and SUBR, cf. my forthcoming paper on the mints of Sudbury and Southwark
3432	The moneyer is Mansi, cf. preceding reference
3442	The mint is Stamford
3550	The mint is Tamworth, cf. *BNJ* VI (1909) p. 39
3551–3553	That there was a mint at Torksey is now accepted, cf. *NC* 1956 pp. 293–5, but these coins seem not to be English
3565	The moneyer appears to be 'Gærman'
3566	The mint is Totnes, cf. *BNJ* XXIX i (1958) pp. 58–60
3567	The mint is not English
3582	The mint is Wallingford
3589	The mint is Ilchester
3622	The moneyer is Man, and the obverse reads a 8, ir. 54
3624–3626	The coins are not English, cf. *BNJ* VI (1909) p. 45
3701, 3703	The mint is probably Worcester, cf. *SNC* 1956 col. 324
3741	The mint is Worcester, cf. *SNC* 1956 col. 324, and *BNJ* XXVIII ii (1956) p. 274
3780	The coin is a Danish imitation, cf. *SNC* 1956 col. 324
3789	The mint is Northampton, cf. *SNC* 1956 col. 324
3867	The mint is Newark, cf. *NNUM* 1956 pp. 215–19
3868, 3869	The mint is Warminster, cf. *BNJ* VI (1909) pp. 41–3

HAROLD I

1	The mint is Barnstaple, cf. *NC* 1897 pp. 302–8, and *NC* 1898 pp. 274–7
121, 122	The first N of GONWINE has been changed into D
133	The mint is Malmesbury
255–257	The mint is in the West Country, perhaps Castle Gotha in Cornwall, cf. *BNJ* XXVIII ii (1956) pp. 270–7
278–289	The mint is Northampton, cf. *SNC* 1955 cols. 159–61
323	The mint is Langport, cf. *BNJ* VI (1909) pp. 27, 28
324–326	The mint is problematical
327–356, 358–364	The mint is Chester, cf. *NC* 1885 pp. 258, 259, *NC* 1891 pp. 12–24
357	The mint is Lincoln
365	The mint is Leicester

Some Corrections to and Comments on B. E. Hildebrand's Catalogue

366–371	The mint is Leicester, cf. *NC* 1885 pp. 258, 259; *NC* 1891 pp. 12–24
762, 763, 765	The mint is doubtful
775	The mint is Dover
959	The mint is Derby
1048	The mint is Warminster, cf. *BNJ* VI (1909) pp. 41–3

HARTHACNUT

7	The mint is Bridport, cf. *BNJ* xxviii i (1955) pp. 92–9
15	The mint is Axbridge, cf. *BNJ* xi (1915) pp. 46, 55
20, 21	The coins are of type B, cf. *BNJ* xi (1915) pp. 24, 25
27	The mint is Derby
61, 62	The mint is Northampton, cf. *SNC* 1955 cols. 159–61
68	The coin is one of Harold I, cf. *BNJ* xxvii iii (1954) pp. 267, 268
73	The mint is Huntingdon
74–79	The mint is Chester, cf. *NC* 1885 pp. 258, 259; *NC* 1891 pp. 12–24
80, 81	The mint is Leicester, cf. preceding reference
164	The mint is Axbridge, cf. *BNJ* xi (1915) pp. 46, 55
169	The mint is not English, cf. *BNJ* xi (1915) pp. 17–19
173	The coin is one of Harold I, cf. *BNJ* xxvii iii (1954) pp. 267, 268
184	The moneyer is Boiga
212	The mint is Winchcombe, cf. *BNJ* VI (1909) p. 53
213	The mint is Worcester
215	The coin is one of Harold I and the mint is Hereford, cf. *BNJ* xxvii iii (1954) pp. 267, 268

EDWARD THE CONFESSOR

1	The mint is Maldon
3	The mint is Langport
4	The mint is Barnstaple, cf. *NC* 1897 pp. 302–8, and *NC* 1898 pp. 274–7
11	The mint is Bedwyn, cf. *BNJ* xxviii i (1955) p. 217
12	The mint is Watchet
18	The coin is an electrotype from a unique coin now in the Copenhagen Cabinet
34	The mint is Lewes
54	The mint is Lincoln (obverse die-link with 377)
81–84	The mint is Derby

Anglo-Saxon Coins

116	The mint is 'Fro', cf. *BNJ* xxviii iii (1957) pp. 504–8
126	The mint is Hertford
174	The moneyer is Dunberd
210–219	The mint is Northampton, cf. *SNC* 1955 cols. 159–61
213	The coin is probably not English
255–274	The mint is Chester, cf. *NC* 1885 pp. 258, 259; *NC* 1891 pp. 12–24
275–278	The mint is Leicester, cf. preceding reference
279	The mint is Lincoln (obverse die-link with 345)
407	The mint is Lydford, cf. *SNC* 1958 pp. 161–2
634	The mint is Petherton, cf. *BNJ* vi (1909) p. 34
682	The mint is Steyning
707	The moneyer is Burred, cf. *BNJ* xx (1929–30) p. 96
750	The mint is Warwick
781	The mint is Winchcombe, cf. *BNJ* vi (1909) p. 53

Supplement (*Tillägg*)

ÆTHELRÆD

4376	The coin is Irish

CNUT

3871	The mint is Lewes
3881	The mint is Cricklade
3884	The coin is not English
3903	The mint is Warwick, cf. *SNC* 1959 p. 4

B. ANALYSIS OF THE PLATES

EDWARD THE MARTYR

Plate 2, Type B — The only known coin of this type is a modern forgery, cf. *BNJ* xvi (1921–2) pp. 8–10

ÆTHELRÆD II

Plate 2, Type A — Of this type three separate emissions are to be distinguished, i.e. 'First Small Cross', 'Intermediate Small Cross', and 'Last Small Cross', cf. *BNJ* xxviii i (1955) pp. 75–92, *SNC* 1956 cols. 5–8, and *Ant. Arkiv* 9

Plate 2, Type A, var. b — The type is a '*Crux*/Intermediate Small Cross' mule (C/A), cf. *Ant. Arkiv* 9 p. 9 and pp. 38, 39

Plate 2, Type A, var. c and d — These are not legitimate varieties, cf. *Ant. Arkiv* 9 pp. 39, 40

Plate 3, Type A, var. f — The type is Scandinavian, cf. *Ant. Arkiv* 9 p. 9

Some Corrections to and Comments on B. E. Hildebrand's Catalogue

Plate 3, Type B 1, var. b	The type is a 'Second Hand/First Hand' mule (B 2/B 1)
Plate 3, Type B 1, var. c	The variety is regional (East Anglia)
Plate 3, Type B 2, var. a	The type is not English

There are several transitional types between the 'Benediction Hand' type (B 3) and the '*Crux*' type (C) which were not distinguished by Hildebrand; cf. a forthcoming paper by Dolley and Elmore Jones: 'The transition between the "Hand of Providence" and "*Crux*" types of Æthelræd II' and *SNC* 1957 cols. 57, 58

Plate 3, Type C, var. a	For a discussion of this variety, cf. *BNJ* xxviii i (1955) pp. 83 f. and *BNJ* xxviii iii (1957) pp. 509–17
Plate 4, Type C, var. b	The variety is an 'Intermediate Small Cross/*Crux*' mule (A/C); cf. *SNC* 1956 col. 7, and *Ant. Arkiv* 9 pp. 7–9
Plate 4, Type C, var. c	The variety is a 'Second Hand/*Crux*' mule (B 2/C); cf. *SNC* 1957 cols. 57, 58
Plate 4, Type C, var. d	The variety is a 'Benediction Hand/*Crux*' mule (B 3/C)

A late variety of the '*Crux*' type which was not distinguished by Hildebrand is the 'Curly-headed' variety; cf. *BNJ* xxviii i (1955) pp. 81–3, and *SNC* 1956 cols. 7–8

Plate 4, Type D, var. a	The type is not English
Plate 4, Type E, var. a	The variety is a 'Helmet/Last Small Cross' mule (E/A)
Plate 4, Type E, var. b	The variety is a 'Helmet/Long Cross' mule (E/D) and is certainly Scandinavian
Plate 4, Type E, var. c	This is a very rare transitional variety between 'Long Cross' and 'Helmet'
Plate 4, Type F	The type is Scandinavian; cf. *BNJ* xvi (1921–2) p. 26
Plate 5, Type F, var. a	The type is Scandinavian; cf. *BNJ* xvi (1921–2) p. 26
Plate 5, Type G	R. H. M. Dolley is devoting a monograph to this type
Plate 5, Type G, var. a	The variety is an '*Agnus Dei*/Last Small Cross' mule (G/A)

CNUT

Plate 5, Type A	
Type A, var. a	
Type A, var. b	
Type A, var. c	All these types are non-English; cf. a forthcoming paper in *BNJ*
Plate 6, Type B	
Type C	
Type D	
Type D, var. a	
Plate 6, Type E	For a discussion of regional styles in this type; cf. *SNC* 1956 cols. 321–5 and 373–6
Plate 6, Type E, var. d	This is a regional variety along the River Severn; cf. *SNC* 1956 cols. 321–5

Anglo-Saxon Coins

Plate 6, Type E, var. e	The type is probably Scandinavian
Plate 7, Type E, var. f Type E, var. g Type E, var. h Type E, var. k Type E, var. l	The types are not English; cf. a forthcoming paper in *BNJ*
Plate 7, Type F	The type is a mule of the 'Arm-and-Sceptre' type of 'Cnut' (=Harthacnut) and the '*Pacx*' type of Edward the Confessor (Cnut I/Edward the Confessor D)
Plate 7, Type G, var. b	The type is not English
Plate 8, Type G, var. c	The type is not English
Plate 8, Type H, var. c	The type is probably Scandinavian
Plate 8, Type H, var. d	The type is not English
Plate 8, Type I	The type is one of Harthacnut; cf. *BNJ* xxviii i (1955) pp. 111–46
Plate 8, Type I, var. a	The type is not English
Plate 8, Type I, var. b	The type is a modern forgery; cf. *BNJ* xxviii ii (1953) (*Proc.*) p. 231
Plate 8, Type I, var. c	The type is not English
Plate 9, Type K, var. a	The variety is a 'Short Cross/Jewel Cross' mule (H/K)

For a discussion of Type K of Cnut, Type A of Harold I, and Type A of Harthacnut; cf. *BNJ* xxvii iii (1954) pp. 266–75

HAROLD I

Plate 9, Type A, var. a	The type is not English
Plate 9, Type B, var. b	The variety is a 'Jewel Cross/Fleur-de-Lys' mule (A/B); cf. *SNC* 1958 pp. 160, 161
Plate 9, Type B, var. c	The type is not English; cf. *BNJ* xv (1919–20) pp. 1–48
Plate 10, Type C Type D Type D, var. a Type E	The types are not English; cf. *BNJ* xv (1919–20) pp. 1–48

HARTHACNUT

Plate 10, Type B, var. a	The type is not English; cf. *BNJ* xi (1915) pp. 21–35
Plate 11, Type C Type D Type E Type F Type G Type G, var. a Type G, var. b	The types are not English; cf. *BNJ* xi (1915) pp. 21–35

Some Corrections to and Comments on B. E. Hildebrand's Catalogue

Plate 11 Type H Type H, var. a Type H, var. b	The types are not English; cf. *BNJ* XI (1915) pp. 21–35
Plate 12, Type I	The variety is a mule of Harthacnut's 'Arm-and-Sceptre' type and Edward the Confessor's '*Pacx*' type (Harthacnut B/Edward the Confessor D)
Plate 12, Type I, var. a	The type is not English; cf. *BNJ* XI (1915) pp. 21–35

EDWARD THE CONFESSOR

For a discussion of the sequence of the first four types of Edward the Confessor (1. Type D, 2. Type A, 3. Type C, 4. Type B) cf. *BNJ* XXVIII i (1955) pp. 111–46

Plate 12, Type A, var. a	The variety is a '*Pacx*/Radiate Small Cross' mule (D/A)
Plate 12, Type A, var. b	The variety is a 'Hammer Cross/Facing Small Cross' mule (G/A, var. c)
Plate 12, Type A, var. c	This is a substantive type which comes in between types G and I; cf. *NC* 1867 pp. 75, 76
Plate 13, Type C, var. a	The type is not English
Plate 13, Type C, var. b	The variety is a 'Radiate Small Cross/Trefoil Quadrilateral' mule (A/C)
Plate 13, Type C, var. c	The variety is a mule of Edward the Confessor's '*Pacx*' type and Harthacnut's 'Arm-and-Sceptre' type (Edward the Confessor D/Harthacnut B)
Plate 13, Type C, var. d	This is a transitional type of the beginning of Edward the Confessor's reign; cf. *BNJ* XXVIII i (1955) pp. 115 and 134
Plate 14, Type I, var. a	The variety is a transitional emission of type I; cf. *SNC* 1957 cols. 157–60
Plate 14, Type K	The type is a variety of type I
Plate 14, Type L	The type is a mule of Edward the Confessor's 'Pyramids' type and Harold II's '*Pax*' type (Edward the Confessor I/Harold II A)

C. NOMENCLATURE AND CONCORDANCE OF TYPES

The following names are now generally used for the types discussed above:

EADGAR

'Reform' type (Hild.*) C2, *BMC*† VI, Br.‡ 6, Hawkins§ 200), 973–5

---

* B. E. Hildebrand op. cit.
† H. A. Grueber *Catalogue of English Coins in the British Museum, Anglo-Saxon Series* II 1893.
‡ G. C. Brooke *English Coins* 1932.
§ E. Hawkins *Silver Coins of England* (Third Edition, R. Ll. Kenyon 1887).

Anglo-Saxon Coins

EDWARD THE MARTYR
'Normal' type (Hild. A, *BMC* I, Br. 1, Hawkins 202), 975-8

ÆTHELRÆD II
'First Small Cross' (Hild. A, *BMC* I, Br. 1, Hawkins 205), 978-9
'First Hand' (Hild. B1, *BMC* IIa, Br. 2, Hawkins —), 979-85
'Second Hand' (Hild. B2, *BMC* IId, Br. 2, Hawkins 206), 985-91
'*Crux*' (Hild. C, *BMC* IIIa, Br. 3, Hawkins —), 991-7
'Intermediate Small Cross' (Hild. A, *BMC* I, Br. 1, Hawkins 205), 997 (transitional type)
'Long Cross' (Hild. D, *BMC* IVa, Br. 5, Hawkins 207), 997-1003
'Helmet' (Hild. E, *BMC* VIII, Br. 4, Hawkins 203), 1003-9
'*Agnus Dei*' (Hild. G, *BMC* X, Br. 6, Hawkins —), 1009 (transitional type)
'Last Small Cross' (Hild. A, *BMC* I, Br. 1, Hawkins 205), 1009-17

CNUT
'Quatrefoil' (Hild. E, *BMC* VIII, Br. 2, Hawkins 212), 1017-23
'Pointed Helmet' (Hild. G, *BMC* XIV, Br. 3, Hawkins 213), 1023-9
'Short Cross' (Hild. H, *BMC* XVI, Br. 4, Hawkins 208), 1029-35
'Jewel Cross' (Hild. K, *BMC* XX, Br. 6, Hawkins 211), 1035 (posthumously?)

HAROLD I
'Jewel Cross' (Hild. A, *BMC* I, Br. 1, Hawkins —), 1035-8
'Fleur-de-Lys' (Hild. B, *BMC* Vc, Br. 2, Hawkins 214), 1038-40

HARTHACNUT
'Jewel Cross' (Hild. A and Aa, *BMC* I and Ia, Br. 1, Hawkins 216), 1035-6
'Arm-and-Sceptre' (Hild. B of Harthacnut and I of Cnut, *BMC* II of Harthacnut and XVII of Cnut, Br. 2 of Harthacnut and 5 of Cnut, Hawkins 217 of Harthacnut and 209 of Cnut), 1040-2

EDWARD THE CONFESSOR
'*Pacx*' (Hild. D, *BMC* IV, Br. 4, Hawkins 221), 1042-4
'Radiate Small Cross' (Hild. A, *BMC* I, Br. 2, Hawkins 226), 1044-6
'Trefoil Quadrilateral' (Hild. C, *BMC* III, Br. 1, Hawkins 220), 1046-8
'Short Cross' (Hild. B, *BMC* II, Br. 3, Hawkins 229), 1048-50
'Expanding Cross' (Hild. E, *BMC* V, Br. 5, Hawkins 219), 1050-3
'Pointed Helmet' (Hild. F, *BMC* VII, Br. 6, Hawkins 227), 1053-6
'Sovereign/Eagles' (Hild. H, *BMC* IX, Br. 7, Hawkins 228), 1056-9
'Hammer Cross' (Hild. G, *BMC* XI, Br. 8, Hawkins 222), 1059-62
'Facing Small Cross' (Hild. Ac, *BMC* XIII, Br. 9, Hawkins 225), 1062-5
'Pyramids' (Hild. I, *BMC* XV, Br. 10, Hawkins 223), 1065-6

HAROLD II
'*Pax*' (Hild. A, *BMC* I, Br. 1, Hawkins 230), 6 January 1066-14 October 1066

The provisional dates given above are based on the latest researches on the subject.

Some Corrections to and Comments on B. E. Hildebrand's Catalogue

The most important recent papers dealing with the chronology and dating of the above types are:

R. H. M. DOLLEY 'The Sack of Wilton in 1003 and the Chronology of the "Long Cross" and "Helmet" Types of Æthelræd II' *NNUM* May 1954

R. H. M. DOLLEY *Some Reflections on Hildebrand Type A of Æthelræd II*, Antikvariskt Arkiv 9 Stockholm 1958

R. H. M. DOLLEY 'The "Jewel-Cross" Coinage of Ælfgifu-Emma, Harthacnut, and Harold I' *BNJ* xxvii iii (1954) pp. 266–75

R. H. M. DOLLEY 'The Stockbridge Down Find of Anglo-Saxon Coins' *BNJ* xxviii ii (1956) pp. 283–7

R. H. M. DOLLEY and F. ELMORE JONES 'An Intermediate "Small Cross" Issue of Æthelræd II etc.' *BNJ* xxviii i (1955) pp. 75–87

P. SEABY 'The Sequence of Anglo-Saxon Coin Types, 1030–50' *BNJ* xxviii i (1955) pp. 111–46

ADDENDA

CNUT

130	The moneyer is Winræd
235	The mint is London (die-duplicate of 2782)
500	The mint is most probably Nottingham
1109	The mint is Malmesbury (die-duplicate of 2891 and 2892)
1169	The moneyer is Lifwine
1595–1598	The mint is Winchester
1650	The mint is Norwich
1658	The type is type G var. a with 'Right-facing bust'
1698	The moneyer is Harthacnut
1898, 1900	The moneyer is Æedric
2279	The moneyer is Ælwerd
2513	The type is type G var. a with 'Right-facing bust'

X

The Numismatic Interest of an Old English Version of the Legend of the Seven Sleepers

by D. WHITELOCK

The Legend of the Seven Sleepers of Ephesus, which is first recorded early in the sixth century, became very popular. It survives in many versions, in Greek, Latin, Syriac, Arabic, and other Oriental languages, and it was translated into many of the modern European languages. It tells how seven youths hid in a cave from the persecution of the Emperor Decius, and, after a miraculous sleep, woke up in the reign of Theodosius, which it declares to be 372 years later. On awaking, they sent one of their number to buy food in Ephesus, where he was suspected of having found ancient treasure because he offered coins of the reign of Decius. He was therefore dragged before the bishop and the magistrate, and threatened with torture to make him reveal his secret, but eventually the truth was discovered, and he led the way back to the cave. The Seven Sleepers lived long enough to be visited by the Emperor in person, and then died. Thus the story provides an early instance of Treasure Trove. It makes it clear that to be in secret possession of ancient treasure is an offence, though it is not specified whether the treasure ought to belong, in whole or in part, to the State or to the owner of the land where it was discovered. All that is shown for certain is that the finder was not allowed quietly to pocket it, but one may well wonder if the possession of ancient coin would have created such a commotion if it was only the rights of a private individual – the owner of the land where it was found – which were involved.

The Old English version of this story is contained in the principal manuscript of Ælfric's *Lives of Saints*, British Museum Cotton MS. Julius E. vii, which belongs to the beginning of the eleventh century.[1] It was also in British Museum Cotton MS. Otho B. x, but this was almost entirely burnt in the fire of 1731, and only fragments remain, which allow it to be assigned to the first half of the eleventh century.[2] The style shows that this piece is not the work of Ælfric. Dr P. Clemoes, who is engaged on a study of it, has kindly informed me that he would assign its composition to the last quarter of the tenth century.[3]

Since the account of the accusation brought against the possessor of ancient coins is taken over from the Latin source, it cannot be regarded as safe evidence for the attitude in Anglo-Saxon England to the finding of buried treasure. Yet one would have expected the translator to have offered some comment or words of explanation to his readers if this attitude had not seemed to him perfectly natural. He is not slavishly wedded to his original. He expands it considerably, making the whole tale much more vivid and the dialogue more natural. He makes several additions from contemporary English conditions. Thus, when describing the persecution of the Christians, he adds that anyone who sheltered them would be condemned to death.[4] This is the serious crime of *fliemanfeorm* in Anglo-Saxon law, the sheltering of fugitives and the king's enemies, one of the pleas of the Crown. Other additions are that the Emperor announced his orders by beadles, and that these expected payment for tracking down the delinquents, and that a reward was offered to informers.[5] When he takes from his source the statement that the heads of the executed Christians were set on stakes outside the walls, he adds 'like others [who were] thieves'.[6] The accused kinsmen merely reply to the Emperor in the Latin version; in the English they swear great oaths.[7] When the Latin says that Dalius's shepherds built huts on the Caelian Hill, the translator explains 'that they might lie there close to their master's cattle, and shield themselves against cold and heat'.[8] The incident of the examining of the money is greatly expanded. For example, the short sentence *tulerunt argenteos et mirabantur eos* becomes:

> they took his pennies and examined them before the people and wondered greatly, for they had never before seen with their eyes such money, which was struck in old days in the Emperor Decius's time, and his image [*anlicnys*] was engraved thereon, and his name written there all around.[9]

If the translator had felt that the incident of Treasure Trove required any elucidation he would not have been debarred from giving it by fidelity to his source. So we may assume from his lack of comment that in Anglo-Saxon England, as in Ephesus in the story, the concealment of the discovery of treasure was a crime. This does not in itself prove that Treasure Trove belonged already to the Crown. The first evidence that it did comes from the reign of Henry I.[10] Yet there is nothing to suggest that this is an innovation then, and it is probable that Anglo-Saxon law, like that of some other Germanic nations, regarded ancient treasure as belonging to the king.[11]

Among the passages in which the translator appears to go beyond his source is one more closely concerned with numismatics. It is the description of the coins taken by Malchus, the emissary, to the town after the saints have awakened. It is as follows:

nam þa mid him sumne dǽl feos. swá micel swá hit mihte béon. ðeah swilce hit wǽre sum twá 7 sixtig penega. 7 wæs þæs feos ofergewrit ðæs ylcan mynet-sleges þe man þæt feoh onslóh sona þæs forman geares þa Decius feng to ríce; Feower siðon man awende mynet-isena on his dagum. þe ðás halgan ðagyt wunodon onmang oþrum mannum. 7 on þam frum-mynet-slæge wæron twá 7 sixtig penega gewihte seolfres on ánum penege. 7 on þæm æftran em sixtig. 7 on þæm þryddan feower 7 feowertig. 7 on þam feorþan git læsse swa hí hit þær heoldon; Đa wæs þæt feoh þæt Malchus hæfde þæs forman mynet-slæges on Decies naman; Đonne betweonan Decies frum-mynet-slæges dagum þa þas halgan into þam scræfe eodon. 7 betweonan Theodosius timan þe ða wæs casere[12] þa Malchus þæt feoh bær to porte. be ealdum[13] getele wæron þa agane ðreo hund geara. 7 twá 7 hundseofontig wintra of ðam dæge þe ða halgan slepon. to ðam dæge þe hí eft awócon;[14]

TRANSLATION

He then took with him a certain sum of money, as much as was available – as if it were some sixty-two pence, however. And the legend on that money was of that same minting with which the money had been struck immediately in the first year when Decius succeeded to the throne. Four times were the dies changed in his days, when those saints still lived among men; and in the first minting were sixty-two pennyweights of silver in one penny, and in the second exactly sixty, and in the third forty-four, and in the fourth even less, as they reckoned it there. Now the money which Malchus had was of the first minting in Decius's name. Then, between the days of Decius's first minting, when these saints went into the cave, and the time of Theodosius, who was emperor when Malchus took the money to the town, there had passed by the old reckoning[15] three hundred and seventy-two years from the day when the saints slept to the day when they woke up again.

One naturally wishes to compare this passage with its source, if only to find out what gave rise to the nonsensical statement that there were sixty-two penny-weights in a single penny. The Old English text is derived from that version of the story which Huber, the scholar who has studied this legend in great detail, calls Latin group I.[16] His text of this passage, taken from a ninth-century Munich manuscript, Cod. lat. 14540, is as follows:

Surrexit Malchus mane, ut habuit consuetudinem, et accepit argenteos LXII; et quidam quidem fuerant numero LX, quidam vero XLIV. Erat autem superscriptio argentorum primi anni imperii Decii. – Hi enim fuerunt in diebus Decii et sanctorum istorum martyrum. In tempore, quo manifestati

An Old English Version of the Legend of the Seven Sleepers

sunt, invenerunt, quoniam habuerunt CCCLXXII annos a die, ex qua requieverunt usque in diem, qua expergefacti sunt sancti martyres.[17]

Among the manuscripts from which Huber prints variants is one, British Museum Harley MS. 3037, of the thirteenth century, which is closer than the others to the Latin text which must have lain before the Old English translator, and I am indebted to Dr Clemoes for calling my attention to the existence of an earlier manuscript, unknown to Huber, of this version of the Latin text. This is the British Museum Egerton MS. 2797, of the eleventh century. Its version of the passage with which we are concerned reads:

> Et surrexit malchus mane ut habuit consuetudinem. et accepit argenteos sexaginta duos et quidam quidæm [sic] fuerunt numero sexaginta. quidam
> or
> uero quadraginta IIII; Erat autem superscriptio argenteorum primi anni imperii decii. Quator enim fuerunt in diebus decii anni et sanctorum istorum martirum in tempore quo manifestati sunt. Inuenerunt quoniam habuerunt ccclxxii annos a die ex qua requieuerunt usque in diem quo [sic] expergefacti sunt sancti martires.;

The faulty punctuation of the latter part of this suggests that the scribe did not understand what he was copying.[18] The interest for us is that here *Quatuor* occurs at the very point where the English translator speaks of four issues. It would be unlikely that this was mere coincidence, and, as it happens, many other readings prove that the translator used a Latin text of the group represented by the Egerton and Harley manuscripts. When other manuscripts read *misit deus* (or *dominus*)[19] *in corde Dalii domini montis*, Egerton and Harley have the corrupt reading *misit dominus* (*deus* Harley) *talem dominum montis*,[20] which accounts for the English rendering: 'God Almighty provided a very prudent man, who had possession of all the plot on the Caelian Hill'[21]. Again, when the various manuscripts differ regarding an embassy sent to Theodosius, some saying that the bishop sent the proconsul to him, others that the bishop and proconsul sent to him, only these two manuscripts supply the text corresponding to the English, namely *Marinus vero episcopus misit ad Theodosium imperatorem scribens ei epistolam* ... which is rendered: 'And the Bishop Marinus immediately after sent a letter to the good Emperor Theodosius.'[22] We are therefore justified in assuming that the Latin version used by the translator was similar to that in the Egerton and Harley manuscripts. But, as Dr Clemoes has pointed out to me, it avoided some of their errors,[23] and it seems likely that, though it had the word *Quatuor*, it had not got the word *anni* in the sentence we are examining. *Quatuor* is most easily explained as a misreading of *hi*, written without division between the letters and so misread as 'Iu',[24] while *anni* represents somebody's attempt to supply something to go with the *Quatuor*.[25] If, then, our translator found himself faced with a statement 'For there were four in the days of Decius', he would ask himself the question 'Four what?' He has taken the answer to be 'Four issues.'[26]

Thus, though one might have preferred to take the alteration of the two issues of the original into four as having a bearing on Anglo-Saxon numismatic history, it turns out on examination to be only an attempt to make sense of a corrupt text. Yet it may have been familiarity with an English coinage which changed at frequent regular intervals that led to this interpretation, and the translator may have welcomed an opportunity to depict a persecuting Emperor as issuing a steadily deteriorating coinage. His source supplied him with values for only two issues. He required two more. The sixty and forty-four in the Egerton and Harley texts occur in most manuscripts of the Latin group I, and in all of Greek group II. A Brussels manuscript of the Latin group has sixty-two instead of sixty, but this is probably an accidental replacement of the number sixty by the figure given just previously for the number of coins Malchus had with him.[27] Huber suggests that the sixty-two given in the Old English version, in addition to the normal sixty and forty-four, is a sign that the translator was collating two different texts, and took sixty-two from one like this Brussels manuscript. But this is improbable; he would hardly have gone to so much trouble, and he is more likely to have chosen sixty-two because that figure was in his text, though there with reference to the number of coins, and not to their value. He did not venture to invent a figure for the fourth issue, merely saying vaguely 'even less'.

If the extant manuscripts of the Old English version represent accurately what the translator wrote, his attempt to remedy the silence of his source regarding the units in which they were reckoning cannot be regarded as a success. I suppose that his words 'as if it were some sixty-two pence' express his knowledge that *argenteos* were not really pennies, though he wished to use a term familiar to his readers. But it is a pity that he chose pennyweight for the unexpressed unit of weight, instead of grains, which would not have given such nonsense. Or, if he had said 'sixty-two pennyweights in a single coin' (as Skeat translates it), using the general term *mynet*, instead of the specific *pening*,[28] they would have been enormous coins, but he would not have written such a contradiction in terms. Perhaps he did not pause to consider the size of the coins he is describing; the native poetry describes the works of the men of antiquity as 'the works of giants', but the rest of his version is so closely related to contemporary Anglo-Saxon conditions that gigantic pennies strike an odd and jarring

An Old English Version of the Legend of the Seven Sleepers

note. Is it possible that his clause, 'as they reckoned it there', which has no counterpart in the Latin, implies an awareness that what he has written does not make good sense as applied to English currency?

The pennyweight, which is sometimes called simply 'penny', was presumably a fixed weight by this time, not varying with the actual weight of different issues of pennies. A small picture of its use as a weight is given in an Anglo-Saxon homily, attributed, though wrongly, to Archbishop Wulfstan. There we read:

> Then let each man consider how much the soul will be tormented on Doomsday when the sins and the soul will be placed on the scales and weighed as gold is weighed against pennies; and if the pennies weigh more than the gold, it soon turns out badly for the man. So will it be with the soul and the sin; if the sin weighs more than the soul, they will both go to destruction.[29]

Though the passage on the four issues in the Seven Sleepers' legend proves on examination to have less interest for numismatics than at first sight it promised, it nevertheless adds to our knowledge of contemporary terminology. The word *mynet-slege*, 'minting, issue', literally 'coin-striking', is unique, as is its compound, *frum-mynet-slege*, 'first issue'. Similarly, we are given the word used for a die, *mynet-isen*, 'coin-iron'. The word for a legend, *ofergewrit*, and that later used in the text for a portrait, *anlicnys*, are, however, recorded elsewhere. They both occur, for example, to translate *superscriptio* and *imago* in Matthew xxii. 20 in relation to the tribute-money to Caesar.

REFERENCES

1. W. W. SKEAT (ed.) *Aelfric's Lives of Saints* I pp. 488–541
2. See N. R. KER *Catalogue of Manuscripts containing Anglo-Saxon* pp. 224–9
3. Dr Clemoes has already published his views on the inclusion of this piece in Ælfric's *Lives of Saints*, and shown that there are reasons to believe that this was not done by Ælfric himself, but that it became associated with this set of *Lives* for the first time in Julius E. vii. See 'The Chronology of Ælfric's Works', P. CLEMOES (ed.) *The Anglo-Saxons. Studies in some Aspects of their History and Culture presented to Bruce Dickins* p. 219 n. 2
4. SKEAT op. cit. lines 49–51
5. Ibid. lines 47, 51–3
6. Ibid. lines 75 f.
7. Ibid. line 299
8. Ibid. lines 418–20
9. Ibid. lines 656–60

Anglo-Saxon Coins

10. See SIR GEORGE HILL *Treasure Trove in Law and Practice* Oxford 1936 pp. 187f., 225 and n. 6; but see above p. 15
11. Ibid. pp. 31, 52–73, 173–6; F. LIEBERMANN, *Die Gesetze der Angelsachsen* II *Glossar* s.v. *Schatzfund*
12. Omitted in the Otho text, interlined in Julius
13. Otho reads *be getealdan*
14. SKEAT op. cit. lines 473–88
15. Or, in the Otho text, 'by estimated reckoning'
16. MICHAEL HUBER, O.S.B. *Die Wanderlegende von den Siebenschläfern* Leipzig 1910
17. Idem, *Beitrag zur Visionsliteratur und Siebenschläferlegende* I Teil *Lateinische Texte* (Programm des. humanist. Gymn. Metten, 1902/1903) p. 61
18. As the Harley text agrees in having no stop after *istorum martirum*, and has an inverted semicolon before *Inuenerunt*, this corruption must belong to their common source
19. This reading is in the Munich manuscript
20. Egerton adds *nomine dailum*, but since neither the Harley nor the Old English versions give the name, this is unlikely to have been in their common source
21. SKEAT op. cit. lines 414–16
22. Ibid. lines 791–2
23. e.g. *geþwærlice* (line 210) is translating an *omnes* omitted in Egerton and Harley, and *he swiðe micelne truwan hæfde* (line 628) renders *fidens*, where Egerton and Harley have *uidens* (corrected later in Egerton to *conuidens*)
24. Father Paul Grosjean has suggested to me that the error could have arisen from a text which wrote XL *quatuor*, for XLIIII, but it comes too far from this figure for this to be probable
25. Dr Clemoes suggests that the peculiar position of *anni* in the sentence may point to its being originally a gloss, at the end of a line
26. It is possible that his Latin text had tried to supply the apparent gap with some word for issues; but in any case it is clear that the translator greatly expanded the source at this point
27. It is improbable that this single manuscript should have retained sixty-two from some older version, though Syrian manuscripts and some of Greek group I give the figures as sixty-two and forty-four
28. It is tempting to suggest that *penege* has replaced *mynete* by scribal error, owing to the preceding *penega*, but the reading of the Otho fragment supports that of the Julius text
29. A. NAPIER *Wulfstan: Sammlung der ihm zugeschriebenen Homilien* pp. 239f.

XI

The Metrology of the Late Anglo-Saxon Penny: The Reigns of Æthelræd II and Cnut

by V. J. BUTLER

The purpose of this essay is to present as clearly as possible the results of a systematic weighing of all the coins of Æthelræd II and Cnut in the British Museum Collection. The evidence is presented principally in the form of frequency tables arranged chronologically according to types. In compiling these tables, certain peculiarities have been noted, and for these I shall

TABLE I

Table of weights for 'Small Cross' type of Eadgar, Edward the Martyr, and 'First Small Cross' of Æthelræd II

GRAINS:	Eadgar	Edward the Martyr	Æthelræd
less than 16·0			
16·0–16·49			xx
16·5–16·99		x	x
17·0–17·49	x	x	x
17·5–17·99		xxx	x
18·0–18·49	x	xx	
18·5–18·99	x	xx	
19·0–19·49	x	xxxx	xxx
19·5–19·99		xxx	
20·0–20·49	xxxxx	xxx	xx
20·5–20·99	xxx	xxxxxx	xx
21·0–21·49	xx	xxxxx	xxx
21·5–21·99		xxxxxx	x
22·0–22·49	xxxxx	xxxxx	xx
22·5–22·99	xxxx	xxx	x
23·0–23·49	xx	xxxxx	
23·5–23·99	xxxx	xxxxx	x
24·0–24·49	xxx	xxx	
24·5–24·99	xx	xx	
25·0–25·49	xxxxx		
25·5–25·99	xxxx	x	
26·0–26·49	xx		
26·5–26·99			
27·0–27·49			
27·5–27·99	x		
28·0 or more			

attempt to offer comments and explanations. These remarks have sometimes occasioned other tables which divide the coins of one type still further under groupings of style or mint. Whatever importance may be attached to these interpretations, I venture to hope that a certain evidential value attaches to the tables themselves.

In the first issue which is exclusive to Æthelræd, i.e. 'First Hand', the coins are struck on a heavy standard of about 25·5 grains. This shows a substantial increase on the preceding 'Small Cross' type which (though the number of coins bearing Æthelræd's name is scanty) seems to have been struck under Æthelræd on a standard of perhaps only 21, and certainly not more than 23 grains. These 'First Small Cross' coins of Æthelræd in their turn appear much lighter than other pennies of this type which were issued as the 'Reformed' type of Eadgar, and throughout the short reign of Edward the Martyr. (See Table 1, p 195.)

There is in this type a very noticeable progressive decline in the weight standard throughout the three reigns, Eadgar striking 'Small Cross' coins on a presumptive weight standard of about 25 grains, with over sixty-five per cent of the coins weighing 22 grains or more, while Edward seems to have struck at about 23 grains.

In the next table (p. 197), which also deals with the 'First Small Cross' type but brings together the whole issue from the three reigns, the coins are divided according to mints. It was felt that a difference in pattern might emerge for various parts of the country, either because of deliberate practice or on account of weakness of control away from administrative centres. A word must first be said about the method of grouping adopted, which is one that will also be used in subsequent tables. *Wessex* includes, as well as the country of the West Saxons, the mints that fall within the counties of Kent, Sussex and Surrey. *Mercia* denotes Old Mercia and all the Anglian territory not conquered by the Danes. *East Anglia* embraces not only Old East Anglia but also Essex and Danish Anglia. The *Danelaw* here means simply the country of the Five Boroughs. *London, Winchester*, and *York* cover, of course, the output of single mints.

The Danelaw, because of the large number of coins of Stamford and Lincoln that chance to be available for this study, presents the most satisfactory conclusive picture. In spite of the slightness of the material for the other areas, the Seven Boroughs appear to be striking fairly light. The trend in the table for East Anglia seems to show that area following the Danelaw. All the coins for London are heavy; Winchester is undistinguished by any outstanding feature of heaviness or lightness, and in fact all London coins are here heavier than all Winchester ones. The evidence for Wessex seems to favour a heavy standard being in use there. Mercia is very indecisive, but seems, if such a division is to

The Metrology of the Late Anglo-Saxon Penny

TABLE 2

GRAINS:	Wessex	Mercia	East Anglia	Danelaw	London	Winchester	York
less than 16·0							
16·0–16·49				xx			
16·5–16·99		x		x			
17·0–17·49			x	xx			
17·5–17·99	x		xx	x			
18·0–18·49		xx		x			
18·5–18·99	x	x	x	x			
19·0–19·49	xx		x	xxxx			x
19·5–19·99	x			xx		x	x
20·0–20·49	xx		xx	xxxx		x	x
20·5–20·99			x	xxxxxxx		x	xx
21·0–21·49	xx		x	xxxxxx			x
21·5–21·99			x	xxxx		x	x
22·0–22·49	xxx		xxx	xxxx			xx
22·5–22·99	xx			xxx		xx	xx
23·0–23·49	x	x		xx		x	xx
23·5–23·99	x	xx	x	xx	xx		
24·0–24·49	xxx	x	x		xx		
24·5–24·99				xx	xx		
25·0–25·49	x	x	x	x	x		
25·5–25·99	x		x		x		xx
26·0–26·49				x			
26·5–26·99							x
27·0–27·49							
27·5–27·99							x
28·0 or more							

be allowed, to follow English rather than Danelaw practice. Most of the York coins cover the same range as Winchester, but there are also some very heavy coins, and since if these are placed with the Danelaw pennies they tend only to blur the curve of the table, I should prefer to allow to York the heavy standard more likely in a centre where there was considerable overseas trade.

The comparatively heavy weight standard of 'First Hand' has already been mentioned. (See Table 3, p. 198.)

If the weights of 'First Hand' coins are split up under the seven areas, the tables seem to show all these areas making a real effort to keep to a 25·5-grain standard, with the possible exception of York. (See Table 4, p. 198.)

There are thus no grounds for dividing off East Anglia and the Danelaw from the rest of the country in this type, as in the preceding issue. The lack of very light coins for Winchester and Mercia may be only fortuitous, but a consistently good standard at Winchester would fit very well the pattern set in succeeding types.

Anglo-Saxon Coins

TABLE 3

Table of weights for 'First Hand' type of Æthelræd II

GRAINS:		GRAINS:	
less than 16·0	x	23·0–23·49	xxxxxx
16·0–16·49		23·5–23·99	xxxxxxxxxxxx
16·5–16·99		24·0–24·49	xxxxxxxxxxxx
17·0–17·49		24·5–24·99	xxxxxxxxxxxx
17·5–17·99	xx	25·0–25·49	xxxxxxxxxxxxxxxxx
18·0–18·49	xx	25·5–25·99	xxxxxxxxxxxxxx
18·5–18·99	x	26·0–26·49	xxxxxxxxx
19·0–19·49		26·5–26·99	x
19·5–19·99	x	27·0–27·49	x
20·0–20·49	xxxx	27·5–27·99	xx
20·5–20·99	xxxxxx	28·0–28·49	
21·0–21·49	xxx	28·5–28·99	
21·5–21·99	xxxxxxxxx	29·0–29·49	x
22·0–22·49	xxxxxxxxxxx	29·5 or more	
22·5–22·99	xxxxx		

TABLE 4

GRAINS:	Wessex	Mercia	Danelaw	East Anglia	London	Winchester	York
less than 17·5							1 at 15·0
17·5–17·99							xx
18·0–18·49	x						x
18·5–18·99	x						
19·0–19·49							
19·5–19·99					x		
20·0–20·49	xxx		x				
20·5–20·99	xxx		x	xx			x
21·0–21·49	xx		x				
21·5–21·99	x		x	x	xxx		xxx
22·0–22·49	xx			xx	xxxxx	x	x
22·5–22·99				x	x	x	xx
23·0–23·49				x	xxxxx		
23·5–23·99	xx		x	xxxx	xxx	x	x
24·0–24·49	xx	xx		x	xxxxx	x	x
24·5–24·99	xxx	x		xxxxxx	xx		
25·0–25·49	xxxxxx	x		xxxxxxxx		x	
25·5–25·99	x		x	xxxxxxxxxx		x	
26·0–26·49	xxx		xxxxx	x			
26·5–26·99				x			
27·0–27·49	x		Plus				
27·5–27·99	x	x	1 at				
28·0 or more			29 grains (Lincoln)				

The Metrology of the Late Anglo-Saxon Penny

It was at one time hoped that the semblance of light striking at York and of the erratic striking of Lincoln which appears on the evidence of the coins in the British Museum might account for the mysterious failure of these two major mints to strike in the next type. These hopes were dashed to the ground when we came to add figures for these mints arrived at on the basis of coins in the Systematic Collection in Stockholm, these being supplied through the kindness of my friend Miss G. van der Meer:

TABLE 5

GRAINS:	Lincoln			York	
	British Museum	Stockholm	British Museum and Stockholm combined	Stockholm	British Museum and Stockholm combined
less than 15·0					
15·0–15·49					x
15·5–15·99					
16·0–16·49					
16·5–16·99					
17·0–17·49					
17·5–17·99				x	xxx
18·0–18·49					x
18·5–18·99				xx	xx
19·0–19·49					
19·5–19·99				x	x
20·0–20·49	x		x		
20·5–20·99	x		x	xx	xxx
21·0–21·49		xx	xx		
21·5–21·99		xxxx	xxxx	x	xxxx
22·0–22·49		xxx	xxx	xxx	xxxx
22·5–22·99		xx	xx	xxx	xxxxx
23·0–23·49		xxx	xxx	xx	xx
23·5–23·99				x	xx
24·0–24·49				x	xx
24·5–24·99				xxx	xxx
25·0–25·49				xxx	xxx
25·5–25·99					
26·0–26·49	x		x		
26·5–26·99					
27·0–27·49					
27·5–27·99					
28·0–28·49		x	x		
28·5–28·99					
29·0–29·49	x		x		
29·5 or more					

Anglo-Saxon Coins

Although both mints are striking somewhat below the hypothetical standard of the type, this comparison removes some of the more exaggerated features found in the case of the coins in the British Museum.

Passing on to 'Second Hand', one of the most marked features of differentiation between the two 'Hand' issues must surely be the drop in weight so characteristic of 'Second Hand':

TABLE 6

Table of weights for 'Second Hand' type of Æthelræd II

GRAINS:		GRAINS:	
less than 14·5		20·0–20·49	xx
14·5–14·99	x	20·5–20·99	xxxx
15·0–15·49		21·0–21·49	xxxxx
15·5–15·99		21·5–21·99	xxxxxx
16·0–16·49	x	22·0–22·49	xx
16·5–16·99	xx	22·5–22·99	xxx
17·0–17·49	xxx	23·0–23·49	
17·5–17·99	x	23·5–23·99	xxx
18·0–18·49	xxxxx	24·0–24·49	
18·5–18·99	xxxx	24·5–24·99	
19·0–19·49	xxxxx	25·0 or more	
19·5–19·99	xxxx		

Although this table has no recognizable peak, the standard can hardly have been more than 22·5 grains. There are in the British Museum Collection no coins of this type which weigh more than 24 grains, whereas in the preceding type over fifty per cent of the coins weighed 24 grains or more.

TABLE 7

GRAINS:	Wessex	East Anglia	London	Winchester
less than 14·5				
14·5–15·49	x			
15·5–16·49	x			
16·5–17·49	xxx		xx	
17·5–18·49	xxxx		xx	
18·5–19·49	xxx		xxxx	
19·5–20·49	xxx	x	xx	x
20·5–21·49	xxxxxx		x	x
21·5–22·49	x	xxx	xx	xx
22·5–23·49			x	xx
23·5–24·49			xxx	
24·5 or more				

The Metrology of the Late Anglo-Saxon Penny

In an analysis of the coins under mints, it was found that the bulk of them came into the groups of Wessex and London, with a few from Winchester, and an even smaller number from East Anglia. The Danelaw claimed one coin of Leicester, at 18·9 grains, and the column for English Mercian mints remained empty. York and Lincoln, as is well known, mysteriously refrained from striking this type, and whatever the reason for this may have been, the 'First Hand' figures show that it was not a penalty imposed because of dissatisfaction with the standard maintained by those mints.

Thus, if anything is to be shown by splitting the numbers of a poorly represented type into still smaller groups, it is that Wessex follows the national pattern, with a block of coins between 17·5 and 21·5 grains. London shows a peak within this block, but is also responsible for some heavy coins, including the three heaviest for the type. Winchester is heavy for the type, and has no light coins.

The next type, '*Crux*', returns to a heavy standard:

TABLE 8

Table of weights for 'Crux' type of Æthelræd II

GRAINS:
less than 17·0	
17·0–17·49	x
17·5–17·99	xxxx
18·0–18·49	xxxx
18·5–18·99	xxxxx
19·0–19·49	xxxxxx
19·5–19·99	xx
20·0–20·49	xxxxxxxx
20·5–20·99	xxxxxx
21·0–21·49	xxxxxxxx
21·5–21·99	xxxxxxxxxxxxxxxx
22·0–22·49	xxxxxxxxxxxxxxx
22·5–22·99	xxxxxxxxxxxxxx
23·0–23·49	xxxxxxxxxxxxxxxxx
23·5–23·99	xxxxxxxxxxxxxxxxx
24·0–24·49	xxxxxxxxxxxx
24·5–24·99	xxxxxxxxxxxxxxxxx
25·0–25·49	xxxxxxxxxxxxxxxxxxxxxxxxxxx
25·5–25·99	xxxxxxxxxxxxxxxxxxxxx
26·0–26·49	xxxxxxxxxx
26·5–26·99	xxxxxxxxx
27·0–27·49	xx
27·5–27·99	plus 1 of 28·1 grains

Anglo-Saxon Coins

A regional analysis of this type presents quite an interesting picture:

TABLE 9

GRAINS:	Wessex	Mercia	East Anglia	Danelaw	London	Winchester	York
less than 17·0							
17·0–17·49			x				
17·5–17·99	x		x		xx		
18·0–18·49	xxx		x				
18·5–18·99	x		xxx			x	
19·0–19·49	xx		xxxx				
19·5–19·99	x					x	
20·0–20·49	xxxxxx		x	x			
20·5–20·99	xx		xx		x		x
21·0–21·49	xxxx		xx	x	x		
21·5–21·99	xxxx		xxxxxxxxx	x	xx		
22·0–22·49	xxxx		xxxxxx	xx	xxxx		
22·5–22·99	xxxxx		xxxxx	xxxx			x
23·0–23·49	xxxxxxx		xxxxxxxxx		xx		
23·5–23·99	xxxxxxx	xx	xxx		xxx	xx	x
24·0–24·49	xxxx		xxxxx	x		x	x
24·5–24·99	xxxxxxxxx		xxxxx	x	xx		x
25·0–25·49	xxxxxxxxx	xxxxx	xxxxx	x	xxx	xxxx	
25·5–25·99	xxxxx	xxx	xxxxxx		xx	xxxxx	
26·0–26·49	xxx	xxx	xx		x	x	
26·5–26·99	xxxxxx	x			xx		
27·0–27·49		xx					
27·5–27·99							
28·0–28·49	x						
29·0 or more							

Wessex, Mercia, and Winchester, the more strongly English areas of the country, seem to have been responsible for the heavy standard shown in the national table. It is perhaps significant that there are again no light coins from Winchester. On the other hand, East Anglia and the Danelaw behave in the same way, and, if their respective tables are collated, the result is a peak significantly below the national average. London seems on this showing to be following Danelaw practice, but as there are in fact twice as many coins above the peak as there are below, it can safely be included in the Wessex-Mercia group. The York coins are too few to arrange themselves in any significant pattern.

With the change to 'Long Cross' in 997, the penny remained heavy; the standard seems even to have been raised a grain or more, thus giving a penny heavier than at any time since Eadgar's reform.

The Metrology of the Late Anglo-Saxon Penny

TABLE 10
Table of weights for 'Long Cross' type of Æthelræd II

GRAINS:	
less than 17·5	
17·5–17·99	x
18·0–18·49	
18·5–18·99	xx
19·0–19·49	xxx
19·5–19·99	xxxxxxxxxxxx
20·0–20·49	xxxxxxxxxxxxx
20·5–20·99	xxxxxx
21·0–21·49	xxxxxxxxx
21·5–21·99	xxxxxxxxxxxxx
22·0–22·49	xxxxxxxxxx
22·5–22·99	xxxxxxxxxxxx
23·0–23·49	xxxxxxxx
23·5–23·99	xxxxxxxxxxxx
24·0–24·49	xxxxxxxx
24·5–24·99	xxxxxxxxxx
25·0–25·49	xxxxxxxxxxxxxxxxxxxxxxxx
25·5–25·99	xxxxxxxxxxxxxxxxxxxxx
26·0–26·49	xxxxxxxxxxxxxxxxxxxxxxxxx
26·5–26·99	xxxxxxxxxxxxxxxxxxxxxxxxxxxxxxxxxxxxxxx
27·0–27·49	xxxxxxxxxxxxxxxxxxxxxxxxxxx
27·5–27·99	xxxxx
28·0–28·49	
28·5 or more	plus 1 of Chester of 30·8 grains and 1 of London of 39·2 grains

TABLE 11
Weights of 'Long Cross' coins of London and Winchester

GRAINS:	London	GRAINS:	London	Winchester
less than 18·5		23·0–23·49	xxx	
18·5–18·99	x	23·5–23·99	xxxx	
19·0–19·49	xx	24·0–24·49	xx	
19·5–19·99	xxx	24·5–24·99	xx	
20·0–20·49	xxxx	25·0–25·49	xxxxx	
20·5–20·99	xxxxx	25·5–25·99	xx	xx
21·0–21·49	x	26·0–26·49	xxx	xxx
21·5–21·99	xx	26·5–26·99	xx	xxxxxx
22·0–22·49	xxxxx	27·0–27·49		x
22·5–24·99	xx	27·5 or more		

Anglo-Saxon Coins

In all but two of the areas to which enough coins to make an appreciable pattern can be assigned, i.e. Wessex, East Anglia, and Mercia, this pattern is the same as the national one, with a peak between 26·0 and 27·5 grains, and a not inconsiderable scatter of coins in the lighter ranges. London, however, does not share this peak, and its lighter coins form a very much larger percentage of the whole than do those of other areas. Winchester repeats its 'Second Hand' and *Crux* pattern: a peak at or even above the national average, and no light coins. (See Table 11, p. 203.)

After its six-year period of currency this heavy 'Long Cross' type was replaced for some reason by a much lighter penny.

TABLE 12

Table of weights for 'Helmet' type of Æthelræd II

GRAINS:	
less than 16·0	1 at 13·0 grains, 1 at 15·2 grains
16·0–16·49	xxx
16·5–16·99	
17·0–17·49	xx
17·5–17·99	xxx
18·0–18·49	xx
18·5–18·99	xxxxxxx
19·0–19·49	xxxx
19·5–19·99	xxxxxxx
20·0–20·49	xxxxxxxx
20·5–20·99	xxxxxxxx
21·0–21·49	xxxxxxxxxxxx
21·5–21·99	xxxxxxxxxxxxxxxxxxx
22·0–22·49	xxxxxxxxxxxxxxxxxxxx
22·5–22·99	xxxxxxxxxxxxxxx
23·0–23·49	xxxxxxxxxx
23·5–23·99	xxx
24·0–24·49	x
24·5–24·99	
25·0–25·49	x
25·5 or more	

The type seems to have been struck on a 22·0 or 22·5 grain standard. A regional analysis shows the same picture in each district, and Winchester has only one coin out of seven that weighs less than 21 grains. The succeeding 'Last Small Cross' type, Æthelræd's last issue, poses several problems. The most remarkable feature of a metrological table for this type is the extraordinarily wide spread of the weights; over eleven grains separate the heaviest and lightest of the coins which are material to the table.

The Metrology of the Late Anglo-Saxon Penny

TABLE 13

Table of weights for 'Last Small Cross' type of Æthelræd II

GRAINS:	
less than 13·5	
13·5–13·99	xx
14·0–14·49	xxx
14·5–14·99	xx
15·0–15·49	
15·5–15·99	xx
16·0–16·49	xxxx
16·5–16·99	xxx
17·0–17·49	xxxxxxxxxxxx
17·5–17·99	xxxxxx
18·0–18·49	xxxxxxxxxxxxxx
18·5–18·99	xxxxxxxxxxxxxxx
19·0–19·49	xxxxxxxxxxxxxxxxxxxxxxxxx
19·5–19·99	xxxxxxxxxxxxxxxx
20·0–20·49	xxxxxxxxxxxxxxxxxxxxxx
20·5–20·99	xxxxxxxxxxxx
21·0–21·49	xxxxxxxxxxxxxxxx
21·5–21·99	xxxxxxxxxx
22·0–22·49	xxxxxx
22·5–22·99	xxxxxxx
23·0–23·49	xxxxxxxxx
23·5–23·99	xxx
24·0–24·49	xx
24·5–24·99	xxxxx
25·0–25·49	xxxxx
25·5–25·99	xxxxx
26·0–26·49	xx
26·5–26·99	xxxxxxxx
27·0–27·49	xxxx
27·5–27·99	
28·0–28·49	
28·5–28·99	x
29·0 or more	

This spread is so much wider than in other types, and there are so many coins heavier than the peak that some reason other than natural error in striking is needed to explain it. The possibility, therefore, of two peaks should be considered, i.e. that we are dealing with two weight standards instead of one.

A regional analysis, to my mind, fails to give an explanation for the apparent double standard, but nevertheless I reproduce the regional tables as negative evidence, and also because although a regional explanation does not wholly cover the problem, regional considerations do seem to enter into it. (See Table 14, p. 206.)

TABLE 14

GRAINS:	Wessex	Mercia	East Anglia	Danelaw	London	Winchester	York
less than 13.5							
13.5–13.99	x	x					
14.0–14.49	xx						
14.5–14.99	x						
15.0–15.49							
15.5–15.99					x		
16.0–16.49					xxx		
16.5–16.99	x		x		x		
17.0–17.49	xxx		xxxx	xxx	xx	x	
17.5–17.99	xxx		xx		x		
18.0–18.49	xxx		xxxxxx	x	xx	xx	
18.5–18.99	xxx		xxxxxxx	xxxx	x	x	
19.0–19.49	x	x	xxxxxxxxxx	xx	xxxxxx	xxx	x
19.5–19.99	x	x	xxxxx	x	xxxxx	xx	x
20.0–20.49	xxxxxxx	x	xxx	xxxx	xx	x	x
20.5–20.99		x	xxx	xxxx	xxx	xx	xx
21.0–21.49	xxxxx		xx	x	xxxxx	x	x
21.5–21.99	xxx			xx	xx	xx	x
22.0–22.49	x	x	x			xxx	
22.5–22.99	x		x	xx	xxx	x	
23.0–23.49	x		x	xx			
23.5–23.99	xx		x				
24.0–24.49				x			x
24.5–24.99	x	xx	x	x			xx
25.0–25.49	x			xx	xx		
25.5–25.99	x			x	x		
26.0–26.49							
26.5–26.99	xxxxx	xxx					
27.0–27.49	x	xxx				x	
27.5–27.99							
28.0–28.49		x					
28.5–28.99							
29.0 or more							

TABLE 15

Æthelred II 'Last Small Cross'

GRAINS:	London	Northern A	Northern B	Southern A	Southern B	South-western	Western	South-eastern	Eastern
less than 13.5									
13.5–13.99	xx								
14.0–14.49	x					x			
14.5–14.99	x						x		
15.0–15.49									
15.5–15.99	x	x							
16.0–16.49	xxxx	x							
16.5–16.99	x					x			x
17.0–17.49	xxxxx	xxxx		x		xx			xx
17.5–17.99	xx					xxx			x
18.0–18.49	xxxxx	xx			xx	xx			x
18.5–18.99	xxxxx	xxxxx	x	xx		x		x	x
19.0–19.49	xxxxxxxxxxxx	xxxx	x	x				x	xxxxx
19.5–19.99	xxxxxxx	xxx		xxxx		x			x
20.0–20.49	xxxxxx	xxxxxxxx		xxxx		xxx		x	
20.5–20.99	xxxx	xxx	xx	x			xx		
21.0–21.49	xxxxxx	x	x	xxxx	x	xx	xx		xx
21.5–21.99	x	xxx	x	x	x	x		xx	xx
22.0–22.49		x			xxx		x		
22.5–22.99	x	x	x	xx	x	x			x
23.0–23.49	xxxx	xx		x		x	xx		
23.5–23.99						x			x
24.0–24.49		x			x				
24.5–24.99	x	xx	x		x				
25.0–25.49		x	xx		x		xxx		
25.5–25.99	x	x	x		x		x		
26.0–26.49			x				x		
26.5–26.99					xxxx	xx	xxx		
27.0–27.49						x	xx		
27.5–27.99									
28.0–28.49									
28.5–28.99							x		
29.0 or more									

Anglo-Saxon Coins

With the exception of York and Mercia, the regional weight-tables show the same large peak at 19–20 grains as the national; Wessex and Mercia contribute most towards the heavier peak. York seems on this evidence to have struck no coins on the light standard.

A double standard in this type was first noticed by Mr R. H. M. Dolley, when working on coins in the Systematic Collection in Stockholm; the much more extensive material there produces a much more obvious and indisputable double peak. Mr Dolley has made a suggestion, for which he gives evidence in a forthcoming paper, mostly from a study of the moneyers at certain given mints, that the difference in the two standards is chronological, and that in fact 'heavy' 'Last Small Cross' pennies are the earlier. Further, and here I return to the regional considerations I have already mentioned, he has shown that the two standards are associated with certain of the regional styles he has discovered in this type.

For the sake of completeness the weights of the BM coins are here given under Mr Dolley's regional styles. (See Table 15, p. 207.) The pattern is not inconsistent with the views already expressed but obviously detailed interpretation lies outside the scope of the present paper.

Cnut's first issue, 'Quatrefoil', albeit on a lighter standard, seems to follow the pattern of 'Last Small Cross'; here too there is a wide difference in weight

TABLE 16

Table of weights for 'Quatrefoil' type of Cnut

GRAINS:		GRAINS:	
less than 8·5		17·0–17·49	xxxxxxxxxx
8·5–8·99	xx	17·5–17·99	xxxxxxxxx
9·0–9·49		18·0–18·49	xxxxx
9·5–9·99		18·5–18·99	xxxxxxxx
10·0–10·49		19·0–19·49	xxx
10·5–10·99	xx	19·5–19·99	xxxxxxxxx
11·0–11·49	xxx	20·0–20·49	xxxxxxxxxxxxxx
11·5–11·99	xxxx	20·5–20·99	xxxxxxx
12·0–12·49	xxx	21·0–21·49	xxxxxxxxxxx
12·5–12·99	xxxxxxx	21·5–21·99	xxxxxxxxxxx
13·0–13·49	xxxxxxxx	22·0–22·49	xxxxx
13·5–13·99	xxxxxxxxxxx	22·5–22·99	xxxxxx
14·0–14·49	xxxxxxxxx	23·0–23·49	xx
14·5–14·99	xxxxxxxxxxxxxxxx	23·5–23·99	x
15·0–15·49	xxxxxxxxxxxxxxxxxxxxxxxxxxx	24·0–24·49	
15·5–15·99	xxxxxxxxxxxxxxxxxxxxxxxxxx	24·5–24·99	xx
16·0–16·49	xxxxxxxxxxxxxxxxxxxxxxx	25·0 or more	
16·5–16·99	xxxxxxx		

The Metrology of the Late Anglo-Saxon Penny

between the heaviest and lightest coins, and enough coins are heavier than the main peak to form themselves into another secondary peak.

Again a regional analysis does not solve the problem. Wessex, Mercia, East Anglia, London, and the Danelaw give the same pattern as the national table, i.e. a major peak at 15–16 grains, and a secondary peak at 20–23 grains: Mercia and East Anglia at 20 grains, London and the Danelaw at 21–22 grains, and Wessex at 22–23 grains. Winchester and York, however, have their own characteristic pattern, which may be set out in the following table:

TABLE 17

GRAINS:	Winchester	York
less than 13·0		
13·0–13·49	x	
13·5–13·99		
14·0–14·49		x
14·5–14·99		x
15·0–15·49	xx	x
15·5–15·99	x	xxxxxx
16·0–16·49	x	xx
16·5–16·99		x
17·0–17·49	xxx	
17·5–17·99	xx	
18·0–18·49	x	
18·5–18·99	xx	x
19·0–19·49		x
19·5–19·99	xxxxx	
20·0–20·49		
20·5–20·99	x	x
21·0–21·49		
21·5–21·99		
22·0–22·49	x	
22·5–22·99	x	
23·0–23·49		
23·5–23·99		
24·0 or more		

Thus the coins which were weighed for this study show only the light standard at York, whereas Winchester reproduces neither the heavy nor the light national standard, but one between the two, though inclining towards the heavier.

In this 'Quatrefoil' issue it is difficult to attribute a cause to the phenomenon of the two peaks. One must add to the similiarity in this matter of weight-practice between 'Quatrefoil' and the preceding last type of Æthelræd, the further similarity that the use of a number of different regional styles for the portrait on the obverse die continues into 'Quatrefoil'. If we are right in believing that these different styles, as in 'Last Small Cross', were not all in use at the same time, one may also hazard tentatively the same explanation as that for the preceding type, namely that one of the two or even three weight standards apparent in 'Quatrefoil' is earlier than the other.

With the end of 'Quatrefoil' a quite new pattern comes into the metrology of the Late Anglo-Saxon penny, one that speaks of great conformity and stability. The range covered by the weights for one type is narrow, and a very large majority is centred on the peak, showing that the king was able to enforce his appointed standard everywhere.

TABLE 18

Table of weights for 'Pointed Helmet' type of Cnut

```
GRAINS:
less than 10·0
10·0–10·49
10·5–10·99   x
11·0–11·49   x
11·5–11·99   xxxx
12·0–12·49   xxx
12·5–12·99   xxxxx
13·0–13·49   xxxxxxxx
13·5–13·99   xxxxxxxxxxxxx
14·0–14·49   xxxxxxxxxxxxxx
14·5–14·99   xxxxxxxxxxxxxxxxxx
15·0–15·49   xxxxxxxxxxxxxxxxxxxxxxxxxxxxxxxxxxxxxxxxxxxxxxxxxxxxxxxx
15·5–15·99   xxxxxxxxxxxxxxxxxxxxxxxxxxxxxxxxxxxxxxxxxxxxxxxxxxxxxxxxxxxx
16·0–16·49   xxxxxxxxxxxxxxxxxxxxxxxxxxxxxxxxxxxxxxxxx
16·5–16·99   xxxxxxxxxxxxxxxxxxxxxxxxxxxxxxxxxxxxx
17·0–17·49   xxxxxxxxxxxxxxxxxxxxx
17·5–17·99   xxxxxxxxxxxxxxxxxxxxxxxxxxxx
18·0–18·49   xxxxxxxxxx
18·5–18·99   xx
19·0 or more
```

As I stated at the outset of this paper, my main purpose has been to present figures obtained by weighing a large number of coins of all the types issued from the time of Eadgar's reform of the coinage until the death of Cnut. Even at this stage, however, it might be profitable to discuss certain points that have emerged in the course of constructing the tables, if only to air some of the problems that these tables pose.

The Metrology of the Late Anglo-Saxon Penny

TABLE 19

Table of weights for 'Short Cross' type of Cnut

```
GRAINS:
less than 11·0
11·0–11·49    xxx
11·5–11·99
12·0–12·49
12·5–12·99    xx
13·0–13·49    xxx
13·5–13·99    xxxxx
14·0–14·49    xxxxxxxx
14·5–14·99    xxxxxxx
15·0–15·49    xxxxxxxxxxxxxxxxxxxxxx
15·5–15·99    xxxxxxxxxxxxxxxxxxxxxxxxxxxxxx
16·0–16·49    xxxxxxxxxxxxxxxxxxxxxxxxxxxxxxxxxxxxx
16·5–16·99    xxxxxxxxxxxxxxxxxxxxxxxxxxxxxxxxxxxxxxxxxxxxxxxxxxxxxxxxx
17·0–17·49    xxxxxxxxxxxxxxxxxxxxxxxxxxxxxxxxxxxxxxxxxxxxxxxxxxxxxxxxxxxxxxxxxxxxxx
17·5–17·99    xxxxxxxxxxxxxxxxxxxxxxxxxxxxxxxxxxxxxxxxxxxxxx
18·0–18·49    xxxxxxxxxxxxxxxxxxx
18·5–18·99    xxxx
19·0 or more
```

It did not need any elaborate system of frequency-tables to demonstrate to the student who is accustomed to handling the Anglo-Saxon coins of this series in any number that the average weights for the different types vary enormously. The tables presented here confirm and stress this fact, and give it figures for reference; the weights fluctuate from Æthelræd's 'Long Cross' type at 27 grains to Cnut's latter two types which were struck on a standard that cannot have been more than 18 grains. Even more important is the variation between successive types; for 'First Hand' we can assume a standard of 25·5 grains, the next type sinks to 22·5 grains, and following on that *'Crux'* rises to 25·5 grains again. It is noteworthy that three times a heavier issue succeeds a lighter; the Late Anglo-Saxon coinage presents no picture of steady devaluation, but rather would show on a graph a series of rises and falls.

We have the coins themselves and may weigh them, but it is no easy matter to find evidence to back one suggestion rather than another with regard to the reason for these fluctuations. Yet, if it is granted that there was State control of at least the majority of bullion in the country, the explanation must depend on two factors. One is the amount of silver available for minting; the other, the number of coins that would be required during the currency of the new type to cover the financial needs of the country. If, as some of us believe, most of the minting of a new issue was done at the very beginning of the period when the type was current, there must first have been a very careful calculation made by the government of the amount of coins that needed to be issued. If more coins were to be needed than could have been provided at the same weight by the melting down of the coins of the old issue, and if new silver were scarce, the weight of the penny would have had to fall. If, however, either fewer were wanted or new silver had become plentiful, the new type could sustain an increase in weight. From the frequent return to a heavier standard which we have already noted, we can deduce that a heavy penny was considered desirable, probably for the encouragement of foreign trade, since to a foreign merchant the actual weight of silver he was receiving would have been of supreme importance.

I would like to draw one more tentative conclusion from this matter of fluctuation. If we have to imagine some kind of measure to provide the country with an adequate coinage such as is envisaged above, it would argue a more sophisticated grasp of financial affairs than many would grant an Anglo-Saxon government to have possessed.

Another question follows on. It was touched on above where a foreign merchant who would have accepted English coins for the metal they contained entered the discussion. This is the question of the relationship between the face value of a coin and the actual value of its metal as bullion. Were they the same? The evidence of fluctuation between types is not on this point decisive one way or the other, although an assumption of the overvaluation of the penny makes it simpler to understand how a lighter penny could have been as acceptable as its heavier predecessor when the owner was required to trade it in. But such an assumption becomes inevitable when we look at the difference in weight between one coin and another within the same type, especially in those two issues where we have noted two seemingly distinct standards, i.e. Æthelræd II's 'Last Small Cross' and Cnut's 'Quatrefoil' type. What, for example, could make a light 'Quatrefoil' coin, weighing perhaps 13 grains, possess equal availability with a heavy one of the type weighing 22 grains, unless the difference in metal-value between them were minimized by the circumstance that neither contained one pennyworth of precious metal? Admittedly we cannot prove that two such coins did pass with equal value, but to imagine a situation where they did not is to conjure up such a state of confusion as to almost nullify the value of having a coinage at all. Those types could also be mentioned in this connexion where the Danish-dominated part of the country seems to have struck on the whole lighter coins than the strongholds of English influence. Hoard-evidence alone can show to what degree lighter Danelaw pennies were current in areas whose own mints maintained a heavier standard. If they competed on equal terms

The Metrology of the Late Anglo-Saxon Penny

with Wessex or English Mercian minted pence, one might again invoke undervaluation to help explain how it was possible.

Such questions as these are not raised merely to account for peculiarities in a series of metrological tables. It seems that the answers which we give to them are crucial to our understanding the capabilities of the Anglo-Saxon government at this period. It would have been no small achievement for it to have been able to have guaranteed all over the country the buying power of its penny no matter on what weight standard it might decide the coin should be struck.

Even at a cursory glance the tables displayed above seem to divide themselves into two groups. The first and larger group is comprised of those in which the weights, plotted on to a diagram, resolve themselves into a long shallow curve; these continue up to the end of Cnut's 'Quatrefoil' type. The second group, here including only two types (though continuing work indicates there may well be more to follow), have in common a short range and an extraordinarily pronounced peak. There is every reason to believe that the metrological pattern of Cnut's last two types reflects the political circumstances prevailing in the country. The reign of Æthelræd, when enemy armies were continually on the march up and down England, was hardly conducive to a rigid enforcement of a theoretical weight standard, and so the lightest coins in some of Æthelræd's issues are only a wild approximation to the standard. Cnut, on the other hand, after he had pacified the country and had established himself on the throne for some time, seems to have been able to keep an appreciably greater number of his coins on a standard, and to decrease the discrepancy between these and the lightest coins of the type.

It is only possible to draw the most general of historical conclusions from observations of this kind, but it might be profitable to keep in mind the appearance of metrological tables, as evidence for the maintenance or failure to maintain a weight standard, for comparison with the known events of the period when an issue is current. Such a comparison is made much easier now that our knowledge of the dating of coins has become so much more precise. The 'Cnut Pointed Helmet' and 'Short Cross' example is the most obvious, but there might well be a similar political background to the progressive decline in weight of the 'First Small Cross' type in the reigns of Edward the Martyr and Æthelræd from the weight ordained by Eadgar when he issued his 'Reformed' coinage in 973.

One further question should be raised here: foreign imitation of English coins. It has already been noted above that with Æthelræd's 'Long Cross' type the Anglo-Saxon penny of this series reached its highest weight so far, but that this was only a slight increase on the previous type. It is, therefore, significant that the first type which is found extensively imitated in Scandinavia and in Ireland is the '*Crux*' type, and the greatest number of imitations are of 'Long Cross'. These coins, though imitating a heavy type by no means maintain indefinitely the heavy weight themselves. Perhaps, too, it is a pointer to the overvaluation of the penny that the earliest of these imitations were struck on a standard heavier than that of their prototypes.

This paper concludes with a table summarizing all the types that have been discussed. A larger sample of coins might have produced slightly different results, and any consideration of the question of weight standard in the Late Anglo-Saxon penny will of course be far more complete when the figures from the Systematic Collection and hoard-coins from Sweden can be added to those available for this study.

TABLE 20

Summary-table to illustrate the metrology of the Late Anglo-Saxon penny

Period of circulation	Type	Presumptive weight standard in grains	
973–979	'First Small Cross'	24·0	falling below under Edward and Æthelræd
979–985	'First Hand'	25·5	
985–991	'Second Hand'	22·5	
991–997	'*Crux*'	25·5	
997–1003	'Long Cross'	27·5	
1003–1009	'Helmet'	22·5	
1009–1017	'Last Small Cross'	27·0–20·0	two or more parallel standards?
1017–1023	'Quatrefoil'	22·5–16·0	
1023–1029	'Pointed Helmet'	18·0	very well maintained
1029–1035	'Short Cross'	18·0	very well maintained

XII

A New Suggestion concerning the so-called 'Martlets' in the 'Arms of St Edward'

by R. H. M. DOLLEY and F. ELMORE JONES

[Plate XV]

In the April 1959 number of *The Coat of Arms* Mr H. C. Curwen has reverted to the vexed and apparently timeless controversy which concerns the ultimate origin of the anachronistic coat of arms which Plantagenet heraldists ascribed to Edward the Confessor.[1] In common with other modern students, and most recently Dr E. Delmar in the *Burlington Magazine*, he accepts the traditional view that the early heralds derived their inspiration from one of the most striking and individualistic of late Anglo-Saxon coin-types, the so-called 'Sovereign/Martlets' type of the Confessor himself.[2] Since both the obverse and the reverse are relevant to the arguments that follow, we illustrate here by enlarged direct photographs perhaps the most famous coin of the whole issue, the unique penny of Horndon from the 1774 hoard from St Mary Hill (**Plate XV, a**), by good fortune a representative coin of the type.[3] As Mr Curwen very justly remarks, 'no English coin bore the figure of a seated King again until Henry III issued his gold penny 200 years later', and it might also have been observed that seated figures are found on only one other issue in the whole of the Anglo-Saxon silver penny series, the so-called 'Two Emperors' type struck for Ælfred the Great and for Ceolwulf II towards the end of the latter's transitory 'reign'.[4] Elsewhere in this volume these unique coins are discussed in greater detail, and here it is necessary to note only that the prototype was a Roman gold coin of the fourth century A.D.[5] Also in these pages the claim is made that the prototype of the obverse of the 'Sovereign/Martlets' type is adapted from the reverse of a sixth-century Roman coin, and for the purpose of comparison we illustrate here an enlarged direct photograph (**Plate XV, 1**) of the reverse of a Constantinople *solidus* of Justin II.[6] That there is copying must be self-evident, and in particular we would draw attention to the turning to one side of the head, a detail which did not escape Dr F. E. Harmer when she discussed the coins in relation to the Great Seals.[7] Incidentally, the 'Sovereign/Martlets' type is the one late Anglo-Saxon issue where we find an attempt to latinize the very name of the ruler – as a general rule the engravers were content to use a more or less correct West Saxon 'normalization' of the Old English nominative. Another possible pointer to strong Roman influence is the consistent omission from the obverse legend of the 'Initial Cross Pattée'.

The obverse, then, of the 'Sovereign/Martlets' penny must surely be accepted as an adaptation at first hand of the reverse of a Roman gold coin, and the numismatist will have no hesitation in rejecting Mr Curwen's claim that 'it probably had its origin in the Great Seal of King Edward'.[8] The point is not unimportant since if the obverse is derived from a Roman coin there must be a possibility that the reverse too had a numismatic not to say Roman prototype. It is at this point, too, that we would begin to part company from Dr Delmar whose ingenious suggestion that the four birds on the reverse of the 'Confessor' penny are derived from a Coptic motif familiar to the Anglo-Saxon through the medium of embroideries seems to us to ignore a fundamental of the morphology of English coin-types of the eleventh century. At this period all pennies were struck in the knowledge that halfpennies and farthings could be supplied only by cutting the pennies into halves and quarters, and in fact all the substantive types struck between 991 and 1065, twenty of them, have a reverse type which is perfectly symmetrical and singularly adapted to division into four.[9] We feel then that Dr Delmar has failed to attach enough importance to the practical aspects of late Anglo-Saxon coin-design, and our contention is that, granted the choice of a bird for a reverse type, it was almost inevitable that the one bird should become four. Granted, too, that the reverse type should also include a cross – and a cross was a great aid to the accurate division of a penny into halfpennies and farthings – it was no less inevitable that the birds should be disposed in the quarters of a 'voided cross'.

Such a line of argument is implicit in Mr Curwen's note, though nowhere clearly stated, so that it does seem to us that the great merit of his paper is its search for a numismatic prototype. There are two sentences, however, with which we cannot agree:

> The date of this penny is about 1056–1059, and personally I think that the birds represent 'Ravens', the reverse of the coin being the Battle Standard of England at that time [p. 184].
>
> I would suggest that the obverse of the 'Sovereign Regnant' may have been struck because the Scottish and Welsh situations had been brought under control, and the counter-claimant to the throne had died, thus leaving Edward, and the organization of which he was the figurehead, supreme for the time being [p. 185].

Concerning the so-called 'Martlets' in the 'Arms of St Edward'

From the first it must be emphasized that the belief of most orthodox numismatists is not that the 'Sovereign/Martlets' type was struck at an uncertain point of time between 1056 and 1059, but that coins with this design were current over a period, presumptively of three years, which we have reason to think may have begun at Michaelmas 1056.[10] During this period the 'Sovereign/Martlets' coins alone would have been legal tender, and there is the further presumption that large numbers must have been available to put into circulation when the issue was initiated.

This interpretation of late Anglo-Saxon currency is of course to some extent conjectural (though it is hoped that this volume will be considered to have supplied fresh arguments in its support) and still less should it be thought that the absolute chronology has been established beyond all cavil. Nevertheless, both the interpretation and the chronology proposed have been arrived at on the basis of a mass of interlocking evidence which is not easily to be brushed aside. Mr Curwen, however, states a case which implies its wholesale rejection, but advances no positive arguments beyond a claim that his dating would allow us to interpret the types of the 'Sovereign/Martlets' issue to allude to the death of Edward Ætheling – who was incidentally a counter-claimant not to the throne but to the succession – and to victories over the Welsh and the Scots. Edward Ætheling's death is recorded by the *Anglo-Saxon Chronicle* (MSS. D and E) under the year 1057, and Mr Grierson has drawn attention to independent evidence which must be conclusive that the death did not take place before the winter of 1056/7 at the very earliest.[11] If, therefore, King Edward, or the hinted at power behind the throne, had wished to commemorate the death – and there is not one scrap of evidence to suggest that such hypothetical and improbable exultation would not have occasioned very proper revulsion among all right-thinking men – the earliest occasion for the introduction of the 'Sovereign/Martlets' type would be the first time that the coinage was changed after the spring of 1057. Unfortunately Mr Curwen has not thought it necessary to indicate how he would order – and date – the later coins of Edward the Confessor, and so we cannot tell how he would overcome the various difficulties that are occasioned by any but the orthodox arrangement of the different issues.[12] As it happens, too, the hoard-evidence for the period c. 1060–80 is unusually clear-cut, and the numismatic specialist must regard with misgiving the lightly throwing overboard a triennial type-cycle which has Michaelmas 1056 as one of its fixed points.

It is the same with Mr Curwen's suggestion that there is an allusion in the coin-type to Edward's wars with the Welsh and with the Scots. According to accepted numismatic theory, the types of the 'Sovereign/Martlets' coinage must have been agreed on during the early summer of 1056 at the very latest. Again we must stress that the great bulk of the coins of any one issue had to be struck and put in currency at the very outset of each triennium, so that a period of intensive striking coincided with the introduction of each new type. If only to prime the *cambia*, moreover, the mints must have begun converting into the new coin surplus old money and any other accumulated bullion some days at least before the formal date when coins of the new issue were to be proclaimed current. In other words, it is perfectly clear that by mid-September at the latest a very large number of dies not only must have been engraved – itself a labour of weeks if not months – but must have been actually distributed to some seventy mints the length and breadth of the country. We may suppose that the bulk of these dies must have been ready for dispatch by the end of August, and it is not unreasonable to suppose that work on them was well under way by July.[13] If, however, Mr Curwen clings to the 1056 dating which already he has sought to undermine, he is confronted with the situation that the designs for the Michaelmas recoinage would have been being canvassed at precisely the moment that the militia was hastily being mobilized as news trickled through of Gruffydd's success at Glasbury.[14] If this was scarcely the time for Edward to advertise that 'the Welsh situation had been brought under control', the situation on the Scottish frontier was little better. Here there was little to report beyond continued failure to turn to real advantage Siward's last great victory of two years earlier, and it was not until 1057 that Macbeth was to be finally overthrown.

Association of coin-types with historical events is always a perilous business, and we are very reluctant to attach any particular significance to Edward's choice of the 'Sovereign/Martlets' design for the triennial coinage which we still believe to have been introduced at Michaelmas 1056. As we have said, this dating rests on an elaborate structure of interlocking facts, and our submission is that Mr Curwen has failed to make out a case for its rejection. Yet, truly nothing short of rejection of a whole interpretation of numismatic evidence is implied by the whole hypothesis that the types of the 'Sovereign/Martlets' coinage allude to the death of the Ætheling and to the position of the English king *vis-à-vis* the Scots and the Welsh.

There is the further suggestion that the 'birds represent "Ravens", the reverse of the coin being the Battle Standard of England at that time'. It is true that an early, albeit not the earliest, account of the Viking descent on Devon in 878 speaks of the capture of their Raven-banner,[15] and the tradition of such banners borne by heathen Scandinavians will be found to survive into

Concerning the so-called 'Martlets' in the 'Arms of St Edward'

the saga age of Iceland. The *Orkneyinga Saga*, for example, attributes a banner of this description to the notorious Earl Sigurd, one of the pagan leaders at Clontarf.[16] Mr Curwen has cited as a possible numismatic prototype a rare penny of Anlaf Guthfrithsson,[17] though he would seem unaware of recent work which has linked this issue with the whirlwind campaigns of 939–41.[18] It was precisely then that Anlaf's Hiberno-Norsemen made themselves so unpopular with the Danes of Lincoln, Stamford, Nottingham, Derby and Leicester that an English poet could claim that the Danish population regarded the English reconquest as a liberation.[19] There seems really no reason to suppose that a century later the Raven-banner would have been associated with anything other than the most militant paganism, nor that it would have been any less unacceptable to the Danelaw – which had long been Christian – than to the English themselves. Consequently it seems highly unlikely that 'Godwine and Harold might have adopted a modification of the Danish Battle Standard ... for use by England'.[20] Even if we were to concede that in 1056 Harold was in a position to impose violent departures from tradition in matters appertaining not merely to regal dignity but also to national unity – and more and more we wonder whether the picture of Edward as an ineffectual puppet does not reflect in part at least nineteenth-century prejudices against vows of chastity – there is the rather curious if not incontrovertible evidence of the Bayeux Tapestry. The artist, though essentially truthful, had every reason not to suppress any details which put Harold the 'perjurer' in a bad light, and one would have thought that it was excellent evidence for the form of the English standard at a time when Harold was really in a position to have influenced its design. The banner of Harold's choice, however, is precisely the one which Mr Curwen would have us believe had been superseded a decade or so earlier by Harold himself.[21]

The suggestion of this note, therefore, is not simply that Mr Curwen's theories are incompatible with the generally accepted interpretation of late Anglo-Saxon coinage, but that they are implausible on grounds that are not purely numismatic. On the other hand, the rejection of the 'Raven' hypothesis in itself brings us no nearer to an understanding of the significance of the mysterious birds that occupy the quarters of one of the most intriguing of late Anglo-Saxon coin-types. There can be no doubt, of course, that these birds have been interpreted as 'martlets' by the heralds, but the numismatist ought to be the first to remark that on the coins – and on more than one early version of the 'arms of St Edward' – the birds concerned are invariably shown *with feet*.[22] An alternative suggestion is that the birds in the 'arms' at least may have been intended for doves, but we have not been able to find any firm basis for this interpretation which, as regards modern times, we suspect to owe much to the traditional picture of the King's dovelike character.

It is at this point perhaps that we should reconsider briefly the Great Seal of Edward the Confessor. It is the counterseal which is of especial significance, and we trust that we will be pardoned for illustrating (**Plate XV, b**) that of the so-called First Seal, although there is every reason to think that it represents a restitution, albeit a very early one.[23] Our reason for so doing is its relative completeness, though for a detailed study of the stylistic parallels with other seals and coins of the period reference will still have to be made to the more fragmentary Second and Third Seals, the authenticity of certain impressions of which seems beyond cavil even if in some cases they may not be attached to an original document. On the counterseal the English King is shown enthroned and holding what are perhaps the emblems of his temporal sovereignty, the bird-topped sceptre and the sword. Wyon identified the bird of the sceptre as a dove, doubtless on the analogy of the later medieval regalia where there does occur a dove-tipped sceptre, albeit of quite different form.[24] There is, however, no literary reference to a pre-Plantagenet sceptre topped or tipped by a bird, and, in the light of the undoubted prototype, we must be on our guard against any too facile assumption that the depiction of a bird-topped sceptre on the Great Seal implies that a sceptre of that type necessarily was included in the English regalia. There is, too, the further possibility that the dove-tipped sceptre of the Plantagenet regalia could have its origin in a misinterpretation of an earlier sceptre topped by quite another species of bird – one has only to put Rock's *Hierugia* beside Jungmann's *Missarum Solemnia* to realize how rapidly even modern scholarship can vary its interpretation of the most timeless of ceremonies. We need not, then, take too seriously Wyon's unsupported claim that the bird that caps one of the sceptres depicted on Great Seals of the Confessor is a dove, and it is worth noting in this connexion that De Gray Birch was far more guarded, and contented himself with describing the bird simply as a bird.[25]

For many years now numismatists have been aware that 'on the day when King Edward was alive and dead' a royal goldsmith and (?) *cuneator* was a certain Theoderic.[26] Not so generally appreciated is that this Theoderic was almost certainly of German origin, his name ('Dietrich') being quite un-English.[27] Neglected, too, are some very close parallels between the coins of the latter half of Edward the Confessor's reign, those with a bearded 'naturalistic' portrait, and certain German coins of precisely the same period.[28] Dr Harmer, too, has stressed the relationship between the Great Seals of Edward the Confessor and those of the German emperors, and to bring home this point we here illustrate

Concerning the so-called 'Martlets' in the 'Arms of St Edward' the Great Seal of Henry IV (**Plate XV, c**).[29] Clearly the imperial influence is very strong, and the resemblance is even closer if we compare the fragments of the authentic Second and Third Seals, so that it is clear that the German and English seals were cut in the same tradition if not by the same hand.

In his *Catalogue* De Gray Birch seems to suggest that there may be a third parallel of almost exactly the same date in the seal of a Byzantine Empress (? Theodora, *c.* 1055), but we are not convinced that the apparently aviform head to the sceptre there depicted is not in fact a flawed impression.[30] On the other hand, there can be no doubt that De Gray Birch was right when he identified the bird of the German sceptre as an eagle, and we would further remark that contemporary representations of the German 'eagle-headed sceptre' are not confined to seals.[31] The Byzantine sceptre also was eagle-headed, and as numismatists we would draw attention to its appearance on coins as late as those of the early eighth-century Emperor Philippicus (**Plate XV, 2**). No less significantly the eagle as some sort of standard or sceptre figures on certain of so-called Arab-Byzantine coins, and even on 'Post-Reform' copper pieces belonging to the early part of the eighth century.[32] The Late Roman origin of the 'eagle-sceptre' need not detain us here, but there is one particular representation, on a Milan *solidus* of Honorius (**Plate XV, 3**), which merits mention because it is so unequivocal. Of course we do not claim that any of these coins were available as models for the Anglo-Saxon *cuneator* – though a specimen of the Honorius coin could conceivably have occurred in an English hoard and have been brought to the royal treasury as Treasure Trove – but they do bring home the point that a 'bird-headed sceptre' had imperial connotations.

In this connexion we would draw attention to the fact that on the English Great Seal Edward the Confessor uses the quasi-imperializing style of *Basileus*, and it is well known that the Anglo-Saxon kings claimed some sort of dominion over territory that was never effectively under their control – the numismatist at once will recall the style REX TO(*tius*) BRIT(*anniae*) found on so many of the 'Post-Eamont' pennies of Æthelstan. Nor is it uninteresting that the oldest portion of the extant English regalia includes an ampulla of eagle form. While, therefore, we certainly would not commit ourselves to any statement that an 'eagle-headed sceptre' figured among the late Anglo-Saxon regalia, we do suggest that the probably German (or at least very strongly German-influenced) *cuneator* who cut the Great Seal of Edward the Confessor included an 'eagle-headed sceptre' on the counterseal because for him, and doubtless for eleventh-century Europe at large, the eagle was a symbol of imperial dominion. It is at this point of the argument that we would revert to the coins of the so-called 'Sovereign/Martlets' issue. Unfortunately there has still to be written a

Anglo-Saxon Coins

systematic analysis of the numerous minor varieties of the main type that exist, but the fact that William Hunter was able to secure a fine run of the coins of this type from the St Mary Hill hoard means that the accuracy of certain observations we will be making here can easily be checked against the relevant Plates of the Hunter and Coats fascicule of the new *Sylloge*.[33]

On the Byzantine prototype (**Plate XV, 1**) the seated personification of Constantinopolis holds in her right hand a spear. This clearly has troubled the Anglo-Saxon engraver, and on many coins it has been converted into a knobbed staff or a long-handled axe with a curved blade which recalls those which are often found in the case of medieval carvings of St Olaf from Scandinavia.[34] Her foot is set on the prow of a ship, a detail that seems never to have been understood by the copyist, though there are coins where the outline seems still to be preserved. The turreted crown of Constantinopolis has been remodelled to approximate more closely to the open, fleured crown which is found in manuscript 'portraits' of Æthelstan, Eadgar, and Cnut.[35] As regards the reverse, it is noteworthy that there are at least three distinct versions of the 'bird' that occupies each of the four quarters. On a majority of the coins these 'birds' are not characteristically predatory, still less aquiline, and Figure I (a) may be thought to give a very fair impression. On other coins the drawing is much more crude so that Figure I (b) is in nowise an exaggeration. There are coins,

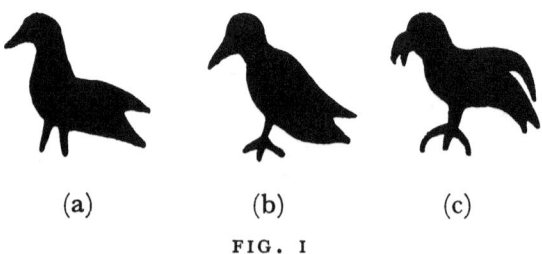

(a)   (b)   (c)

FIG. I

however, where the form of the 'bird' is as in Figure I (c), and it is noteworthy that these coins are among the best executed of the whole series. Such 'birds' simply cannot be considered to approximate to 'doves' or 'martlets', and our submission is that the curved beak and talons too long have been disregarded. On grounds that are purely stylistic, then, the traditional identification of the 'birds' is suspect, and the balance of the evidence must be that they are birds of prey. It is to this conclusion, of course, that Mr Curwen had arrived on quite

Concerning the so-called 'Martlets' in the 'Arms of St Edward'

other grounds, though naturally we would emphasize the discrepancies between the 'birds' of the Edward the Confessor coins and the undoubted ravens that figure on the coins of Anlaf Guthfrithsson. The whole balance of the 'birds' is different, and we believe that this must support our contention that the 'birds' are eagles.

Doubtless it will be objected that any 'Eagle-sceptre' belongs to the obverse rather than the reverse of the coin-type in question, but in reply we would remark that there is a precedent for such a transposition. Probably at Michaelmas 1029, Cnut's die-engraver substituted a more 'naturalistic' (?) fleur-de-lis for the trefoil that had represented the head of the English sceptre on a number of coins struck over the previous fifty years.[36] Within a decade we find on coins of Harold Harefoot (**Plate XV, 5**) this 'Fleur-de-lis sceptre' occupying not only a prominent place on the obverse but also each of the four quarters of a reverse divided by a 'Voided Long Cross'. There is some reason to think, moreover, that the original design of the 'Sovereign/Eagles' obverse contemplated the inclusion of the eagle later transferred to the reverse. There is in an English private collection a unique coin of this issue on which the cross on the orb held by the King is replaced by a 'bird' of precisely the same form as those that appear on the reverse (**Plate XV, d**), incidentally the same 'bird' that appears as our Figure I (c).[37] The variant is rather more involved than the 'simple cross' which it supplants, and must surely represent a deliberate experiment at a time when 'Eagle-sceptres' were very much in the designer's mind. One might even imagine that the choice of a bird to crown the orb reflected a misunderstanding of the miniature 'Winged Victory' found in the same position on late fourth-century gold coins with a very similar reverse, for example, a *solidus* of Arcadius (**Plate XV, 5**), but the resemblance of typical pence to the Justin II reverse is so close that the coincidence is better disregarded even though the Arcadius coin is much the more likely to have occurred in an English 'Treasure Trove'. It must be remembered that there were four symbols of dominion proper to the two versions of the *Majestas* found on the Great Seal, namely the 'Trefoil (? Trinitarian) sceptre' and the '*Globus crucifer*' proper to the obverse, and the 'Eagle-topped sceptre and the sword' found on the counterseal.[38] Already we have noted the copyist of the Justin II *solidus* unhappy about the spear, and it is not impossible than an imaginative engraver experimented to see if it would be possible to bring together on the obverse more of the traditional trappings of imperial sway. On one or two rare coins of this issue, moreover, the orb appears to be 'jewelled', apparently the result of an attempt to substitute a 'Cross Botonnée' for the normal 'Cross Pattée'. It is indeed a pity that at present we have no sure pointer to the date of Edward's Great Seal, but Dr R. Lane Poole has observed that it 'appears to have been in use not much later than 1051', while Dr Harmer has noted authentic impressions of the so-called Second Seal – the only genuine matrix? – on a Canterbury writ which must be dated after 1052 and on the Taynton writ which is datable between 1053 and 1057.[39] The numismatist should be the last to forbear to comment on the coincidence between these dates and the introduction of the first 'Germanizing' coin-type (*BMC* type VII=Brooke 6=Hildebrand F=Hawkins 227), an event almost certainly to be dated to Michaelmas 1053.

Granted, then, that the 'bird' which tops the sceptre on the Great Seal of the German *imperator* is an eagle in the best Roman and Byzantine tradition, there would seem little reason for the English sigillographer to identify as a dove the 'bird' which occupies precisely the same position on the counterseal of the contemporary English *Basileus*. Granted, too, that the 'bird' which figures on the counterseal of Edward the Confessor *c*. 1053 is an eagle, the student must begin to wonder whether it is not in fact an eagle which appears in each of the quarters of the reverse of a novel coin-type introduced in all probability at Michaelmas 1056. Reluctantly, therefore, English numismatists must consider again the validity of their time-honoured nomenclature, and we feel that we have made out a case for abandoning the name 'Sovereign/Martlets'. Strictly, too, the obverse is not a true 'Sovereign' type, the aversion of the head being foreign to a true *Majestas*, but this is a detail which perhaps can be overlooked in the interests of intelligibility. Tradition may well prove too strong in this matter, but we venture to suggest that there is also a greater congruity of the essential criteria if in the future we label the issue presumptively introduced at Michaelmas 1056 the 'Sovereign/Eagles' type.

REFERENCES

1. H. C. CURWEN 'Some Notes on a Penny of Edward the Confessor' *The Coat of Arms* v no. 38 (April 1959) pp. 184 ff.
2. E. DELMAR 'Observations on the Origins of the Arms of Edward the Confessor' *Burlington Magazine* xcv (1953) pp. 359 ff.
3. For the 1774 St Mary Hill find (*not* 1775 cf. *BNJ* xxix i (1958) p. 52) *vide supra* p. 165
4. Cf. *supra* p. 81
5. Cf. *supra* p. 14
6. Cf. *supra* p. 30
7. F. E. HARMER *Anglo-Saxon Writs* p. 103
8. Op. cit. p. 184

Concerning the so-called 'Martlets' in the 'Arms of St Edward'

9. 'Voided Short Cross' 991–7, 1048–50, 1023–9, 1029–35, 1040–2, 1046–8, 1050–3, 1053–6, 1056–9, 1059–62, 1065/1066
   'Voided Long Cross' 997–1003, 1003–9, 1017–23, 1037–40, 1042–4
   'Small Cross Pattée', 1009–17, 1044–6, 1062–5
   'Jewel ("Club") Cross' 1035–7
10. For the principles of Eadgar's monetary reform cf. *supra* pp. 154–58.
11. P. GRIERSON in *EHR* LI (1936) pp. 90–7
12. Cf. *BNJ* xxviii ii (1956) p. 283 ff.
13. Insufficient attention has been paid to the phenomenon that surviving coins from issues which were withdrawn before their official inception – e.g. *'Agnus Dei'* in 1009 and 'Facing Pyramids' in 1065 – almost invariably prove to be from minor mints peripheral to the centre or centres of die-production
14. STENTON op. cit. p. 565
15. *Anglo-Saxon Chronicle* (B, C, D, E), *s.a.* 878. But it is not in the oldest version (A), nor in those used by Asser and Æthelweard. That the heathen associations persisted is brought out by the legendary accretions made in the twelfth-century *Annals of St. Neots*.
16. *Orkneyinga Saga*, cc. 11, 12; with which cf. the *Saga of Burnt Njal*, cc. 155, 156
17. Op. cit. p. 185
18. *Nordisk Numismatisk Årsskrift* 1957–8 pp. 13 ff.
19. *Anglo-Saxon Chronicle s.a.* 942
20. CURWEN op. cit. p. 185
21. F. M. STENTON (ed.) *The Bayeux Tapestry* Pl. 72 where the English centre is drawn up beneath two *dragon* standards. There is also early literary evidence that Harold's personal standard was anthropomorphic
22. For example, the well-known Westminster Abbey relief
23. The evidence is set out in detail by Miss Harmer op. cit. pp. 101–5
24. The dove-tipped sceptre seems first to be mentioned in a document of the reign of King John
25. *Catalogue of Seals in B.M.* I p. 2 no. 5
26. Cf. *NC* 1904 pp. 144–79
27. Cf. *NC* 1953 p. 181
28. Cf. R. GAETTENS *Münzporträts im xi Jahrhundert* ? Heidelberg 1956 *passim*
29. HARMER op. cit p. 96
30. *Catalogue of Seals in B.M.* v p. 3 no. 17 454
31. Ibid. pp. 12–13, nos. 21, 133 and 21, 135
32. We are indebted to Dr John Walker for drawing our attention to this remarkable persistence of imperial symbolism
33. Cf. *infra* p. 228
34. On other coins the identity of the objects capping the 'staff' seems deliberately vague
35. Cf. T. D. KENDRICK *Late Saxon and Viking Art* Pls II, XVIII, LXXIII, XCI, XCV

36. The earliest appearance of a sceptre is on two Kentish coins *c.* 978; cf. *BNJ* XXVIII i (1955) pp. 89–90
37. We are indebted to Mr J. D. Gomm of Ealing for permission to publish the coin which he himself recognized as unique while yet a schoolboy
38. On the obverse of the so-called 'First' Seal the Cross is wanting from the Orb, but the balance of the evidence must be that it was present on the genuine Great Seal
39. HARMER op. cit. p. 99 (Poole quoted) and 104

XIII

Some Remarks on Eighteenth-century Numismatic Manuscripts and Numismatists

by J. S. MARTIN

[Plates facing pp. 232 and 233]

No apologies are offered by the writer for adding this particular essay to this book. In the first place, it is only in this field that her abilities allow her to make a suitable contribution as a mark of her respect for Sir Frank Stenton, and in the second place he himself holds enlightened views of the value of coins as evidence in historical studies generally, as was made abundantly clear when he treated the Numismatic Congress, 1954, to a stimulating address on that very subject.

In his article in the *Centennial Publication*, 1958, of the American Numismatic Society, Mr C. E. Blunt pointed out, with numerous examples, the importance to Anglo-Saxon numismatic studies of manuscript material dating from the seventeenth, eighteenth, and nineteenth centuries. The present paper is to offer certain loosely connected items of information and speculations arising from the study, but lately commenced and still continuing, of two late Georgian manuscripts to which attention had not been drawn at the time Mr Blunt wrote. One of these is, indeed, none other than Ruding's collection of papers, the whereabouts of which Mr Blunt questioned in his article.

(a) CHARLES COMBE'S MANUSCRIPT

Through the generosity of B. A. Seaby, Ltd. the Department of Coins and Medals recently acquired a demy-octavo pocket-book, covered in maroon leather and of some one hundred pages, which contains lists of the coins of English monarchs from the Heptarchy up to 1780 in the reign of George III. It also includes illustrations of about three hundred and fifty coins up to the time of Edward III, most of which have been cut out from printed plates, though there are a large number of drawings in both ink and pencil. Where appropriate, mint-towns and mint-marks are also given, and against nearly every entry there is an indication as to the collection in which a specimen of the coin was, at that time, to be found; unfortunately no mention is made of moneyers.

Anglo-Saxon Coins

A label attached to the first page states that the manuscript came from the library of Taylor Combe, below which, at a later date, Mr P. Carlyon-Britton has noted that Mr F. W. Lincoln, Sen., gave it to him in 1907. This book is undoubtedly the one comprising Lot 2415 at Sotheby's Sale of Taylor Combe's library in 1826, and which was sold to Matthew Young for six shillings. How and when it fell into Mr Lincoln's hands is not known.

Internal evidence shows quite clearly that this manuscript is the work of Dr Charles Combe. The writing is similar to known specimens of his hand, the great majority of entries relate to coins from the Hunter cabinet of which he mainly was in charge, and on the last few pages are some extensive notes relating to the coins of the Seleucid kings, which notes Mr G. K. Jenkins, Deputy Keeper of Coins and Medals, has obligingly connected directly with Dr Combe's celebrated catalogue of Greek coins in the Hunter Collection. External evidence also confirms Dr Combe's authorship, for Ruding in his *Annals* makes occasional reference to 'Dr. Combe's book', a particular instance being in respect of a coin (now known to be false, and about which Ruding himself was in two minds) of Æthelbald. Ruding states that Dr Combe's book shows the coin to be in the cabinet of Mr Austin, and in the manuscript there is the coin listed with the letter A beside the illustration cut out from a plate engraved under the direction of John White!

One or two notes in other hands also appear, particularly in that of Taylor Combe who has initialled one of his entries, the word 'false' against an illustration of an 'Ælfred' coin, moneyer 'Breece', also emanating from the imaginative Mr White.

The material for the manuscript must have taken a number of years to assemble, and appearances suggest that the major part was available before the book was commenced, as the space left for the coins of each monarch is in proportion to the number of entries. One space provided, by all appearances at the time the columns were originally drawn up, is for a penny of Eanred; no illustration was ever put in, though the King's name was inserted and circles, the size of a penny, were drawn. The only penny of Eanred of which Dr Combe could have been aware was that found at Trewhiddle in 1774, hence it is a fair assumption that the book was commenced after that date. Similarly, two rare coins of Edward the Confessor found at St Mary Hill in 1774 are included in their proper places. Furthermore, illustrations cut out from plates published by Strutt and by Gough in 1777 are used, and these also appear to have been in from the start.

The last date shown is 1780 (in respect of Maundy Money) nor does this look

Eighteenth-century Numismatic Manuscripts and Numismatists

like a late addition, thus the original compilation probably continued at least till that year, but not later than 1782 when the catalogue of Greek coins referred to above was published. Dr Combe continued working on his book from time to time for some years, apparently as and when he gained access to various collections, notably that of the Duke of Devonshire. The lists of mint-towns are at first in alphabetical order, but later entries are not so arranged and are sometimes in different ink. These additions continued up to 1812 at least, when he made entries relating to the Royal Collection which he inspected, by invitation, in that year.

The significance of the manuscript lies both in what it is and the information it can yield. As a document it is without doubt quite the most ambitious list of English coins that had at that date ever been attempted, and it must have been of the greatest assistance to Taylor Combe and Ruding, both of whom had recourse to it. For its time it is amazingly comprehensive, particularly in view of the paucity of published information, notably as regards the Anglo-Saxon series which Snelling omitted from his *Views*. Admittedly it contains some errors but, again for its day, it is remarkably accurate. No conclusion has been reached as to its precise purpose; it may have been intended as a basis for the catalogue of Hunter's English coins that Dr Combe at one time proposed to publish, but it is not known whether it contains all of them and in any case it lists coins from at least twelve other collections. It certainly is not intended as a comprehensive list of all English coins, for a number of Anglo-Saxon coins then in the British Museum are omitted, although sixty-two of these are included, nor are any Pembroke coins noted as such.

The only information extracted so far relates to Anglo-Saxon coins, and even here there is a great deal more still to be learned, especially when the *Sylloge* of coins in the Hunterian Museum, now preparing under the capable hands of Miss Anne Robertson, becomes available. It has been possible to identify nearly all the Plates from which illustrations have been cut, one result being the discovery of some Plates, not nowadays generally known, in Strutt's *Chronicles* of 1777. An analysis has been made of all the Anglo-Saxon coins resulting, *inter alia*, in the redating in the provenances of the National Collection of eighteen coins from 'before 1812' or 'undated' to 'before 1782'; these are listed in the Appendix.

The main value of the manuscript, however, is as a record of the disposition of a number of identifiable coins at a given time, thus eliminating the possibility of their coming from finds of a later date, as well as going some way towards confirming their validity, as explained by Mr Blunt in his article referred to at the beginning.

Anglo-Saxon Coins

The number of Anglo-Saxon coins marked as being in various collections is as follows:

Hunter	608	Tyssen	7
Devonshire	85	Langford	6
BM	62	Royal	5
Southgate	27	Austin	2
Hodsol	13	Rebello	1
Bodleian	8	Solly	1
Mason	7		

Only about one hundred and forty can be said for certain to have been in the National Collection at this time, something like half that number are instanced. Only twenty-seven Southgate coins are listed against ten times that number in his collection when he died fifteen years later. What does stand out is the unrivalled richness of Hunter's collection in the series.

(b) RUDING'S MANUSCRIPTS

A short while ago twenty-six bound volumes of various sizes and about two inches thick were located in the Department of Manuscripts, British Museum, and represent the papers of Rev. Rogers Ruding, author of the monumental *Annals of the Coinage of Britain*. This work, first published in 1817, went through three editions and stood unrivalled in its time. The papers represent a vast assembly of material collected by Ruding when preparing the *Annals*, from many sources which he acknowledges in the preface to his book. So far it has not been possible to do more than glance over this material, but two volumes, Additional MSS. Nos. 18093/4, dealing with Anglo-Saxon coins, have been more thoroughly examined.

The first item that came to notice was a drawing of the 'Offering penny' of Ælfred, *BMC* 158, the nature of which was demonstrated by Mr R. H. M. Dolley in an important article in the *Numismatic Chronicle* for 1954. The drawing, which is reproduced as Figure I, is marked 'found near Poole in Dorsetshire' and 'Rough copy of a drawing by Mr [i.e. Taylor] Combe'. Hitherto the earliest reference to this coin has been in Hawkins's *Silver Coins of England*, 1841, where he says that it was owned by a Mr Garland but gives no clue as to its origin. It is now possible to say, therefore, that it was found near Poole at a date not later than 1826, the year when Taylor Combe died.

Next is a list of about two hundred Anglo-Saxon pennies (the majority illustrated by drawings) purchased by Rev. Richard Southgate between 1786 and

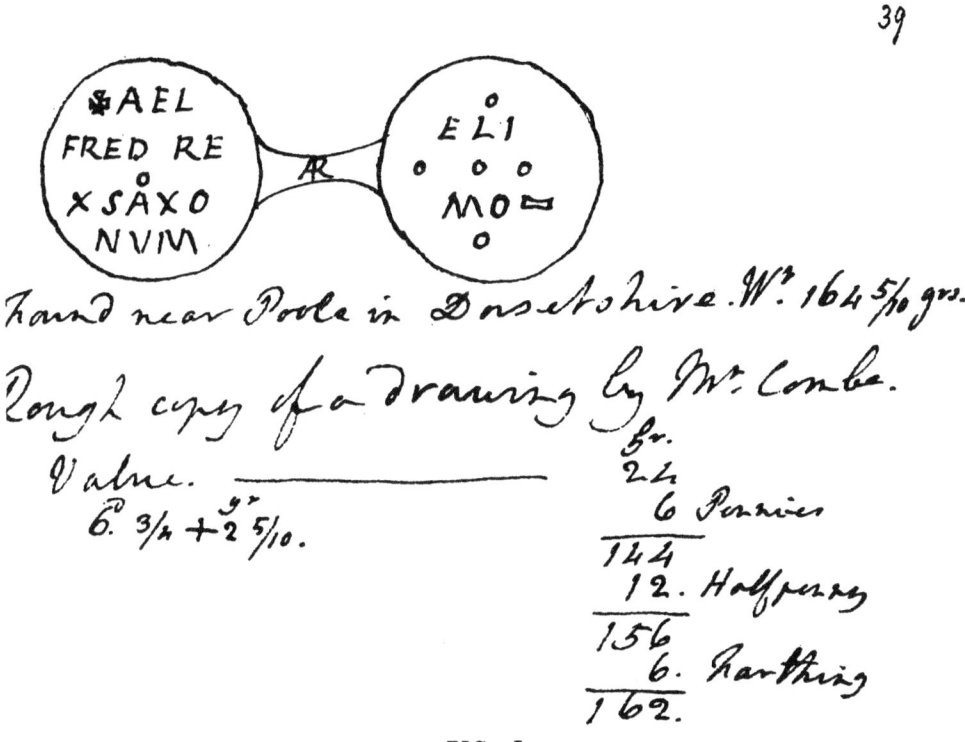

FIG. I

1795 inclusive. It has been possible to identify these, nearly all of which must have come into the National Collection via Tyssen. The first Sale Catalogue of Southgate's coins prepared by Messrs Leigh and Sotheby after his death in 1795 listed, *inter alia*, two hundred and sixty-five Anglo-Saxon pennies, but Edward Hawkins noted in the British Museum copy that Tyssen purchased the collection before the day of the Sale for eighteen hundred guineas. As it stands Hawkins's statement is not correct, for a revised Sale Catalogue published two months after the first shows that a considerable number of Southgate coins did, in fact, come under the hammer, names of buyers and prices paid having been written in. Very few of the Anglo-Saxon pennies came to sale, however, and there is little doubt that Tyssen had the remainder. It has been possible by means of the list to revise the provenances of two hundred coins in the *British Museum Catalogue*; the revisions are given in the Appendix.

Yet another interesting document is headed 'List of 121 Saxon, English, and Scotch Coins presented to the British Museum by his Grace the Duke of Argyle by the hands of the Rt Honble Ld Frederick Campbell. April 24th, 1789.'

Anglo-Saxon Coins

Underneath are given details of the coins except for six noted as 'unknown', there being four of Eadmund, four of Eadred, three of Eadwig, fifty-four of Eadgar, forty-three 'Short Cross' pennies, and seven 'Scotch' coins, the latter not recognizable from the descriptions. At the end of the List is another paragraph, saying:

> The above coins were all found in the Isle of Tiry one of the smaller Hebrides, some in the year 1780, by a tenant of the Duke of Argyle, who, whilst he was digging Potatoes accidentally lighted upon them, concealed as he imagined in some sort of cloth, which however was chiefly mouldered away. The others were found in 1787, likewise by a Tenant of the Duke whilst he was planting Potatoes. These were contained in an earthenware Pot. Both parcels lay between two and three feet below the surface of the earth; and both pots are within a small distance of two Danish Forts. The former near *Dun a Chalish*, and the latter near *Dun Hiadin*. This Island, when Iona was in its flourish state, was called its Granary.

It should be added that the first find contained the Anglo-Saxon pennies, and the other coins were in the second.

This List, which is stated to have been copied from a document in Southgate's possession, allows a satisfactory provenance to be given to sixty-one of the Anglo-Saxon coins; details appear in the Appendix. Six more are insufficiently described, the remaining four (one of Eadwig and three of Eadgar) cannot now be found in the National Collection.

A further twelve Anglo-Saxon coins of Eadgar were given by Lord Frederick Campbell to Miss Banks (an enthusiastic collector and sister of Sir Joseph Banks, for many years President of the Royal Society) in December 1807. These she bequeathed to the British Museum when she died in 1818, but eight which duplicated coins already held were passed on to the Museum of the Royal Mint. The four which remain in the National Collection can, with confidence, be given a Tiree provenance, and are included in the Appendix. It may be observed here that Miss Banks records in her papers that Taylor Combe in 1809 gave her thirty-three plates of Anglo-Saxon coins; these were a set of those annotated as having been published in 1803 but which were not in fact available to the public till Ruding published them with his *Annals*. Ruding must have had the original printing plates as his illustrations are identical with those given by Taylor Combe to Robert Bryer and included in the latter's manuscript of 1812 (see Mr Blunt's article quoted above).

Details of the 'Short Cross' pennies found in the second Tiree hoard will be published at a later date.

DR CHARLES COMBE

REV. RICHARD SOUTHGATE

TAYLOR COMBE

Eighteenth-century Numismatic Manuscripts and Numismatists

There is still much more to be learned from Ruding's Anglo-Saxon papers, and there will be work for years in sifting the rest of the material.

THREE GREAT NUMISMATISTS

Three of the outstanding numismatists of their time, certainly unequalled as regards the Anglo-Saxon series, were the Rev. Richard Southgate, Dr Charles Combe, and his son Taylor Combe. Details of their lives can be found in the *Dictionary of National Biography*, the *Gentleman's Magazine*, and elsewhere, but brief biographical notes will not be out of place here to accompany the three portraits reproduced opposite pages 232 and 233, and which, so far as the writer is aware, have not been reproduced for publication for a century and a half.

REV. RICHARD SOUTHGATE [Plate facing p. 232]

Richard Southgate was born at Alwalton, Huntingdonshire, on 16 March 1729, his father, William, being a substantial farmer in the district. He was educated in schools at Uppingham, Fotheringay, and Peterborough, and entered St John's College, Cambridge, in 1745, taking his degree of Bachelor of Arts four years later. In 1754 he was ordained and presented to the Rectory of Woolley, Huntingdonshire, from which five years afterwards he felt himself obliged to resign, the young patron of the living having himself just taken holy orders.

He served as curate in several parishes, finally becoming curate of St Giles in the Fields, Bloomsbury, in 1765, which office he held thirty years until his death. In 1783 he was given the small Rectory of Little Steeping, Lincolnshire, and in the next year was appointed Assistant Librarian to the British Museum, with a residence, following the death of Dr Andrew Gifford, also a noted numismatist.

Hitherto Mr Southgate had been by no means affluent, but in 1786 he inherited an estate of one hundred pounds a year, and in 1790 was presented to the very valuable living of Warsop, Nottinghamshire, worth some fourteen hundred pounds a year and which he held while he lived. These additions to his income enabled him considerably to extend the collections of books and coins he had already assembled. It is interesting in this connexion to recall from the earlier parts of this article that *c.* 1780 Dr Combe noted only twenty-seven Southgate coins in his manuscript, that the list of Anglo-Saxon pennies acquired by Mr Southgate commences in 1786 and extends to some two hundred coins, and that when he died he was possessed of two hundred and sixty-five. In later life

Anglo-Saxon Coins

he commenced collecting shells and other natural curiosities. In all his acquisitions he followed the wise policy of selecting only the finest specimens available.

He became a Fellow of the Society of Antiquaries in 1791, and later was elected to the Linnean Society, but he did not long grace those learned institutions, for he died, a bachelor, on 22 January 1795, during one of the severest cold spells ever recorded in England.

He was by nature active in mind but sluggish in body, becoming corpulent in later life as may be seen from his portrait. The sweetness of his disposition and his benevolence to the poor (sometimes misplaced, for he seems to have been somewhat gullible) were commented on by many of his contemporaries, while his extensive scholarship was renowned. His knowledge of the Anglo-Saxons was unrivalled in his day and his learning in history and numismatics generally was equalled by few.

Apart from a few sermons Mr Southgate never published anything, although at the time of his death he had been preparing a history of the Anglo-Saxons and Danes in England based largely on their coinage. It is apparent, however, that he rendered valuable assistance to others in preparing their publications, for there is hardly a numismatic work of the period that does not contain some tribute to his help. There was a proposal in 1782 that he should give a description of the Anglo-Saxon coins in the Hunter Collection, but nothing came of this (see the *Gentleman's Magazine*, 1782, p. 519).

The portrait reproduced here is taken from an engraving in the front of Leigh and Sotheby's Sale Catalogue of his books, coins, shells, etc., which is also prefaced by a memoir of his life by Charles Combe.

DR CHARLES COMBE [Plate facing p. 232]

Charles Combe was born on 23 September 1743, in Bloomsbury, where his father John Combe traded as an apothecary. He was educated at Harrow and then studied medicine in London, succeeding to his father's business in 1768. He continued a successful career in medicine, obtained the diploma of Doctor of Medicine from the University of Glasgow in 1783 and practised widely as an obstetrician till his death. In 1769 he married Arthey, daughter of Henry Taylor, and had by her four children; she died in 1799.

He became interested in coins and other antiquities early in life, becoming a Fellow of the Society of Antiquaries in 1771 and of the Royal Society in 1776; he also acted as Secretary of the Society of Arts for a short while in 1806 and 1807. His especial work on coins was in connexion with the magnificent collection assembled by Dr William Hunter, the eminent anatomist and brother of the even more distinguished John Hunter. This collection, which is now in the possession of the University of Glasgow, was formed largely with the advice and selection of Dr Combe who purchased many of the coins on Hunter's behalf. In 1782 he published a descriptive catalogue of the coins of the Greek cities as a first instalment of a complete catalogue of the Collection, but after Hunter's death in 1783 he seems to have lost interest in this project, although under the terms of Hunter's will he retained the right of access to the Collection. He published other numismatic works as well as an edition of Horace.

He died in Bloomsbury on 18 March 1817, leaving two surviving children, one of whom was Taylor Combe.

The portrait is taken from an engraving by N. Branwhite of members of the Medical Society in 1801.

TAYLOR COMBE [Plate facing p. 233]

Taylor Combe, son of the above, was born in 1774 (the exact date has not yet been ascertained) and was educated at Harrow and Oriel College, Oxford, where he obtained the degree of Master of Arts in 1798. In 1803 he was appointed an Assistant Librarian to take charge of the collection of coins and medals in the British Museum, which remained in his care when in 1807 he became Keeper of the newly established Department of Antiquities in which post he served till his death. He was elected a Fellow of the Society of Antiquaries in 1796, becoming a Director of the Society in 1813. He became a Fellow of the Royal Society in 1807 and acted as Secretary from 1812 till 1824.

In 1808 he married Elizabeth, daughter of the late Edward Whitaker Gray, Keeper of Natural History and Antiquities at the British Museum, who had himself been Secretary of the Royal Society in 1797.

He died at the British Museum after a long illness in July 1826.

Under the influence of his father Mr Combe took an interest in antiquities from an early age, particularly ancient coins. His publications included a Catalogue of the Greek coins in the British Museum, and a description of the collection of Ancient Terracottas, as well as a number of articles in *Archaeologia*. After his death his Catalogue of Anglo-Gallic coins in the British Museum was published, as well as the Catalogue of Ancient Marbles which he had in part prepared. Apart from one or two contributions to *Archaeologia* he published no writings on Anglo-Saxon coins, of which he had a deep knowledge, but he made extensive notes which were used by others in their publications and superintended the engraving of the thirty-three plates of coins to which reference has already been made.

A portrait of Mr Combe used to hang in the old Medal Room at the British Museum, but this was destroyed during the Second World War when the

Anglo-Saxon Coins

Museum suffered from enemy attack. Fortunately the National Portrait Gallery had already taken a photograph of the portrait, and from that the picture opposite page 233 is reproduced. It is feared that in the same incident Taylor Combe's papers, together with those of Southgate, Tyssen, and perhaps Dr Combe, were all destroyed for they have not been found since that time.

In conclusion the writer would like to express the general appreciation of the support Sir Frank Stenton has given to Anglo-Saxon numismatics and to the science generally, especially as regards the grand design of the *Sylloge of Coins of the British Isles*. In truth, his sentiments are different from those of Archdeacon Nicolson, who wrote in 1676: 'There's not much to be learned from any Coins we have of our Saxon Kings, their silver coins being all of the same size, and generally very slovenly minted.'

Appendix

Amendments and additions to 'The Provenances of the Anglo-Saxon Coins Recorded in the Two Volumes of the *British Museum Catalogue*', *BNJ* xxviii i (1955) pp. 26–59.

MERCIA
Offa
Before 1777: 32 (found at Winchester and via Gostling, 1777, and Southgate, 1795)
Before 1782 (C. Combe MS.): 31, 42, 58
Southgate Collection (1795): 38 and (via Tyssen, 1802) 30, 35, 48, 51, 54

Coenwulf
Before 1782 (C. Combe MS.): 99
Southgate Collection (1795): 74, 96, and (via Tyssen, 1802) 73

Berhtwulf
Before 1783 (C. Combe MS.): 132

Burgred
Southgate Collection (1795): 168, 185, 300, 349, 381, and (via Tyssen, 1802) 329

KENT
Eadberht Praen
Southgate Collection (1795): 3 (via Tyssen, 1802)

Cuthred
Southgate Collection (1795): 7

Baldred
Southgate Collection (1795): 17

Wulfred
Southgate Collection (1795): 26

Ceolnoth
Southgate Collection (1795): 29 (via Tyssen, 1802)

EAST ANGLIA
Eadwald
Southgate Collection (1795): 3 (via Tyssen, 1802)

Anglo-Saxon Coins

Æthelstan I
Southgate Collection (1795): 8 (via Tyssen, 1802)

Æthelweard
Southgate Collection (1795): 25 and (via Tyssen, 1802) 21

(St) Eadmund
Before 1782 (C. Combe MS.): 84
Southgate Collection (1795): 52, 57

'St Eadmund Memorial Coinage'
Southgate Collection (1795): 108

NORTHUMBRIA
Anlaf
Before 1782 (C. Combe MS.): 1097
Southgate Collection (1795): 1090, 1103 (both via Tyssen, 1802)

Eric Bloodaxe
Southgate Collection (1795): 1112 (via Tyssen, 1802)

'St Peter'
Southgate Collection (1795): 1114 (via Hollis, 1817)

WESSEX
Ecgbeorht
Southgate Collection (1795): 14, 20 (both via Tyssen, 1802)

Æthelwulf
Before 1782 (C. Combe MS.): 85
Before 1812: 18

Æthelbearht
Southgate Collection (1795): 15, 61 (both via Tyssen, 1802)

Æthelræd I
Southgate Collection (1795): 1, 19 (both via Tyssen, 1802)

Ælfred
Before 1782 (C. Combe MS.): 87
Southgate Collection (1795): 86 and (via Tyssen, 1802) 10, 175, 444
Poole find (before 1826): 158 (presented Rev. G. V. Garland, 1875)

Eighteenth-century Numismatic Manuscripts and Numismatists

Edward the Elder
Before 1782 (C. Combe MS.): 9, 113
Southgate Collection (1795): 45
Rome find (1846): 64

ENGLAND
Æthelstan
Before 1782 (C. Combe MS.): 85
Southgate Collection (1795): 14, 63, 84, 117, 154, and (via Tyssen, 1802) 20, 83, 148

Eadmund
Tiree find (1780): 47, 61, 86, 136
Southgate Collection (1795): 66, 103, 140, 144, and (via Tyssen, 1802) 1, 120, 148

Eadred
Tiree find (1780): 48, 50, 62, 102
Southgate Collection (1795): 3, 20, 41, 49, 78, and (via Tyssen, 1802) 24, 39, 57, 69

Eadwig
Tiree find (1780): 21, 28
Southgate Collection (1795): 4, 15 (both via Tyssen, 1802)

Eadgar
Tiree find (1780): 1, 22, 26, 33, 48, 59, 64, 65, 67, 69, 74, 75, 77–9, 83, 84, 86, 87, 91, 94, 97, 98, 100, 115, 118, 119, 131–5, 137, 143, 146, 147, 149, 153, 156, 160, 169, 174, 177, 182, 183, 186, 191, 193, 207, and (via Miss Banks, 1818) 58, 126, 170, 188
Before 1782 (C. Combe MS.): 197
Southgate Collection (1795): 7, 8, 151, and (via Tyssen, 1802) 29, 190

Edward the Martyr
Before 1782 (C. Combe MS.): 12
Southgate Collection (1795): 5, 8, 9, 24

Æthelræd II
Before 1782 (C. Combe MS.): 142, 310, 340, 374
Southgate Collection (1795): 6, 11, 30, 78, 98, 120, 130, 136, 144, 151, 164, 190, 262, 298, 326, 335, 354

Cnut
Southgate Collection (1795): 5, 8, 14, 17, 22, 30, 40, 43, 55, 84, 92, 217, 219, 220, 245, 257, 270, 293, 305, 307, 357–9, 380, 471, 478, 479, 491, 493, 497,

Anglo-Saxon Coins

498, 505, 514, 522, 523, 547, 551, 555, 556, 558, 566, 570, 573, 581, 598, and (via Tyssen, 1802) 60, 158, 200, 218, 279, 597

Harold I
Before 1782 (C. Combe MS.): 92
Southgate Collection (1795): 4, 47, 61, and (via Tyssen, 1802) 19
Dymock Sale (1830): 91 (via Barclay, 1831)

Edward the Confessor
Before 1782 (C. Combe MS.): 715
Southgate Collection (1795): 29, 129, 135, 138, 285, 286, 298, 315, 332, 399, 510, 533, 549, 559, 567, 687, 688, 696, 698, 716, 869, 933, 981, 1115, 1165, 1200, 1226, 1262, 1282, 1283, and (via Tyssen, 1802) 132, 241, 352, 543, 1529, and (via Miles, 1820) 137, 1188

Harold II
Southgate Collection (1795): 15, 20, 37, 42, 52, 63, 94
Soberton find (1833): 93

XIV

Viking Age Coin-Hoards from Ireland and their relevance to Anglo-Saxon Studies

by R. H. M. DOLLEY and J. INGOLD

[Plate XVI]

There can be little doubt that English numismatists have attached too little importance to coin-hoards from Ireland. Twenty-three such finds which contain Anglo-Saxon coins are listed in Mr J. D. A. Thompson's recent *Inventory of British Coin Hoards, A.D. 600–1500*, and there are at least eleven further finds which will have to be incorporated in the second edition. One of these, a small but critical find of the so-called 'St Peter' pennies of York from Geashill, has been the subject of a recent paper in the *Numismatic Chronicle*, and it was there suggested that the composition of the find argues strongly that the traditional chronology of the series can no longer be maintained.[1] Other recent papers have touched on a mid-tenth-century hoard from Co. Meath and another from Monasterboice.[2] As long ago as 1863 another hoard of the same period was published, albeit without find-spot, in the *Numismatic Chronicle*, and reassessments are urgently needed of such important eleventh-century hoards as those from near Dungarvan and from near Kilkenny.[3]

In the National Museum of Ireland we have come across material relating to four further hoards which include one or more Anglo-Saxon coins, and it is this material which we propose to publish in the course of this paper. Our indebtedness to the Director, Mr A. T. Lucas, for permission to publish is obvious, and we feel under no less an obligation to Dr Liam O'Sullivan for his most generous assistance. Not only were all the records and resources of his Department placed at our disposal, but he and his small staff have spared no pains to ensure that we received all the assistance we might require. In particular we are grateful for all the photographs that illustrate this paper, and for photostats and/or transcripts of manuscript material on which many of our arguments are based. For other information we are glad to acknowledge the help and encouragement received from Monsignor M. Moloney of Limerick, from Professor M. J. O'Kelly of Cork, from Mr Liam and Dr Máire de Paor of Dublin, and from Mr W. A. Seaby of Belfast. It should be stressed, however, that we do not claim systematically to have combed the material available in Dublin, let alone in Ireland, and

Anglo-Saxon Coins

in particular we believe that a rich harvest awaits any student with the time to search through the archives of the Royal Irish Academy. In an appendix we have listed fifty hoards from Ireland deposited during the period c. 825–1175, seventeen of them additions to the *Inventory*, and we will be surprised if systematic research over the next few years does not lead to a substantial increase in that total.

It is worth recalling that no fewer than twenty-four of the fifty hoards listed were discovered in the second quarter of the nineteenth century, i.e. during the hey-day of Petrie and O'Donovan. Ten more came to light during the twenty-five years that followed. In other words, two out of every three Irish finds of the Viking period came to light during the period of the abortive Topographical Survey and its aftermath when Irish numismatics were dominated by such figures as Henry Richard Dawson, John Lindsay, Richard Sainthill, and, last but greatest, Aquilla Smith. While it is true that this was also a period of construction-works, and especially of railway-building, there can be little doubt but that the reporting of so many discoveries was engendered by a genuine public interest in antiquities, and we are satisfied that a re-creation of that climate might again transform our understanding of the numismatic evidence for the Viking period of Irish history.

It has been claimed that the Irish finds are also of paramount interest for the Anglo-Saxon numismatist, and especially is this true of the 'Northumbrian' series. Two coins only are known of a shadowy Sihtric, probably the brother of Anlaf Quaran, who seems to have shared the latter's fleeting dominion at York c. 942. One of these coins was found in Ireland. There are but six coins in public and private collections of the historically better-attested Regnald II Guthfrithsson. Five at least of the coins of this ruler are from Irish finds. There are hoard-provenances for sixteen of the 'Raven' coins of Anlaf I Guthfrithsson, and ten prove to be from Irish finds. In the same way it is the soil of Ireland which has produced at least six of fewer than thirty coins of Eric Bloodaxe. There is, indeed, no better commentary on the extent of unpardonable though unofficial spoliation of Ireland in the eighteenth and nineteenth centuries than the circumstances that today no more than four of the post-Brunanburh coins of York are to be found in the museums at Belfast and Dublin, the sole survivors of more than five times that number discovered in Ireland during the last two hundred years.

(a) THE MACROOM (CORK) FIND c. 1840

It is against this sombre background that we should examine the first of our four unpublished hoards, a find of tenth-century Anglo-Saxon coins from near

Viking Age Coin-Hoards from Ireland

Macroom in Co. Cork. The evidence for this hoard is a page bound into a scrapbook kept with the coins in the National Museum of Ireland, and it is indeed to be hoped that publication here may lead to the discovery of the Clibborn notebook to which allusion is made in the caption. On the internal evidence of the volume as a whole we would be inclined to date this hoard before c. 1850, or perhaps even a whole decade earlier, and it is of course precisely this information which the Clibborn manuscript could supply. The page is here reproduced (Figure I) at exactly the same size as the original.

The individual coins are not without interest, and especially since the copyist if not the original artist has omitted or misunderstood several details of great significance for the numismatist as such. Coin (1) is clearly a penny of Æthelstan of the Chester moneyer 'Eadlfe' (=Eadulf). The artist has omitted the 'small crosses' and/or 'rosettes' from the centre of the fields which distinguish *BMC* types V and VI, but the legends and the privy-mark in the reverse field correspond exactly to those found on a penny of *BMC* type V in the British Museum (*BMC* 27 – ex Dean (Dawson) of St Patrick's Sale, lot 251). To the best of our knowledge this coin is unique, and thus the presumptive date of the Macroom hoard may seem carried back before 1842. Coin (2) is a *BMC* type II penny of Edward the Elder by a moneyer Spov. No coin corresponding to the illustration is recorded in *BMC*, and hence we have no opportunity of confirming a suspicion that Dean Dawson may have obtained the whole find except the coins 'supposed to be melted'. Coins (3), (4), and (5) are pennies of Eadmund by the common North-western (Chester?) moneyers Cnapa, Eadmund, and Dorulf respectively. The first and last correspond exactly to coins in the British Museum (*BMC* 38 and 43) which have, however, provenances which take them back well before 1838. Coin (6) is a commonplace penny of the North-eastern (York) moneyer Ingelgar which the failure of the artist to record the obverse prevents one identifying more exactly (but cf. *BMC* 84 and 87 – both from the 1846 Rome hoard). Coin (7), with a blundered and retrograde obverse legend, is a fifth coin of the same King. It is readily identifiable as a die-duplicate of *BMC* 138 (ex Cuff, 1839), if it is not the actual specimen – in which case the *terminus ante quem* for the hoard would have to be put back three years. The artist has taken some licence with the reverse, apparently to assist an attribution to Winchester which we now know to be precluded by the style which is North-western. It is indeed curious how many tenth-century moneyers' names have as their deuterotheme the diminutive '-uc' (Teothuc, Landuc, etc.), and Winuc is by no means the only one to be associated with the Chester area. Coin (8) is a penny of Eadred from the same area by a moneyer Wulfstan. It corresponds exactly to

243

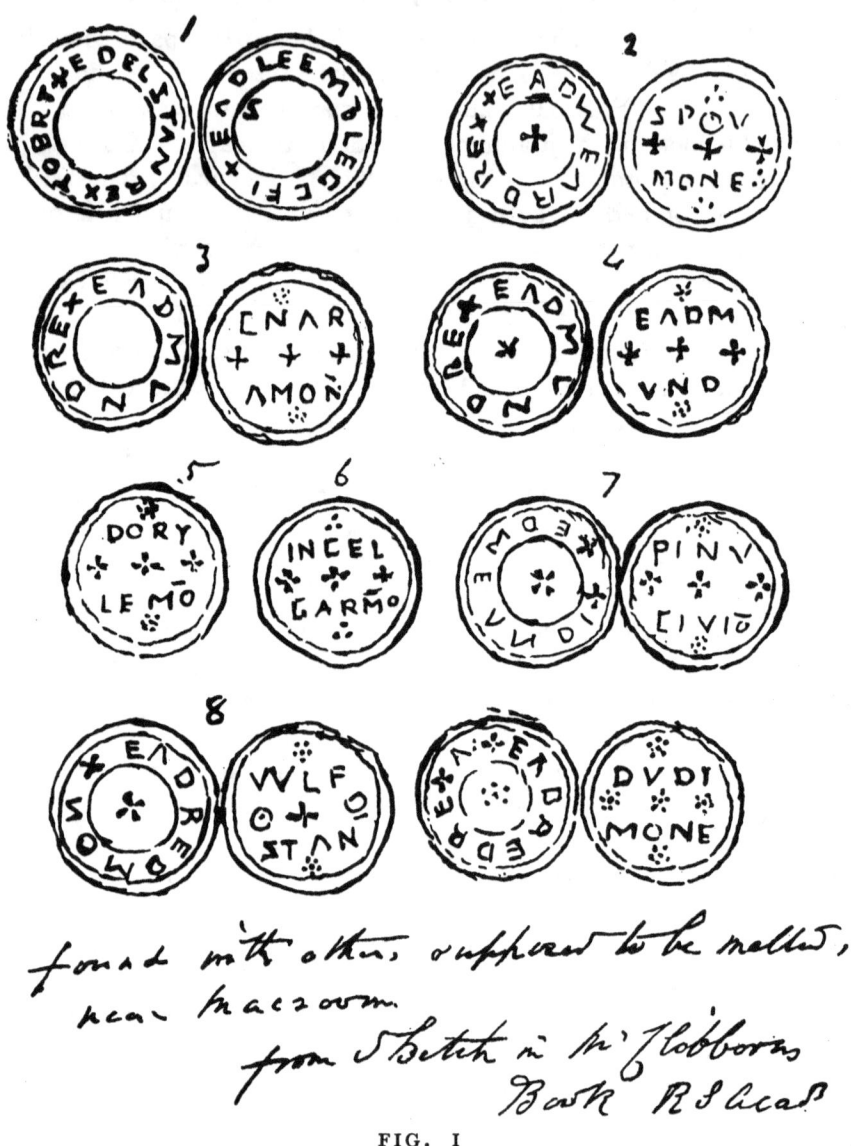

FIG. I

BMC 85, even to the anomalous form of obverse legend, but the British Museum coin is ex Thane, 1819, which would carry the Macroom hoard back rather earlier than the whole of the evidence might seem to warrant. The last coin, unnumbered in the sketch, is also of Eadred and again from the Chester area. It is of the extremely rare variety known as *BMC* type IV and is by the

Viking Age Coin-Hoards from Ireland

well-attested moneyer Dudi(g). Coins of this type hitherto have been known only for Oslac and Thurulf, and it is reasonably certain that no coin corresponding to Clibborn's sketch has passed through the sale room during the last century. None the less, the drawing carries complete conviction, and one can but hope that the reason for its non-appearance is not that the whole of the Macroom hoard in the end found its way to the melting-pot, *BMC* 27 of Æthelstan being derived from another source.

Tenth-century hoards from Munster are extremely rare, and it is curious that none seem to contain coins of Eadwig and Eadgar, though nearly fifty per cent of Irish hoards deposited before *c.* 980 terminate with coins of Eadgar. Moreover, the pennies of Eadgar which occur in Irish finds outnumber those of all other English kings put together. The other Munster finds are both recorded in Thompson's *Inventory*, a small hoard from Mungret (*Inventory* 277) and an even smaller find from Co. Tipperary (*Inventory* 356). The former is given the perhaps needlessly vague dating 'Xth century' – after all it is difficult to see how an Irish find containing Æthelstan could be earlier than the second quarter of the century, while the apparent absence of pence later than Æthelstan might have suggested the unlikelihood of the hoard being deposited much after the middle of the century. Inquiry at the Limerick Museum, moreover, has established that the hoard – which stands in urgent need of republication if only because of its inclusion of a fragment of a penny of Regnald II Guthfrithsson – in fact ends with Eadred, and is thus of precisely the same date as the find from Macroom. The Tipperary hoard should perhaps be dated a quinquennium earlier, and so our three Munster finds would seem to form an entity. The suggestion must be that the liberation of the Munster hinterland from the depredations of the Shannon and Lee Vikings was achieved two decades before the Irish under Mathgamain stormed Limerick, but a detailed discussion of the possible relationship of these three coin-hoards to historical events mentioned in the Irish Chronicles lies outside the scope of the present volume. As numismatists, however, we feel we should draw attention to the fact that in all three hoards coins from the Chester area would appear to have predominated, another reminder of the comparative unimportance of the Severn ports for trade with Ireland before the eleventh century.

For any future edition of the *Inventory* it is suggested that the hoard might be summarized as follows:

MACROOM, Co. Cork, *c.* 1840 (?).
A number of Æ Anglo-Saxon coins (9 illustrated) Deposit: *c.* 950.
WESSEX. Edward the Elder: *BMC* (A) type ii – *no mint-name*: Spov, 1.
KINGS OF ENGLAND. Æthelstan: *BMC* (A) type v – *Chester*; Eadlfe, 1.

Anglo-Saxon Coins

Eadmund: *BMC* (A) type i – *no mint-name*: Cnapa, 1; Dorulf, 1; Eadmund, 1; Ingelgar, 1; Winuc, 1. Eadred: *BMC* (A) type i – *no mint-name*: Wulfstan, 1. *BMC* (A) type iv – *no mint-name*: Dudi(g), 1.

MS. note in the National Museum of Ireland.

Drawings of the above nine coins are endorsed 'found with others supposed to be melted, near Macroom / from Sketch in Mr. Clibborn's / Book R.I. Acad.'

The find is also of interest as providing the most westerly provenance as yet recorded for a Viking Age hoard from Ireland.

(b) THE DERRYMORE (WESTMEATH) FIND 1872

In the same scrapbook that contains the copy of Clibborn's drawings of some of the coins from the Macroom find there are bound a number of quarto pages which represent the first draft of a paper by no less an authority than Aquilla Smith concerning a hoard discovered in 1872. To the best of our knowledge this paper was never completed, and the later pages in particular reveal the author's uneasiness concerning, and lack of mastery of, the comparative material from England and from Scandinavia. It must be remembered that Smith was writing before the appearance of the second edition of Hildebrand's *Anglosachsiska Mynt*, and that for some reason he appears not to have been familiar with the first. Since, therefore, the paper was never sent to the press, and since many of the descriptions are as unnecessarily long by modern standards as much of the discussion is now superfluous, we trust we will be pardoned if we do not begin this account by transcribing in full the Smith draft, nor even the first portion which is dated '7 August 1872'. The actual circumstances of his acquisition of the hoard, however, are recorded by Smith in the following words:

> In the month of June 1872 eleven Silver pennies were discovered by a labouring man on the townland of Derrymore, in the barony of Farbill, County of Westmeath.
>
> I purchased the coins from Mr D'Arcy of Hyde Park, Killucan, who disposed of them for the benefit of the poor man who found them.

It will be noticed that the very idea that there might be a Treasure Trove inquest does not seem to have entered the author's head, and it is only by pure chance that we have today a record of a hoard which happens to be the only one from Ireland known to us to have included a coin of 'Ogsen', and the only one to have contained coins of the equally mysterious 'Thymn'. It is also the

Viking Age Coin-Hoards from Ireland

only Irish hoard to be published which contains the heavy coins of Sihtric Silkbeard's 'Second Coinage' so unaccountably omitted from Lindsay's *Coinage of Ireland*.

All the coins were of 'Long Cross' type, i.e. belonged to, or were imitations of, an English issue which is believed to have been introduced at Michaelmas 997 and to have been withdrawn at Michaelmas 1003. Smith adds the following pertinent observation:

> These coins are in fine preservation, and from the similarity in style of workmanship and type they all appear to have been coined within a limited number of years, by four different kings or petty princes; the letters are distinct and well formed, yet it is not possible to identify the names on the obverses of some of them with any person mentioned in history, or to determine the place of mintage.

In our opinion this homogeneity of style points to the nine Irish coins all having been struck at one mint, Dublin, and we also believe that all the Irish pieces were struck for one ruler, the wily Sihtric III Anlafsson, better known to history as Sihtric Silkbeard.

The find may be listed as follows, Smith's beautiful transcription of the legends of the coins allowing us confidently to associate several of them with pieces recorded by Hildebrand in the 1881 edition of his work.

ENGLAND

ÆTHELRÆD II (978–1016)
'Long Cross' issue (*BMC* IVa=Brooke 5=Hildebrand D=Hawkins 207)

Chester, Ælewine

(1) Obv. +ÆDELRÆD REX ANGLO   Rev. +ÆL=EPIN=EM'O=LEIG

    26·4 grains   cf. Hildebrand 1475

Brooke has normalized this moneyer's name as Ælfwine, but we feel that this is against the numismatic evidence, and a recent note has suggested that ÆLE- may be a Mercian writing for ÆDEL-.[4] It is understood that Miss G. van der Meer will be discussing the whole problem in her forthcoming study of the linguistic significance of the personal names appearing on Late Anglo-Saxon pence.

Dover, Leofhyse

(2) Obv. +ÆDELRÆD REX ANGL   Rev. +LEO=FHYS=EM'O=DOFR

    23·5 grains   cf. Hildebrand 417

Smith, it should be said at once, read the first letter of the mint-signature as an R, and consequently attributed the coin to Rochester. Leofhyse, however, is not known for the Medway mint, but is known at Dover in this very type, and we have had no hesitation in emending Smith's reading. A Rochester coin of this type occurs in the Fourknocks find described below, while one of Bath found near Dungarvan completes the tally of Irish finds of 'Long Cross' pence of Æthelræd II – unless that is we add pennies of Huntingdon and Hertford on the rather dubious authority of White's plate, a second state of which is included in the second edition of Simon. It is indeed remarkable that coins from two Kentish ports should comprise not less than thirty-three and a third per cent and perhaps fifty per cent of those of the 'Long Cross' issue found in Ireland.

IRELAND

HIBERNO-NORSE KINGDOM OF DUBLIN

SIHTRIC SILKBEARD (?–994–c. 1035)

Mint of Dublin

Second Coinage (c. 998–1005?)

(a) *In the name of Sihtric*
Moneyer: 'Fænimin' (Faraman?)

(3) *Obv.* +SIHTRIC RE+ DYFLIN   *Rev.* FÆ=NEMI=NMO=DYEN
Two small pellets at the back of the King's neck
22·8 grains   cf. Hildebrand 19

(b) *In the name of Æthelræd*
Moneyer: 'Emirnie'

(4) *Obv.* +ÆDEL RE+ ANGMENI   *Rev.* +EMI=RNIE=M'OE=NNMD
An annulet at the back of the King's neck
18·2 grains   Hildebrand —

Moneyer: 'Færemin' (Faraman?)

(5) *Obv.* +ÆDELRÆD REX AIGO   *Rev.* +FÆ=REMN=NM'O=DYFLI
23·0 grains   cf. Hildebrand 374

Moneyer: Niomnren

(6) *Obv.* +ÆDLERD RE+ ANGN   *Rev.* +NI=OMN=REN=ONM
An hour-glass-shaped object at the back of the King's head
23·3 grains   Hildebrand —

Moneyer: Siel

(7) *Obv.* +ÆDLRED REX AIO   *Rev.* +SIE=LOM=DILS=EGN
23·5 grains   Hildebrand —

The apparently unpublished coins of Emirnie and Siel are of especial interest to the Irish numismatist because of their obvious relationship to certain coins of 'Thymn' and of Sihtric respectively.

Viking Age Coin-Hoards from Ireland

(c) *In the name of 'Thymn'*[5]
Moneyer: Emirnie

(8) *Obv.* +DYMN ROE+ MNEGM   *Rev.* +EMI=RNIE=M'OI=VND
   A rosette of pellets at the back of the King's head
   19·1 grains   cf. Hildebrand 5

Moneyer: Fiemenin

(9) *Obv.* From the same die as (8)   *Rev.* +FIE=MENI=MNO=DYFII
   20·8 grains   Hildebrand —

(10) *Obv.* +DYMN ROE+ MNEDI   *Rev.* +FIE=NEMI=NMO=DIMI
   20·8 grains   cf. Hildebrand 12

(d) *In the name of 'Ogsen'*
Moneyer: Færem(i)n

(11) *Obv.* +OGSENHEAMELNEM   *Rev.* +FÆ=REM=NM'O=DYFL
   23·0 grains   Hildebrand —

Among the Irish coins especially notable are nos. (9) and (11). The former is a die-combination which we have been unable to trace elsewhere, and which is the more welcome for muling a 'Dublin' reverse with an obverse normally found with a 'London' die. It is to be hoped that this will be yet another nail in the coffin of attempts to read the names of Irish mints into the blundered versions of English legends which occupy the reverses of the coins of Sihtric III – it is not so very long since there was being canvassed in England the possibility that LVND could stand for Londonderry. Even more critical is the coin of 'Ogsen'. Only two coins of this 'ruler' are recorded in Hildebrand, and the only hoard-provenance known to us is the 1836 find from Årstad (Eigersund) in Norway deposited at the end of Cnut's reign. The Norwegian coin appears to be a duplicate of the second of the Stockholm coins which are from the same obverse die, and which both have completely blundered reverse legends. The Derrymore coin, on the other hand, appears to be still from the same obverse die but from an incontrovertible 'Dublin' reverse. It is, moreover, securely dated by its companions. There is need perhaps for a separate note concerning the problems of the 'Ogsen' coins, on the lines perhaps of the forthcoming paper on 'Thymn', but it is worth stressing here that the essential accuracy of Aquilla Smith's transcription of the legends of the Derrymore coin is more than vindicated by reference to a coin in the National Museum of Ireland. This could well be the Derrymore coin itself, though the weight is recorded as being half a grain heavier, and it is illustrated by Dr Liam O'Sullivan as no. 11 on Plate XVII of the *Centenary Volume* of the *Journal of the Royal Society of Antiquaries of Ireland*.

Anglo-Saxon Coins

The date of deposition of the Derrymore hoard can be established with considerable precision. The presence of English 'Long Cross' coins alone places it after some date in 997, and the fact that the Irish coins are imitations of these means that it is unlikely that the hoard can have been deposited much before the millennium. On the other hand, there are metrological arguments which can be adduced which place the Irish coins concerned early in a series which clearly got under way very soon after the introduction of the English prototypes. The obvious historical occasion for such a hoard would be the Irish victory at Glen Mama in 999, and the possibility of some connexion is one that cannot be excluded. If we seem reluctant to accept it on the present evidence it is because we are not satisfied as yet that the coins of 'Thymn' and 'Ogsen' may not represent a temporizing coinage in the months immediately after Glen Mama when Sihtric's prospects must have seemed bleak indeed. However this may be, we feel that a date for the Derrymore find $c.$ 1000 ± 2 is close enough for the present, and it is satisfactory indeed to have new evidence of the virtual contemporaneity of many of the 'Dublin' coins which purport to have been struck not only by Sihtric but also by Æthelræd and by more shadowy princelings about the identity of whom there has been far too much speculation.

Reduced to slightly modified *Inventory* format, the find may be summarized as follows:

DERRYMORE, Co. Westmeath, June 1872

11 Æ Anglo-Saxon and Hiberno-Norse pennies. Deposit: $c.$ 1000

ENGLAND: Æthelræd II. *BMC*(A) type iva – Chester: Elewine, 1; Dover: Leofhyse, 1. HIBERNO-NORSE: *temp.* Sihtric III. 'Heavy' 'Long Cross' coinage in the name of Sihtric, 1; of 'Æthelræd', 4; of 'Thymn', 3; of 'Ogsen', 1.

MS. notes by Aquilla Smith in National Museum of Ireland.

The coins (? the whole find and ? no container or hacksilver) passed from the finder to a Mr D'Arcy of Killucan, who sold them to Dr Smith.

(c) THE FOURKNOCKS (MEATH) HOARD 1950
(Plate XVI)

In 1950 and 1951 some highly successful excavations were conducted by Dr Harnett in respect of certain prehistoric barrows at Fourknocks close to the mearing of Co. Meath and Co. Dublin. In the course of these excavations there was unearthed just below the surface of one of the mounds a small hoard of silver coins of the Viking period. They were sent to the National Museum of Antiquities and reported on by Dr O'Sullivan. Since clearly dissociated from the Stone Age objects discovered in the lower levels, they do not figure in

Viking Age Coin-Hoards from Ireland

Dr Hartnett's publication of the excavations, and we are particularly indebted to Dr O'Sullivan for foregoing his obvious prior claim to publish a hoard which is of such exceptional importance for the Irish as well as the Anglo-Saxon numismatist. The hoard may be listed as follows. The numbers correspond to those appearing on the Plate, and it must be emphasized that the transliteration of the legends is only approximate.

(i) SILVER INGOT

(1) A small bar apparently of coinage silver weighing 3 dwt. 2·5 g.

(ii) COINS

ENGLAND

ÆTHELRÆD II (978–1016)

'Long Cross' issue (*BMC* iva=Brooke 5=Hildebrand D=Hawkins 207)

Rochester, E(a)dsige

(2) *Obv.* +ÆDELRÆD REX ANGLORX   *Rev.* +ED=SIGE=M O=ROFEC
    Broken and chipped   Die-axis 180°
    cf. Hildebrand 3285

'Last Small Cross' issue (*BMC* I=Brooke 1=Hildebrand A=Hawkins 205)

Lincoln (Boga?)

(3) *Obv.* +ÆDELRÆ . . . L   *Rev.* + . . . LINCOLN
    Fragment   Die-axis 0°

The only 'Last Small Cross' coin recorded by Hildebrand to combine the mint-signature LINCOLN with the 'a 4' obverse legend is Hildebrand 1676, and the Fourknocks coin appears to be from the same reverse die.

The two English coins can be dated, of course, with considerable precision, the Rochester penny belonging to an issue believed to have been current for six years from Michaelmas (?) 997, and the Lincoln penny to one initiated at Michaelmas (?) 1009 and continued apparently until Æthelræd's death.

IRELAND

'SUB-SIHTRIC' COINAGE c. 1020–30?

(a) With a small cross pattée behind the neck (cf. Roth 35, 36)
    (1) In imitation of earlier coins of Færemin

(4) *Obv.* +SIHTRCRE=DI.L   *Rev.* +FÆ=REMI=NMO=DYFLI
    Three fragments   Die-axis 270°

(5) *Obv.* +SITRCRE+IN   *Rev.* +FIE=RIN=NFO=DIM
    Four pieces (15 grains)   Die-axis 0°

Anglo-Saxon Coins

(6) *Obv.* +HITRCRE+DNII   *Rev.* +IFN=RIIF=INIO=DHII
     18 grains   Die-axis 180°

(2) In imitation of earlier coins of 'Steng'

(7) *Obv.* +SIHTRCRE+DYFL   *Rev.* +STE=NGM=ODYF=LINR
     17 grains   Die-axis 0°

(b) With a small cross pattée behind the neck and a pattern of three pellets on the neck (cf. Roth 51–3)

(1) In imitation of earlier coins of 'Steng'

(8) *Obv.* +SIHTRCRE+DIFL   *Rev.* From the same die as (7)
     Four pieces (15.5 grains)   Die-axis 90°

(c) With a small cross botonnée and an arc of three pellets behind the neck (cf. Roth 40)

(1) In imitation of earlier coins of 'Færemin'

(9) *Obv.* +NITRCRE+IDIHI   *Rev.* +FNE=RIME=IEMO=MEITH
     12.5 grains   Die-axis 90°

(10) *Obv.* +INTRCRH+IF   *Rev.* +FÆ=R.=NIO=NEFI
     Three fragments   Die-axis 90°

(11) *Obv.* +I . . .   *Rev.* +FE . . .
     Fragment   Die-axis 180°

(2) With a name 'In(d)remin', etc.

(12) *Obv.* +HITRCRE+IIEL   *Rev.* +IH=REMI=NEO=LIEN
     17.5 grains   Die-axis 0°

(13) *Obv.* From the same die as (12)   *Rev.* From the same die as (12)
     Three fragments   Die-axis 180°

(14) *Obv.* +IHTRCRE+DIFL   *Rev.* +ND=REMI=NHO=DYFN
     Two fragments   Die-axis 270°

(15) *Obv.* +NTR...+NDIFL   *Rev.* From the same die as (16)
     Two fragments   Die-axis 90°

(d) With a small cross botonnée and an arc of three pellets behind the head, and a pattern of three pellets on the neck (cf. Roth 58)

(1) In imitation of earlier coins of 'Færemin'

(16) *Obv.* +IHTRCRE+NEDIH   *Rev.* +INE=REM=NFIO=MELI
     Chipped (12 grains)   Die-axis 90°

(17) *Obv.* From the same die as (16)   *Rev.* +FÆ=RIN=NIO=HEI
     15 grains   Die-axis 0°

Viking Age Coin-Hoards from Ireland

(18) *Obv.* +NE+... *Rev.* +REH=NIE=MH
    Four fragments   Die-axis 270°

(19) *Obv.* +HITRCRE+IFID *Rev.* +NE=RFM=DIE=INIO
    Three fragments   Die-axis 270°
    Variety with trefoil for three pellets on neck

(20) *Obv.* +IHTRERTE+IFIH *Rev.* +ML=ARE=IDIF=ELM
    12·5 grains   Die-axis 90°

    (*e*) *With a small cross botonnée and an arc of three pellets behind the head, and a small cross pattée on the neck* (cf. *Roth 58 but a variant*)

        (1) In imitation of earlier coins of 'Indremin'

(21) *Obv.* +HITRCRE+HEITH *Rev.* +ND=REM=NMO=DIFL
    17 grains   Die-axis 270°

        (2) In imitation of earlier coins of 'Færemin'

(22) *Obv.* From the same die as (21) *Rev.* ...Æ=REM=MHIo=DIFL
    Two fragments   Die-axis 270°

    (*f*) *With a pattern of three large and two small pellets behind the neck,* (?) *an arc of three pellets behind the head, and* (?) *a pattern of three pellets on the neck* (cf. *Roth 54 but a variant*)

(23) *Obv.* +HITRCRE+IDNI *Rev.* +IFL=RIH=NHIO=RML
    Two pieces (15 grains)   Die-axis 180°

    (*g*) *With a small cross botonnée behind the neck, but other symbols (if any) doubtful*

(24) *Obv.* +H...EM *Rev.* +IFL=RHF=
    Two fragments   Die-axis 90°

    (*h*) *Apparently with a large and small pellet behind the neck, but coin incomplete*

(25) *Obv.* +H...DI *Rev.* =EMI=NMO=
    Two fragments   Die-axis 0°

    (*i*) *Reading* 'ÆNRED' *and with a small cross botonnée behind the head and a triangle of three pellets on the neck*

(26) *Obv.* +IENREDRE+DIF *Rev.* +FÆ=REM=N O=DIFL
    Five fragments   Die-axis 180°

    (*j*) *With an arc of three pellets behind the head* (cf. *Roth 40 but a variant*)

(27) *Obv.* +HNTRCRE+MEIDI *Rev.* +ND=REMI=NHO=DYFN
    15 grains   Die-axis 0°

(28) *Obv.* From the same die as (27) *Rev.* From the same die as (27)
    Fragment   Die-axis 0°

Anglo-Saxon Coins

(29) *Obv.*   Again from the same die   *Rev.* +HD=RI=HNO=RIFN
              Three fragments   Die-axis 90°

(*k*) *Uncertain fragment*
(30) *Obv.*   ?   *Rev.* =NMO=
              Fragment   Die-axis 0° (?)

We believe that this is the first occasion on which there has been published an Irish hoard in which the Hiberno-Norse element is confined to Roth's classes 6 and 7, and the fact that all the latter coins have a pellet in each of the quarters of the reverse field confirms our suspicion that this was a deliberate 'difference' intended readily to distinguish the lighter coinage of 'Long Cross' type to which we would attach the name 'Sub-Sihtric'. In the Scandinavian hoards the odd coin of this type occurs, but we freely admit that it has come as something of a surprise to us that the coinage was struck on the scale implied by this hoard. The twenty-seven coins prove to be from twenty-two obverse and twenty-three reverse dies, and the diversity is the more remarkable when it is recalled that not a dozen Roth numbers are involved. It is significant, too, that more than two-thirds of the Irish coins have an arc of three pellets behind the head as part of the obverse type, and this cannot but foster the hope that the more fundamental criteria may one day be found to contain a clue to the sequence of issue during the period *c*. 1010–*c*. 1030 to which most coins of Roth's classes 6 and 7 would appear to belong. In the absence of other hoards of this type, the elucidation of the order of striking will not be easy, but it is clear that much could be established by patient analysis of the 'Sub-Sihtric' coins which are found mixed with later issues in various as yet unpublished parcels from the Dunbrody hoard of 1837.

To establish the date of the Fourknocks hoard is not too difficult a matter. An absolute *terminus post quem c*. 1010 is provided by the presence of the broken 'Last Small Cross' penny of Æthelræd II. Absent from the find are the very characteristic Hiberno-Norse issues with one or more 'hands' on the reverse, the issue of which cannot have begun much before 1035 to judge from the evidence of the mixed Hiberno-Norse and English hoards from Co. Kilkenny, Dunbrody, and Andreas. The evidence of Scandinavian finds has still to be sifted systematically, but enough work has been done to suggest that we can accept the evidence of the Tjore hoard from Norway which argues that the issue of the 'differenced' coins of Roth's classes 6 and 7 did not begin substantially earlier than *c*. 1015. It is, then, between 1015 and 1035 that the numismatist will seek to place the Fourknocks hoard, and it is indeed to be deplored that the

Viking Age Coin-Hoards from Ireland

fragmentary condition of so many of the coins precludes metrological argument. We feel, though, that the weight standard apparently indicated and the degree of blundering of the legends would be most consistent with a date fairly late within our bracket, and that, on the present evidence, a dating *c.* 1030 ±5 would be reasonable.

For *Inventory* purposes it is hoped that the following summary may prove adequate:

FOURKNOCKS, Co. Meath, 1950
29 Æ Anglo-Saxon and Hiberno-Norse pennies   Deposit: *c.* 1030
and one Æ ingot.
ENGLAND: Æthelræd II: *BMC* (A) type iva – *Rochester*: Edsige, 1.
BMC (A) type i – *Lincoln*: Boga ?, 1. IRELAND. *temp*. Sihtric III (or a little later?): Roth Class 6: 16. Roth Class 7: 10. Roth Class 6 or 7: 1.

The hoard was discovered during excavations on a prehistoric barrow. The ingot (wt. 3 dwt. 2·5 grs.) and the coins, the latter mainly fragmentary, are in the National Museum of Ireland. This seems to be the latest context in which one of these little ingots has occurred in the whole of the British Isles.

(d) THE BALLYCASTLE (ANTRIM) HOARD *c.* 1894

The evidence for this medium-sized hoard is to be found in the same scrapbook as contained the drawings of the coins found near Macroom and the unpublished paper by Aquilla Smith on the hoard from Derrymore. It consists of a letter dated '29:xii:1896' from a Mr S. G. Milligan of Belfast to Dr William Frazer of Dublin. The letter runs as follows:

> Dear Dr. Frazer,
> I send enclosed 4 coins found in a Burial Mound near the sea shore not far from Ballycastle, Co. Antrim. It was about 2 years ago the mound was opened and about 70 coins of this kind were found of which I got 4 and now ask you to accept of them as I know you are interested in coins – and I think these are Danish & very sharp and clear and very fresh for their age.
> I have been told one of them is Canute or Cnut of England & others the Danish King of Dublin. But you will know all about them. The Head has a kind of Corona & if the features are likenesses they had good big noses.
> Wishing you the compliments of the Season – I am faithfully
> S. G. Milligan

At first sight this may not seem the most promising of material for the numismatist. True, we are given an unusually precise indication not only of the date and place of finding of the hoard but also of its size, but the sender of the coins does not describe them in any detail. On reflection, however, it is not impossible that sufficient clues in fact are given for us to hazard a guess at the types of Irish and English penny represented in the hoard.

Coins of Cnut are not often found in Ireland, but it is instructive to note that such as are found are virtually all of one type, his last (*BMC* XVI=Brooke 4 =Hildebrand H=Hawkins 208). Substantial numbers of pennies of this class occurred in the half-forgotten 1792 find from near Kilkenny, and it is not without significance that this type and this type alone seems to have been imitated on any scale in Ireland (cf. O'Sullivan groups 6 and 29 which constitute the bulk of the 1834 Kirkmichael find from the Isle of Man). It is interesting too that the same type also occurs, albeit with a few later English coins, in a second predominantly Irish hoard from the Isle of Man, the 1874 find from Andreas Churchyard. In both the Kilkenny and the Andreas Churchyard hoards the Irish element is the same, namely coins of O'Sullivan group 3 of the class with the 'Branched hand', the variety that we propose to call the 'Ballylinan' type after the 1786 Irish find from that place, a find where coins of this class appear to have predominated to the exclusion of all others. Prima facie, therefore, the Cnut coins were of 'Short Cross' type, and there is the further presumption that the Irish coins correspond to O'Sullivan Plate XVII, 16–20.

In the National Museum of Ireland, albeit unprovenanced, there is at least one Cnut penny of *BMC* type XVI which could be the Ballycastle coin sent to Dr Frazer – though this is admittedly pure hypothesis – and a very large number of the 'Ballylinan' coins, the great majority of them almost certainly from the great 1837 hoard from Dunbrody, among which Milligan's three 'Danish' pieces could well be lurking. There is the additional argument that 'Ballylinan' coins are virtually the only Irish coins likely to be found with English coins of Cnut, on which the legends invariably are blundered. Had the Ballycastle coins been coins of Sihtric – or even the Sub-Sihtric issues described above in our account of the find from Fourknocks – we feel that Milligan's informants who had identified the coins of Cnut would have recognized the name of the legendary Sihtric Silkbeard.

Finally we would draw attention to the significance of Milligan's ingenuous remark that 'the Head has a kind of Corona & if the features are likenesses they had good big noses'. It is in the 'Ballylinan' type that the dots which had ended the formal strands of hair run together into a beaded arc which might well be described as 'a kind of Corona', while it is in this type that for the first time there can be detected that progressive elongation of the hitherto more or less

Viking Age Coin-Hoards from Ireland

naturalistic nose which was eventually to culminate in the fantastic proboscis of O'Sullivan groups 13 and 14.

It is perfectly true that the bulk of the coins of O'Sullivan group 3 with 'Branched hand' which are known today come from four hoards from southern Leinster, those from Ballylinan, Dunbrody, and Kilkenny already mentioned and the nineteenth-century hoard from near Baltinglass. However, the mint is indubitably Dublin, and there is good evidence that coins of this type circulated freely around the shores of the Irish Sea. For example, single-finds have been recorded from the Meols Sands at the mouth of the Dee, and mention has already been made of the significant Manx hoard from Andreas Churchyard. It is worth noting, too, that at least one example has occurred in a hoard from the Faroes, one of the three latest Irish pennies to be found in Scandinavia.[6] There is nothing, then, that is presumptively improbable about the discovery of a hoard of such coins from north-eastern Ulster, and we believe that any future edition of the *Inventory* should include an entry on the following lines:

BALLYCASTLE, neighbourhood, Co. Antrim, *c.* 1894.

70 Æ Hiberno-Norse and Anglo-Saxon pennies. Deposit: *c.* 1035.

MS. letter in National Museum of Ireland. The coins are not described, but are said to be of 'Cnut of England' and of 'the Danish King of Dublin'. The probability is that the former were of *BMC* type XVI, and the latter of the 'Branched hand' variety of O'Sullivan group 3.

Disposition: 4 coins were sent to Dr Frazer at Dublin by Mr S. C. Milligan. The hoard was discovered during the 'opening' of a tumulus by the sea – for similar anachronistic provenances cf. the 1950 hoard found in excavation of Stone Age barrows at Fourknocks, Co. Meath, and the two ninth-century coins found in an apparently prehistoric context at Cushendall, Co. Antrim.

DISTRIBUTION MAP
OF IRISH VIKING AGE COIN-HOARDS
[Map 1]

On the accompanying map there are indicated all the Viking Age coin-hoards from Ireland of which we have come across a mention in the course of researches extending over several years. It has no pretensions to completeness – though it seems to be rather more complete than anything heretofore attempted – but there is no reason to think that the pattern which emerges is other than representative. The first thing to be noticed is the disproportion in which hoards have occurred as between the different counties. There are no fewer than thirteen counties from which a Viking Age coin-hoard has still to be recorded:

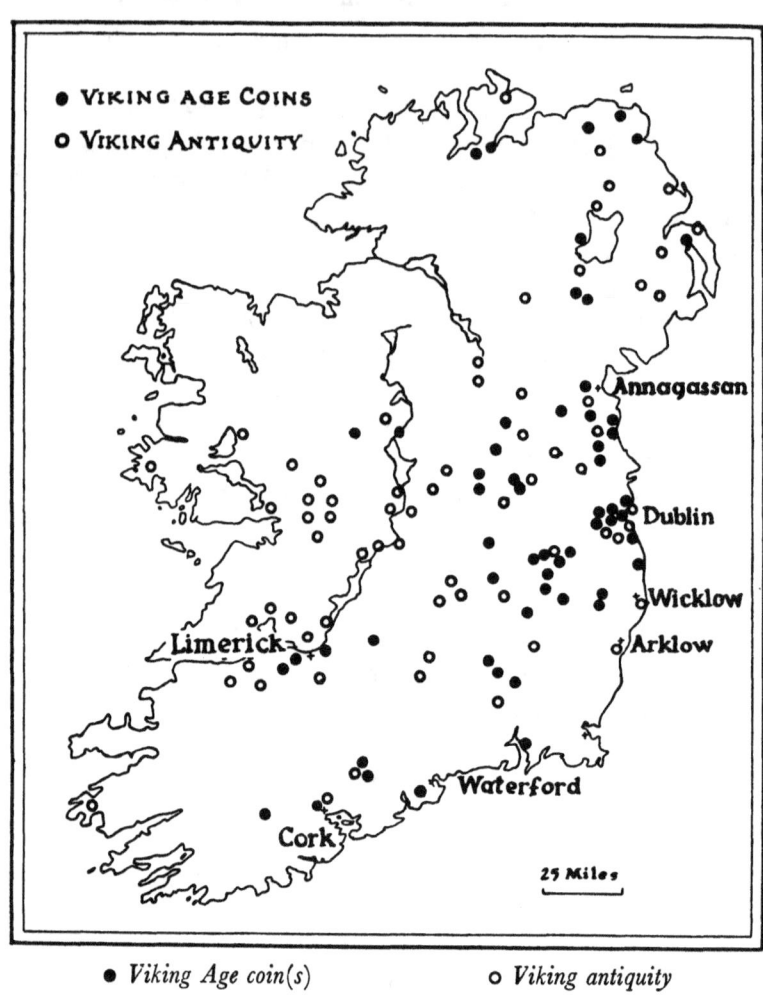

• *Viking Age coin(s)* ○ *Viking antiquity*

MAP I

Carlow, Cavan, Clare, Derry, Fermanagh, Galway, Kerry, Leitrim, Longford, Mayo, Monaghan, Roscommon, and Sligo. From six counties only one coin-hoard of this period is known to us, Donegal, Down, Tipperary, Tyrone, Waterford, and Wexford, and from six no more than two, Antrim, Armagh, Cork, Kilkenny, Laois, and Offaly. In marked contrast seven counties, Dublin, Kildare, Limerick, Louth, Meath, Westmeath, and Wicklow, have furnished between them no fewer than thirty-one coin-hoards, and of these a further check establishes that Dublin, Kildare, Louth, Meath, and Wicklow account for no fewer than twenty-five. In other words, half the recorded Irish coin-

Viking Age Coin-Hoards from Ireland

hoards of the Viking Age are from five out of the thirty-two modern counties. All five counties are contiguous, and together form the eastern half of the province of Leinster. Almost in the centre of their eastern seaboard is Dublin, still the only Viking Age mint in Ireland of which the existence has been proved beyond all doubt. It is no less illuminating to tot up the Viking Age hoards under provinces:

CONNAUGHT	—
LEINSTER	35
MUNSTER	7
ULSTER	7
Uncertain	1
	50

It is at once apparent that Leinster has provided just over two-thirds of the known hoards of the period. At this stage a reasonably complete distribution map of single-finds of coins is not practicable, but those known to us fully bear out the overall accuracy of the picture presented by the larger hoards.

The picture if anything gains in precision when the hoards are divided up into two chronological groups, the valid point of division being the establishment of the Viking mint at Dublin c. 995. The pattern is then as follows:

	Before 995	After 995
CONNAUGHT	—	—
LEINSTER	23	12
MUNSTER	4	3
ULSTER	3	4
Uncertain	1	—
	31	19

In the period before 995 there are twenty-three hoards of which the approximate find-spot is known. Their position in relation to the coast is as follows:

	0–10 miles	10–20 miles	More than 20 miles
CONNAUGHT	—	—	—
LEINSTER	6	3	9
MUNSTER	1	—	1
ULSTER	2	—	1
	9	3	11

Anglo-Saxon Coins

For the period after 995 the approximate find-spot is known in the case of twenty-one hoards, and the distribution is as follows:

	0–10 miles	10–20 miles	More than 20 miles
CONNAUGHT	—	—	—
LEINSTER	5	2	7
MUNSTER	3	—	—
ULSTER	2	—	2
	10	2	9

In other words, three out of every seven Irish hoards of the Viking Age have been found within ten miles of the sea. Only in the case of Leinster do hoards found more than ten miles from the sea heavily outnumber those from the immediate littoral. In the case of the thirteen hoards from Munster and Ulster, only four were deposited more than a day's march from the coast.

Two things seem clearly to emerge. In the first place the use of coin would appear to have been confined to the Ostmen, and it may be taken as reasonably certain that money did not circulate among the native Irish. In the second place the Viking hold of the enclave around Dublin seems to have been far more secure than any control the Scandinavians may have exercised over the hinterland of the other principal Viking colonies at Limerick, Cork, Waterford, and Wexford. What the battle of Clontarf meant to the Dubliners is well shown by the fact that of the seventeen hoards deposited after c. 1020, only five are from Ireland north of Dublin, and two of these are from the coast. In contrast no fewer than twelve pre-Clontarf hoards are known from the triangle formed by the counties of Meath, Westmeath, and Louth alone, and the numismatic evidence must be that it was Malachy and not Brian who wrested the plain of North Leinster from the Dublin Ostmen.

On the map Dr Máire de Paor and her husband have been kind enough to incorporate the find-spots of the principal Viking antiquities found in Ireland. As we have seen, coins, whether Anglo-Saxon or Hiberno-Norse, represent Ostmannic activity, and thus the comparison is valid. Scanty though the evidence of the antiquities undoubtedly is, it is clear that the pattern of distribution by no means coincides with that of the coins, and we regard this as welcome corroboration of our claim that money was not in use by the native Irish. A sword or a brooch it appears could pass freely, as booty or by barter, but for coin there seems to have been one fate, the melting-pot. Indeed, there are Celtic parallels for this reluctance of the Irish to adopt a monetary economy. From

Viking Age Coin-Hoards from Ireland

Scotland we know no coin struck there before 1135, and in the name of even a nominally independent Welsh prince there exists one solitary silver penny – and that struck at an English mint by an Hiberno-Norse moneyer.[7]

REFERENCES

1. *NC* 1957 pp. 123–32
2. Meath *JRSAI* 1960 pp. 41–7: Monasterboice *NC* 1957 p. 195
3. Dungarvan Bonser 9245: Kilkenny *GM* 1792 pp. 122, 195, and 221
4. *NC* 1957 pp. 215–16
5. For a detailed study of the coins of ÐYMN see forthcoming paper in *BNJ*
6. We are grateful to Mrs Fritze Lindahl of the Royal Danish Collection for establishing these provenances. In *Aarboger for nordisk Oldkyndighed og Historie* 1929 pp. 283–315 there is published a coin claimed to be Irish from the Store Frigård find (cf. G. GALSTER *Coins and History* 1959 p. 96) which must be fifty years later in date than the coin from the Faroes
7. The pattern of Viking Age hoards from Scotland is no less suggestive, a majority of the finds being from the Islands and even those from the mainland from the immediate littoral; cf. foldout table opposite *NC* 1951 p. 80

Appendix

SUMMARY LISTING OF COIN-HOARDS FROM IRELAND c. 825–1175

NOTES

For the purposes of this listing 'hoard' is defined as THREE or more coins believed to have been concealed on the same occasion.

The term 'hacksilver' is used in its widest sense to include unmutilated ornaments *and* small ingots.

The probable size of the hoards is indicated by the following code:

(A) More than one hundred and twenty coins.
(B) Fewer than one hundred and twenty but more than thirty coins.
(C) Fewer than thirty coins.

TABLE

No.	Location	Year	Thompson No.	Bonser No.	English	Continental	Kufic	Hiberno-Norse	Hacksilver	Probable Size of Hoard	Approximate Date of Deposit
1	Delgany, Co. Wicklow	c. 1874	117	8892	x	x	–	–	–	B(A?)	c. 830
2	Mullaboden, Co. Kildare	1871	276	–	–	x	–	–	–	C	c. 850
3	Drogheda, Co. Louth	1864	129	–	–	x	–	–	–	A?	c. 910?
4	Nobber, Co. Meath	1843	263	9134	x	–	x	–	–	C	c. 920
5	Geashill, Co. Offaly	1862	–	–	x	–	x	–	–	C	c. 920
6	Claremont, Co. Dublin	1838	89	–	x	–	x	–	–	C	c. 930
7	? Co. Dublin	1883	133	9135	x	–	–	–	x	B	c. 930
8	? Co. Kildare	1840	205	–	x	–	x	–	–	C	c. 930
9	? Co. Tipperary	1844	356	8901	x	–	–	–	–	C	c. 945
10	Armagh, Co. Armagh	1831	13	–	x	–	–	–	–	C(B?)	c. 950
11	Ballitore, Co. Kildare	1837	29	–	x	–	–	–	–	B	c. 950
12	Macroom, Co. Cork	c. 1840?	–	–	x	–	–	–	–	C(B?)	c. 950
13	Monasterboice, Co. Louth	1746	–	–	x	–	–	–	x	C(B?)	c. 950
14	Mungret, Co. Limerick	c. 1840?	277	–	x	–	–	–	x	C	c. 950
15	Killyon Manor, Co. Meath	1876	215	9111	x	–	–	–	–	B	c. 955
16	Oldcastle, Co. Meath	1900	298	9130	x	–	–	–	–	C	c. 960
17	Killincoole, Co. Louth	1864	212	9128 / 9138	x	–	–	x	–	B	c. 965
18	Lough Lene, Co. Westmeath	1844	260	8890	x	x	–	–	–	C	c. 965
19	'Ireland'	1862	–	9112	x	–	–	–	–	B	c. 965
20	Carrowen, Co. Donegal	1864	75 / 261	9119 / 9126	x	–	–	–	–	C(B?)	c. 970

Supplementary Remarks

1 A MS. letter in the archives of the National Museum of Ireland suggests that students would do well to be cautious when basing arguments on the provenance of this characteristically 'Kentish' hoard.
2 See *JRHAAI*, 1872–3, pp. 13–16, where coins are minutely described.
3 There is good reason to think that the size of this find may have been grossly exaggerated.
4 The bulk of the hoard is preserved in the National Museum of Ireland.
5 *NC*, 1957, pp. 123–32.
6 Lindsay's account has still to be consulted if only because of the illustrations.
7 The *Inventory* dating is impossible if only because Æthelstan did not obtain York until 927. The objects in fact consisted of one ingot and *two* pieces of hacksilver.
8 The *Inventory* dating is impossible if only because Æthelstan did not become king until 924.
9 The BOEG EBBC coin cannot be of York. Some of the coins figure in Linsay's Sale, Sotheby, 14–17: viii: 1867.
10 Add Lindsay (I), p. 136. The coins associated with this find in *NNA*, 1957/8, are now seen to be from Derrykeighan.
11 For the York element see *NNA*, 1957/8, p. 29.
12 MS. note (with drawings) in the archives of the National Museum of Ireland.
13 *NC*, 1957, p. 195.
14 Part of the hoard is in the Limerick Museum and it included at least one coin of Eadred. The critical publication is the *Memorials of Adare* (Oxford, 1865), pp. 150–1, and a full study is in preparation.
16 The bulk of this find is in the Belfast Museum, and the penny of Anlaf in the British Museum.
17 The coin of Eadwig is *not* of York.
18 Some of the coins figure in Lindsay's Sale, Sotheby, 14–17: viii: 1867.
20 For reassessment of this find see forthcoming paper by R. H. M. Dolley (*UJA*).

No.	Location	Year									Class	Date
21	Smarmore, Co. Louth	1929	333	9199	x	–	–	–	–		B	c. 970
22	?, Co. Meath	c. 1845	–	–	x	–	–	x	–		C	c. 975
23	?, Co. Offaly	1828	–	–	–	–	–	–	x		C?	Before 975
24	Dalkey, Co. Dublin	1838	115	–	x	–	–	–	–		B	c. 980
25	Derrykeighan, Co. Antrim	1843	119	8886	x	–	–	–	–		B	c. 980
26	Glendalough, Co. Wicklow	c. 1835	174	–	x	–	–	–	–		C	c. 980
27	?, Co. Kilkenny	c. 1823	207	–	x	–	–	–	–		B	c. 980
28	Marl Valley, Co. Westmeath	1841	265	–	–	–	–	x	–		A	c. 985
29	Kildare, Co. Kildare	1923	134	9157	x	–	–	–	–		B	c. 991
30	Clondalkin, Co. Dublin	c. 1830?	91	–	–	–	x	–	–	B(A?)		c. 995
31	Dungarvan, Co. Waterford	1912	–	9245	x	x	x	–	–		C	c. 1000
32	Derrymore, Co. Westmeath	1872	–	–	x	–	x	–	–		C	c. 1000
33	Fourknocks, Co. Meath	1950	–	–	x	–	–	–	x	C(B?)		c. 1030
34	Kilkenny, Co. Kilkenny	1792	–	–	x	–	–	?	–		A	c. 1035
35	Ballycastle, Co. Antrim	c. 1894	–	–	–	–	–	x	–		B	c. 1050
36	Dunbrody, Co. Wexford	1836	141	9183	x	–	–	x	–		A	c. 1050
37	Ballylinan, Co. Laois	1786	–	–	x	–	–	x	–		A?	c. 1050
38	Baltinglass, Co. Wicklow	1862	30	–	–	–	–	x	–		B	c. 1050
39	Adare, Co. Limerick	1834	6	–	–	–	–	x	–		B	c. 1050
40	Clondalkin, Co. Dublin	1816	–	–	–	–	x	–	–		C?	c. 1070
41	Limerick, Co. Limerick	1833?	233	–	–	–	–	x	–		B	c. 1070
42	Dunamase, Co. Laois	1758	–	–	–	–	–	x	–		B	c. 1080
43	Glendalough, Co. Wicklow	1639	174	–	–	–	–	–	x	C(B?)		c. 1080
44	Kilcullen, Co. Kildare	1305	213	–	–	–	–	x	–		A?	c. 1100?
45	Donough Henry, Co. Tyrone	1830	122	–	–	–	–	x	–		A?	c. 1100?
46	Dublin, Co. Dublin	c. 1870	–	–	–	–	–	–	x		C	c. 1100?
47	Castlelyons, Co. Cork	1837	160	–	–	–	–	x	–		A	c. 1150?
48	Kildare, Co. Kildare	c. 1840	–	–	–	–	–	x	–		C	c. 1150?
49	Scrabo Hill, Co. Down	1855	326	9240 9243 9247	x	–	–	x	–		B	c. 1160?
50	'Buttack', Co. Armagh	1847	–	–	–	–	–	x	–		C	Before 1150

21 *BNJ*, xxxvii, ii (1953), pp. 161–6.
22 For account of this small hoard see recent note by R. H. M. Dolley on the earlier find from Glendalough (*JRSAI*, xc, i (1960), pp. 41–7).
23 *PRIA*, 32, p. 291.
24 For reassessment of this find see forthcoming paper by R. H. M. Dolley (in preparation).
25 For reassessment of this find see forthcoming paper by W. A. Seaby (*BNJ*). The *Inventory* dating is impossibly early.
26 For reassessment of this find see recent paper by R. H. M. Dolley (*JRSAI*, xc, i (1960), pp. 41–7).
27 For reassessment of this find, from the west of the county, see forthcoming paper by R. H. M. Dolley and J. S. Martin (*NC*).
28 See also R. Sainthill, *Olla Podrida*, I, p. 184 – a number of coins are in the National Museum of Ireland.
29 For the provenance ('near Kildare') cf. MS. Registers of the National Museum of Ireland where the bulk of the hoard now is.
31 The coins are now no longer on loan to the Public Library of Waterford.
32 MS. note in the archives of the National Museum of Ireland.
33 Hoard from the 1950–2 excavations (*PRIA*, 58, pp. 197–277) in National Museum of Ireland.
34 'Near Kilkenny', *GM*, pp. 122, 195, and 221.
35 MS. letter in the archives of the National Museum of Ireland.
36 An important parcel from this hoard is in the British Museum.
37 *NC*, 1957, pp. 183–5: cf. *TRIA*, 1787, pp. 139–60. The exact find-spot seems to have been nearer Kilmaroney, cf. *Anthologia Hibernica*, iv (July–December 1794), p. 106.
40 MS. note in the archives of the National Museum of Ireland.
41 There is some reason to think that this hoard in fact was discovered in 1832.
42 *NC*, 1958, p. 81.
43 The *Inventory* identifications of individual coins are deficient – largely because of failure to consult the *editio princeps* of Ware.
46 'Christchurch Cathedral'. Coins in the Belfast Museum – information from Mr W. A. Seaby.
47 Also known as the Fermoy hoard.
48 Kildare Tower, Petrie, *Round Towers*, p. 210.
50 *UJA*, I (1953), p. 166. 'Buttack' being a misprint for 'Outlack'?

Anglo-Saxon Coins
REGISTER OF THE HOARDS BY COUNTIES

Co. Antrim	Ballycastle; Derrykeighan
Co. Armagh	Armagh ('near'), 'Buttack'
Co. Cork	Castlelyons; Macroom
Co. Donegal	Carrowen
Co. Down	Scrabo Hill
Co. Dublin	Claremont; Clondalkin (2); Dalkey; Dublin ('Christchurch Cathedral'); unknown site
Co. Kildare	Ballitore; Kilcullen; Kildare ('Tower'); Kildare ('near'); Mullaboden; unknown site
Co. Kilkenny	Kilkenny ('near'); unknown site ('west of County')
Co. Laois	Ballylinan; Dunamase
Co. Limerick	Adare; Limerick ('near'); Mungrett
Co. Louth	Drogheda; Killincoole; Monasterboice; Smarmore
Co. Meath	Fourknocks; Killyon Manor; Nobber; Oldcastle; unknown site
Co. Offaly	Geashill
Co. Tipperary	Unknown site
Co. Tyrone	Donough Henry
Co. Waterford	Dungarvan
Co. Westmeath	Derrymore; Lough Lene; Marl Valley
Co. Wexford	Dunbrody
Co. Wicklow	Baltinglass; Delgany; Glendalough (2)
Unknown	1862

INCIDENCE OF DISCOVERY

Before 1800	13, 34, 37, 42–4
1800–1824	27, 40
1825–1849	3, 4, 6, 8–12, 14, 18, 22–6, 29, 30, 36, 39, 41, 45, 47, 48, 50
1850–1874	1, 2, 5, 17, 19, 20, 32, 38, 46, 49
1875–1899	7, 15, 16, 35
1900–1924	29, 31
1925–1949	21
1950–	33

Viking Age Coin-Hoards from Ireland

ALPHABETICAL INDEX OF THE HOARDS

Adare	39	Kilcullen	44
Armagh	10	Kildare	8
		Kilkenny	34
Ballitore	11	Kilkenny (Co.)	27
Ballycastle	35	Killincoole	17
Ballylinan	37	Killyon Manor	15
Baltinglass	38		
'Buttack'	50	Limerick	41
		Lough Lene	18
Carrowen	20	Lugga	see Nobber
Castlelyons	47		
Claremont	6		
Clondalkin	30, 40	Macroom	12
		Marl Valley	28
Dalkey	24	Meath (Co.)	22
Delgany	1	Monasterboice	13
Derrykeighan	25	Mullaboden	2
Derrymore	32	Mullingar	see Marl Valley
Donough Henry	45	Mungrett	14
Drogheda	3		
Dublin	46	Nobber	4
Dublin (Co.)	7		
Dunamase	42	Oldcastle	16
Dunbrody	36		
Dungarvan	31	Scrabo	49
		Smarmore	21
Fermoy	see Castlelyons		
Fourknocks	33	Tipperary (Co.)	9
Geashill	5		
Glendalough	26, 43	Unknown site	19

POSTSCRIPT

MS material in the Royal Irish Academy suggests that the Armagh and Ballitore hoards should be dated c. 970, and that the Claremont hoard in fact was found at Glasnevin. It also postulates an earlier hoard from Glendalough (c. 940) and a later hoard from Armagh (c. 1100).

XV

Sterling

by P. GRIERSON

The etymology of the word *sterling* is one of the long-standing puzzles of English numismatics. Ruding very helpfully collected the various views regarding it which had been put forward up to the date at which he was writing, but while himself preferring the derivation from 'Easterling' he left it to the reader to make up his own mind on the subject.[1] *The Oxford English Dictionary*, which for most English readers represents the ultimate authority, admits its inability to provide a satisfactory explanation.[2] Edward Schröder, in the only scholarly discussion of the subject in the present century, argued ingeniously that it was not English at all but Romance, and in the last resort a loan-word from the Greek στατήρ.[3] The latest edition of Kluge's *Etymologisches Wörterbuch* found this acceptable and contented itself with summarizing Schröder's article.[4] Gamillscheg, who as an expert on Romance philology could speak with authority, dismissed it bluntly as phonetically impossible, but was unable to suggest anything in its place.[5] The problem is still unsolved.

The historical background to the early employment of the word and the variant forms under which it appears are well known. It does not occur in Old English. In Middle English we find *sterling* or *sterlinge* from the thirteenth century onwards, the forms *starling* or *starlynge* only later (fourteenth century). The Latin form *sterilensis* appears in the eleventh century and *sterlingus*, *esterlingus* and so forth in the twelfth, as also does the French *esterlin*. Middle High German *sterlinc* is found in the opening years of the thirteenth century, Italian *sterlino* in its second half.[6] There need be no cause for surprise that the word appears in its Latin form a considerable time before it is met with in the vernacular, since the great bulk of the written material is in Latin and its early occurrence in a vernacular source would be a matter of chance. The meaning was primarily an English penny and secondarily the mark or pound based upon this (*marca sterlinorum, libra sterlinorum*). The name was also applied to the pennies of Scotland and Ireland, the design of which was based on that of the English sterling, and to the innumerable imitations of these types which proliferated on the Continent between the late twelfth and the middle of the fourteenth century.[7] In the purely literary sources it was used in a general way to imply

Sterling

coin of high quality. The earliest reference in Middle High German, in Wolfram von Eschenbach's *Parzival*, occurs in a passage where Artus gives Gewan *silbers manegen staerlinc*,[8] though in this case the British connexion of Arthur may have been in the author's mind as well.

Neither in Latin nor in English is the word found in pre-Conquest records; allegations to the contrary break down upon closer examination.[9] It is generally believed that it first occurs in a charter of the Norman abbey of Les Préaux, in which a certain Richard recognizes that he has mortgaged to the monks an inheritance he had received from his uncle in return for 8*s. de esterlins* which had been paid him by the monk Warin, who despite his name is described as being *de Anglia*.[10] The charter is dated the third year of the nineteen-year cycle, better known as the Golden Number, which could be 1085, 1104, or conceivably 1123, but hardly later, since the document clearly belongs to the Norman period. Even if it is dated 1085, however,[11] it can be shown that certain other references are older still, though not by many years. Ordericus Vitalis, who wrote in the 1130's, records three instances of its use which can be dated respectively shortly before 1079, between 1077 and 1089, and 1081. All three refer to gifts to the abbey of St Evroul's at Ouche, the first of forty *libras sterilensium* by William de Ros, a clerk of Bayeux, who became Abbot of Fécamp in 1079 and who gave the money while still no more than a clerk,[12] the second of the same sum by Archbishop Lanfranc some time between 1077 and his own death in 1089,[13] and the third of sixty *solidi sterilensium* by Mabel, daughter of Roger de Montgomery, Earl of Shrewsbury, which was confirmed in a charter obtained by Abbot Mainer from William I in 1081.[14] In the last case we have the actual words of the charter, the authenticity of which there is no reason to doubt,[15] and in the other two there are no grounds for supposing that Ordericus altered the wording of the terms in which he found the gifts recorded in the abbey archives. The earliest appearance of the word, therefore, is in the form *sterilensis* and can be dated *c*. 1078.[16]

The meaning of the word in each of these early cases is up to a point perfectly clear. It signifies English coin and was an alternative way of saying *denarii monetae Angliae* or *denarii anglicani* or something similar, being intended to distinguish English pennies from those of Rouen or Maine or Anjou. Ordericus, in the same list of gifts in which those of Lanfranc and William de Ros are recorded, mentions one of the Countess Matilda of one hundred *libras Rodomensium* (of Rouen, *Roumois*),[17] while charters of Les Préaux refer to shillings *Romeisinorum* in that of Richard and in others of 1093 (?) and 1119 and to shillings *monete Cenomannice* (of Le Mans) in one of 1106.[18] *Moneta Angliae* was a perfectly possible phrase; Ordericus refers to a gift of forty-four *libras Anglicae monetae* from Lanfranc in 1077,[19] the phrase occurs in an undated charter of Les Préaux which can be placed between 1087 and 1095,[20] and the famous treaty of 1101 between Henry I of England and Count Robert II of Flanders assured to the latter an annual pension of five hundred *libras anglorum denariorum*.[21] There is room for doubt, however, on one point. The fact that the word *sterling* only appears in the post-Conquest period makes it possible that, in addition to distinguishing English coins from those of Normandy and its neighbours, it may also have served to distinguish the coins struck in England by the Norman kings from those of their Anglo-Saxon predecessors. Its success, indeed, in displacing such more obvious terms as *denarii monetae Angliae* encourages the belief that this may have been its original function.

Nearly a century ago the German numismatist Grote put forward a tentative classification of coin-names, dividing them into twenty-four classes according to their nature or origin.[22] His system was reproduced in a simplified form by Engel and Serrure.[23] In the Middle Ages such names for the most part derive from one or other of the following sources: (1) the value or weight of the coin; (2) the form, nature, colour, or sound of the metal employed; (3) the name or title of the prince who issued it; (4) the name of the mint official directly responsible for the striking; (5) the country or mint where the coin was struck; (6) some feature of the type; (7) some feature of the legend. The sixth of these possibilities is by far the commonest source, and two of the traditional etymologies for *sterling*, those from 'star' and 'starling', belong to this group. A third traditional etymology, that from 'Easterling', would be related to the fourth group, though not fitting into it precisely. An etymology of the fifth class, deriving it from the place-name Stirling in Scotland, has been occasionally suggested, but is so clearly disproved by the early incidence of the word that it need not be discussed.

The alternative derivations from 'star' or 'starling' are put forward by the Renaissance scholar Polydore Vergil in his *Anglica Historia*,[24] and evidently date from the later Middle Ages.[25] The context in which the word 'sterling' is explained, that of the creation of the 'Long Cross' penny by Henry III in 1247, is obviously irrelevant, and despite Polydore's assertion that coins bearing either the star or the starling were found from time to time it seems likely that the etymologies were invented on the basis of the verbal resemblance and that the coins to fit them were identified later. Modern writers who have discussed the question have cited, for the star, a number of later Anglo-Saxon or early Norman issues where the complex cross-patterns of the reverse types might be vaguely thought of as having a stellar appearance,[26] and for the starling the so-called 'Sovereign' type of Edward the Confessor, which has on the obverse

Sterling

the King seated and on the reverse four birds arranged around a cross in the field.[27] The fact that these birds are presumably not starlings[28] would not affect the issue, for the public has never treated coin-emblems with much respect when transforming them into coin-names.[29]

Neither of these etymologies has greatly commended itself to modern scholars. 'Star' was *steorra* in Old English, so phonetically there would be no difficulty over its transformation into *ster-*, while the suffix *-ling* would be fulfilling its common function of conferring identity or acting as a diminutive.[30] 'Starling' is likewise admissible, for the Old English form is *staer*, which would be *ster* in Kentish and some Midland dialects; the bird is indeed sometimes called a *sterling* in sources of the fourteenth and fifteenth centuries. It is untenable, however, on numismatic grounds. The reverse type of a single issue of Edward the Confessor, which was in circulation for only three years at a period before the word *sterling* is known to have existed and of which the most distinctive feature was not the birds on the reverse but the seated monarch on the obverse[31] could not possibly have been regarded by anybody as the typical 'English penny' and given its name to the denomination in general. In the case of the 'star', however, though the argument that the reverse type of many late Anglo-Saxon and early Norman pennies were sufficiently star-like in form to give rise to the name must be abandoned, there is what appears at first sight to be a strong argument in its favour. We have seen already that the earliest recorded appearance of the word can be dated *c.* 1078. It is probable that the previous year had seen the introduction of the coinage of *BMC* type V of William I, of which a conspicuous and quite unusual feature is the presence of two large stars in the obverse field on either side of the facing bust of the King.[32] Some thirty years earlier an exactly similar feature on one of the issues of *nomismata* of the Emperor Constantine IX (1042–55)[33] had caused these coins to be referred to as *stellati* in South Italian documents.[34] The fact that a penny with such a design was being issued in England at precisely the moment when we first meet with the word *sterilensis* suggests strongly that the traditional derivation of *sterling* from 'star' may be correct.

The reasons against it, however, seem to be conclusive. The word occurs first in a group of Latin documents, and if the coins had in fact been known as 'star-pennies' they would undoubtedly have been described in these documents as *stellati*, as were the *nomismata* of Constantine IX. A latinization of an English word would have occurred only if the latter were long established, which if it were based on the design of the coins of *BMC* type V could not have been the case, or if its meaning were not understood, which would equally not have been true of a name based upon the star on the coins. Further, it is inconceivable that a name given to a single issue of *stellati*, lasting for only three years, could have come to be regarded as suitable for describing English coinage as a whole. There are, indeed, instances in which a coin-name has survived the circumstances that gave rise to it or been extended to a much larger group of coins than that which it at first denoted, but there is always a good reason behind such phenomena when they occur. Either the name has been applied to a new denomination and is treated as descriptive of the denomination and not the type, or the issues of a particular mint have been so enormous that the name used for them is regarded as sufficiently descriptive of all coins of the same class.[35] Neither of these conditions obtained in England. *BMC* type V of William I was a regular issue like any other, and can scarcely have obtruded itself upon the consciousness of the public in any decisive fashion. The presence of the two stars on the pennies of 1077–80 must be written off as a coincidence, like that of the word *ducatus* on the reverse legend of the Venetian *ducat* which gave rise to the popular belief that it was to this that the coin owed its name.[36]

The derivation from 'Easterling', the name given to North German merchants trading in England,[37] was suggested as early as the last quarter of the thirteenth century, when it appears in a group of documents connected with the great recoinage of 1279. The anonymous author of the *Tractatus novae monetae* in *The Red Book of the Exchequer* observes that while the word *nummus* is believed to be derived from Numa, the first who struck coins in Rome, *moneta* and *sterlingi* are derived from those of the workmen who actually made them.[38] The group of documents of the same date in the Register of Walter of Pinchbeck relating to the monetary rights of the abbey of Bury St Edmunds contains a similar but more specific passage. After deriving *nummus* from Numa – this was common tradition[39] – it explains that just as the *florins* are so called from the Florentine workmen who made them, *sterlings* are called from the Easterlings who were the first to make these coins in England.[40] The two documents are related to each other,[41] and the etymology proposed for *sterling* was evidently the result of speculation as to how the word originated. The two analogies were omnipresent and misleading; to derive *moneta* from *monetarii* was to put the cart before the horse with a vengeance, and the *fiorino* took its name from the city where it was struck and not from the Florentines who made it.[42] But the error is easily intelligible, for Florentine moneyers, their prestige enhanced by the phenomenal success of the *fiorino d'oro* as a vehicle of international trade and business accounting, were in demand everywhere in Europe in the late thirteenth and fourteenth centuries and working in many mints. It was natural to assume that they had given their name to the *florin* and they had been preceded as international mint-masters by the Easterlings, who had equally given their name to

Sterling

the *sterling*. Historically, however, such a belief is completely without foundation. The word *sterling* is applied to the English penny at a period when moneyers' names still appeared on the coins, and the presence of an 'Easterling' element in English minting can be absolutely excluded. Further, although Skeat[43] was prepared to accept the 'Easterling' etymology, Bradley[44] has pointed out that it is untenable on phonetic grounds, for the stress on the first syllable of Easterling would not have allowed this to be dropped.[45] On both historical and linguistic grounds, therefore, the etymology 'Easterling' must be regarded as unacceptable. The early date at which it is put forward in the written sources is no good argument to the contrary, for medieval assertions regarding etymology take little account of either reason or history and are based on nothing more than the resemblance between the words in question.[46]

Two further etymologies have been proposed in recent years, one from 'steer' (Old English *stēor*) and the other from the latinized form *stater* of the Greek στατήρ. The first of these, suggested by L. F. Salzman,[47] was prompted by the fact that cattle have been in many societies the earliest form of 'money', at least in the limited form of money as a symbol of wealth, and very frequently the words for cattle and money have remained the same. This is most obviously so in the relationship between *pecus* and *pecunia* in Latin, but it occurs in many other languages as well; our own *fee* is cognate with German *Vieh*, 'cow', and in Old English *feoh* meant indifferently cattle, wealth, and money. The late date of the appearance of the word *sterling*, however, seems to put this derivation out of court. Such a transfer of meaning takes place at a much earlier stage in the development of society than that achieved by eleventh-century England, and there is no trace of the existence of the word *sterling* in Anglo-Saxon times. Further, while the transfer of meaning from 'cattle' to 'money' is of frequent occurrence, I know of no case of individual coins being called after some particular kind of livestock, the reason being no doubt that between the stage of cattle-money and coin-money there is normally that of ingot-money, so that the notion of weight plays the predominant role in the earliest naming of coins. One cannot lay too much stress upon this, for there are examples of coin-names being derived from their equivalents in primitive money – the Greek *drachma* and *obolus* are cases in point – but one can at least say that such a phenomenon would be a very unusual one. The fundamental objection to this etymology for *sterling* is the late date at which the word appears.

Finally, of the various etymologies proposed or accepted by serious scholars, there is that put forward by Schröder.[48] His argument is that the background of the word is continental, not English, and that it goes back to στατήρ. This was familiar, at least in its Latin dress, to the learned world; it is used in the

Anglo-Saxon Coins

Vulgate for a large silver coin – the 'tribute penny' found in the fish's mouth (Matt. xvii. 27) is so described – it is explained by Isidore, and where it occurs in the Bible it is frequently glossed as 'penny' (*phennige, phennich, phennigo*).[49] In Late Latin it could acquire a prosthetic *i* as *istater*, in which form it occurs in the so-called 'Keronian Glossary' of the eighth century.[50] One can envisage a further development from *istater* or **estater* to **estedre* and thence to **ester(e)*, analogous to the attested evolution from *patre(m)* to *pedre* and ultimately *père*.[51] The addition to this of the suffix *-ling* would give *esterling, esterlin, sterling*, and so forth. The precise way in which these came to be applied to the English penny escapes us. Perhaps there was a word **staterling* in eighth- or ninth-century German meaning a coin of guaranteed weight which was later taken over for the English penny. Perhaps – and this is the view to which Schröder inclines – the evolution took place on the Continent and not in England, since the word is first found in Norman sources and, if the copy of the Les Préaux charter can be trusted, *esterlin* appears earlier than the precise form *sterling*. In that case the English word would be a borrowing – and modification – of a pre-existing Romance word.

The objections to this theory are of a serious character. In the first place, *stater* was a learned word, and a rare one at that; we have no reason for ascribing to it a period of continuous daily use from the late Roman period, and without such use it would not have undergone a phonetic evolution analogous with that of *pater*. When comparable words for weights, measures, and values were borrowed at an early date their evolution has left abundant traces behind. *Pondus, libra, uncia, amphora, sextarius, solidus*, and *denarius* were all incorporated into the vernacular of the Romance languages, and some of them into those of the Germanic languages, and evolved accordingly, while *stater* belongs to the same class as *talentum* and *obolus* which were never absorbed into the vernacular and remained unchanged. Schröder cites several examples of the use of *stater* or *steter* occurring in a vernacular setting in documents of the later Middle Ages and the sixteenth century, while such forms as **stedre* or **stère* whose existence he postulates are never found at all. On linguistic grounds, therefore, the evolution of *stater* into *sterling* is hard to imagine.

The historical objections are equally cogent. The word *sterling* was applied specifically to English coins, or to continental imitations of these, and it apparently came into existence within a decade of the Conquest to denote the Anglo-Norman penny. If *stater* were a learned word for 'penny' and *sterling* its diminutive, there seems no reason why the latter should have been applied to English coins and their derivative only. *Stater* in its Biblical sense – and so far as the Middle Ages were concerned it had no other – simply meant a silver

Sterling

coin, and any pedant might have applied it to the penny of any country of western Europe. *Talentum, obolus*, and other words of a similar character were applied everywhere to local units of measurement or value, while the meaning of *sterling* was quite specific. The fact that this was the case seems to dispose completely of the proposed derivation of the word from *stater*.

If none of the etymologies generally current can be regarded as satisfactory, it is worth attacking the problem from a different angle. The traditional approach has been that of picking out words which resemble *sterling* and then trying to find some feature of English coinage to which they might be supposed to refer. A more promising procedure would be to start with the coinage, attempt to isolate such features of this as appear to be distinctive, and then inquire whether any element in the word *sterling* can be regarded as referring to them. We have seen that *sterling* seems originally to have implied one of two things: either 'English coin' as distinct from coin of Rouen or Le Mans or Angers or some other mint in northern France, or 'Anglo-Norman coin' as distinct from that struck by the Anglo-Saxon monarchs before 1066. What differences existed between these that would have made a sufficient impression on users of the coins in question to give rise to a special name for them?

When we try to enumerate the features that differentiated Anglo-Saxon and Anglo-Norman coinage from that of the Continent, we find at once that we can make no generalizations regarding type but that we can on organization and to a limited degree on fineness and weight. The coinage of all England was under royal control; though the moneyers were many and coins were struck in every locality of any importance, the types were changed punctually at three-yearly intervals, the fineness and weight of each issue was regulated by the Crown, and the moneyers procured their dies from agents of the central authority and were answerable to the king for the use that was made of them.[52] None of this was true on the other side of the Channel. Though individual feudal magnates might control their own coinage as strictly as did the King of England, the coinage of France and Germany had lost all semblance of unity, so that type, fineness, and weight varied from one feudal principality to the next. No continental coinage still maintained the weight of the Carolingian *denier*, and most of them had sunk to only a fraction of the weight of the English penny at the time of the Conquest.

The uniformity of English coinage over a large area is the only one of these features that could conceivably have supplied a name to it as a whole. There was no distinctiveness of type, and though English coins were in general heavier and of better metal than those of the Continent, this could not be regarded as a sufficiently specific feature, for there were a few mints – that of Cologne is the most conspicuous example – whose issues were in neither respect inferior to those of Edward the Confessor and William I.[53] Uniformity was a distinguishing characteristic, but it was one that would strike a foreigner, not an Englishman, who would take it for granted, so that if the notion of uniformity lay behind the word *sterling* one would expect the latter to have an Old French rather than a Teutonic root. The vocabulary of Old French, however, is one on which we are fairly well informed, and there does not in fact seem to have been any word in use which resembles *sterling* and could be applicable in this sense to English coins. We must then look at the alternative possibility, that *sterling* derived from some feature that differentiated Anglo-Norman coinage from that which had gone before.

There are in fact two very striking differences between Anglo-Saxon and Anglo-Norman coinage. Anglo-Norman coins were substantially heavier than the majority of the later Anglo-Saxon issues, and were much more stable in weight.

These two features of the coinage over the period 1042–87 can best be illustrated in the table on p. 275. The sequence of Edward the Confessor's issues as shown in it may now be regarded as certain, though the actual dates proposed, which are based on the view of Mr P. Seaby that up to 1051 the issues were biennial and only thereafter triennial,[54] may perhaps be modified in the future. The weights of the first six issues of Edward's reign are based on the table compiled by Mr Seaby[55] and those for William's reign from that in Brooke's Catalogue;[56] the intervening weights are based on the published material in the British Museum and that in the Fitzwilliam Museum, Cambridge. There is, at least about some of them, an element of approximation, for the moneyers were probably instructed to strike so many pennies to the pound of metal by weight, and this would not necessarily work out at an even figure in grains. The allowance for wear, once one has composed a frequency table for each issue, is also a matter of guesswork, especially since the number of coins available is often too small to allow of any rigorous statistical treatment; I have assumed in general that an allowance of 0·5 grain should be sufficient. In any case, though the details may not always be absolutely correct, the general pattern is clear. The weight of the penny in Edward's reign was frequently altered while that of William was extraordinarily stable. The first five issues were all of the same weight, apparently 21·5 grains. The weight was then increased with *BMC* type VI to 22·5 grains – this figure may be regarded as certain[57] – at which it remained fixed, at least so far as law and policy were concerned,[58] for two centuries, down to the great recoinage of 1279/80. This stabilization of the weight of the penny was apparently an act of deliberate policy, contrasting with the

Sterling

Type	BMC type	Date	\	\	Weight	\	\	\
			17	18	20.5	21.5	22.5	27
Edward the Confessor								
'Pax'	IV	1042–44		x				
'Radiate – Small Cross'	I	1044–46	x					
'Trefoil Quadrilateral'	III	1046–48		x				
'Long Cross'	II	1048–50		x				
'Expanding Cross'	V							
(a) Light Series		1050–51		x				
(b) Heavy Series		1051–53						x
'Pointed Helmet'	VII	1053–56				x		
'Sovereign'	IX	1056–59			x			
'Hammer Cross'	XI	1059–62				x		
'Facing Head – Small Cross'	XIII	1062–65	x					
'Pyramid'	XV	1065–66				x		
Harold II								
'Pax'	I	1066				x		
William I	I	1066–68				x		
	II	1068–71				x		
	III	1071–74				x		
	IV	1074–77				x		
	V	1077–80				x		
	VI	1080–83					x	
	VII	1083–86					x	
	VIII	1086					x	
Later Norman and Plantagenet kings							x	

frequent changes of Anglo-Saxon times, and the Norman kings compensated themselves for any financial loss it might involve by levying a general tax, the *monetagium commune*, which we know from the Coronation charter of Henry I to have been collected *per civitates et comitatus* and to have been an innovation of William I (*non fuit tempore regis Eadwardi*).

The date at which the word *sterling* first appears had, therefore, already seen the creation of a substantially heavier penny than that normal in the later Anglo-Saxon period and the establishment of the custom, perhaps even the acceptance of the principle, that its weight should not be altered from issue to issue. Either of these, and particularly the last, was sufficiently distinctive to have resulted in the giving of a special name to the new penny, and there happens to be a parallel case which suggests the form that such a name might take. The gold coin of the Roman Empire, from the time of Nero onwards, was struck forty-five to the pound and known as the *aureus*, the word being initially an adjectival qualification of *denarius* in the general sense of coin subsequently transmuted into a noun in its own right. In the third century the weight of the *aureus* became very variable, so that by its end it is often impossible to say what weight was intended by the moneyers or indeed whether any definite weight was intended at all. Diocletian attempted to restore a definite standard, but since the coins appear to have been struck *al marco* and not *al pezzo*, i.e. without adequate control of the weight of each piece, no real stability was achieved. It was left to Constantine to create a new denomination in gold, struck seventy-two to the pound and six to the ounce, which was to remain an enduring standard for centuries to come. This coin was first called an *aureus solidus*, but *aureus* was quickly dropped and the coin was simply known as a *solidus*.[59] The meaning behind the word was essentially that which we ourselves mean in such a phrase as 'solid worth': it denoted a coin of pure gold and unchanging weight, something as good as could be made and on which one could depend. Its unchanging character, its 'integrity', was the quality which was fundamental to it. *Solidum nuncupatum*, wrote St Isidore, *quia nihil illi deesse videtur; solidum enim veteres integrum dicebant et totum*.[60] For once his explanation of a word is quite correct.

Here we have a clear lead, for *solidus* translates into Greek as στερεός, 'stiff', 'hard', 'solid', used in such phrases as 'solid gold' and having the secondary metaphorical meanings of 'stern', 'harsh', 'stubborn', and so forth. The root of στερεός is the Indo-Germanic *st(h)er-, meaning to be stiff or rigid, and it connects up with a very large and miscellaneous series of words in all the Indo-Germanic languages which have as their basic idea the notion of hardness or stiffness, either in a literal or a metaphorical sense.[61] The cognate word in Middle English – it survives as *steer* only as a dialect word in Scotland and the northern counties[62] – was *ster* (*stere*, *steer*),[63] meaning 'strong' or 'stout' and attested from the thirteenth century onwards. Christ at His scourging was 'Beten with scourges stronge and ster' in *Ipotis*,[64] and in the second version of *Guy of Warwick* 'dewke Raynere' is described as 'an hardy knyght and a stere'.[65] The Old English progenitor of the word is not known, but in view of the widespread ramifications of the root in the Indo-Germanic languages one may presume its existence in the form of *stēre* or *stiēre*, with the meaning of 'strong', 'rigid', or 'fixed'.[66]

The existence of such a word, taken in conjunction with the circumstances in which *sterling* first appears in the documents, provides an eminently satisfactory explanation of the latter's etymology. The pennies of the Anglo-Norman period would have been *stere penegas* in contrast to those of the pre-Conquest period, partly perhaps in the sense of being heavier but mainly in that of being stable in weight, as the Constantinian *solidus* was in contrast to the *aureus* of the preceding reigns. The three gifts to St Evroul's recorded by Ordericus would

Sterling

have consisted of such *stere penegas*, and it would be natural for the Anglo-Norman scribes to latinize this expression as *sterilenses*, the more so since they may well not have understood themselves what *stere* was intended to signify. It would also be natural for *stere penega* in the vernacular to become *sterling*, on the analogy of *feorðan-pening* becoming *feórþling*.[67] This in turn would give rise to the familiar Latin *sterlingus*, which replaced the earlier form found only in Ordericus and be turned into French as *esterlin* by the addition of a prosthetic *e-* and the elimination of the final consonant.

How would such a word spread? It was obviously not at first the official name of the coin: penny or *denarius* would be sufficient for all ordinary purposes, and it is natural that *denarius* alone should be employed in Domesday Book. It is difficult to believe that it was at first a local nickname which subsequently passed into general use. More probably, amongst the legislation of William I, there were provisions relating to *monetagium* by which the King undertook to leave the weight of the penny unchanged,[68] and the English version of the document referred to the stable penny as a *stere pening*, rather like the *Ewiger Pfennig* which was so much in demand in Germany in the later Middle Ages. In this way the expression would have become widely current, so that in the course of the next hundred years it became, in its latinized form, the name by which the coinage of England was regularly referred to in official documents where coinages of several different types were in question.[69]

Etymologies are in the nature of things not easily susceptible of either proof or disproof; one must usually content oneself with showing that the phonetic changes and the developments in the sense which seem to have occurred fit into a pattern which, while it may admit of exceptions, holds good for a large number of words of the same type. The etymology here proposed for *sterling* is one that satisfies both the linguistic and the historical requirements; it explains what the word originally meant and how it came to be employed. It has also a striking parallel in the origin and meaning of the word *solidus*, and though arguments from analogy can never be pressed it must be remembered that there are a limited number of ways in which people have used and thought about money and that patterns of behaviour and terminology with regard to it have an unexpected way of repeating themselves at widely separated periods of time. There are, therefore, strong reasons in its favour, and if it is accepted it carries with it two rather curious corollaries. One, disconcerting perhaps only to numismatists, is that the term cannot properly be applied to the Anglo-Saxon penny, but must be reserved to those of post-Conquest date. The other is that the metaphorical sense of the word *sterling* was inherent in it from the first, even though in its actual form with the *-ling* ending the word derives this secondary meaning from the high quality of English currency in the later Middle Ages and more modern times.[70]

REFERENCES

1. R. RUDING *Annals of the coinage of Great Britain* Third Edition London 1840 I pp. 7-9
2. *O.E.D.* x Oxford 1933 s.v. 'Sterling'. This section in the original version of the dictionary was the work of Henry Bradley
3. 'Sterling' *Hansische Geschichtsblätter* XXIII 1917 pp. 1-22. This article was one of a number which Schröder devoted to Germanic coin-words. Though not all of their conclusions are correct, the articles are amongst the most valuable contributions that have been made to the subject
4. F. KLUGE *Etymologisches Wörterbuch der deutschen Sprache* Seventeenth Edition by W. Mitzka Berlin 1957 s.v. 'Sterling'
5. E. GAMILLSCHEG *Etymologisches Wörterbuch der französischen Sprache* Heidelberg 1928 s.v. 'Sterling': 'lautlich nicht möglich'
6. *O.E.D.* as above; SCHRÖDER art. cit. pp. 2-9. There is a good selection of passages in Old French in A. TOBLER and E. LOMMATZSCH *Altfranzösisches Wörterbuch* III (2) Wiesbaden 1952 s.v. 'Esterlin'
7. The standard work on these, now badly out of date, is J. CHAUTARD *Imitations des monnaies au type esterlin frappées en Europe pendant le XIIIe et XIVe siècles* Nancy 1871; there is a good analytical summary in A. ENGEL and R. SERRURE *Traité de numismatique du moyen âge* III Paris 1905 pp. 1427-31. On the history of the imitations in certain particular regions see P. BERGHAUS 'Die Perioden des Sterlings in Westfalen, dem Rheinland und in den Niederlanden' *Hamburger Beiträge zur Numismatik* I 1947 pp. 34-53 and S. E. RIGOLD 'The trail of the Easterlings' *BNJ* XXVII 1949 pp. 31-55
8. WOLFRAM VON ESCHENBACH *Parzival* VI 335, line 29, ed. K. Lachmann. Seventh Edition by E. Hartl Berlin 1952 p. 164
9. E. MARTINORI *La moneta: vocabolario generale* Rome 1915 p. 496 quotes a passage referring to sterlings from the *Vita dominae Hildeburgis* (in L. D'Achery *Spicilegium* First Edition Paris 1657 II p. 690), which he declares to be of the tenth century. It is in fact of the early twelfth century. J. H. BAXTER and C. JOHNSON *Medieval Latin word-list* (London 1934) p. 401, allege that it occurs as early as the eighth cencentury, but Mr R. E. Latham kindly informs me that this assertion depends upon a passage in Hector Boece's *Scotorum Historia* (Paris 1574), fo. 204 v., to the effect that King Osberht minted pennies at Stirling, whence the name of the coin. This is no more than a late attempt to explain the origin of the word, and is without historical value
10. J. H. ROUND *Calendar of documents preserved in France illustrative of the history of Great Britain and Ireland* London 1899 no. 327 pp. 111-12. The charter is known only from the copy in the thirteenth-century cartulary

Sterling

11. Actually 1104 seems more likely, despite the fact that at that date Normandy and England had separate rulers, since Richard refers to a journey which he is about to undertake and which may entail an absence of ten years or even cost him his life. This sounds like an expedition to the Holy Land
12. ORDERICUS VITALIS *Historia ecclesiastica* III 12 (ed. A. Le Prevost II Paris 1840 p. 129)
13. Loc. cit.
14. ORDERICUS VITALIS op. cit. VI 5 (ed. Le Prevost III p. 21)
15. H. W. C. DAVIS *Regesta regum Anglo-Normannorum, 1066–1154* I no. 140 Oxford 1913 p. 37
16. There is a reference to 15,000 *libras sterilensium* in the context of William's Breton expedition of 1075 (ORDERICUS VITALIS op. cit. IV 17; ed Le Prevost II p. 291), but there is here no guarantee that the word occurred in Ordericus' source. The same is true of the reference in ibid. IV 7; ed. Le Prevost II p. 223 and the speech recorded in ibid. V 14; ed. Le Prevost II p. 419
17. ORDERICUS VITALIS op. cit. III 12 (ed. Le Prevost II p. 129)
18. ROUND op. cit. nos. 322, 327, 328, 332 (pp. 110, 112, 113)
19. ORDERICUS VITALIS loc. cit.
20. ROUND op. cit. no. 321 p. 110. The exact formula is not given
21. F. VERCAUTEREN *Actes des comtes de Flandre, 1071–1128* Brussels 1938 no. 30 §18 p. 94. The date is not 1103, as given there, but 1101 (F. L. GANSHOF 'Note sur le premier traité anglo-flamand de Douvres' *Mélanges dédiés à la mémoire de Raymond Monier* (≡*Mém. de la soc. d'hist. du droit des pays flamands, picards et wallons* IV Lille 1958) pp. 113–16
22. H. GROTE *Münzstudien* IV Leipzig 1865 Part 2 'Die Geldlehre' pp. 151–7
23. Op. cit. I Paris 1891 pp. lxvi–lxix
24. *Anglicae Historiae libri XXVI* Basel 1534 p. 304: 'Habeo autem autores, qui tradunt, per idem tempus percussum est denarium argentum, quod vulgo sterlyng, ab effigie sturni aviculae vocitatur, quae in altera parte numi impressa esset, nam sturnus Anglice sterlyng dicitur. ... Quare omnis Anglica moneta etiamnum sterlyngorum nomine putatur ... vel numulus in altera parte haberet notam stellae, quam Angli ster vocant. Et isti denari etiam hodie reperiuntur.' It should be said that Polydore took a lively interest in origins and etymologies, and was the author of a work entitled *De rerum inventoribus* in eight books
25. I have not been able to trace Polydore's source. It does not seem to be Matthew Paris or any of the better known medieval chroniclers
26. SCHRÖDER art. cit. p. 12 cites *BMC* A/S II 1893 Plates XVII–XXIX *passim*, and notes that the resemblance to a star is closer on some of the types of William I and William II. It is nowhere very convincing, however, and there is no likelihood at all that these patterns were thought of as stars by those who designed them
27. *BMC* A/S II 1893 Plate XXIII 2 Plate XXIV 10 etc.
28. They are usually described by the heraldic term of martlet, but it is more

probable that they were intended to represent eagles. See R. H. M. DOLLEY and F. ELMORE JONES 'A new suggestion concerning the so-called "martlets" in the "Arms of St Edward"' *supra* pp. 215–26

29. e.g. the groat bearing an eagle which was struck at Deventer by Frederick of Blankenheim, Bishop of Utrecht (1394–1423), and which was known as a *deventergans*, a 'Deventer goose'

30. It is generally regarded as essentially a diminutive (cf. W. W. SKEAT *Principles of English etymology* Oxford 1887 p. 223), but the element of making of an object a separate entity is often present. It is much used in Germanic languages in the formation of coin-names, especially in German itself, where the proliferation of denominations in the later Middle Ages gave rise to *Halbling, Zweiling, Dreiling, Vierling,* and *Sechsling*

31. This is the only occasion on which a seated monarch appears on English coinage prior to the issue of the gold penny of Henry III. The model appears to have been the seated Constantinopolis on the *solidi* of Justin II (565–78), one of which must by some chance have come into the hands of the official who was responsible for deciding the design of the coinage; cf. P. D. WHITTING 'The Byzantine Empire and the Anglo-Saxons' *supra* p. 35

32. G. C. BROOKE *A catalogue of English coins in the British Museum. The Norman kings* London 1916 I Plates XI–XIV. The dates of the issue cannot be determined with absolute certainty, but on the assumption that William continued the triennial system of his predecessors this type should have been issued from 1077 to 1080

33. W. WROTH *Catalogue of the Imperial Byzantine coins in the British Museum* London 1908 II Plate LVIII 9, 10

34. e.g. in 1059 the price of some land acquired by the church of Trani was fixed at forty-seven *nomismata*, eighteen of these being *skifati*, sixteen *stellati*, and thirteen *romanati* (*Le carte che si conservano nello Archivio del Capitolo Metropolitano della città di Trani* ed. A. di Gioacchino Prologo Barletta 1877 no. 16 p. 54). The three terms employed afford a good illustration of the diverse sources from which coin-names could be drawn, *skifati* being so called from their form, *stellati* from their type, and *romanati* from the name of the Emperor who issued them (Romanus III, 1028–34)

35. An example of the first of these is the retention of the name of *cavallo* for the Neapolitan copper coins of Charles VIII, though these no longer bore the effigy of the horse which had characterized the *cavalli* of Ferrante, who had introduced this denomination. Obvious examples of the second class are the *ducat*, the *testone*, and the *thaler*

36. H. E. IVES *The Venetian gold ducat and its imitations* New York 1954 pp. 5–6. The falsity of the traditional etymology is here proved by the fact that the term *ducat* was first applied to the silver *grosso* of Venice, which existed for over three-quarters of a century before the gold *ducat* and had no reverse legend at all

37. According to the *O.E.D.* the word *Easterling* for North German merchants is not attested for the vernacular before the sixteenth century, but in Latin it is known

Sterling

as early as the thirteenth; cf. *The Pinchbeck Register* ed. Lord Francis Hervey, Brighton 1925 II 6

38. 'Moneta vero fertur dicta fuisse a nomine artificis, sicut sterlingi Angliae a nominibus opificum nomina contraxerunt' *The Red Book of the Exchequer* (ed. H. Hall Rolls Series London 1896 III 991)
39. e.g. ISIDORE OF SEVILLE *Etymologiae* XVI 18 10
40. 'Moneta Anglie fertur dicta fuisse a nominibus opificum, ut florenus a nominibus Florentinorum, ita sterlingus a nominibus Esterlingorum nomina sua contraxerunt, qui huiusmodi monetam in Anglia primitus componebant' *The Pinchbeck Register* loc. cit.
41. Though there are similarities of substance and sometimes of wording between the two works they seem to be drawing on a common fund of information rather than to be copying one another. The Abbot of Bury was at the time engaged in a lively dispute with the Master of the Mint regarding his minting privileges, and it is probable that the representatives of the two sides had each been airing their knowledge for the others' benefit
42. Though the canting badge of the city, the fleur-de-lis, also appears on the coins, this was not the origin of the name itself
43. W. W. SKEAT *Etymological Dictionary of the English Language* Oxford 1888 s.v. 'sterling'. His references to the appearance of the term Easterling in the *Liber Albus* are not correct
44. In *O.E.D.* s.v. 'sterling'
45. The initial *e* of *esterlin* is of course no part of the original word, but the prosthetic *e* (earlier *i*) added to words of Latin or Germanic origin beginning with an *s* followed by a consonant (spiritus, *esprit*, scutum, *écu*, etc.)
46. The fourteenth-century author of the *Eulogium Historiarum*, for example, explains the name of the Emperor Vespasian on the supposition that as a child he suffered from the singular disease of wasps (*vespae*) in the nose (*Eulogium Historiarum*, ed. F. S. Haydon Rolls Series London 1858 I 145)
47. *English Trade in the Middle Ages* Oxford 1931 p. 8 n. 3
48. Art. cit. pp. 15 ff.
49. E. G. GRAFF *Althochdeutscher Sprachschatz* III Berlin 1837 col. 343. 'Penny' is here being used, however, in the general sense of 'a coin', as was normal in the Middle Ages, so that not much stress can be laid on it
50. E. STEINMEYER and E. SIEVERS *Die althochdeutschen Glossen* I Berlin 1879 p. 254 line 35. This form is quite exceptional – the normal *stater* (without prosthetic *i*) occurs on p. 253, line 34 – and the word is understood as being a weight (*uuaka*, 'Wage')
51. The analogy, however, is not as close as Schröder suggests, for the accusative of *stater* was not *statrem* but *staterem*, which would affect the subsequent development of the word
52. The details of the highly efficient organization of the coinage during the last

period of the Anglo-Saxon monarchy have been worked out by Mr Dolley, Mr Elmore Jones, and others only in recent years, and no comprehensive study has yet been published. The best account is that of R. H. M. DOLLEY and D. M. METCALF, 'The reform of the English coinage under Eadgar' *supra*, pp. 136–68. The length of the separate issues had varied somewhat in the period between Eadgar's reform and the Conquest; it started as six years, and only in the middle of Edward the Confessor's reign was it fixed at three years

53. The Cologne penny of the later eleventh century weighed some 1·45 grammes (=22·3 grains) and was of about the same fineness as the English sterling (W. HÄVERNICK *Die Münzen von Köln* I Cologne 1935 pp. 8–10). It is possible that when William I increased the weight of the English penny to 22·5 grains he was deliberately bringing it into line with that of Cologne

54. P. SEABY 'The sequence of Anglo-Saxon coin-types, 1030–1050' *BNJ* XXVII, 1955–7 p. 128

55. Ibid. pp. 129–30

56. BROOKE op. cit. I pp. cli–cliv. He is inclined to believe that the theoretical weight of the coins was fixed at 22·5 grains from the Conquest onwards, and that the lower weight of the early types of William I denotes laxity in the control of the moneyers and not the existence of a lower standard. If this is correct it would only reinforce my conclusions, but on the evidence it looks as if a standard intended to be permanent was fixed at the Conquest, only to be modified slightly in the light of experience some years later

57. Owing to the fact that it gave rise to the Tower pound of 5,400 grains (i.e. 22·5 grains × 240). This was in its origin nothing other than the weight of the actual stone or metal 'poise' used in the Tower mint for checking the exactness of the weight of 240 pennies

58. The complaints over the state of the coinage under Henry I and Stephen were aroused by the misconduct of the moneyers, not by any change in the official standard

59. E. BABELON *Traité des monnaies grecques et romaines. 1ère Partie. Theorie et doctrine* I *Introduction* Paris 1901 coll. 532–4. *Solidus* had been occasionally applied to *aureus* even earlier, implying an *aureus* of full weight, but as a substantive it does not occur before the fourth century. The gold coins of Alexander Severus (222–35) are termed *solidi* in the *Historia Augusta*, but anachronistically; Lampridius was writing under Constantine

60. *Etymologiae* XVI 25 14

61. The most obvious cognate word in a modern tongue is German *starr*, 'stiff', 'motionless', but with different consonantal endings the root is held to lie behind such words as *sterben*, to die (i.e. become stiff), *stark* (strong in the sense of rigid), *stare* (i.e. look fixedly), and so on. Cf. E. BOISACQ *Dictionnaire étymologique de la langue grecque* Third Edition Heidelberg-Paris 1938 s.v. 'στερεός'; G. CURTIUS *Principles of Greek etymology* Fifth Edition (English translation by A. S. Wilkins

and E. B. England London 1886) 1 p. 253; P. PERSSON *Beiträge zur indogermanischen Wortforschung* (Skrifter utgivna af K. Humanistiska Vetenskaps-Samfundet i Uppsala 10: Upsala-Leipzig 1912) pp. 428–46 and R. GRANDSAIGNES D'HAUTERIVE *Dictionnaire des racines des langues européennes* Paris 1948 pp. 204–5

62. J. WRIGHT *The English Dialect Dictionary* v London 1904 s.v. 'steer'
63. *O.E.D.* s.v. 'steer'
64. C. HORSTMANN *Altenglische Legenden: Neue Folge* Heilbronn 1881 p. 346 line 440
65. *The Romance of Guy of Warwick* ed. J. Zupitza Early English Texts Society Extra Series nos. xxv–xxvi London 1876–7 p. 19 line 662. The rarity of the word is shown by the fact that Zupitza was unacquainted with it, and queried whether it should not be amended to 'fere'
66. Francis Junius also suggested that *sterling* was connected with στερεός, but as a loan-word from the Greek, implying 'the good English penny' in contrast to the poor-quality continental ones (*Etymologum Anglicanum* Oxford 1743 s.v. 'sterling'). Basically the idea seems to me correct, but there can be no question of there being a loan-word; rather there is a common root. Junius's suggestion was corrected by his editor, Edward Lye, who preferred 'Easterling' on the authority of Spelman and Skinner
67. This word was displaced by *feorþung*, the ancestor of our *farthing*. One may conjecture that *healfling* also existed, like German *Halbling*, but it apparently does not occur in surviving documents
68. Our knowledge of the legislation of this period is very haphazard, and we need not be surprised that the precise provisions regarding *monetagium* have not survived, though the terms of Henry I's Coronation charter indicate that they must have existed. I know of no continental parallel as early as this, but cf. the undertaking of Philip Augustus in 1187 (?) not to alter the money of Orléans during his lifetime in return for a triennial tax ('monetam Aurelianensem quae in morte patris nostri currebat, in tota vita nostra non mutandam concessimus, et eam neque mutari neque alleviari patiemur'; L. DELISLE *Catalogue des actes de Philippe Auguste* Paris 1856 no. 201 pp. 498–9)
69. e.g. the agreement of 11 March 1186 on the marriage portion of Margaret of France, widow of the young Henry of England, defined this in terms of money of Anjou but allowed for its being paid in silver marks *bonorum sterlingorum*, 13*s*. 4*d*. sterling being taken as equal to 54*s*. in Angevin money (ROUND op. cit. no 1084 p. 383)
70. I should like to express my thanks to Professor Whitelock, Mr Blunt, and Mr Dolley for reading the draft of this paper and for commenting upon and greatly improving those sections concerned with their several specialities

Index Personarum

(a) Kings, Bishops, Chroniclers, etc.

Adam of Bremen, chronicler, *d.* 1076? 112, 116
Ælfred, King of Wessex, *d.* 899 13, 14, 24, 30, 34, 35, 45, 65–7, 75, 77–96, 98, 99, 110, 111, 124, 156, 160, 215, 230, 238
Ælfric, homilist, *fl.* 1000 129, 188, 193
Bata, scholar, *fl.* 1005 128
Æthelbald, King of Wessex, *d.* 860 63, 228
Æthelberht, King of Kent, *d.* 616 8
King of East Anglia, *d.* 794 13, 49, 50, 54
King of Wessex, *d.* 865 65, 66, 69, 78, 238
Æthelflæd, Lady of Mercia, *d.* 917 86
Æthelheard – see Æthilheard
Æthelræd, King of Wessex, *d.* 871 66, 80, 238
uncertain ruler, *c.* 875 96, 97
II, King of England, *d.* 1016 14, 33, 42, 118, 124–30, 140, 141, 146–8, 152, 153, 167, 171–7, 182, 183, 186, 195, 196, 198–207, 209, 211–14, 239, 247, 248, 250, 251, 254, 255
King of Mercia – see Æthilræd 254, 255
Archbishop – see Æthered
Æthelstan, King of England, *d.* 939 24, 34, 43, 82, 85, 96, 111, 119, 123, 126, 127, 130, 140, 144, 149, 221, 222, 238, 239, 243, 245
Æthelwald, Ætheling, *d.* 902 108, 113, 116
Æthelweard, chronicler, *d.* 998? 115, 119, 238
Æthelwulf, King of Wessex, *d.* 858 63–76, 156, 238
Æthered, Archbishop of Canterbury, *d.* 888 80–3, 85, 95, 96
Æthilheard, Archbishop of Canterbury, *d.* 805 48, 651, 54, 60
Æthilraed, King of Mercia, *d.* 704 39
Alexander Severus, Emperor, *d.* 235 282
Alf- – see Ælf-
Al Mansur, Caliph, *d.* 775 34, 50
Al Mu'tamid, Caliph, *d.* 892 32
'Alvaldus', ruler?, *c.* 900 98, 100, 101, 108, 113
Anastasius, Emperor, *d.* 518 26, 27, 37
Andronicus II, Emperor, *d.* 1328 27
Anlaf I, King of York and Dublin, *d.* 981 238
II, King of York and Dublin, *d.* 941 115, 219, 223, 238, 242
Anthemius, Emperor, *d.* 472 21
Arcadius, Emperor, *d.* 408 3, 223
Athel- – see Æthel-, etc.
Avitus, Emperor, *d.* 456 21

Baldred, King of Kent, *fl.* 825 237
Basil II, Emperor, *d.* 1025 32

Bede, chronicler, *d.* 735 8
Belisarius, general, *d.* 564 24
Beornred, eighth-century missionary 24
Berhtwulf, King of Mercia, *d.* 852 69, 71, 72, 237
Bertha, Queen of Kent, *fl.* 600 8
Brian Borumha, King of Ireland, *d.* 1014 260
Burghard, eighth-century missionary 24
Burgred, King of Mercia, *d.* 874 65, 66, 80, 82, 95, 237

Cædwalla, King of Wessex, *d.* 689 24
Cen- see Coen-
Ceol, King of Wessex, *d.* 597 29
Ceolnoth, Archbishop of Canterbury, *d.* 870 65, 66, 73, 80, 96, 97, 237
Ceolwulf II, King of Mercia, *fl.* 785 30, 32, 35, 52, 80–2, 95, 96, 156, 215
Charlemagne, Emperor, *d.* 814 40, 42, 47, 126
Charles the Bald, Emperor, *d.* 877 63, 96–8
the Fat, Emperor, *d.* 887 96–8
the Simple, Emperor, *d.* 929 96–8
VIII, King of France and Naples, *d.* 1498 280
Clovis, King of France, *d.* 495 21
'Cnut', Viking ruler, *c.* 900 32, 96, 97, 99, 100, 102, 105, 107–19
Cnut, King of England, *d.* 1035 115, 129, 130, 146, 148, 152, 171, 172, 177–80, 182–4, 186, 187, 208–13, 222, 223, 239, 255–7
Coenred, King of Mercia, *fl.* 705 24
Coenwulf, King of Mercia, *d.* 822 45, 48–55, 72
Constans II, Emperor, *d.* 668 12, 22, 25, 31
Constantine the Great, Emperor, *d.* 337 2, 276
III, Emperor, *d.* 411 3, 4
VII, Emperor, *d.* 959 32
IX, Emperor, *d.* 1055 29, 269
Constantius II, Emperor, *d.* 361 22
Crispus, Emperor, *d.* 326 11
Cuthbert, Bishop of Lindisfarne, *d.* 687 14
Cuthred, King of Kent, *d.* 807 237
Cynethryth, Queen of Mercia, *fl.* 790 41, 46, 51, 52, 54, 59

Decius, Emperor, *d.* 251 188, 190
Diocletian, Emperor, *abd.* 305 276
Dunstan, Archbishop of Canterbury, *d.* 988 156

Ead- – see Ed-
Eanred, ruler, *fl.* 850 228

285

Index

Ecgbe(o)rht, King of Kent, *fl.* 775 39–41, 44, 51, 53, 55, 56, 61
   King of Wessex, *d.* 839 44, 71, 72, 74, 75, 238
Ecgfrith, King of Mercia, *d.* 796 54
Edberht, Bishop of London, *fl.* 785 42–4
   Præn, King of Kent, *d.* 798 48, 50, 55, 237
Edgar, King of England, *d.* 975 34, 88, 93, 127, 129, 130, 136–68, 172, 185, 195, 196, 210, 213, 222, 232, 239, 245
Edmund, King of East Anglia, *mart.* 869 91, 92, 96, 98, 99
   King of England, *d.* 946 232, 239, 245
   Ironside, King of England, *d.* 1016 155
Edred, King of England, *d.* 955 232, 239, 243–5
Edwald, King of East Anglia, *fl.* 796 49, 50, 54, 237
Edward the Elder, King of England, *d.* 924 14, 83, 85–8, 95, 96, 98, 110, 130, 161, 163, 239, 243, 245
   the Martyr, King of England, *d.* 978 139–41, 163, 172, 182, 186, 195, 196, 213, 214, 239
   the Confessor, King of England, *d.* 1066 14, 35, 125, 129, 132, 146, 152, 157, 172, 181, 182, 184–6, 215–26, 228, 240, 268, 269, 274, 275
   Ætheling, *d.* 1057 217, 218
Edwig, King of England, *d.* 959 140, 160, 232, 239
Edwin, King of Northumbria, *d.* 633 14
Eric, King of York, *d.* 954 238, 242
Eudes, Emperor, *d.* 898 96–9

Frederick, Bishop of Utrecht, *d.* 1423 280

Gildas, chronicler, *fl.* 550 5
Godwine, Earl, *d.* 1053 219
Gruffydd, King of Wales, *d.* 1063 219
Guthfrith, King of York, *d.* 895 97, 116, 119
Guthred – see Guthfrith
Guthrum, King of East Anglia, *d.* 890 84, 85, 88, 90, 92, 95, 96, 116, 119

Hadrian, seventh-century missionary 25
Halfdan – see Halfdene
Halfdene, Viking, *fl.* 870 37, 80
   Viking, *fl.* 895 30, 37, 80, 82, 90, 96
Harold I, King of England, *d.* 1040 172, 180, 181, 184, 186, 223, 240
   II, King of England, *d.* 1066 14, 125, 185, 186, 219, 240, 275
Harthacnut, King of England, *d.* 1042 115, 119, 172, 181, 184–6
Heaberht, King of Kent, *fl.* 765 39, 40, 53, 55, 56, 61
Helena, Empress, *fl.* 325 10
Hengist, Jutish invader, *d.* 488 6

Henry I, King of England, *d.* 1135 89, 189, 268, 275, 282
   III, King of England, *d.* 1272 215, 280
Heraclius, Emperor, *d.* 641 8, 28, 32, 99
Heraclius Constantine, Emperor, *d.* 641 32, 99
Hincmar, canonist, *d.* 882 66
Honorius, Emperor, *d.* 423 3, 4, 221
Horsa, Jutish invader, *d.* 455 6
Hundeus, Viking, *fl.* 895 117
Hygeburg, eighth-century nun 24

Iænberht, Archbishop of Canterbury, *d.* 792 47, 51, 53, 54, 59
Ine, King of Wessex, *abd.* 726 24
Innocent IV, Pope, *d.* 1254 62
Isidore, canonist, *d.* 636 272, 276

Jænbrereht – see Iænberht
John, Emperor, *d.* 425 4
John Zimisces, Emperor, *d.* 976 33
Justin, I, Emperor, *d.* 527 31
   II, Emperor, *d.* 578 28, 215, 223, 280
Justinian I, Emperor, *d.* 565 10, 21, 25, 27, 28, 30
   II, Emperor, *d.* 711 11, 28

Ken- – see Coen-

Lanfranc, Archbishop of Canterbury, *d.* 1089 267, 268
Leo I, Emperor, *d.* 474 17
   III, Emperor, *d.* 740 13, 28
   III, Pope, *d.* 816 45, 51
   IV, Pope, *d.* 855 24
Leofgyth, eighth-century nun 24
Leofwine, eighth-century missionary 24
Liudhard, Bishop, *fl.* 600 8
Louis the Pious, Emperor, *d.* 840 23, 97
   the Child, Emperor, *d.* 911 97, 117
   IX, King of France, *d.* 1270 62
Lullus, eighth-century missionary 24

Macbeth, King of Scotland, *d.* 1057 218
Magnentius, Emperor, *d.* 353 22
Magnus Maximus, Emperor, *d.* 388 4
Mainer, Abbot, *fl.* 1080 267
Malachy, King of Leinster, *d.* 1022 260
Mathgamain, King of Munster, *d.* 976 245
Matilda, Countess, *fl.* 1080 267
Maurice, Emperor, *d.* 602 28, 29, 37
Maxentius, Emperor, *d.* 313 21
Maximian, Emperor, *d.* 305 14
Mellitus, Bishop of London, *d.* 624 9
Montgomery, Mabel de, *fl.* 1080 267
   Roger de, *fl.* 1080 267

Index

Offa, King of Mercia, d. 796 13, 24, 34, 39–62, 237
'Ogsen', Irish ruler (?) c. 1000 246, 249, 250
Olaf, King of Norway, d. 1030 222
   King of Sweden, fl. 1010 158
Ordericus Vitalis, chronicler, d. 1143? 267, 276, 277
Oswald, King of Northumbria, d. 642 11

Pada, King of Mercia, fl. 656 39
Perctarit, King of Lombardy, d. 688 24
Philip Augustus, King of France, d. 1314 283
Philippicus, Emperor, d. 713 221
Phocas, Emperor, d. 610 9, 28
Pippin, King of France, d. 768 40, 45, 62, 87
Plegmund, Archbishop of Canterbury, d. 914 83, 85, 86, 96
Polydore Vergil, chronicler, d. 1555 268, 279
Priscus Attalus, Emperor, d. 455 3
Procopius, chronicler, d. 565 24, 25

'Raienalt', Viking, fl. 915 110, 112
Regnald I, King of Dublin and York, d. 921 92
   II, King of York, d. 943 92, 242, 245
Robert II, Count of Flanders, fl. 1100 268
Roger of Wendover, chronicler, d. 1236 124, 136, 155
Romanus I, Emperor, d. 944 32

Siefred, Viking, fl. 895 86, 96, 98–103, 107–11, 113–18
Sievert – see Siefred
Sigeferth – see Siefred
Sigurd, Viking, d. 1014 219
Sihtric, Viking, fl. 895 96
   King of Dublin, fl. 942 242
   King of Dublin, d. 1042? 158, 247–50, 255

Simeon of Durham, chronicler, fl. 1130 116
Siward, Earl, d. 1055 218
Stephen, King of England, d. 1154 147, 152, 282

Theodebert, King of France, d. 547 8
Theoderic, goldsmith, fl. 1060 220
Theodore, Empress, fl. 1055 221
Theodore, Archbishop of Canterbury, d. 690 25
Theodosius I, Emperor, d. 395 3, 21, 26, 30, 35
   II, Emperor, d. 450 4, 35, 188, 190
Theophilus, Emperor, d. 842 33
Thorkell, Viking, d. 1025? 153
'Thymn', Irish ruler? c. 1000 246, 248–50
Tiberius II, Emperor, d. 582 28, 37

Valentinian I, Emperor, d. 375 30
   II, Emperor, d. 392 30
   III, Emperor, d. 455 4, 15
Vitalian, Pope, d. 672 25

Waldburg, eighth-century nun 24
Wigmund, Archbishop of York, fl. 840 34
Wilfrid, eighth-century missionary 24
Willebald, eighth-century missionary 24
Willehad, eighth-century missionary 24
William I, King of England, d. 1087 14, 33, 34, 124, 129, 269, 270, 274, 275, 277, 279
   II, King of England, d. 1100 279
de Ros, Abbot, fl. 1080 267
Willibrord, eighth-century missionary 24
Wulfred, Archbishop of Canterbury, d. 832 72, 737
Wulfstan, Archbishop of York, d. 1023 129, 193
Wynfrid, eighth-century missionary 24
Wynnebald, eighth-century missionary 24

(b) Moneyers

In an index a degree of normalization is inevitable, and the forms that appear more or less consistently here do not necessarily agree with those that appear in the text.

Æedric 187
Ælewine 247, 250
Ælfnoth 142
Ælfsige 178
Ælfwig 173
Ælwerd 187
Æthelgeard 73, 76
Æthelhere 71–3, 76
Æthelmod 55, 58, 73, 76
Æthelmund 73, 76
Æthelnoth 47, 48, 55, 57, 58, 73, 76
Æthelred 43, 142

Æthelstan 92
Æthered – see Æthelred
Alh- – see Ealh-
Alvaldus? 113 – see also Index (a)

Babba 40, 55, 56, 58
Beaghard 55, 56, 58
Beagmund 70–2, 76
Beorht- – see Byrht-
Beorn- – see Bern-, Biarn-
Bernwald 91
Biarnnoth 67, 72, 76

Index

Boga, Boiga, etc. 251, 255
Botred 49, 54, 59
Brid 71, 72, 76
Bur(h)red 182
Burhstan 142
Byrhtlaf 174
Byrhtric 172

Ciolh(e)ard 42, 55, 56, 58
Cnapa 243, 246
Cuthberth 55, 56

Dægberht 73, 76
Deiheah 67, 71-3, 76
Deimund 55, 58
Deor- – see Dor-, Dur-
Diar 67, 70-3, 76
Dorulf 243, 246
Dud 43, 53, 55-7
Dud(d)a 53, 55
Dudwine 73, 76
Dun 70-2, 76
Dunberd 182
Dunstan 179
Dunun 71
Dursig(e) 179

Eadberht 55, 57
Eadhun 55, 57
'Eadlfe' – see Eadulf
Eadmund 243, 246
Eadnoth 50
Eadred 246
Eadsige 251, 255
Eadulf 243, 245
Eadwerd, 175, 179
Eadwig, 176
Eadwine 175
Ealhmund 41-3, 55-8, 73, 76
Eal(h)ræd 41, 55-7
Eama 48, 55, 58
Eanmund 48, 71-3, 76
Eanwald 64
Ed- – see Ead-
Elf- – see Ælf-
'Emirnie' 248, 249
Eoba 40, 47, 55-9
Eofermund 161
Ethel- – see Æthel-

'Fænimin' 248
'Færemin' 248, 249, 251-3
Faraman 248
'Fiemenin' 249

Gærman 180

Gelda 92
Godman 179
Godwine 179

Harthacnut 187
Heaberht 46, 55, 57
Hebeca 73, 76
Herebeald 70-3, 76
Hildulf 161
'Hun..c' 49, 54, 59
Hunbearht 71-3, 76
Hunred 73, 76
Hun(e)wine 179

Ibba 55, 57-9
'Indremin', etc. 252, 253
Ingelgar 243, 246

Leofhyse 247, 250
Leofwine 177
Lewerd 179
Liaba 71, 72, 76
Lifwine 187
Ludoman 55, 59
Lul 43, 49, 50, 54, 59
Lulla 43, 55, 58

Man 180
Mania 142
Manan 142
Man(n)a 70-3, 76
Man(n)inc 71-3, 76
Mansi(ge) 180

'Niomnren' 248

Œthilred 43, 55, 58
Oslac 245
Osmod 41, 55, 56, 58, 59
Osmund 70-3, 76
Oswine 161
Oswold 174

Pada 11
Pehtwald 55, 58
Pendred 43, 55, 58

Rendred 43

Seberht 48
'Siel' 248
Spov 243, 245
'Steng' 252
Swegn(n) 180
Swetric 179
Swota 177

Index

Thurulf 245
Tidwald 43
Tilewine 83, 85, 90
Tirwald 43, 47, 55, 58, 73, 76
Torhtulf 73, 76
Torhtwald 70, 76

Udd 40, 43, 53, 55, 56

Welheard 66, 71, 72, 76

Wermund, 73, 76
Wihtred 49, 50, 54, 59
Wilheah 70-3, 76
Wilhun 55, 59
Winoth 55, 58, 59
Winræd 187
Winuc 243, 246
Wulfhath 55, 59
Wulfstan 243, 246

(c) Modern Authorities, Collectors, etc. (See also pp. 60-1)

Adelson, H. L. 26
Akerman, J. 5, 28
Allan, J. 51
Andrew, W. J. 119
Austin, 'Mr.' 228, 230

Baldwin, A. H. F. 105
Banks, D. 232
Bergsoë, V. 110, 119
Birch, W. de G. 220, 221
Blanchet, A. 39
Bliss, T. 65
Blundell, W. 86
Blunt, C. E. 37, 38, 75, 98, 105, 161, 170, 227, 229, 283
Boon, G. C. 27, 37
Borrell, H. P. 67
Bradley, H. 271, 278
Brooke, G. C. 42, 49, 64-6, 68, 93, 116, 274
Bryer, R. 232
Butler, V. 171

Calori Cesis, F. 44, 61
Carlyon Britton, P. W. P. 93, 228
Clemoes, P. 188, 191, 193, 194
Clibborn, E. 243-6
Collingwood, R. G. 3
Combe, C. 227-30, 234-6
  T. 65, 228-30, 232, 235, 236
  Mrs. T. 66
Corbet Anderson, J. 65, 81
Cotton, Sir Robert 52
Curwen, H. C. 215-19, 222

Dawson, H. R. 242
Delmar, E. 215, 216
De Longpérier, A. 50, 119
De Paor, L. 241
  M. 241, 260
Devonshire, Duke of 229, 230
Dieudonné, A. 39
Dolley, R. H. M. 37, 38, 45, 75, 118, 124, 170, 171, 183, 187, 208, 230, 282, 283

Elmore Jones, F. 38, 170, 183, 187, 282
Engel, A. 39, 268
Evans, Sir John 6, 33, 61, 62, 44, 48

Fountaine, Sir Andrew 52, 61
Frazer, W. 255-7

Galster, G. 261
Gamillscheg, E. 266
Garland, H. 230
Gifford, A. 233
Gomm, J. D. 226
Grabar, A. 37
Grierson, P. 9, 30, 37, 53, 80, 89, 90, 122, 124, 217
Grosjean, P. 194
Grote, H. 268
Grueber, H. A. 92

Haigh, D. H. 33, 44, 45, 97, 110, 116, 117, 119
Harmer, F. E. 215, 220, 224, 225
Hartnett, P. T. 250, 251
Hawkins, E. 64, 67, 96, 97, 105, 110, 231
Hildebrand, B. E. 169-87
Hill, P. V. 7, 11, 31
Hodsol, J. 230
Huber, M. 190-2
Hunter, W. 52, 139, 222, 228, 230, 234, 235

Jenkins, G. K. 228
Junius, F. 283

Keary, C. F. 28, 29, 42, 46, 92, 116
Kendrick, Sir Thomas 25
Kent, J. P. C. 28, 30, 37, 38
Kluge, F. 266

Lagerqvist, L. O. 171
Lane Poole, R. 223
Langford, A. 230
Latham, R. E. 278
Le Gentilhomme, P. 11, 12
Lelewel, J. 111

Index

Lewis, A. R. 23, 32
Lincoln, F. W. 228
Lindahl, F. 261
Lindsay, J. 66, 67, 242
Lockett, R. C. 44, 46
Lopez, R. S. 25, 29
Lucas, A. T. 241
Lye, E. 283

Mallinson, A. 38
Martin, J. S. 66, 93, 141
Mason, C. A. 230
Mattingly, H. 6
Meer, G. van der 199, 247
Megaw, B. R. S. 166
Metcalf, D. M. 45, 282
Milligan, S. C. 255, 257
Milne, J. G. 18
Moloney, M. 241
Mossop, H. R., 187

Nelson, P. 105, 116
Nicolson, W. 236

O'Donovan, J. 242
O'Kelly, M. J. 241
Oman, Sir Charles, 42, 116
O'Neil, B. H. St J. 15
O'Sullivan, L. 241, 249–51

Pegge, S. 52
Pembroke, Earl of 52
Petrie, G. 242
Pirenne, H. 23
Pownall, A. 61
Prou, M. 97
Puttock, J. 65, 66

Rashleigh, J. 33, 67, 75, 116, 119
P. 67
Rasmusson, N. L. 32, 171

Ravetz, A. 15
Rebello, I. 230
Roach Smith, C. 5, 6
Robertson, A. S. 229
Ruding, R. 65, 89, 228–33, 266

Sabatier, P. 33
Sainthill, R. 67, 242
Salzman, L. F. 271
Seaby, B. A. 227
P. 187, 274
W. A. 116, 241, 263
Serrure, C-A. 119, 268
Schröder, E. 266, 271, 272
Skeat, W. W. 192, 271
Skinner, S. 283
Smith, A. 242, 246–50, 255
Snelling, T. 229
Solly, E. 230
Southgate, R. 230–4, 236
Spelman, Sir Henry 283
Stainer, C. L. 91
Stenton, Sir Frank 30, 45, 49, 63, 122, 127, 170, 227, 236
Stephenson, C. 132
Stevenson, W. H. 81
Sutherland, C. H. V. 6, 9, 17, 28

Taffs, H. 93
Tait, J. 132
Talbot Rice, D. 25, 34
Thompson, J. D. A. 27, 28, 94, 241, 245
Tyssen, S. 52, 139, 230, 231, 236

Walker, J. 31, 225, 228
White, J. 248
Whitelock, D. 56, 116, 119, 167, 283
Wilson, D. M. 75
Wyon, A. B. 220

Young, M. 228

Index Locorum

(a) Finds

Abingdon 19, 20, 22
Adare 263–5
Andreas 138, 141, 162, 165, 254, 256, 257
Armagh 262, 264, 265
Årstad 249
Ash 18, 20

Baggiovara 44
Ballaquayle 162
Ballitore 262, 264, 265
Ballycastle 164, 255–7, 263–5
Ballylinan 256, 257, 263–5
Baltinglass 257, 263–5
Bangor 139, 162, 167
Barfriston 20
Barham Down 20
Barrington 20
Barrowby 164
Beeston Tor 78
Bekesbourne 20
Betham 165
Birdoswald 15
Birka 32, 118
Bishopsbourne 20
Blood Moore Hill 20
Breach Down 20
Brighthampton 18–20
Broadstairs 18, 19
Bucklersbury – see London
Burray 139, 141, 162, 165, 167
Burt (see also Carrowen) 138, 141, 162
Burwell 20
'Buttack' 263–5

Caerwent 37
Caistor 20
Caldale 157, 164
Campsey Ash 163
Canterbury – St Martin's 8, 16, 30, 37
Carrawburgh 15
Carrowen (see also Burt) 162, 262, 264, 265
Castle Dore 5
Castlelyons 263–5
Castor 164
Chancton 158, 163, 165
Chartham 20
Chatham 20
Cheltenham 78
Chessel Down 20

Chester 84, 122, 137–9, 153, 155, 160, 162, 164, 166
Chesterford 43
Cimiez 12, 13
Claremont (Glasnevin) 262, 264, 265
Clondalkin 263–5
Coleraine 16
Constantine 164
Crondall 8–11, 16, 28
Croy 67
Croydon 20, 33, 63, 65, 68, 78, 81
Crundale 20
Cuerdale 27, 32, 33, 80–8, 90–2, 96–121
Cushendall 257

Dalkey 138, 141, 162, 263–5
Dean 84, 90
Delgany 51, 262, 264, 265
Denge Marsh 163
Derrykeighan 137, 141, 162, 166, 263–5
Derrymore 164, 246–50, 263–5
Donough Henry 263–5
Dorking 63, 65, 68–70
Douglas 137, 141, 160, 162
Dransau 118
Driffield 19
Drogheda 118, 262, 264–5
Droxford 20, 22
Drwsdangoed 163, 165, 166
Dublin 262–5
Dunamase 263–5
Dunbrody 157, 165, 167, 254, 257, 263–5
Dungarvan 139, 141, 162, 165, 167, 241, 248, 261, 263–5
Dunrossness 162, 163
Dunsforth 78
Dunstable Downs 20

East Shefford 20
Erith 82, 85, 87

Fairford 20
Faroes 257
Fermoy 265
Fitful Head 162, 163
Fourknocks 165, 248, 250–7, 263–5
Frilford 22
Frisia 12

Index

Gainford 78
Geashill 241, 262, 264, 265
Gilton 18, 20
Girton 20
Glasnevin 265 – and see Claremont
Glendalough 139, 141, 162, 263-5
Goldsborough 78
Gotland 32
Gracechurch St – see London
Gravesend 63, 66-8, 70, 78
Great Burton 163
Guildown 20

Halton Moor 157, 164
Harewood 158, 163
Harkirke 84-7, 91, 110, 118
Harnham Hill 20
Harting Beacon 163
Hatherop Castle 93
Holywell Row 20, 22
Hon 32
Honey Lane – see London
Hook Norton 78
Howletts 20

Ilanz 51, 56, 57
Ilchester 27
Inchkenneth 138, 139, 141, 162, 165
Ingatestone 84
Iona 137, 139, 141, 153, 157, 160, 162, 165
Ipswich 153, 163
Isleworth 164
Italy 52

Kent 6, 8, 59
Kilcullen 263-5
Kildare 164, 262-5
Kilkenny 138, 141, 162, 164, 241, 254, 256, 257, 261, 263-5
Killincoole 138, 141, 162, 262, 264, 265
Killyon Manor 262, 264, 265
Kingsholm 163
Kirk Maughold 165
Kirkmichael 163, 256
Knockmaon Castle 162
Koldemosen 118

Laugharne 138, 162, 164
Leckhampton 78
Leigh-on-Sea 84-6, 91, 92
Limerick 263-5
Little Wilbraham 20
London – area 27 142, 161
  Bucklersbury 82, 85
  Gracechurch St 165
  Honey Lane 163
  London Wall 67
  Middle Temple 51, 63, 64, 68-71
  St Martin's-le-Grand 163
  St Mary Hill 165, 215, 222, 224, 228
  St Pancras 16
  St Paul's Churchyard 81
  Stamford Hill 51
  Walbrook ('City') 33, 158, 165
  Waterloo Bridge 78
Long Wittenham 20
Lough Lene 138, 141, 162, 262, 264, 265
Lugga 265
Lympne 142

Macroom 242-6, 262, 264, 265
Mackrie 138, 141, 162, 166
Maiden Castle 15
Markshall 10
Marl Valley 164, 263-5
Marston St Lawrence 20
Meath 139, 141, 162, 241, 261, 263-5
Meols Sands 257
Middle Temple – see London
Milton Street 165
Mitcham 20, 22
Monasterboice 241, 261, 262, 264, 265
Morley St Peter 82, 84-7, 91, 92, 110, 111, 118, 122
Mullaboden 262, 264, 265
Mullingar 265
Mungret 245, 262, 264, 265

Netley Abbey 51, 52
Nobber 262, 264, 265
Northampton 142
North Uist 165
Nottingham 163, 164

Offaly 263
Offham 164
Oldcastle 262, 264, 265
Ouse (Yorkshire) 94
Outlack 263
Oving 164
Ozingell 18, 20

Penarth Fawr 163
Penrice 164
Plas Gwyn 93
Poole 78, 230, 238

Quendale 139, 141, 162, 163, 165, 167

Richborough 2, 5, 6, 15, 16, 57, 59
Rogaland 52

Index

Rome – area 50, 52, 67, 239, 243
   Forum 82, 84, 87
   Vatican 82, 84, 86, 87
Rotherham 135, 164
Rushen 164

St Martin's – see Canterbury
St Martin's-le-Grand – see London
St Mary Hill – see London
St Paul's Churchyard – see London
Salisbury 142
Sarre 18–20, 22
Scaldwell 163
Scrabo Hill 263–5
Sedlescombe 158, 165
Sevington 63, 64, 68–70
Shaftesbury 129, 164
Shudy Camps 20
Sibertswold 18, 20
Sleaford 18, 20, 22
Smarmore 138, 141, 159, 162, 263–5
Soberton 164, 240
Southampton 63, 66, 68, 70, 81, 142
Stafford 165
Stamford 84, 85, 87, 88, 90–2
Stamford Hill – see London
Stapenhill 20
Store Frigård 261
Stowting 20

Sullington 163
Sutton Hoo 8, 14, 16, 18, 19, 26, 29

Tarbat 139, 141, 162, 167
Terslev 84
Tetney 137, 144, 156, 162
Thwaite 163, 165
Tipperary 245, 262, 264, 265
Tiree 137, 138, 141, 162, 163, 232, 239
Tirling, 16
Tjore 254
Trewhiddle 51, 63, 67–70, 75, 78, 84, 228

Vaalse 118
Voss 52

Walbrook – see London
Washington 80
Waterloo Bridge – see London
Wedmore 165
Westerham 28
West Stow Heath 20
Wheatley 19, 20
Whitchurch 165
Winchester 237

Yeavering 11
York 11, 91, 94, 139, 162–5

(b) *Anglo-Saxon mints*

Axbridge 135, 146, 172, 181
Aylesbury 146

Barnstaple 135, 146, 172, 177, 180, 181
Bath 87, 90, 145, 248
Bedford 145, 172
Bedwyn 135, 146, 181
Berkeley 147, 167
Bridgnorth? 134, 146, 172
Bridport 146, 172, 177, 181
Bristol 146, 149
Bruton 131, 146, 148, 178
Buckingham 146, 149
Bury St Edmunds 147

Cadbury 131, 146, 148
Caistor 146, 177
Cambridge 144, 145, 173
Canterbury 17, 40, 41, 44, 48, 49, 54, 70–2, 74, 80–2, 84–6, 90, 91, 95, 99, 112, 124, 145, 173, 178, 179
Castle Gotha? – see 'Gothabyrh'
'Castle Rising' – see 'Roiseng'

Chester 85, 124, 125, 127, 133, 141, 142, 145, 159, 174, 177, 178, 180–5, 247, 250
Chichester 145
Cissbury 146, 175, 179
Colchester 146, 173
Crewkerne 131, 146
Cricklade 146, 182

'Darent' 145
Derby 145, 173, 176, 177, 181
Dorchester 146
Dover 144, 145, 181, 247, 248, 250

'Eanbyrh' 177
'Ebraice Civitas' – see York
Exeter 87, 88, 95, 124, 127, 133, 145, 172

Frome? 146, 177, 182

Gloucester 144, 145
'Gothabyrh' 146, 148, 173, 178, 180
Guildford 146, 176

Hastings 146, 158, 172

293

Index

Hereford 125, 127, 144, 145, 181
Hertford 145, 173, 174, 176, 179, 182, 248
Horncastle 146
Horndon 132, 147, 215
Horsforth? – see 'Orsnaforda'
Huntingdon 145, 177, 181, 248
Hythe 147

Ilchester 131, 144–6, 173, 177, 179, 180
Ipswich 144, 145, 149, 174, 177, 179

Langport 146, 178, 180, 181
Launceston 146, 148
Leicester 144, 145, 160, 174, 176–8, 180–2, 201
Lewes 125, 144, 145, 172, 174, 178, 181, 182
Lincoln 90, 124, 127, 133, 144–6, 158, 176, 180–2, 196, 199, 201, 251, 255
London 11, 12, 80, 82–90, 95, 127, 133, 145, 156, 160, 173, 174, 177, 179, 187, 196–8, 200–4, 206, 207, 209
Louth? 146
Lydford 146, 172, 173, 179, 182
Lym(p)ne 144, 145, 174, 178

Maldon 146, 181
Malmesbury 145, 180, 187
Milborne Port 135, 146, 175, 179

Newark 146, 175, 180
Newport 145
Northampton 145, 174, 178, 180–2
Norwich 127, 133, 144, 145, 173, 187
Nottingham 146, 174, 187

'Orsnaforda' 91, 110
Oxford 91, 145, 179

Pershore 135, 147
Peterborough 146
Petherton 147, 182

Quatford? – see Bridgnorth

Reading 147, 167
Rochester 44, 144, 145, 247, 248, 251, 255
'Roiseng' 90
Romney 146, 179

Salisbury 146, 153
Sandwich 147
Shaftesbury 145, 178
Shrewsbury 125, 145, 161, 177, 179
Southampton 17, 145, 174, 178
Southwark 146, 176, 179, 180
Stafford 144, 145, 179
Stamford 90, 144, 145, 180, 196
Steyning 146, 182
Sudbury 146, 176, 179, 180

Tamworth 145, 176, 180
Taunton 146
Thetford 124, 127, 133, 145, 173
Torksey 146, 176, 180
Totnes 145, 149, 176, 180

Wallingford 145, 180
Wareham 144, 145
Warminster 135, 146, 177, 180, 181
Warwick 144, 145, 173, 176, 182
Watchet 146, 181
'Weardbyrh' 145
Wilton 145, 153
Winchcombe 144, 145, 176, 181, 182
Winchester 71, 78, 84, 87, 88, 95, 124, 133, 142, 145, 161, 178, 196–8, 200–4, 206, 209
Worcester 125, 135, 146, 174, 180, 181

York 97–100, 103, 105, 107–12, 116, 117, 124, 133, 142, 145, 146, 158, 173, 174, 196–9, 201, 202, 206, 208, 209, 241, 242

(c) General

Angers 97, 98, 273
Anjou 267
Aquitaine 117
Arles 3
Arundel 135
Athelney 156

Baltic 32
Boulogne 24
Bourges 98
Brie 16
'Brunanburh' 32
Burpham 146

Bury St Edmunds 270
Byzantium 2, 23–38, 99

Calne 135
Campbon 17
Canterbury 69, 224
Carthage 29
Castle Clifford 135
Clare 135
Clontarf 149, 219, 260
Cologne 273, 282
Constantinople – see Byzantium
Cork 260

294

Index

Danelaw 89–92
Deventer 280
Droitwich 135
Dublin 247, 248, 259, 260
Dunwich 135

East Anglia 49, 50, 54, 59
Evreux 97, 112
Eye 135

Fordwich 135

Gaul 4, 14, 39
Glasbury 218
Glen Mama 250
Grantham 135
Grateley 127, 147
Gunnersbury 131

Humber 90

Ireland 241–65

Kent 40, 41, 248

Le Mans 98, 267, 273
Les Préaux 267, 268, 272
Lichfield 44, 45
Limerick 245, 260
Limoges 97, 98
Lincoln 149
Loire 117
London 63, 81, 83, 88, 124–6, 130
Lucca 42
Lyons 3, 8, 14

Maine 267
Marsal 21
Melle 97, 98
Milan 2, 30, 221

Neustria 117
Newport 134
Norwich 149

Orléans 17, 98, 283
Otford 41
Ouche 267

Pavia 24
Pevensey 135
Pontefract 135

Quentovic 96–8, 100, 103, 110, 111

Ravenna 2, 9, 29
Rhuddlan 135
Rome 24
Rouen 267, 273

St Evroul 267, 276
Severn 245
Sigtuna 158
Spain 32
Stirling 268, 278
Sweden 32
Syracuse 33

Tamworth 45
Taynton 224
'Thule' 24
Trani 280
Trier 3, 4, 10
Tutbury 135
Twineham 135

Verdun 21

Waterford 260
Wexford 260
Whitby 24
Wilton 26
Wimborne 135
Winchester 66
Wroughton 83

Yarmouth 135
York 119, 149, 242

Index Rerum

'Agnus Dei 153, 154
al marco 276
al pezzo 276
amphora 272
Annales Vedastini 117
aureus 275, 276, 282

cavallo 280
'Cunnetti' 32, 33, 99–101, 105, 108–14, 118

Danegeld 153, 154
denarius 5, 9, 272, 275, 277
denier 8, 15, 39, 111, 123
deventergans 280
dinar 13, 32, 34, 50, 51, 56
dirhem 32
dreiling 280
ducat 280
ducatus 270

'Easterling' 270
electrum 11
esterlin 272
Ewiger Pfennig 277

florin 270
follis 21, 127, 147, 167

halbling 280
heregeld 154

Keronian Glossary 272

libra 272

mancus 45, 51
miliaresion 13, 33, 99
minimus 6
monetagium 275, 277, 283

nomisma 269, 280
Notitia Dignitatum 4

obolus 5, 272, 273

penny, introduction of 12, 13, 39
Peter's Pence – see Romescot
pondus 272

romanati 280
Romescot 77, 167

'St Peter' coinage 107, 109, 110, 112, 238, 241
sceatta 7, 11–13, 26, 31, 39
scyphates 280
Seal, Great 220, 221
sechsling 280
semissis 9
sextarius 272
shilling 9
siliqua 2, 4, 5, 31
skifati – see scyphates
solidus 2, 4, 7–10, 26, 28–32, 35, 221, 223, 272, 276, 282
stater 272, 273
stellati 8, 269, 280
sterilenses 277
sterling 266-83
styca 13

talent 272, 273
testone 280
thaler 280
thrymsa 9, 10, 12, 26
Tower pound 282
treasure trove 15, 155, 180, 189
tremissis 8, 9, 11, 15, 28–30, 93
type cycle 152-8

uncia 272

vierling 280
Vulgate 272

zweiling 280

I. FROM ROMAN BRITAIN TO SAXON ENGLAND I

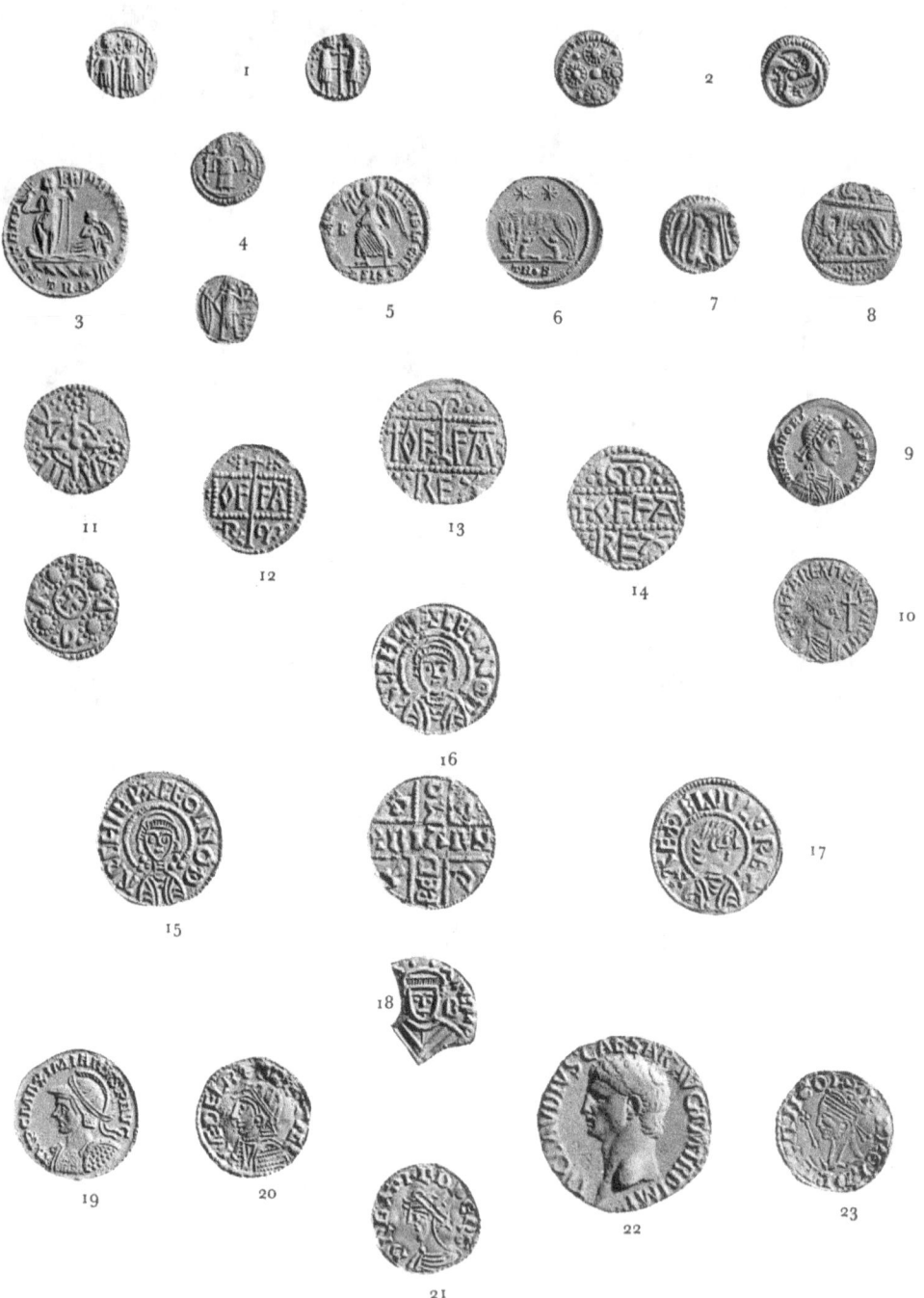

II. FROM ROMAN BRITAIN TO SAXON ENGLAND II

III. BYZANTINE PROTOTYPES AND FINDS

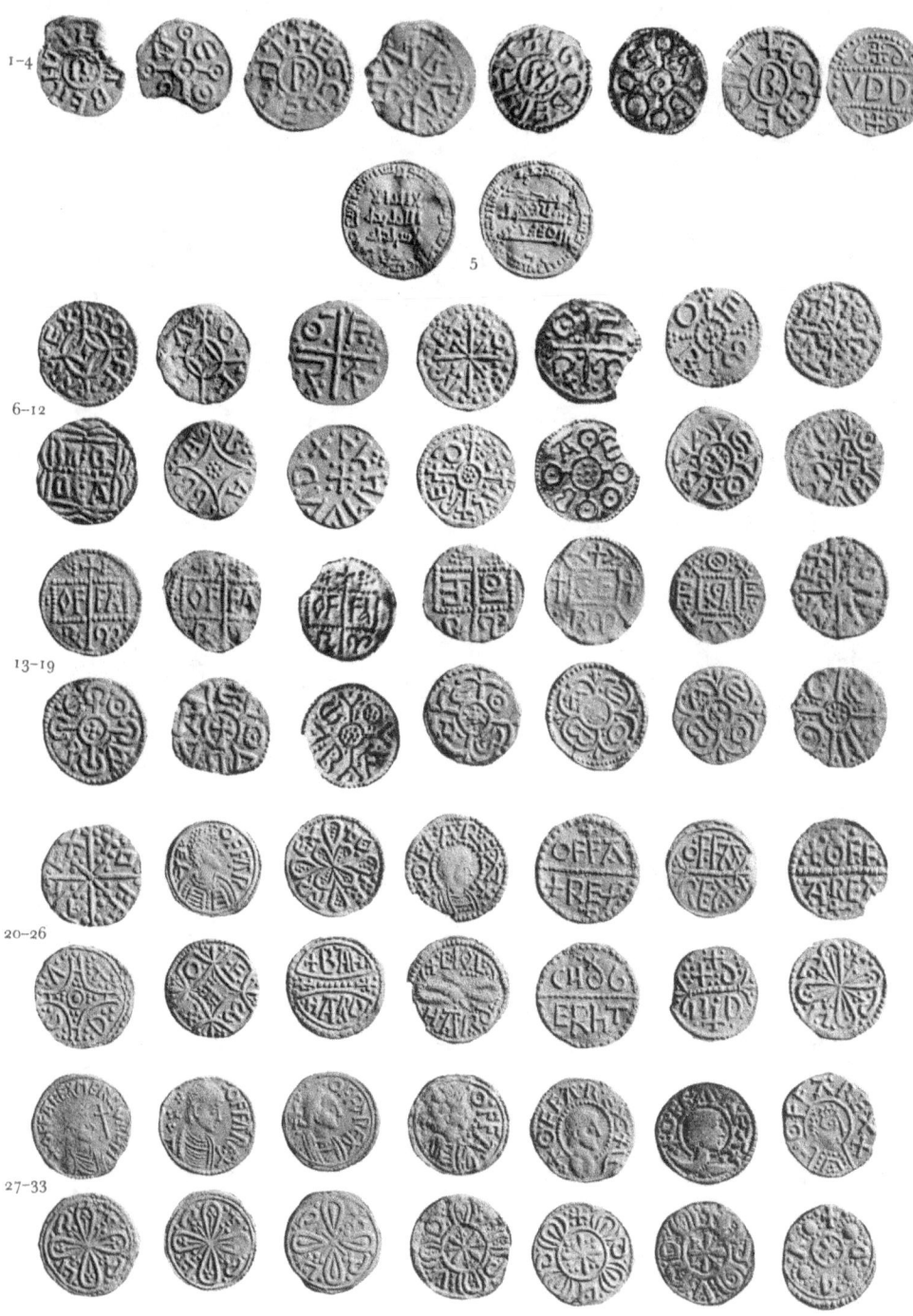

IV. THE COINAGE OF OFFA I

V. THE COINAGE OF OFFA II

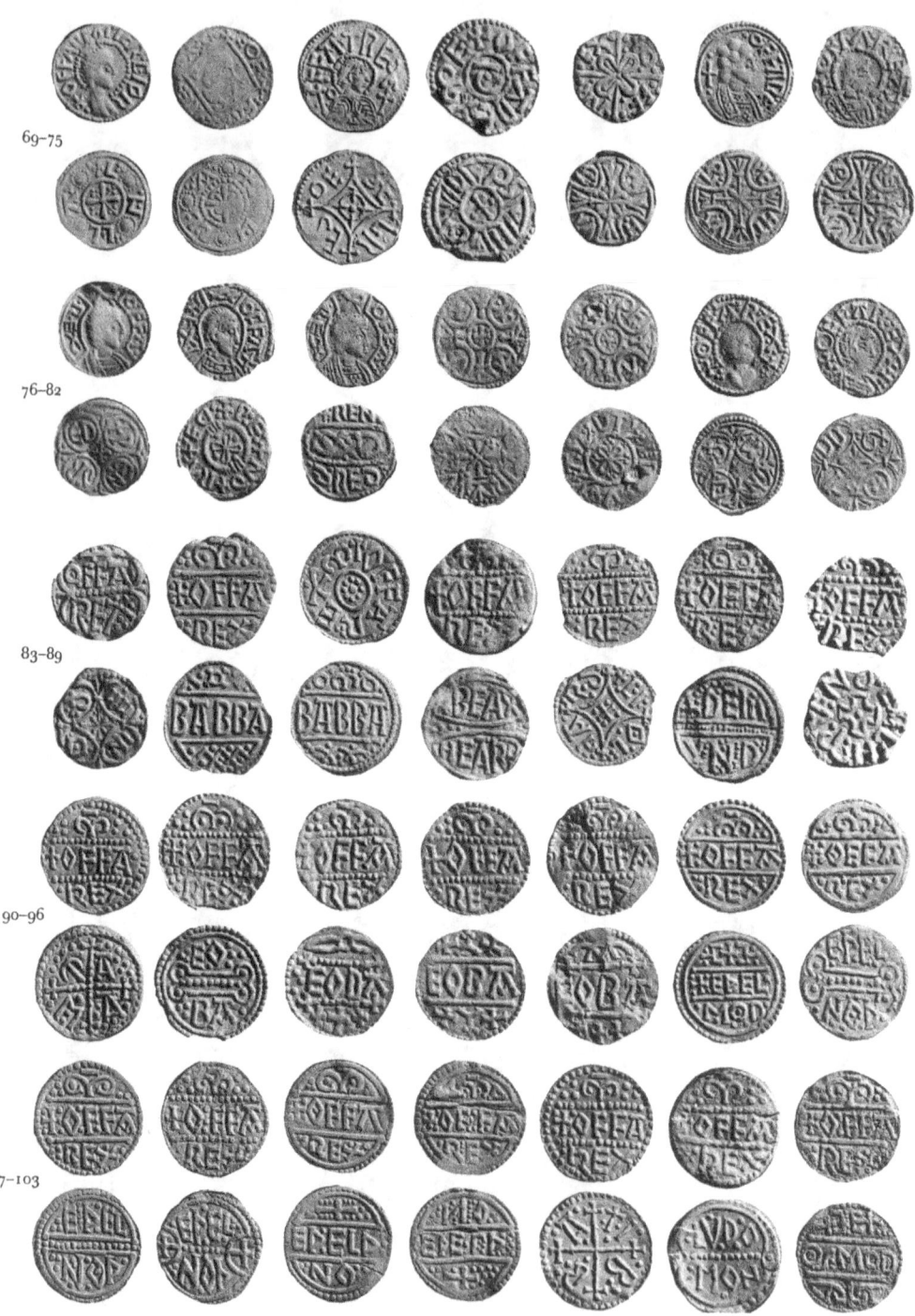

VI. THE COINAGE OF OFFA III

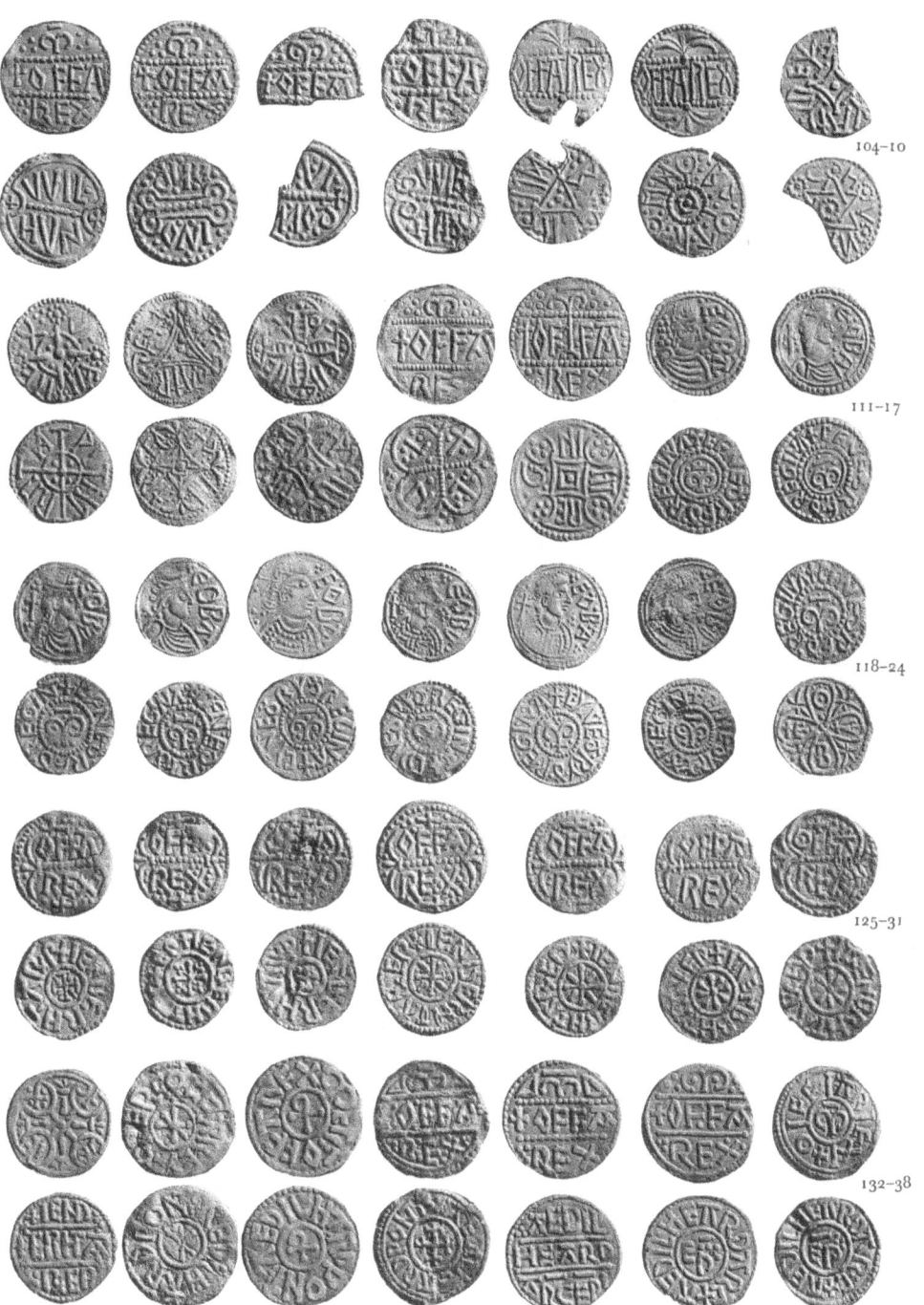

VII. THE COINAGE OF OFFA IV

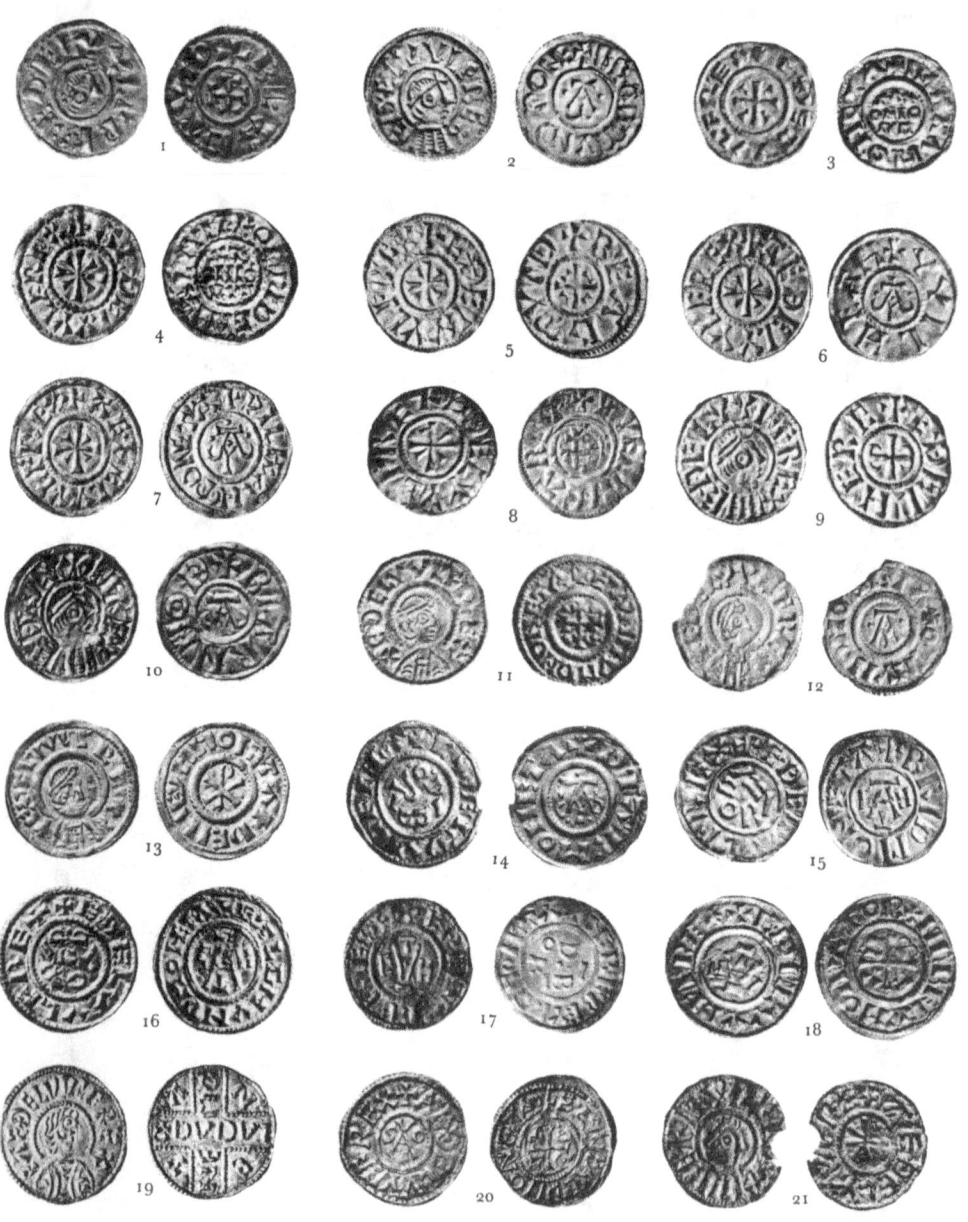

VIII. THE COINAGE OF ÆTHELWULF

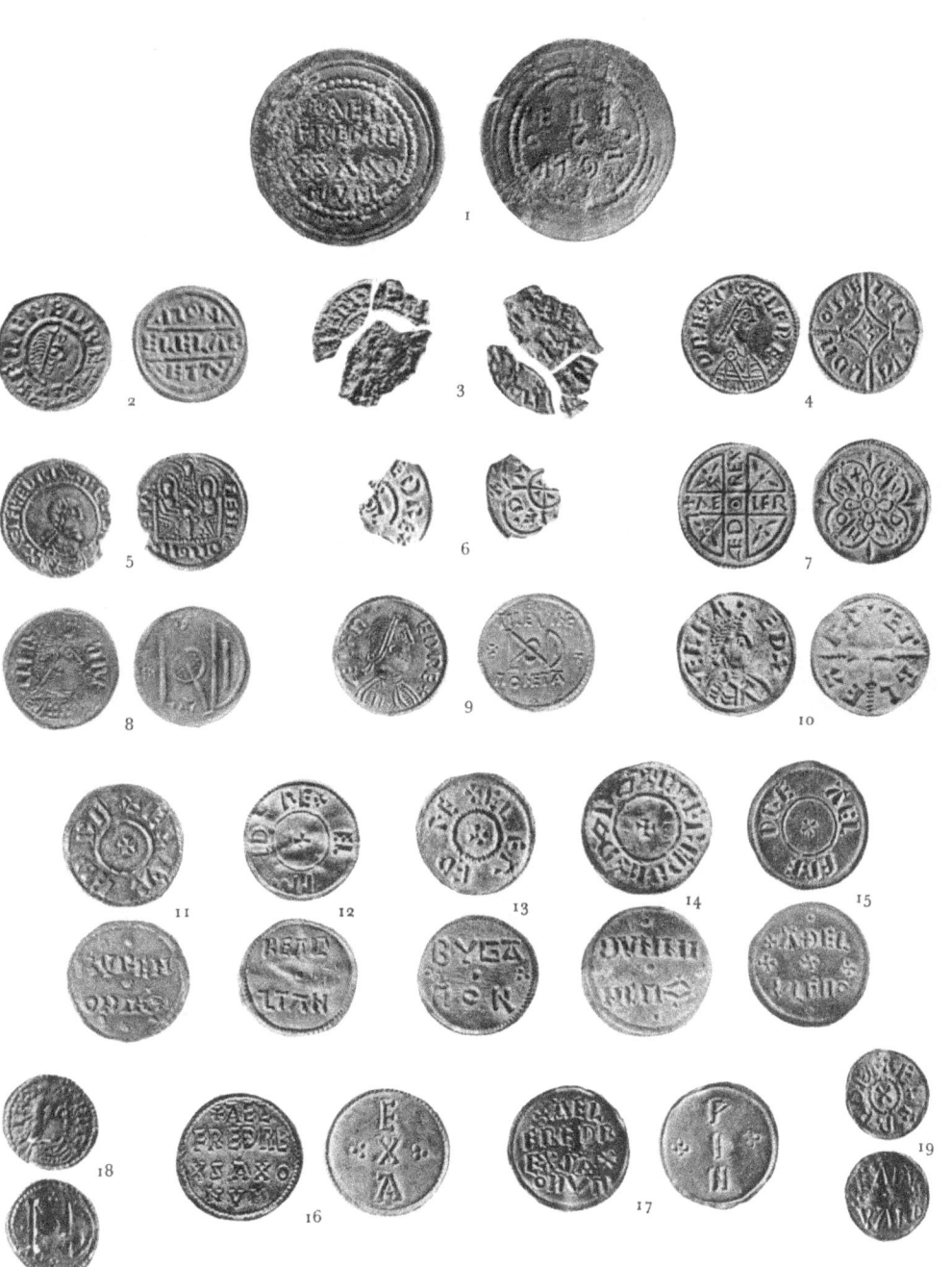

IX. THE COINAGE OF ALFRED THE GREAT

X. VIKING IMITATIONS OF THE COINS OF ALFRED THE GREAT

XI. NORTHUMBRIAN VIKING COINS IN THE CUERDALE HOARD I
1–20 Obverse types and varieties, 21–45 Reverse types and varieties, 46–7 'Quentovici'

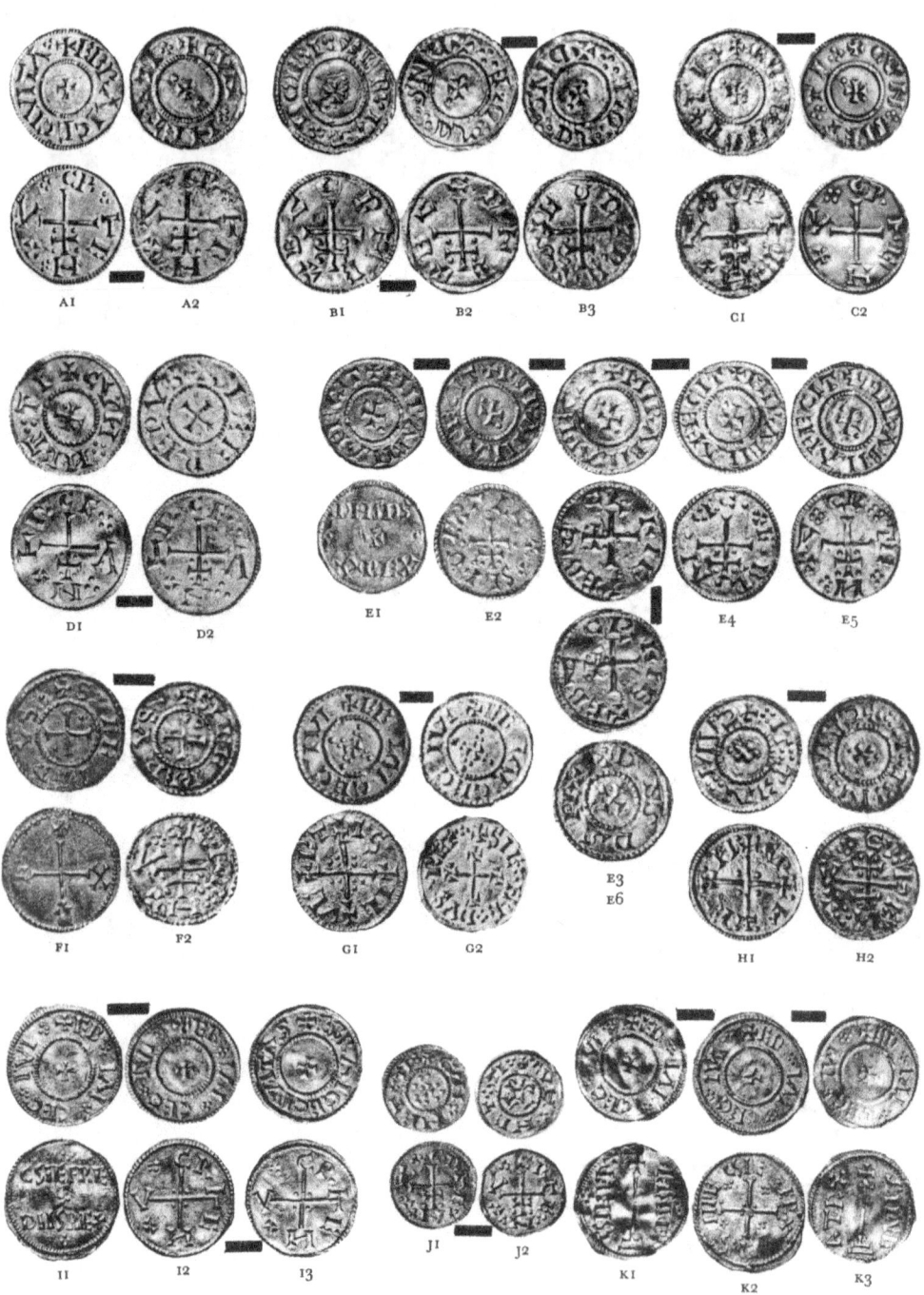

XII. NORTHUMBRIAN VIKING COINS IN THE CUERDALE HOARD II
Examples of die-links

XIII. THE COINAGE OF EADGAR.
A. Principal types and styles

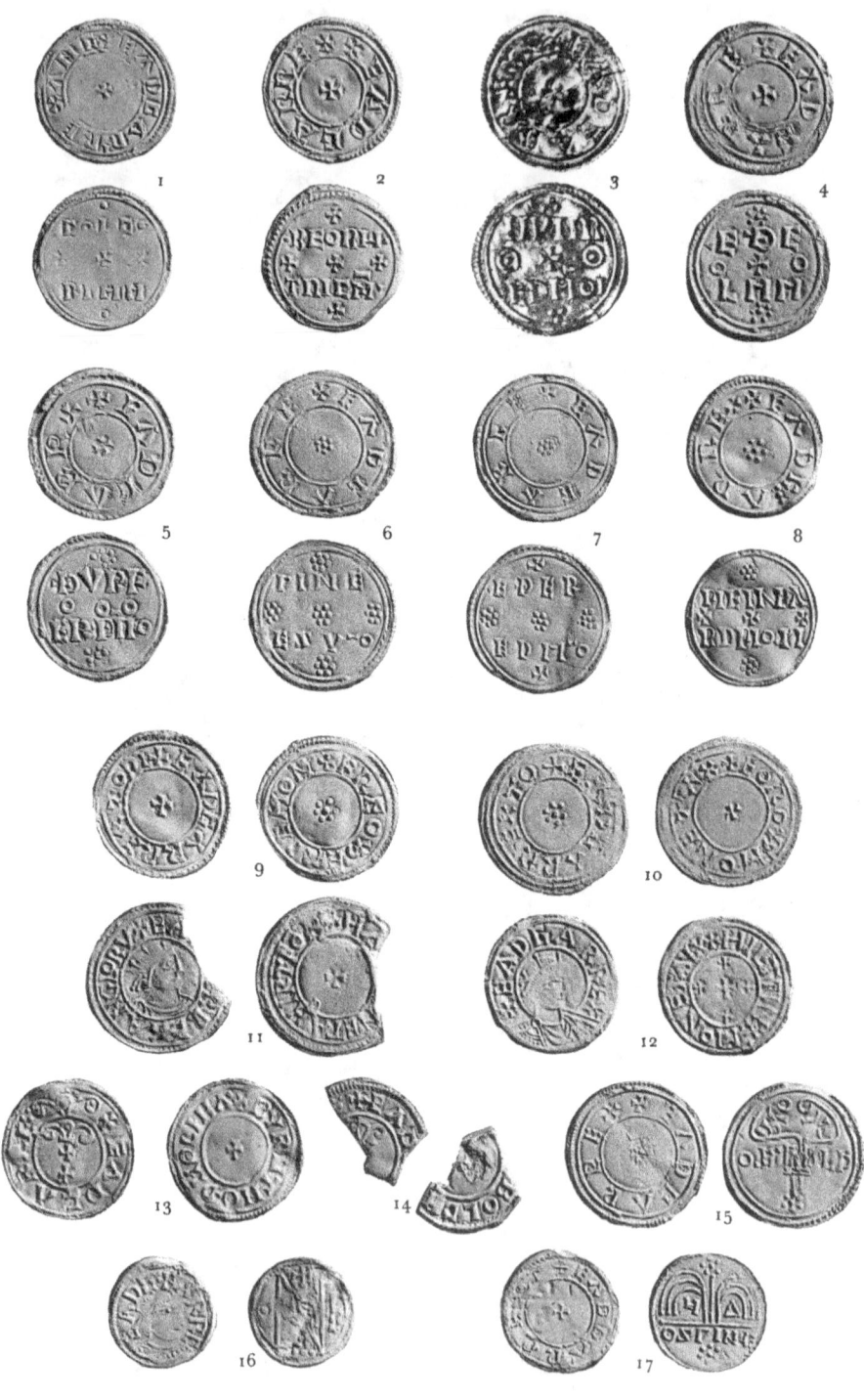

XIV. THE COINAGE OF EADGAR
A. Minor varieties etc., halfpence

XV. THE ORIGIN OF THE 'MARLETS' IN THE ARMS OF ST EDWARD
a and d enlarged 2×: b and c reduced ⅔: 1–5 actual size

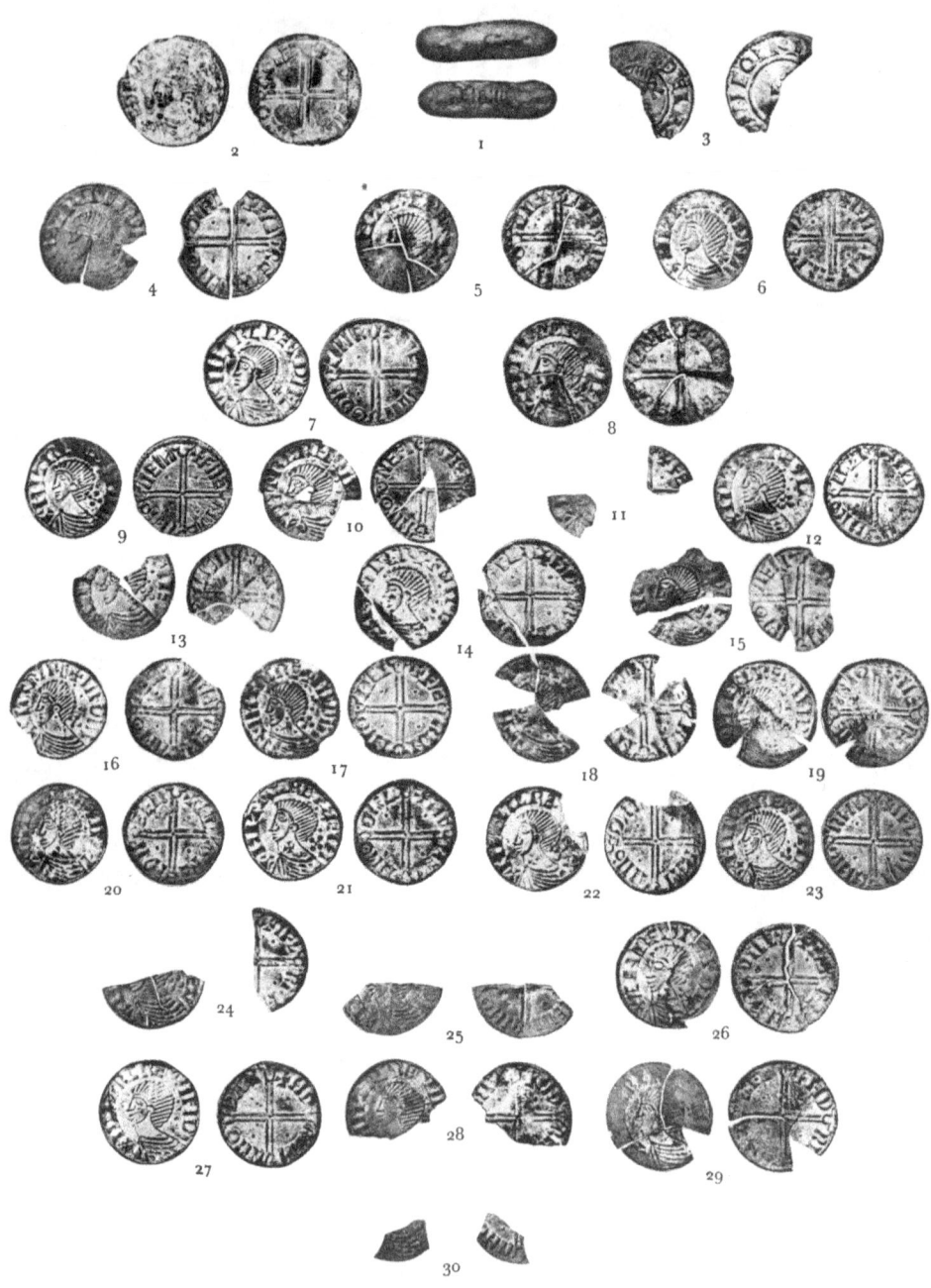

XVI. THE 1950 HOARD FROM FOURKNOCKS, CO. MEATH

For Product Safety Concerns and Information please contact our EU representative GPSR@taylorandfrancis.com
Taylor & Francis Verlag GmbH, Kaufingerstraße 24, 80331 München, Germany